Introductory VHDL: From Simulation To Synthesis

PRENTICE HALL XILINX DESIGN SERIES

CILETTI	*Modeling, Synthesis, and Rapid Prototyping with Verilog HDL*
DUCKWORTH	*VHDL Synthesis (2002)*
HARRIS/DICK	*DSP with FPGA's (2002)*
MANO & KIME	*Logic and Computer Design Fundamentals, 2/e*
WAKERLY	*Digital Design Principles and Practices, 3/e*
XILINX	*Xilinx Student Edition: Foundation Series Software*
YALAMANCHILI	*Introductory VHDL: From Simulation to Synthesis*

Introductory VHDL: From Simulation To Synthesis

Sudhakar Yalamanchili
Georgia Institute of Technology

PRENTICE HALL
Upper Saddle River, New Jersey 07458

Library of Congress Cataloging-in-Publication Data on file

Vice President and Editorial Director: Marcia Horton
Publisher: Tom Robbins
Acquisitions Editor: Eric Frank
Editorial Assistant: Jennifer Diblasi
Executive Managing Editor: Vince O'Brien
Managing Editor: David A. George
Vice President of Production and Manufacturing: David W. Riccardi
Editorial supervision: Scott Disanno
Page composition: Eileen Clark
Cover director: Jayne Conte
Cover: Bruce Kenselaar
Marketing Manager: Danny Hoyt
Manufacturing Buyer: Pat Brown

© 2001 by Prentice-Hall, Inc.
Upper Saddle River, New Jersey 07458

Trademark Information
Xilinx is a registered trademark of Xilinx, Inc. XC4000 is a trademark of Xilinx, Inc.

Printed in the United States of America

10   9   8   7   6   5   4   3   2   1

ISBN 0-13-080982-9

Prentice-Hall International (UK) Limited, London
Prentice-Hall of Australia Pty. Limited, Sydney
Prentice-Hall Canada Inc., Toronto
Prentice-Hall Hispanoamericana, S.A., Mexico
Prentice-Hall of India Private Limited, New Delhi
Prentice-Hall of Japan, Inc., Tokyo
Prentice-Hall (Singapore) Pte. Ltd., Singapore
Editora Prentice-Hall do Brasil, Ltda., Rio de Janeiro

To

my parents

Janardhana Rao and Kusuma

Table of Contents

Preface

Good judgement comes from experience
Experience comes from bad judgement
—Proverb

It is often pointed out that some things are best learned by "doing" and that the use of computer-aided design (CAD) tools in the design of digital systems is one such body of knowledge. Over the years, hardware description languages have evolved to aid in the description, modeling, and design of digital systems. The steady advances in microelectronics continues to increase the power and complexity of digital systems, which in turn places increasing demands on the associated CAD environments. Early in the next century silicon die are projected to pack in excess of one billion transistors. At the forefront of modern systems research are methodologies for the design of systems composed of these billion transistor chips. The intellectual capacity of human designers is limited and has led to the use of the principles of hierarchy, abstraction, and modularity in handling the increasing complexity of digital systems. The semiconductor industry's continued relentless march towards increasing densities and speeds will only increase the designers reliance on design tools to manage the complexity of future designs. Hardware description languages such as VHDL (VHSIC Hardware Description Language) form an integral part of such design environments.

My earlier book, *VHDL Starters Guide,* focused on the use of VHDL as a language for describing digital systems for the purpose of simulation in tasks such as performance evaluation and design verification. This book attempts to expand that point of view to encompass the use of a VHDL description as a point of departure for the synthesis of digital hardware. The emergence of an IEEE Standard for VHDL and the rapid development and use of the IEEE Standard VHDL language in industry makes it imperative that we provide opportunities for electrical and computer engineering students to learn the language and become proficient in its application both in simulation and synthesis environments.

There are many excellent books on the VHDL language and its use for the purpose of building accurate models of complex digital systems. These books have been largely complete treatments of the language and generally have been written for practicing engineers, and more recently for use in graduate and undergraduate courses. In the last few years the use of hardware description languages in the undergraduate classroom has become more common; it is no longer unusual for students to use VHDL or Verilog in their junior or senior design projects.

Even with all these developments in education, I find the usage of hardware descriptions languages in the classroom for the purposes of synthesis at the same point that I found the treatment of simulation modeling five years ago. Texts that treat the synthesis of digital hardware from high-level language descriptions focus on the intellectually challenging problem of synthesis from abstract specifications, whether they are executable language specifications or other formal specifications. Thus, courses dealing with synthesis tend to be at the advanced graduate level. At the same time introductory digital logic courses make use of synthesis tools for boolean expressions and state machines. The courses may start from prior generation specification languages or even a hardware description language such as VHDL and will target programmable logic arrays and the rapidly expanding area of field programmable gate arrays (FPGAs). The focus on synthesis in this book is motivated by the rapid growth of FPGAs in all manner of digital systems from low-cost controllers to high-speed special purpose co-processors. It is my belief that FPGAs will become a mainstay in the digital designers tool chest, and synthesis from high-level languages will be a dominant design methodology. Hence I foresee a need for the integration of FPGAs into courses in digital logic and computer architecture.

This text is not intended to be a comprehensive coverage of the VHDL language. Rather, it is intended to provide an introduction to the *basic* language concepts, and a framework for *thinking about* the structure and operation of VHDL programs from the point of view of modeling and simulation as well as synthesis. The book introduces key VHDL constructs that are motivated by the behavioral and physical properties of digital systems. Each language construct is studied from two opposing points of view: i) for the purpose of simulation the physical or behavioral attribute of a digital system that is *captured* by the language construct and ii) for the purposes of synthesis the digital hardware that is *implied* by the construct.

Programming idioms from conventional programming languages by themselves are insufficient for productively learning to apply hardware description languages such as VHDL. Through laboratory exercises, students can very quickly come up to speed in building useful, non-trivial models of digital systems. As their experience grows, so will their need for more comprehensive information and modeling techniques, which can be found in a variety of existing textbooks and the standard language reference manual.

This book is intended to support a first look at the language and as such I have decided to focus on what I felt were the most commonly used aspects of the language. VHDL has often been accused of being bulky, overly complicated, and difficult to use. Although the language may possess a large number of features I have found that I can focus on a core set of language constructs that can enable to students to rapidly become productive in its application. By packaging the Xilinx Foundation CAD tools with this text I hope students will be provided with a productive learning experience.

Intended Audience

The style of the book is motivated by the need for a text for sophomore- through senior-level texts used in courses in digital logic, computer architecture, and capstone design projects. The ability to construct simulation models of, or synthesize, the building blocks studied in these courses is an invaluable teaching aid.

Students learn the most about digital systems if they have to build them, in this case using VHDL models. I have found it valuable in my own courses to provide concurrent laboratory exercises that reinforce foundational material taught in the classroom. The scope and complexity of hardware laboratory exercises are limited by the available time in a semester- or quarter-long course. The VHDL language provides an opportunity for students to experiment with larger designs than would be feasible in a hardware laboratory, using a development environment that is rapidly being adopted throughout the industrial community. In the case of VHDL I like an approach that enables students to adjust quickly to the basic language concepts such that they could construct models of basic logic and computer architecture components productively in sophomore- and junior-level courses. The full power of the language is not necessary at this point, nor should it be. As students progress to more advanced courses and their needs grow, they will be able to use productively the more advanced language features and their corresponding texts as references.

Style of the Book

VHDL is a complex language that could easily be worthy of a course in its own right. However, curricula are usually strapped for credit hours, and devoting a course to teach VHDL would mean eliminating existing material from the curricula. The style of this book is intended to permit integration of the basic concepts underlying VHDL into existing courses without necessitating additional credit hours or courses for instruction. In order to fill the need for a companion text for digital logic and computer architecture courses and to serve as an early introduction to the basic language concepts the book must satisfy several criteria. First, it must relate VHDL concepts to those already familiar to the student. Students learn best when they can relate new concepts to ones that are already familiar to them. In this case we rely on concepts from the operation of digital circuits. Language features are motivated by the need to describe specific aspects of the operation of digital circuits, for example, events, propagation delays, and concurrency. Second, each language feature must be accompanied by examples. Simulation exercises address one or more VHDL modeling concepts. To keep with the idea of a companion book, tutorials for two VHDL environments are provided in the Appendices. Finally, the text must be *prescriptive*. Chapter 4, Chapter 6, and Chapter 8 each provide a prescription for writing classes of VHDL models. This is not intended to produce the most efficient models, but serves the purpose of rapidly bringing the student to a point where he or she can construct useful simulation models for instructional purposes. By enabling a look at the detailed operation of digital systems, VHDL reinforces the foundational concepts taught in the classroom. At this point, students begin to think about alternative, more creative, and often more efficient approaches to constructing the models.

This book, *Introductory VHDL: From Simulation to Synthesis*, attempts to develop an intuitive and structured way of thinking about VHDL models without necessarily spending a great deal of time on advanced language features. Students should be able to learn enough quickly through exercises and association with classroom concepts to be able to construct useful models with the help of this book. During development, portions of *Introductory VHDL: From Simulation to Synthesis* have been utilized in a two-course sequence on computer architecture at Georgia Tech. Sophomore students typically start with no background in VHDL but with a good background in high-level programming languages such as C or Pascal. By the end of the second quarter they will have built a model of a pipelined RISC processor with hazard detection, data forwarding, and branch prediction. Early in the second quarter the students make the transition from knowing VHDL as a new language to knowing how to use it as a tool for studying computer architecture. The goal is to integrate VHDL into the curriculum early in a manner that strengthens the learning of the concepts while concurrently providing training in the use of VHDL simulation tools.

The approach I take in this book is a bit unusual in that I do not begin with a discussion and presentation of language syntax and constructs, that is, identifiers, operators, and so forth. In fact, the book presents core constructs via examples and the syntax is not presented until late in the text with the notion that this chapter will be used more as a reference. The premise is that readers who have had experience with programming in high-level languages simply need an accurate syntactic reference to these language constructs. I believe that the road to building useful models is built on an understanding of how we can describe those aspects of hardware systems that require constructs that are not typically found in traditional programming language definitions, such as signals and the concept of time; this is where the bulk of this book is focused. As a result, a syntactic reference to the core programming language features has been reduced to a single chapter. My goal is to focus on the concepts underlying the VHDL language. If I can capture the novel features of the language in a manner that appeals to the reader's intuition and is based on thinking in hardware or systems terms, then a reference to the syntax of core constructs is sufficient to get students started in building useful models. My hope is that this text can apply this approach successfully and fulfill the goal of getting students at the sophomore level excited about the use of such languages in general and the evolving design methodologies in particular. Once they have reached this goal, they are then capable of more rapidly expanding their understanding to the full scope of the language.

Organization of the Text

As a result of this view, the text starts with concepts from the operation of digital circuits. This text assumes that the reader is comfortable with introductory digital logic and programming in a block-structured, high-level language such as Pascal or C. The subsequent chapters introduce various VHDL constructs. Each set of language constructs are first introduced as representations of the operational and physical attributes of digital systems. Then the same set of language constructs are discussed from the point of view of inferring digital circuit implementations that correspond to the behavior captured by the language construct. This dual interpretation is carried on throughout the text as new language constructs are introduced. For example Chapter 4 and Chapter 5 discuss basic language constructs from the point of view of simulation and synthesis respectively. Though VHDL is often criticized as a bulky and complex language in its entirety, the associations between language features and digital are intuitive and therefore easy to pick up. Once the basic concepts are understood a good syntactic reference to the language is sufficient for the students to be able to build models quickly of digital circuits including higher-level objects such as register files, ALUs, and simple datapaths.

Chapter 4, Chapter 6, and Chapter 8 provide recipes for building basic VHDL models. These models are not necessarily the most efficient but are intuitive and easy to get students started. Each of these chapters provide simulation exercises that can be exercised by the student to reinforce the concepts. Chapter 5, Chapter 7, and a part of Chapter 8 discuss the construction of models from the point of view of synthesis. The concepts are reinforced by exercises.

Completion of the exercises provides the student with an ability to proceed to more complex language features and productive use of any of the existing comprehensive VHDL language texts. In our curriculum, the students proceed to senior design projects where they describe systems in VHDL, synthesize their designs, and emulate the resulting designs using hardware emulators. Chapter 9 through Chapter 12 present language features as additional functionality that serve a specific purpose, for example, input–output and procedures. A syntactic reference to the common language features is provided in Chapter 12.

Several appendices have been added to support the material in the text. For example, a tutorial for the Xilinx Foundation tools and a tutorial for Aldec's Active VHDL simulator are provided. Another appendix provides a detailed template for a VHDL model illustrating the relative ordering of program constructs. This can serve as a handy reference toward the end of the student's experience. A third appendix provides a description of a model of the SPIM processor datapath described in "Computer Organization & Design: The Hardware Software Interface" by D. Patterson and J. Hennessey [9]. Students in a first-quarter architecture course can modify this datapath by adding instructions or modifying the controller to implement a more complex state machine. A fourth appendix provides a synthesizable model of a pipelined version of this datapath. The model can be used in a second-quarter computer architecture course as the starting point for the addition by the students of hazard detection, forwarding, and simple branch prediction. This has been invaluable in enabling students to gain a deeper understanding of these concepts since they must actually make them work.

If a professor so chooses, he or she can use this book to teach VHDL only for simulation by not covering Section 3.2, Section 3.3, Chapter 5, Chapter 7, and Section 8.5. The SPIM models provided in the appendix are synthesizable models but can certainly be used with a functional simulator. However it may be desirable to introduce some timing information to the simulation model.

This book may be used as a companion text in digital logic and computer architecture courses for gradually enabling students to learn VHDL "as they go." It may also be used in laboratory courses where VHDL is sometimes taught and used in the pre-laboratory exercises that ensure that the students have designed a functionally correct circuit prior to using valuable laboratory time and resources. I hope that the text will enable more curricula to productively introduce VHDL early in the curriculum while serving as a teaching aid for classroom material. Students are thus prepared for advanced courses dealing with state-of-the-art techniques such as rapid prototyping of digital systems, high-level synthesis, and advanced modeling.

Caveats

VHDL'93 This text follows the model described in the 1993 VHDL standard. The language was revised from the 1987 VHDL standard. Those features that are only available in VHDL'93 or VHDL'87 are explicitly identified in the text and marked in the margin as shown here. However, I do not cover the full set of VHDL'93 features. This text is based on the idea that at the sophomore and junior level it is best to limit coverage to those features of the language that can be used to build useful models that provide insights into the behavior of digital systems, particularly at the architectural level. Students can subsequently can move onto a broader coverage of the language in many excellent textbooks, some of which are listed in the bibliography. As a result, the reader should be aware that complete coverage of the language features is not provided in this text. Furthermore, early in the text the IEEE 1164 standard data types are introduced and utilized in all of the examples rather than staying with the relatively simpler **bit** and **bit_vector** types. We hope that this will expose students to standard practice and not compromise the goals of focusing on core language features and types.

Finally, all of the models shown in the text have been compiled and tested under Aldec's Active VHDL 3.5 simulator and the synthesis examples were compiled and tested using Xilinx's Foundation Express 2.1*i*. The synthesis examples were compiled and simulated for the Xilinx XC4000XL components.

Acknowledgments

This book grew out of a perceived need in the classroom, the encouragement of colleagues, the participation and feedback from students, and the never-ending accommodations of my family. It is a pleasure to acknowledge the contributions of the many people who contributed to its generation.

I am grateful to Tom Robbins of Prentice Hall who had the courage to sign me for a second text after completing my previous book, *VHDL Starter's Guide,* as late as I did. Tom's vision extended to the involvement of Xilinx Inc. and he encouraged me to adopt the same *Starter's Guide* approach toward the introduction to high-level synthesis concepts in early digital and computer architecture courses.

I am especially grateful to those colleagues who were generous with their time in reading early drafts of the manuscript and forthcoming with their comments and suggestions. I am grateful to Mike Furman and Jim Hamblen for their comments, insights, and overall diligence in the classroom. Peter Flur and John Lockhart were as always generous with their time and patient in their responses in helping me with the nuances of typesetting and managing document preparation across platforms and tools. I am also grateful to Diana Fouts for the figures and proofreading of the text.

I am once again grateful to numerous sophomore and junior students in CmpE 2510, CmpE 3510, and ECE 4170 for their patience with the early draft of the text. I continue to learn from them as I hope they do in the courses I have the good fortune to teach. The conscientiousness of the reviewers was evident in the depth of their critique, and improvements over early drafts were largely due to their diligent appraisals in identifying inconsistencies, suggesting illustrative exercises, and improving the presentation style.

Projects such as this text are impossible without the indulgence of my family. I hope the resulting quality of this text and associated benefits to users can do justice to the sacrifices they have had to make.

My colleagues, students, and family share any successes from the completion of this text, whereas any omissions and errors remain solely with the author.

Sudhakar Yalamanchili
Atlanta, GA

CHAPTER 1

Introduction

1.1 What is VHDL?

The acronym VHDL stands for the **V**HSIC **H**ardware **D**escription **L**anguage. The acronym VHSIC, in turn, refers to the **V**ery **H**igh-**S**peed **I**ntegrated **C**ircuit program. This program was sponsored by the Department of Defense (DoD) with the goals of developing a new generation of high-speed integrated circuits. During the course of this program the increasing complexity of digital systems that were made possible by continuous advances in semiconductor and packaging technologies were found to have a fundamental impact on the economics of the design of military and space electronic systems. When the life-cycle cost of these systems were examined the cost of maintenance was becoming significant. Furthermore it was becoming increasingly difficult to share designs of subsystems across contractors. The need for a standardized representation of digital systems became apparent. A team of DoD contractors was awarded the contract to develop the language and the first version was released in 1985. The language was subsequently transferred to the IEEE for standardization after which representatives from industry, government, and academe were involved in its further development. Subsequently the language was ratified in 1987 and became the IEEE 1076–1987 standard. The language was reballoted after five years and with the addition of new features forms the 1076–1993 version of the language. This text adheres to the 1076-1993 standard while attempting to point out differences with the 1076-1987 version, because simulation and synthesis compilers will generally support both versions and one is bound to encounter legacy models.

Ever since VHDL became an IEEE standard it has enjoyed steadily increasing adoption throughout the electronic systems computer-aided design (CAD) community. The DoD requires that VHDL descriptions be delivered for all application-specific integrated circuits (ASICs). The interoperability between models developed using VHDL environments from different CAD vendors has been improved by the establishment of the IEEE 1164 standard package. Synthesis support has been similarly supported through the establishment of a version of the IEEE 1164 package for synthesis. Practically every major CAD vendor supports VHDL. This status of VHDL as an industry standard provides a number of practical benefits including model interoperability among vendors, third party vendor support, and design re-use.

Conventional procedural programming languages such as C or Pascal typically describe procedures for computing a mathematical function or manipulating data, for example, matrix multiplication or sorting respectively. A program is a recipe or a sequence of steps for *how* to perform a computation or manipulate data. The execution of the program results in the computation or rearrangement of data values. On the other hand VHDL is a language for *describing* digital systems. Such descriptions can be used by a simulator for simulating the behavior of the system without having to actually construct the system. Alternatively synthesis compilers can utilize such a description for creating descriptions of the digital hardware for implementing the system. Although VHDL has been investigated for its use in describing and simulating analog systems, the language is predominantly used in the design of digital electronic systems.

1.2 Digital System Design

The design of digital systems is a process that starts from the specification of requirements and proceeds to produce a functional design that is eventually refined through a sequence of steps to a physical implementation. Both simulation and synthesis are complementary activities employed in the design process although the specific relationship is a function of the target implementation. Consider the design of an ASIC for processing digital images. This is a custom chip designed for a specific task, unlike a microprocessor that may be programmed for a variety of tasks. Custom ASICs are generally the highest performing solution for any computation but often the most expensive. An example of the sequence of activities that typically takes place during ASIC design is shown in Figure 1-1.

The first step is the specification of the requirements. Such a specification will typically include the performance requirements derived from the number of images to be processed/sec and the operations to be performed on them, as well as interface requirements, cost constraints, and other physical requirements such as system size and power dissipation. From these functional requirements, a preliminary high-level functional design can be generated. Simulation is often used at this level to converge to a functional design that can meet the performance requirements. This initial functional design is now refined to produce a more detailed design description at the level of registers, memories, arithmetic units, and state machines. This is the register transfer level (RTL) of the design. Subse-

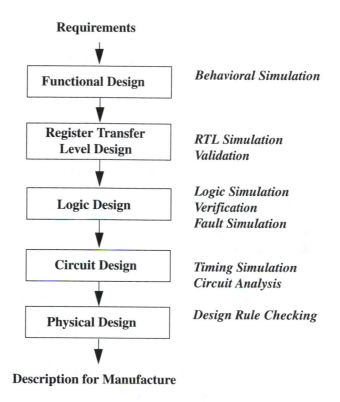

Requirements

| Functional Design | *Behavioral Simulation* |

| Register Transfer Level Design | *RTL Simulation* *Validation* |

| Logic Design | *Logic Simulation* *Verification* *Fault Simulation* |

| Circuit Design | *Timing Simulation* *Circuit Analysis* |

| Physical Design | *Design Rule Checking* |

Description for Manufacture

FIGURE 1-1 Typical activity flow in top-down digital system design

quent refinement of this RTL description produces a logic design that implements each of the RTL components. Both RTL and logic level simulation may be used to ensure that the design meets the original specification. Fault simulation can model the effects of expected manufacturing defects as well as faults that may be induced due to the environment. For example, if this image-processing chip is to be flown in a satellite, radiation effects in space can cause devices to change state and lead to single bit errors. If the error rate in the intended orbit is relatively high the design can be modified to accommodate such bit errors using techniques tuned to the particular physical phenomena. Finally, the logic level implementation is transformed into a circuit level implementation and hence to a physical chip layout from which accurate physical properties of the design, such as chip area and power dissipation, can be evaluated. Design rule checks, circuit parameter extraction, and circuit simulation activities can be performed at this level.

At each level of this design hierarchy there are components that are used to describe the design. At the higher or more abstract levels we have a smaller number of more power-ful components such as adders and memories. At the lower and less abstract levels we have a larger number of simpler, less-powerful components such as gates and transistors. Each level of the design hierarchy corresponds to a *level of abstraction* and has an associated set of activities and design tools that support the activities at this level. Some of the activities at each level are shown in Figure 1-1. The accuracy with which we can predict the behavior, physical properties, and performance of the circuit increases at the lower levels of the hierarchy with considerably longer simulation times. Imagine having to simulate the behavior of 100 million transistors on a chip!

If design errors are discovered at these finer levels of detail, changes in the design may be expensive to make, particularly if we have to move back several levels in the design process to correct these errors. This can lead to longer development times and consequently increased cost, not to the mention loss of revenues by being late to market. Much of the motivation for the development of hardware description languages in general stems from the evolving economics of the marketplace for electronic systems and the methodologies used to design these systems. With the ability to simulate designs at multiple levels of abstraction, errors can be discovered and corrected early. Moreover it is important to note that throughout this hierarchy simulation is a commonly used technique. Hardware description languages such as VHDL are targeted for use throughout this design hierarchy and provide some degree if uniformity across the various levels.

A typical design flow that employs automated synthesis depends on the target hardware. Let us consider our digital image processing chip, only this time we wish to implement the chip in a field programmable gate array (FPGA). For the moment we can think of an FPGA as hardware device that provides a large number of gates and flip flops that we can connect as we wish. This is not an accurate image but will do for the moment (at least until we get to Section 3.3). Now our design flow changes to the example shown in Figure 1-2. A functional design is created, say in VHDL, and can be simulated as before to verify functional correctness. This functional design may be refined to an RTL description where data flows and basic hardware functional units are defined. Once we have created the RTL design a synthesis compiler creates a gate level implementation of the system described by the VHDL code. At this point a logic level simulation can performed to obtain preliminary performance estimates. This logic implementation is now placed on the FPGA using the gates and flip flops provided by the chip. The corresponding gates and flip flops must now be connected by routing signals between them on the chip. Once this placement and routing processes have been completed we can derive accurate estimates of the delays through the wires and gates since these delays are available from the chip specification. This timing information can be extracted from the design and stored in an industry standard format. We can now conduct a realistic timing simulation.

The growth in the FPGA marketplace has been explosive as they potentially provide very low-cost programmable hardware solutions for many tasks currently performed by embedded controllers. However they are also making headway in the market for high-performance custom solutions. In fact FPGA solutions have been proposed that can outperform current generation ASIC chips and at a significantly reduced cost. It is this potential cost-performance advantages in several niche markets that is garnering significant interest in the research, development, and product communities. In particular it is the ASIC replacement market that is fueling much the current development. Thus the synthesis focus in this text is motivated by, and on occasion only relevant to, FPGAs, although the emphasis is on general principles that must be addressed by most any synthesis compiler.

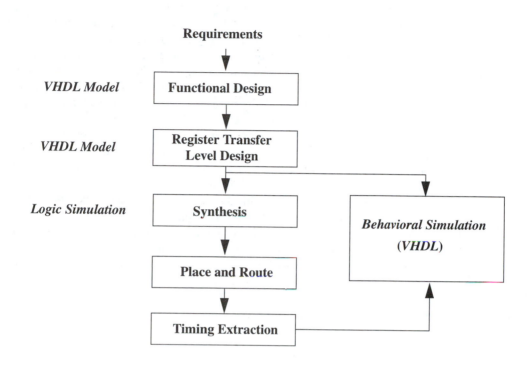

FIGURE 1-2 An Example of a synthesis design flow for FPGAs

1.3 The Marketplace

The use of CAD environments in general and hardware description languages in particular is driven by the technology marketplace. After all, these tools and languages are intended to enable the cost-effective and profitable development of electronics products. The key question with respect to the state of the art is: where are the costs, both in terms of costs incurred and revenues lost due to design paradigms that are not as efficient or effective as they could be?

The costs incurred are directly a function of the available technology. Both the semi-conductor industry and software industry have been in overdrive during the last three decades and show no signs of abatement in the next decade. Memory densities have been quadrupling every three years and processor speeds doubling every eighteen months. As chip densities increase, new products are becoming available at a faster rate and development cycles are becoming shorter. The importance of time to market is captured in an illustrative manner and described by Madisetti as shown in Figure 1-3 [8]. For every product there is an optimal time for introduction into the marketplace in a manner that will maximize the revenue generated. Early in the life cycle of the product, market share should rise, peak, and then begin to decline as newer products emerge. If the product is delayed to market, then the trajectory of its performance relative to the maximum may be depicted as shown in the figure. In summary Figure 1-3 shows that it is very difficult to make up for lost ground. Many organizations measure lost opportunity cost in terms of thousands to tens of thousands of dollars per day in lost revenue. An unfortunate side effect of such economics is that time to market pressures may reduce the quality of the first version of the product; with the increasingly faster rate of technology evolution approaches to reduce time to market are critical. New CAD tool environments and hardware description languages are an integral part of any solution.

Given this emphasis on the time-to-market and the resulting need for shorter design cycles, what are the impediments to shortening the time to market? Historically, the CAD tool industry has developed in a bottom-up fashion and has been driven by the development of point tools and processes: design rule checking, layout, verification, and so forth. Digital design was a manual process in that designs needed to be transformed manually between levels of abstraction and at each level of abstraction we would be assisted by the

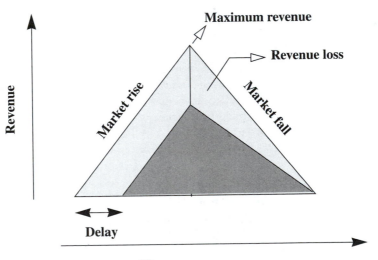

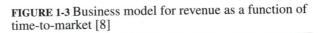

FIGURE 1-3 Business model for revenue as a function of time-to-market [8]

appropriate tools. This is partly a by-product of the fact that for chip and board designs there has been an understanding of the specific design problems, which include layout, design rule checking, test vector generation, and so on. Advances have focused on better tools to address these problems spurred by the new challenges of faster, denser, and more complex technologies. In contrast, very few tools exist at the architectural level for addressing system design issues. The problems are not as well defined, but the impact can be overwhelming. It has been observed that the first 10%–20% of the design cycle can determine 70%–80% of the final system cost. Further, it has been reported that only 5%–10% of the design cycle time is spent in studying and formulating requirements, whereas 70% of the manufacturing costs are affected by customer requirements [8].

New methodologies are needed to address the issues of requirements capture, system specification, and early analysis via rapid prototyping. Such new design methodologies are emerging, and VHDL is becoming an integral part of such design approaches.

1.4 The Role of Hardware Description Languages

Traditional design methodologies have been structured around a hierarchy of representations of the system being designed. Distinct representations at differing levels of detail are necessary for the various tasks encountered during design. One of the best-known representations of the different views and levels of abstraction in a digital system is the Y–chart shown in Figure 1-4 [3,13,14] and illustrated through the following example.

Imagine we are a part of a company, DSP, Inc., in the business of designing a next-generation digital signal-processing chip, code name Cyclone. Given the current costs of fabrication and the time window within which the chip must be brought to market to be competitive, we wish to verify prior to fabrication that the chip can support the intended applications. From the design flow shown in Figure 1-1, we know that this behavior can be described at multiple levels of abstraction, that is, at the functional level, RTL level, logic level, and so on. Behavioral descriptions are necessary early in the design so that simulations can ensure that the chip is functionally correct. This functionality may be verified at more than one level of abstraction. The advantage of this approach is that we can make this assessment independent of the many possible physical implementations. Once we have verified the functionality, the design can be translated to a structural description composed of the major components of this chip: memories, registers, arithmetic units, logic units, and so forth. Simulation can be employed again to ensure that the Cyclone structural design correctly performs the intended functions using the components that we have selected. As shown in Figure 1-4, the structural description may also be provided with varying levels of detail. This design can be refined until we translate this description to a physical description that can be further refined to produce a manufacturable specification.

Historically, hardware description languages have been targeted to a certain level of abstraction such as the gate level or RTL. Tools have been developed and targeted for tasks at a specific level of the design. For example, some tools may be optimized for implementing state machines that describe data movement at the RTL. Other tools may be developed

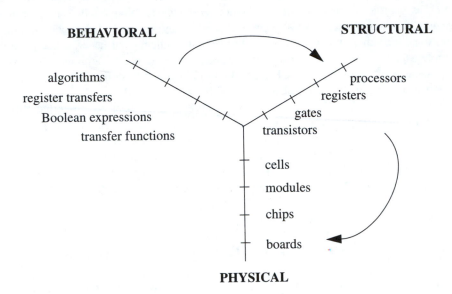

FIGURE 1-4 Design views and corresponding levels of abstraction

for verification at the gate level by generating test vectors used for final chip verification. The tools at the different levels of abstraction may employ different descriptions of the Cyclone. Such *point tools* are focused on a single aspect of the design and on a single level of abstraction. Often these tools came with their own languages and associated compilers and simulators. However, as chips become more complex and design processes start using an increasingly diverse set of tools, the time taken to move information between tools has become a concern. Recently, estimates of the lost productivity due to incompatibility between design tools has been estimated as high as $4.5 billion dollars/year [8]. Although simulation has been used at all levels of system design designated in Figure 1-4, synthesis attempts to move in an automated fashion between the three domains and levels of abstraction. The use of hardware description languages such as VHDL can help address several aspects of this fundamental problem of design refinement.

Interoperability => The VHDL language provides a set of constructs that can be applied at multiple levels of abstraction and multiple views of the system. This significantly expands the scope of the application of the language and promotes a standardized, portable model of electronic systems. Thus, the complexity of the movement of data and design information between tools is significantly reduced. The net effect is a reduction in the time to design the Cyclone and bring it to market. We may also expect that the reduction in the number of distinct types of tools and languages realizes a reduction in the cost of the design infrastructure and therefore a reduction in the product unit cost.

Technology is a rapidly moving target. We cannot anticipate innovations in technology design styles or products. Therefore an attractive philosophy is to develop a design environment that is independent of technology. The industry is characterized by a number of distinct technologies and associated design styles that target specific points in the continuum of time to market, cost, and performance. For example, the use of programmable logic devices (PLDs) FPGAs has the attributes of low cost and quick time to market. ASIC products incur higher non-recurring engineering development costs and therefore usually higher product costs. However, they can deliver substantially higher performance. These distinct design styles leads to environments with a distinct set of CAD tools and methodologies.

Technology Independence => The VHDL descriptions of the design are not tied to a specific methodology or target technology. The language is rich enough that it can be used to describe a chip at the instruction set level, register transfer level, or switching transistor level. DSP Inc. must produce a high-performance version for use in a real-time radar processing system for the military. Design tools for custom and ASIC chips utilize VHDL in their suite to simulate and validate their designs prior to detailed physical design. Prior to physical design we would wish to have detailed timing information to ensure that the performance requirements of the application can be met. However, the application software developers may simply want a functionally accurate instruction set simulation of the Cyclone chip so that development of application software may begin immediately – hardware/software co-design. Eventually when a detailed physical design is available, the software may be tested on an associated simulation to determine the performance that can be achieved for the applications of interest—two widely differing levels of detail, both easily supported within the same language.

Now imagine it is six months later and you have found a commercial market for the Cyclone to implement video compression algorithms. The only problem is that they have to cost one-tenth of the cost of the military part but the processing constraints are much looser. The major CAD vendors have tools that can synthesize designs to FPGA and complex PLD (CPLD) devices. The Cyclone is re-implemented within an FPGA using synthesis from the VHDL models. The result is a cheaper, slower, higher volume product.

Now let us say that your company develops a model of the Cyclone using CAD tools from vendor Tools'R'Us. Now your company wishes to have a subcontractor use this chip in the design of a second product, say a voice recognition board for personal communicators. Their design environment is completely different, using archaic design tools from StoneAge CAD Tools, Inc. You now need to send them detailed schematics and operational specifications and educate them on the Cyclone design so that they may use this description to design and validate the board level product using their design tools. However, they do support the VHDL language. Because VHDL is a standard, rather than having them reconstruct the design in their environment, the preceding instruction set models of the Cyclone can be directly used and simulated, and will produce identical results using the StoneAge's simulators.

Design Re-use=> We can see libraries of VHDL models of components emerging and being shared across platforms, toolsets, organizations, and technical groups. Engineers working on a large design can be independently designing subsystems with considerably less concern for design environment or design tool compatibly issues. As we will see in later chapters the language possesses many features that enable us to separate the interface of a components from its internal implementation.

Hardware/Software Prototyping => Part of the difficulty with a board design is that the software for processing the data streams cannot be tested until hardware is available. But what if we have detailed hardware descriptions of the components on the board that behave exactly as the Cyclone chip to the level of detail of a clock cycle? We could simulate the system to a sufficient level of detail so that the simulator could take the place of the hardware for software development purposes. Application programs could be executed on a software simulation. This would permit trade-offs between the hardware and software implementations even before a single chip or board was designed! Such an approach based on this concept of Virtual Prototyping is an example of a newly emerging design methodology for systems in general, but is currently being applied to digital signal processing systems in particular [8,11].

Hardware description languages are at the core of modern digital systems design methodologies. Proficiency in their use will be necessary for designers and familiarity a must for electrical and computer engineering students.

1.5 Chapter Summary

Digital system design is a process of creating and managing multiple descriptions of systems representing distinct views and varying levels of abstraction. Historically, design environments grew around point tools for solving specific problems at each level of abstraction. Design methodologies governed the application of these tools and the flow of information between them. The evolution of distinct methodologies and modeling styles can hinder interoperability and make it difficult to share models. As electronic systems grew in complexity, the need to integrate these point tools into a cohesive design process determined a large component of the economics of product design. The advent of hardware description languages such as VHDL and their acceptance as industry standards has had an enormous impact on the economics of product development.

We see that VHDL modeling can be used to model hardware and software systems at multiple levels of abstraction (Figure 1-5). The language is independent of technology and design methodologies or styles, and therefore promotes portable descriptions, rapid prototyping, and free exchange of models among organizations and individuals. The result has been the promise of reduced design cycle times, faster time-to-market and reduced cost. We can expect to see the use and growth of the language continue as a widely used hardware description language for both military and commercial systems for some time to come.

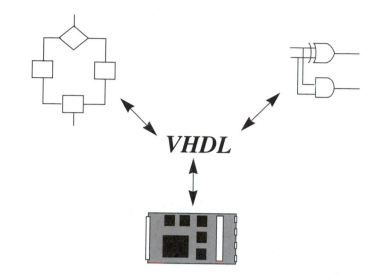

FIGURE 1-5 The VHDL language can be applied at multiple levels of abstraction

Within the purview of the design of electronic systems the VHDL language is accompanied by several other hardware description languages. One of the more widely used is Verilog. The goals and motivation for the Verilog language parallel those of VHDL, although Verilog shares a distinct developmental heritage. The major CAD tool vendors support both the VHDL and Verilog languages as well as a number of homegrown and specialized languages for specific design activities.

CHAPTER 2 — Modeling Digital Systems

VHDL programs are unlike programs written in Pascal, C, or Fortran. Conventional programs are based on thinking in terms of algorithmic sequences of calculations that manipulate data toward a specific computational goal. The thought process that goes into writing such programs is inherently procedural, a direct result of the serial computing model embodied in most modern computers. Writing VHDL programs is very different. We are not interested so much in how a function is computed, rather we are interested in *describing* the behavior of some physical system such as a digital circuit. This behavioral description can be used for at least two purposes, both of which are addressed in this text. The first purpose is the simulation of digital circuits. A simulator uses the VHDL description to conduct a simulation that "behaves like" the physical system. Such simulations can be used to verify the behavior of the digital circuit prior to expensive fabrication. The simulation can in fact serve as a virtual prototype in making and evaluating design trade-offs prior to finalizing the design. The second purpose is for the synthesis of digital circuits. Design tools analyze the VHDL description and produce a digital circuit that implements the behavior captured in the VHDL description. The resulting circuit descriptions can be processed rapidly to produce custom hardware or can be used to configure re-programmable hardware components to implement the design. Thus the VHDL descriptions can in fact be used to support two complementary processes found in the design of digital systems: simulation and synthesis.

The VHDL language was motivated by the desire to describe digital systems. Thus this chapter discusses the significant structural, physical, and behavioral characteristics of digital systems. The characteristics that are captured in the VHDL language constructs are described in the following chapters.

2.1 Motivation

Physical systems such as digital circuits do not necessarily behave in a manner that is easily described by sequential programs that we are used to writing. They are characterized by interactions between potentially thousands to millions of concurrently operational components. For example, consider describing a modern microprocessor, which at the time of this writing can be represented by a Pentium III, at the gate level. If we could formally prove the correctness of a design from the design specification and implementation we would not need simulation. However formal proof techniques cannot currently, nor in the foreseeable future, handle designs of such complexity. Thus we rely on simulation. In fact, many times the reason we want to simulate a physical system is because we cannot otherwise evaluate the system. For example, if we need to know the average time a person must wait at a bus stop, we cannot obtain some mathematical function that will accurately compute this value for us. Traffic patterns, whimsical pedestrians, and riders with incorrect change all contribute to a degree of unpredictability and complexity that prevents us from writing an accurate mathematical expression for the waiting time at a bus stop. However, we can simulate the transit system and observe how long people wait in the simulation. If our simulation is accurate, then we will be able to predict reliably the delays that will occur in practice.

The digital systems that we will consider do not exhibit probabilistic or random behavior but are comprised of many constituent subsystems whose interactions can be quite complex, and there are several compelling reasons for simulation. We may wish to simulate a design prior to implementation to ensure that the system meets its specification. For example, we may design a board-level product that interfaces to a camera and processes images in real time. A VHDL simulation of the board may be used to establish that the design can indeed operate fast enough to keep up with the rate at which images are being received from the camera. Given the cost of modern fabrication facilities and the increasing complexity of digital systems it has become necessary to be able to rely on accurate simulation models to design and test chips and systems prior to their construction. How can we be sure that the design will function as intended or that the design is indeed correct? The VHDL simulation serves as a basis for testing complex designs and validating the design prior to fabrication. The overall effect is that of reducing redesign, shortening the design cycle, reducing the probability of design error, and bringing the product to market sooner.

The features of a language for describing digital systems are quite different from procedural languages. Whereas early simulators for digital systems have been written in C or Pascal, developers had to provide new functions, operations, and data types to enable one to write simulation applications. The definition of the VHDL language provides a range of built-in features in support of the simulation of digital systems.

As a result of the motivation to model digital systems, many of the language concepts and constructs can be identified with the structural, behavioral, and physical characteristics of digital systems. We learn best when we can identify concepts with which we are already familiar. In this chapter we will review the operational characteristics of digital systems and identify several key attributes that will be subsequently linked to major language features. In Chapter 3 we will describe the models underlying the use of the VHDL descriptions for simulation and synthesis, namely discrete event simulation and hardware inference respectively. The remainder of the text focuses on the presentation, description, and application of the major language features.

2.2 Describing Systems

The term *system* is used in many different contexts to refer to anything from single chips to large supercomputers. Webster's dictionary defines a system as: "an assemblage of objects united by some form of regular interaction or interdependence."

We are interested in being able to describe digital systems at any one of several levels of abstraction, starting from the switched transistor level to the computing system level. To do so requires us to identify attributes of systems common to all of these levels of abstraction. For example, imagine that you are in the business of selling sound cards for personal computers. You are trying to make a sale to Personal Computer, Inc. and have them include this sound card as a part of their product line, thus making it available in all of their personal computers. A sample design of your card might appear as shown in Figure 2-1. In order to make this sale, you must be able to provide a concise description of this card to the engineers of Personal Computer, Inc., How could you describe such a card? What do the engineers need to know to evaluate your design? They certainly need to understand the *interface* to the card. For example, what can you connect to this card? Speakers, microphones, or even a stereo amplifier? How does the processor communicate with this card? You must be able to describe all of the signals that may pass through the card interface to ensure compatibility with the internal bus used for communication between components within their system. A second component of this description is the behavior of the card itself. This could be communicated in one of several ways. One way

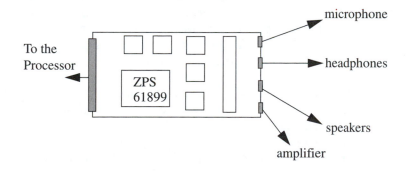

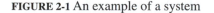

FIGURE 2-1 An example of a system

is to describe component chips and their interconnection; this description assumes that the engineers were familiar with the operation of the individual chips. Such a description is commonly referred to as a *structural* description and can be easily conveyed in a block diagram. Alternatively, we can describe the behavior of the card in terms of the type of processing it performs on the input signals and the type of output signals it produces, for example, audio output for the speakers. Such descriptions are referred to as *behavioral* descriptions. You are describing what the card does independent of the physical parts that make up the card. Depending upon who you are talking to, one description or the other is preferable. For example, marketing would be interested in the latter description and engineering would be interested in the former.

Structure and behavior are complementary ways of describing systems. The specification of the behavior does not necessarily tell you anything about the structure of the system or the components used to build it. In fact, there are usually many different ways in which you can build a system to provide the same behavior. In this case, other factors such as cost or reliability become the determining factors in choosing the best design. We would expect that any language for describing digital systems will support both structural and behavioral descriptions. We would also expect that the language would enable us to evaluate or simulate several structural realizations of the same behavioral description. The VHDL language provides these features.

2.3 Events, Propagation Delays, and Concurrency

Let us look a little closer at these structural and behavioral descriptions. Digital systems are fundamentally about *signals*, specifically binary signals that may take values 0 or 1. Digital circuits are comprised of *components* such as gates, flip-flops, and counters. Components are interconnected by wires and transform input signals into output signals. A machine-readable (i.e., programming language) description of a digital circuit must be able to describe the components that make up the circuit, their interconnection, and the behavior of each of the components in terms of their input and output signals and the relation between them. This language description can then be simulated by associated computer aided design tools or used to synthesize a hardware description.

Consider the gate level description of a half adder shown in Figure 2-2. There are two input signals, a and b. The circuit computes the value of two output signals, sum and carry. The values of the output signals, sum and carry, are computed as a function of the input signals, a and b. For example, when a = 1 and b = 0, we have sum = 1 and carry = 0. Now, suppose the value of b changes to 1. We say that an *event* occurs on signal b. The event is the change in the value of the input signal from 0 to 1. In our idealized model of the world this transition takes place instantaneously at a specific, or discrete, point in time. Real circuits take a finite amount of time to switch states, but this approximation is still very useful. From the truth tables for the gates, we know that such an event on b will cause the values of the output signals to change. The signals sum and carry will acquire values 0 and 1 respectively, that is, events will occur on the signals sum and carry. A basic ques-

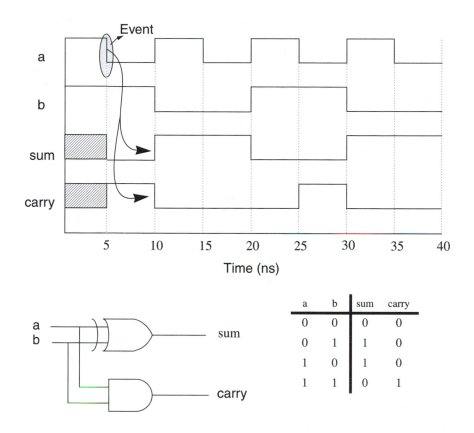

FIGURE 2-2 Half-adder circuit

tion then becomes the following: When will these events on the output signals occur relative to the timing of the events on the input signals?

Electrical circuits have a certain amount of inertia or natural resistance to change.
Physical devices such as transistors that are used to implement the gate level logic take a
finite amount of time to switch between logic levels. Therefore, a change in the value of a
signal on the input to a gate will not produce an immediate change in the value of the output signal. Rather, it will take a finite amount of time for changes in the inputs to a gate to
propagate to the output.   This period of time is referred to as the *propagation delay* of the
gate. The time it takes for changes to propagate through the gates is a function of the physical properties of the gate, including the implementation technology, the design of the gate
from basic transistors, and the power supplied to the circuit. From the timing behavior
depicted in Figure 2-2, we can see that the gate propagation delay is 5 ns. Electrical cur-
rents that carry logic signals through interconnect media, such as the wires, also travel at a
finite rate. Thus, in reality, signals experience propagation delays through wires and the

magnitude of this delay is dependent upon the length of the wire. This delay is non-negligible particularly in very high-speed, high-density circuits. It is interesting to note that wires have considerably less inertia than gates. The resulting physical phenomenon is therefore quite different. However, as device feature sizes have become increasingly smaller, wire delays have become non-negligible in modern high-density circuits. As we shall see in later chapters, VHDL provides specific constructs for handling both types of delays. The timing diagram shown in Figure 2-2 does not include wire delays.

A third property of the behavior of the circuit shown in Figure 2-2 is *concurrency* of operation. Once a change is observed on input signal b, the two gates concurrently compute the values of the output signals sum and carry and new events may subsequently occur on these signals. If both gates exhibit the same propagation delays then the new events on sum and carry will occur simultaneously. These new events may go on to initiate the computation of other events in other parts of the circuit. For example, consider two half adders combined to form a full adder, shown in Figure 2-3. Events on the input signals In1 or In2 produce events on signals s1 or s3. Events on s1 or s3 in turn may produce events on s2, sum, or c_out. In effect, events on the input signals In1 or In2 propagate to the outputs of the full adder. In the process many other events internal to the circuit may be generated. In the associated timing diagram, every $0 \rightarrow 1$ and $1 \rightarrow 0$ transition on each signal corresponds to an event. Note the data-driven nature of these systems. Events on signals lead to computations that may generate events on other signals.

2.4 Waveforms and Timing

Over a period of time, the sequence of events that occur on a signal produces a *waveform* on that signal. The effects of each event may in turn propagate through the circuit, producing waveforms on internal signals and eventually producing waveforms on the output signals. The timing diagram shown in Figure 2-3 is a collection of waveforms on signals in the full-adder circuit, where each waveform is an alternating sequence of $0 \rightarrow 1$ and $1 \rightarrow 0$ transitions or events.

The model of the operation of digital circuits in terms of events, delays, concurrent operation, and waveforms extends to sequential circuits as well as combinational circuits. Consider the operation and timing of a positive edge-triggered D flip-flop shown in Figure 2-4. The output values are determined at the time of a $0 \rightarrow 1$ transition on the clock signal. At this time the input value on signal D is sampled and the values of Q and $\overline{Q}$ are determined. Events on the asynchronous set ($\overline{S}$) and reset ($\overline{R}$) lines produce events on the output signals independent of events on the clock. The unique aspect of the behavior of this model is the dependency on the clock signal. Computation of output events is initiated at a specific point in time determined by a $0 \rightarrow 1$ event on the Clk signal, independent of events occurring on the D input signal. This need to *wait for* a specific event is an important aspect of the behavior of sequential digital circuits. Such circuits are referred to as *synchronous* circuits. Synchronous circuits operate with a periodic signal commonly

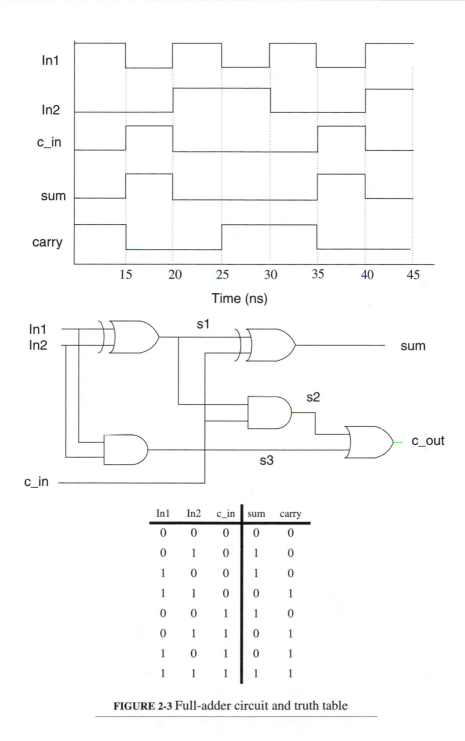

FIGURE 2-3 Full-adder circuit and truth table

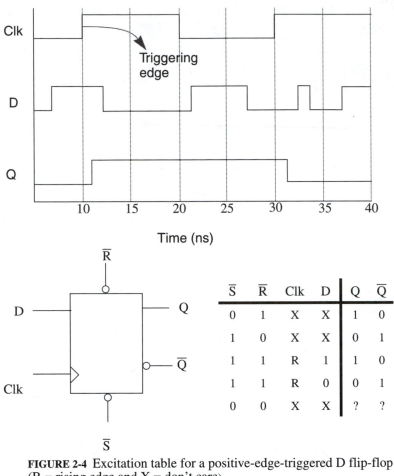

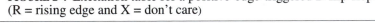

FIGURE 2-4 Excitation table for a positive-edge-triggered D flip-flop
(R = rising edge and X = don't care)

referred to as a clock that serves as a common time base. Clocks are an important aspect of digital circuits and deserve special attention

Alternatively, in the absence of a global clock signal many digital systems operate asynchronously with request–acknowledge protocols. This is most easily understood in the context of a communication channel between two chips. The transmitting chip may assert a TRANSMIT signal when it is ready to transmit data. The receiving chip will be monitoring the TRANSMIT signal and when asserted will read the data and then assert an ACK signal. On seeing the event on the ACK signal the transmitter can stop transmitting the data. The timing is shown in Figure 2-5 where the causal relationship between signal transitions is shown by the arrows. Such "handshaking" operations are very common in the operation of digital logic implementation of communication channels and it is clear that both the transmitter and receiver have to wait for specific events on a signal.

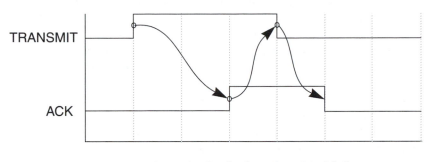

FIGURE 2-5 An example of a four-phase handshake

2.5 Signal Values

Signal values are normally associated with the outputs of gates. Wires transfer these values to the inputs of other gates, which, as a result, may drive their outputs to new values. In general, we tend to think of signals in digital circuits as being binary valued and being driven to these values by a source such as the power supply or the output of a gate. These logical values are physically realized within a circuit by associating logical 0 or 1 values to voltage or current levels at the output of a device. For example, in some circuits a voltage occurring between 0 and 0.8 volts is recognized as a logical 0 signal, whereas a voltage occurring in the range 2.0 to 3.3 volts is recognized as logical 1 signal. However, what happens when a signal is not driven to any value, for example, if it is disconnected? What is the value of the signal? It is neither 0 or 1. Such a state is referred to as the high-impedance state and is usually denoted by Z. This is a normal, inactive condition and occurs when a signal is (temporarily) disconnected.

What happens when a signal is concurrently driven to both a 0 and a 1 value? This is clearly an abnormal or error condition and should not occur, and if it does, it is indicative of a design error. How do we denote the value of the signal? Remember that our overall goal is the accurate description of digital systems often for the purpose of testing a design to ensure that it is correct prior to fabrication. If this condition were to occur during the simulation of a circuit the simulator must be able to represent the value of the signal and propagate the effects of this design error through the circuit. Such unknown values are typically denoted by X. What if the initial value of a signal is undefined? How can we represent this value and propagate the effects of uninitialized signal values to determine the effect on the operation of the circuit? Such values are typically denoted by U.

At the very least, we see that for the purpose of simulation 0 and 1 values alone are insufficient to accurately capture the behavior of digital systems. We will see that the

VHDL language is flexible enough to enable the definition of a range of values for single-bit signals. Early in the evolution of VHDL, CAD tool vendors defined their own value systems. Some vendors even had as many as forty-six distinct values for a single-bit signal! This made it difficult to share VHDL models. Imagine if different C compilers had different definitions of the values of integers. The same C program could produce different results depending upon the compilers that were used. In addition to 0, 1, Z, X, and U values, it is useful to denote the concept of *signal strength*. The strength of a signal reflects the ability of the source device to supply energy to drive the signal. This strength can be weakened or attenuated by, for example, the resistance of the wires giving rise to signals of different strengths. Although the range of strength values can be large, only two levels are sufficient to characterize certain types of transistor circuits. The use of strength values facilitates certain styles of design. The VHDL language is being widely used to describe the behavior of circuits that can be automatically synthesized by design tools. A value system that incorporates the concept of signal strength is therefore necessary.

Value	Interpretation
U	Uninitialized
X	Forcing Unknown
0	Forcing 0
1	Forcing 1
Z	High Impedance
W	Weak Unknown
L	Weak 0
H	Weak 1
-	Don't Care

FIGURE 2-6 IEEE 1164 value system

In an attempt to establish common ground and enable the construction of portable models, the IEEE has approved a nine-value system. This is the IEEE 1164 standard, which has gained acceptance and widespread usage. In this system single-bit signals take on functional values of 0, 1. However, they can also be unknown (X), uninitialized (U), or not driven (Z). If we include two levels of signal strength and the don't-care value (-), we have the IEEE 1164 value system shown in Figure 2-6. It is important to note that this value system is not a part of the VHDL language but rather a standard definition that vendors are motivated to support and users are motivated to use because it enables reuse of designs and sharing of models between users. Practically all vendors support the IEEE 1164 value system.

From the perspective of the synthesis of digital circuits from VHDL descriptions, the effect of the value system is a bit different. For example, when circuits are synthesized the unknown and uninitialized values do not have any meaning for a signal. A signal must be represented by a wire or a storage element, such as a latch or flip flop, and the signal value is represented by the state of the wire, latch, or flip flop. There is no physical implementation for the unknown or uninitialized signal values. Synthesis compilers must address this issue while the IEEE has approved an 1164 standard-based package for synthesis.

2.6 Shared Signals

It is common for components in a digital circuit to have multiple sources for the value of an input signal and multiple destinations for the value of an output signal. However, connecting all component inputs and outputs by dedicated signal paths can be expensive. Therefore many designs will utilize *buses*: a group of signals that can be time shared among multiple source and destination components. Consider the simple case of a single-bit signal shared among multiple sources and destinations as shown in Figure 2-7. This is an efficient design in the sense that it minimizes the interconnect wiring among communicating components. Sources and destinations time share the bus using transceivers– transmitter/receiver pairs. At any given time only one transmitter is enabled whereas multiple receivers may be enabled at the same time. The tri-state buffers can be controlled by a decoder to ensure that only one source is driving the bus at a time. The architecture of personal computers and workstations is built around one or more multi-bit buses. The microprocessor may drive a data bus to communicate addresses to memory, whereas, at other times, the memory controller may drive the bus to return values to the processor. The Input/Output buses in PCs interconnect many devices such as CD ROMs, floppy disk drives, and hard disk drives, that share the Input/Output bus.

Although buses only permit one transmitter at one time, certain forms of switching circuits are carefully designed based on *wired logic* and permit multiple, concurrent transmitters or drivers on a bus. In these circuits, the interconnection of wires can produce AND and OR Boolean functions. For example, if several devices drive a shared signal to either 0 or Z, then the signal value will be determined by the interactions among all of the values applied to it: in this case if at least one device is driving the signal to a 0, the value of the signal will be 0. Thus, the interconnection can be regarded as implementing a wired-OR function. Similarly it also possible to implemented wired-AND logic.

The key issue here is that some signals may be driven to a value by one or more sources rather than a single source such as the output of gate. Hardware description languages must be expressive enough to describe such circuits for the purpose of accurate simulation. Language constructs must be capable of capturing the interaction between multiple drivers for a signal, for example, is the resulting value of the signal the AND, OR, or maximum value of all of the drivers?

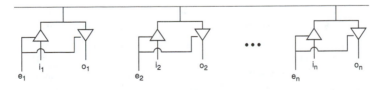

FIGURE 2-7 An example of a signal driven by multiple sources— buses

Similarly synthesis compilers must be able to process such descriptions and produce logic that arbitrates among accesses to shared signals in a manner that is correct. For example, if only one source is permitted then a decoder must be synthesized to control the multiple drivers.

2.7 Chapter Summary

This chapter is based on the premise that to most effectively use the VHDL language we must understand the distinguishing physical, structurally and behavioral attributes of the digital systems that the language is designed to describe. I hope that this approach will provide an intuitive basis for the reader to learn and apply language constructs described in succeeding chapters. The key attributes discussed in this chapter include:

- System descriptions
  - interface
  - function
    - structural
    - behavioral
- Events
- Propagation delays
- Concurrency
- Timing
  - synchronous
  - asynchronous
- Waveforms
- Signal values
- Shared signals

The VHDL language provides basic constructs for representing each of the above attributes. An associated simulator implements a discrete event simulation model, manages the progression of simulated time, and maintains internal representations of the waveforms being generated on signals. Synthesis compilers process the VHDL descriptions and a set of target hardware components to create a circuit that implements the behavior captured in the VHDL description. These underlying simulation and synthesis models are described in Chapter 3, whereas language constructs to specify these attributes are described in the remaining chapters.

Simulation vs. Synthesis

The effective use of modern programming languages is predicated upon an understanding of several underlying abstractions. For example, when writing C programs we understand the sequential flow of control of the host processors and the notions of memory addresses in our use of pointers. In a similar fashion, if we are to understand how to effectively utilize hardware description languages we must be comfortable with the underlying models for their application. This chapter addresses two main uses of hardware description languages, namely simulation and synthesis, and the models underlying the use of VHDL for these two purposes.

Simulation and synthesis are complementary design processes. In both cases we start with the specification of the behavior of a digital system and we construct a VHDL model of this system. For example we might describe the behavior of a digital circuit in terms of the input signals, the output signals, and knowledge of the delays in computing the value of the output signals. A VHDL simulator executes this model to mimic the behavior of the physical circuit where the behavior is described in terms of the occurrence events and waveforms on signals. In this manner many alternative designs can be formulated, analyzed, and eventually discarded in favor of one design option. We can answer many questions about each design option, such as correctness or performance of the design, without having to actually construct the circuit. Simulation is particularly useful in the design of future generations of digital systems where the cost of hardware and software prototyping renders physical prototyping clearly infeasible.

In contrast, digital circuit synthesis is the reverse process. A VHDL program is the input to a synthesis compiler that can process this description to generate the physical design of a circuit. The compiler must infer the hardware structures necessary to implement the behavior described by the VHDL code. Essentially the synthesis compiler mimics the activities of a human designer who generates a hardware design from an initial specification. However, automated synthesis, when feasible, can be much faster than a designer and can help reduce the overall product design time and product cost.

Figure 3-1 captures the relationship between simulation and synthesis. The VHDL model provides a description of the behavior of a digital circuit. From the perspective of simulation this model is used to study the properties of the circuit. In a sense, this model is generated from knowledge of the physical and behavioral properties of the circuit. In synthesis, this model is used as the first step in generating a physical design.

The remainder of this chapter first presents a discussion of the execution model for simulating circuits described in VHDL. As a practical issue this understanding is invaluable in debugging VHDL simulations. This discussion is followed by the description of a hardware inference model that illustrates the use of VHDL for synthesis of digital circuit implementations.

vhdl model

entity my_ckt **is**
port(x, y :**in bit**;
       z : **out bit**)
end entity my_ckt;
architecture behavioral **of** my_ckt **is**
begin
-- *some code here*
--
end architecture behavioral;

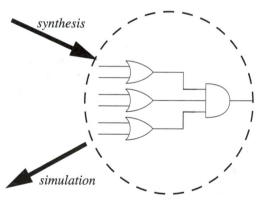

synthesis

vhdl model

entity my_ckt **is**
port(x, y :**in bit**;
       z : **out bit**)
end entity my_ckt;
architecture behavioral **of** my_ckt **is**
begin
-- *some code here*
--
end architecture behavioral;

simulation

FIGURE 3-1 Simulation vs. synthesis

3.1 The Simulation Model

Chapter 2 presented a description of the behavior of digital systems in terms of events that take place at discrete points in time. Some events may cause other events to be generated after some delay and many events may be generated concurrently. *Discrete event simulation* is a programming-based methodology for accurately modeling the generation of events in physical systems. The operation of a physical system such as a digital circuit is described in a computer program that specifies how and when events—changes in signal values—are generated. A *discrete event simulator* then executes this program, modeling the passage of time and the occurrence of events at various points in time. Such simulators often manage millions of events and rely on well-developed techniques to keep track accurately of the *correct order* in which the events would have occurred in the physical system. We can view VHDL as a programming language for describing the generation of events in digital systems supported by a discrete event simulator. The following describes a simple, discrete, event simulation model that captures the basic elements of the simulation of VHDL programs. Understanding the VHDL model of time is a necessary prerequisite to writing, debugging, and understanding VHDL models.

3.1.1 A Discrete Event Simulation Model

Discrete event simulations utilize an event list data structure. The event list maintains an ordered list of all future events in the circuit. Each event is described by the type of event— for example a $0 \rightarrow 1$ or $1 \rightarrow 0$ transition—and the time at which it is to occur. Although we generally think of transitions as a change of value between 0 and 1, recall that signals may have other values. In general, an event is simply a change in the value of a signal. Let us refer to the time at which an event is to occur as the *timestamp* of that event. The event list is ordered according to increasing timestamp value. This enables the simulator to execute events in the order that they occur in the real world, that is, the physical system. Finally, the simulator clock records the passage of simulated time. The value of this clock will be referred to as the current *timestep,* or simply timestep. Imagine what would happen if we froze the system at a timestep and took a snapshot of the values of all of the signals in the system. These values would represent the *state* of the simulation at that point in time.

Example: Discrete Event Simulation

Let us consider one approach to the discrete event simulation of the half-adder circuit shown in Figure 2-2. Assume that we have been able to specify waveforms on the inputs a and b. In a physical circuit these waveforms would likely be generated as the output of another component. At timestep 0 ns, initial values on inputs a and b will cause events that set the values of the sum and carry signals. Assuming that the propagation delay of a gate is 5 ns, these events will be scheduled to occur 5 ns later. Figure 3-2 (a) shows these events

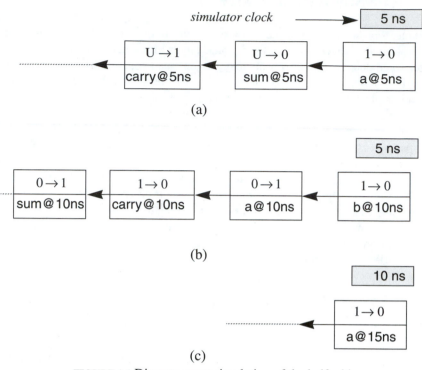

FIGURE 3-2 Discrete event simulation of the half adder

at the head of the event list at time 5 ns. Note that both sum and carry are scheduled to receive values at this time. Prior to this time the values of the sum and carry are undefined, as represented by the shaded areas in the timing diagram shown in Figure 2-2. Input a is also scheduled to make a transition at the same time (for the moment let us ignore how these events on the input signal are generated). These events correspond to the signal transitions shown on the timing diagram in Figure 2-2 at 5 ns. The simulator removes these events from the event list, and the current values of these signals are updated. Due to a change in the value of signal a, the simulator determines that the values of the output signals, sum and carry, have to be recomputed. The computation produces new values of sum and carry, which are scheduled in the event list at timestep 10 ns. The head of the event list now appears as shown in Figure 3-2(b), with all of the events scheduled for timestep 10 ns. The global clock is now updated to 10 ns, all events scheduled at timestep 10 ns are removed from the event list, the corresponding signal values are updated, and any new events are computed and scheduled. Figure 3-2(c) shows the head of the event list after event computations at timestep 10 ns, and prior to the update of the global clock. The simulator clock will now be updated to 15 ns and the process repeated. This process is continued until there are no more events to be computed or until some predetermined simulation time has expired.

Example End: Discrete Event Simulation

This behavior of a discrete event simulator as captured in the preceding example can be described in the following steps:

1. Advance simulation time to that of the event with the smallest timestamp in the event list. This is the event at the head of the sorted event list.

2. Execute all events at this timestep by updating signal values.

3. Execute the simulation models of all components affected by the new signal values.

4. Schedule any future events.

5. Repeat until the event list is empty or a preset simulation time has expired.

In general, there is substantial concurrency in a digital circuit and many events may take place simultaneously. Thus, many signals may receive values at the same timestep and more than one event is executed at a timestep. We see that the simulator employs a two-stage model of the evolution of time. In the first stage, simulation time is advanced to that of the next event and all signals receiving values at this time are updated. In the second stage, all components affected by these signal updates are re-evaluated, and any future events that are generated by these evaluations are scheduled by placing them into the event list in order of their timestamp.

It is apparent that this model is quite flexible and general. We can think of modeling gate-level circuits as well as higher level circuits such as arithmetic logic units (ALUs), decoders, multiplexors, and even microprocessors. We simply need to describe the behavior of these components in terms of input events, computation of the output events from input events, and propagation delays. If we can describe a digital system in these terms, we can develop computer programs for implementing this behavior. Note that discrete event simulation itself is only a model or approximation of the behavior of real systems. In real circuits signals do not make instantaneous transitions between logic 0 voltage levels and logic 1 voltage levels. For that matter there are no such things as truly digital devices. There are only analog devices wherein we interpret analog voltage levels as 0 or 1! In practice for many purposes, such a discrete event model is adequate. However, often more detailed and accurate models are required; in such cases complementary techniques and models are employed. To distinguish the discrete event model from the real system, we will refer to the former as the *logical model* and the latter as the *physical system*.

The basic data structures and concepts are common across discrete event simulation systems. The VHDL simulators will provide facilities for setting the duration of a simulation timestep and to query the contents of the event queue at points during the simulation. The user can also typically examine the event at the head of the event queue and force signals to specific values prior to the next timestep. An understanding of this underlying simulation model and the basic data structures is invaluable in debugging VHDL simulations.

3.1.2 Accuracy vs. Simulation Speed

In the context of the discrete event simulation model it is now clear why there is an natural trade-off between simulation accuracy and simulation speed. Suppose we wish to construct a simulation of a 32-bit adder. Our first VHDL model may be at the level of an adder component that is described by the delay in computing a sum of its input values. The behavior of the box is to simply add the two inputs and produce an output value. In later chapters we will see how we can write such a simple, one-line, VHDL model. When the two input values are available an output value is computed and scheduled for some time, say 5 ns, into the future. The presence of input values causes one event, namely the change in the value of the output, to be scheduled for some point in time in the future. An alternative and relatively more accurate model of the adder might describe a gate-level implementation of a 32-bit adder. Now when new inputs become available a sequence of events are generated along the internal signals that connect the inputs and outputs of gates in the design. We can imagine that if we add up the total number of events that are generated in this discrete event model it would be on the order of tens of events. Each of these events must be inserted in the event queue and eventually removed as simulated time progresses. The amount of work, and therefore time, performed by the simulator is proportional to the number of events that are handled. One step in the simulation now will correspond to a gate delay rather than the full delay through the adder.

The key observation is that in the gate-level model the discrete event simulation must process one to two orders or magnitude more events. Accuracy is improved because we monitor gate-level events. However the amount of work that the simulator must perform is much greater and hence simulation time is increased. Scale this simple example up to the context of 10 million gate designs and we have non-negligible differences in simulation times!

Accuracy has traditionally been a function of simulation time and it is not unusual for simulations to run overnight or even for days. In fact for many years there were vendors that sold special-purpose hardware just for logic simulation. That technology has now evolved to use new classes of commercial hardware whereas many vendors still rely on the leading high-performance workstations.

3.2 The Synthesis Model

Whereas simulation is the process of using a model to mimic the behavior of a physical system, synthesis is the complementary process of constructing a physical system from a model. The physical design is automatically generated from an abstract description using a pre-defined set of basic building blocks such as logic gates. For example, we might simply state we wish to add two 32-bit signed binary numbers. The synthesis process will determine the detailed gate-level design of a 32-bit adder. Although complete design environments will generate a transistor-level design, in this text we focus on a higher level of abstraction as the target of synthesis compilers – a VHDL model is synthesized to a digital circuit constructed from a set of gate level primitives, namely logic gates, flip-flops, latches and small blocks of memory. For quite some time there have been computer-aided design tools that can translate such gate-level descriptions to a physical layout or into a form for programming configurable logic devices to implement the same circuit.

Synthesis is a design process that operates on three types of information. The first is the model of the circuit, which in our case is a VHDL model. The second is a set of constraints on the resulting circuit, such as speed and area. The third input is the set of components that are to be used to construct the circuit. This is analogous to a C compiler needing information about the target microprocessor instruction set. For example, the C compiler needs to know what types of logic gates do we have at our disposal. Do we have three-input NAND gates? Do we have D-type, positive-edge-triggered flip-flops and do they have asynchronous preset and clear inputs? Is the design to be implemented using only two-input NOR gates? Synthesis compilers must operate with these three pieces of information.

Just remember, automated synthesis is simply replacing what you would otherwise be doing manually. In our digital logic classes we have seen how we can generate or synthesize a gate-level implementation of a boolean function from a truth table. We have studied techniques for taking a state diagram and designing a sequential circuit that implements the behavior captured in this state diagram. Modern day CAD tools do automate these design processes and in this sense are also synthesis tools. The more recent trend in synthesis research is to raise the level of abstraction at which we describe our systems. Rather than providing boolean expressions, truth tables, or state diagrams, we would describe computations at the level of programming languages. Our descriptions may be at the level of addition and multiplication of integers or real numbers, sorting of unsigned numbers, or masking and shifting operations on boolean strings. As we raise the level of abstraction of our description we find that there are many hardware implementations for a given description. Just remember the number of different types of adders that you covered in your digital logic class or the large number of ways you could encode the states in a state machine. The high-level synthesis problem becomes much more challenging because in the process you must choose between alternative feasible hardware implementations. However, by rasing the level of abstraction we can describe the desired hardware more compactly and typically in less time, thereby significantly reducing the length of the design cycle. It is also hoped that automated processes can improve the time required to verify the design by eliminating certain types of design errors, promote design re-use, and reduce the time to react to future changes in the design as the products evolve.

As with simulation, where discrete event simulation is an underlying model that can help us write and debug VHDL models, is there a fundamental way of thinking about synthesis that can be helpful in writing and debugging synthesis models? The answer is yes, and is described in the following subsection.

3.2.1 Hardware Inference

The definition of VHDL provides a rich set of language artifacts for the description of digital systems. In fact we can construct several equivalent VHDL models of the same circuit much in the same way that we can describe a circuit in different but equivalent mathematical forms. For example, a combinational circuit may be described by a truth table or a boolean expression. Furthermore digital systems can be described at multiple levels of abstraction, for example at the switch, gate, or register transfer level. Such flexibility is desirable when we wish to construct simulation models where we can trade accuracy for simulation speed. However, the fact that a single circuit can be described in so many ways does present many challenges to synthesis compilers that must *infer* a single hardware implementation from a VHDL description. Just as discrete event simulation is the underlying execution mechanism for the simulation of models expressed in VHDL, synthesis from VHDL models is based on the process of *inference*. Synthesis compilers must infer typical hardware components and their interconnection from the VHDL code. Inference is followed by optimization to reduce the size or increase the speed of the circuit. This process is best illustrated with an example.

Example: Operator Inferencing

Let us suppose we wish to design a circuit for a single-bit that can perform the operations of addition, subtraction, logical AND, and logical OR. We can describe such an ALU in many ways, however, a language description with a precise syntax and semantics is the most desirable. Let us consider the description shown in Figure 3-3. For the moment ignore the absence of standard programming language constructs such as declarations and **begin...end** constructs. Imagine we are asked to synthesize hardware that implements the computations described by the code. We must be able to infer hardware structures required to implement each of the statements. Some inferences appear quite obvious. From the first two lines of the code we know we require a two-input AND gate and a two-input OR gate. The next two lines compute the sum and carry from the addition of the two-input bits. The last statement requires a bit more thought. The statement describes an operation wherein the output signal Out is one of the three-input signals, S1, S2, or S3; the choice depends on the value of the signal Sel. Sounds suspiciously like a 3-to-1 multiplexor! The compiler may infer a multiplexor from such a statement. By analyzing the data dependencies we can also infer that the output of the logical and arithmetic operations form the three inputs to the multiplexor. The result is the circuit shown in the figure.

Example End: Operator Inferencing

The preceding example produced purely combinational logic. The data dependency abstraction is very natural and translation to combinational logic is an intuitive one. What about circuits that use latches or flip-flops such as state machines? The issue here is being able to infer latches or flip-flops from the VHDL code. The following example illustrates the process of inferring storage from a language model.

```
--
-- pseudo code for a single-bit arithmetic/logic unit
--
s1 <= in1 and in2;
s2 <= in1 or in2;
s3 <= in1 xor in2; -- perform the sum operation
c_out < (in1 and c_in) or (in1 and in2) or (in2 and c_in);
out <= s1 when sel = "00" else
       s2 when sel = "01" else
       s3 when sel = "10" else
       '0';
```

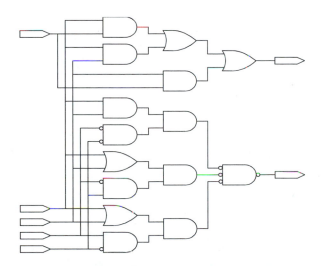

FIGURE 3-3 An example of the synthesis of a single-bit ALU

Example: Storage Inferencing

Consider the semantics of the block of code shown in Figure 3-4. If the condition is true, then the signal Z will acquire the value of the expression on the right hand side. However, if the condition is false then we can only infer that Z will retain its previous value. Because the value of Z may not change, we must infer storage to retain the value of Z, that is a latch or flip-flop. This process of inferring storage is more subtle than operator inferencing described earlier.

Example End: Storage Inferencing

```
--
-- a simple conditional code block
--
if (sel = '0') then
z <= in1 nor in2;
end if;
```

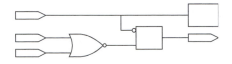

FIGURE 3-4 An example of latch inferencing

When writing code for synthesis we must remember that we are describing hardware. There is often a tendency to allow conventional programming techniques to creep into the structure and style of programs written in hardware description languages. These techniques are intended to optimize the sequential execution model of programs; they are not usually compatible with the hardware inferencing process required of synthesis and they often increase the complexity of the inference process. We should approach VHDL model development from our digital logic background and not from our C or Java background. The sequential flow of control found in these languages promotes a code development style where successive computations are orchestrated to be dependent on each other in the interest of execution speed. Digital logic on the other hand is inherently concurrent. By adopting such a "hardware aware" approach to writing VHDL models we can expect to generate designs that are generally faster and often smaller.

3.2.2 Target Primitives

An important issue is the set of components that serve as the target for synthesis. Just imagine that you are given a state machine and you are tasked with designing the hardware implementation. The implementation depends on the set of hardware primitives that we have to begin with. We might be able to go to the proverbial hardware store and purchase various types of hardware building blocks with which to build our circuits. Our building blocks may only include positive-edge-triggered D flip-flops. Or perhaps the components all rely on two-phase non-overlapping clocks. In general we cannot rely on the synthesis compiler having access to the complete range of digital components including all types of combinational and sequential components. Thus the synthesis process becomes a bit more interesting. Now the synthesis compiler must not only create a physical design but must also create a design using only those components that you have available. For example, suppose we are provided with the following boolean equation

$$\overline{A}BC + \overline{B}C + DB$$

This equation can be implemented in several different ways, three of which are illustrated in Figure 3-5. The first implementation is a straightforward two-level gate implementation that represents the structure of the expression. The second implementation reduces to the implementation of the same expressions and the third implementation uses inverters and only NAND gates. This example illustrates a simple fact, namely that the circuit produced by a synthesis compiler depends on the set of building blocks that are used. Furthermore we see that the implementations are not necessarily unique. How does the compiler or user select the building blocks? Usually building blocks are chosen based on performance metrics such as area or speed.

You may recall spending many hours in your digital logic course performing logic minimization with automated tools or experimenting with manual techniques using Karnaugh maps or algebraic methods. In modern CAD tools these and more powerful techniques are automated and applied across very large designs. Throughout the course of this book we are mainly focused on understanding VHDL synthesis using a particular set of target hardware primitives. These are the class of circuits known as field programmable gate arrays. Synthesis coupled with reprogrammable logic has emerged as a powerful tool for constructing low-cost systems. As these components continue to become denser and more powerful they are beginning to displace many custom integrated circuits in embedded applications. They have been found to be well suited for digital circuits that imple-

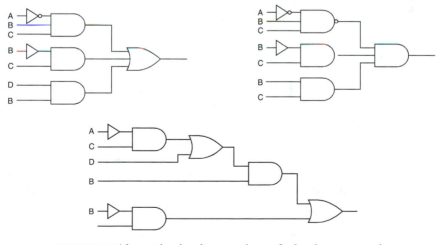

FIGURE 3-5 Alternative implementations of a boolean expression

ment state machines, pattern matchers, and integer arithmetic. Although the main focus of this book is on generic issues in synthesis, the implementation bias is towards FPGAs described in the following section.

In summary, the focus of the sections of this text that discuss synthesis is on inference from VHDL language constructs. In subsequent chapters we study each major language construct from the point of view of inferring hardware structures. From this we derive some general suggestions for writing VHDL models for synthesis so that we might be able to exercise some control over the synthesis process and at the very least enable our expectations to be largely consistent with the results.

3.3 Field Programmable Gate Arrays (FPGAs)

During the last decade there has been rapid development of many different types of reprogrammable hardware devices. Such devices go by many names: reconfigurable hardware, configurable hardware, reprogrammable hardware, and so on. Without a tour of all forms of programmable logic devices in this book we will simply describe the one specific class of devices that we are interested in, namely FPGAs.

The basic idea underlying the architecture of an FPGA is very simple. In general combinational and sequential circuits can be implemented directly in silicon. Such ASICs produce the highest performance but can perform only one function. Because the development cost cannot be spread across multiple applications, the cost of ASICs are generally higher than, for example, conventional microprocessor-based solutions. What we would like is hardware that is programmable much in the same way you can change a program by changing the instructions. The ideal hardware analogy would be the ability to reconfigure the interconnections between millions of transistors that comprise these chips to compute a new function for a new application. Although this is not currently feasible we can get pretty close with the following, rather simple, idea (although the implementation is far from trivial!),

Let us suppose that we had a basic hardware cell that could be reprogrammed to implement any "small" combinational or sequential circuit. Now let us tile the surface of a silicon die with an array of such configurable hardware blocks as shown in Figure 3-6. Running vertically and horizontally between this two-dimensional array of hardware blocks are wires. At the intersection of the horizontal and vertical wires are switches. Collectively the switches form a switch matrix. Each of the hardware blocks can connect themselves to any set of the horizontal or vertical signals that are adjacent to the block. The switch points can connect horizontal signal lines to vertical signal lines and vice versa.

Given this hardware infrastructure consider a gate-level design. We can use the chip illustrated in Figure 3-6 as follows. Partition the design into small sub-circuits so that each sub-circuit can be implemented in a single configurable hardware block. Assign each sub-circuit to a configurable hardware block. Now establish the original connections between the sub-circuits through the switching matrix. The hardware blocks on the periphery of the

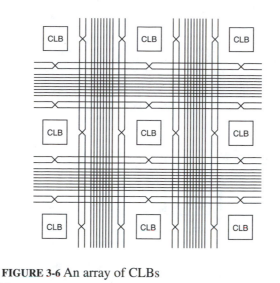

FIGURE 3-6 An array of CLBs

chip are different from those in the interior because they must be used to drive signals off the chip as well as read signals coming from off the chip. These blocks are referred to as input/output (I/O) blocks. Thus the FPGA is comprised of two configurable block types. If you wish to implement a different gate-level design, repeat the partitioning, placement, and programming process with a different gate-level design. We now have an architecture that is hardware reprogrammable! The real question now is how are these configurable logic blocks (CLBs) implemented? How can they be configured to implement different logic functions? Although practically all FPGA designs resemble the architecture shown in Figure 3-6 they differ in the structure of the individual CLBs, the I/O blocks, and the specifics of the switching matrix. In fact vendors differ in the terminology they use to describe their reprogrammable hardware components. The following sections describe each of the basic components in greater detail using the Xilinx XC 4000 series of FPGAs.

3.3.1 Implementation of CLBs

In the Xilinx terminology the internal hardware blocks of Figure 3-6 are referred to as CLBs. The I/O blocks are abbreviated as IOBs and the wiring is referred to as the switch matrix. The basic structure of an XC 4000 CLB is illustrated in Figure 3-7. The major digital logic components are two 16x1 random access memory (RAM) blocks, a single 8x1 RAM block, and two edge-triggered D flip-flops. Several multiplexors are used to configure the interconnections between the CLB components and the inputs and outputs to the CLB. The RAM components can be structured as look up tables (LUTs) to implement combinational logic by implementing the truth tables corresponding to the logic circuit. The flip-flops clearly are used as sequential components and can be configured to

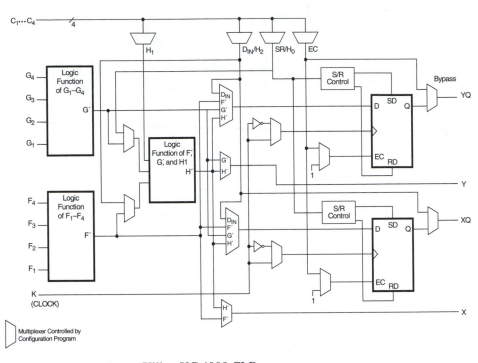

FIGURE 3-7 Xilinx XC 4000 CLB

operate on either edge of the clock or as latches (only in the 4000X series of parts). Let us now consider the configuration of this CLB to implement combinational or sequential components.

Combinational circuits are implemented using the 16x1 RAM modules, also referred to as LUTs. Consider a gate-level circuit shown in Figure 3-8. This circuit has four inputs and one output. The behavior of this circuit can be represented by a 16-entry truth table also shown in the figure. The truth table can be realized in one of the 16x1 bit LUTs in the following manner. The four inputs serve as the 4-bit address to the memory and the single-bit memory contents at that location is set to the value of the corresponding truth table output value. Thus in this case the contents of memory location 1100 is 0 whereas the contents of memory location 1001 is 1. The 16x1 LUT can implement any boolean function of four variables and is also referred to as a function generator. Each CLB has two 4-bit function generators F and G. A third function generator H can implement any boolean function of three variables. Two of these inputs can come from the outputs of the F and G function generator or from outside the CLB. A third input must come from outside the CLB. By using all three function generators a single CLB can implement any boolean function of five variables and some functions of up to nine variables. Figure 3-8 also graphically illustrates the effect of implementing a gate-level design using the function generators.

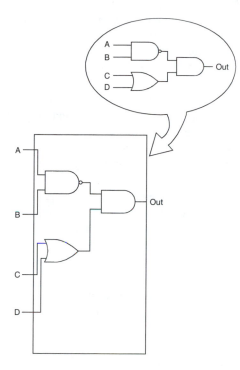

A	B	C	D	Out
0	0	0	0	0
0	0	0	1	1
0	0	1	0	1
0	0	1	1	1
0	1	0	0	0
0	1	0	1	1
0	1	1	0	1
0	1	1	1	1
1	0	0	0	0
1	0	0	1	1
1	0	1	0	1
1	0	1	1	1
1	1	0	0	0
1	1	0	1	0
1	1	1	0	0
1	1	1	1	0

FIGURE 3-8 Implementation of combinational functions using LUTs

In some of the newer components the LUTs can be configured to operate as a memory block. Various configurations are possible such as two 16x1 RAM modules, one 32x1 module, or as a dual ported 16X1 memory module. Both synchronous-edge-triggered as well as asynchronous-memory interfaces are supported. The CLB also contains two D flip-flops. These flip-flops can be configured to be triggered on either edge of the clock and also possess clock enable inputs. In the XC4000X series of parts these two flip-flops can also be configured as latches with a common clock and clock enable inputs. In addition to the four inputs to each of the F and G function generators a CLB has four additional inputs and a clock input. From the figure we see that the CLB also produces four outputs. Two from the function generators and the two outputs from the flip-flops. In addition you will note that there are external signals that can be passed through to facilitate placement and routing. For example trace the sources of the outputs XQ and YQ.

The CLB structure shown in Figure 3-7 does not show one important set of signals, the carry chain. The F and G function generators contain logic for the fast generation of carry and borrow signals that are passed to the adjacent CLBs. This dedicated carry chain runs along the CLBs in a column and can significantly speed up arithmetic and counting operations. All vendors typically supply implementations of common building blocks that are optimized to the structure of their hardware components. Xilinx, in fact, has a core generator utility that can create common building blocks from parameterized descriptions provided by the user. Adders, subtractors, multipliers, and memories are common building blocks often supplied by FPGA vendors.

We can now begin to regard the FPGA as a sea of flips-flops and function generators. A gate-level design can be "placed" on this array by mapping combinational components to function generators and sequential components to flip-flops. A CLB can be configured to implement the combinational and sequential components that have been assigned to it. The CLB is configured by setting configuration bits associated with the CLB. Loading these configuration bits for each CLB within the FPGA is referred to as the process of programming the FPGA. Once we have placed the combinational and sequential components with the CLBs we need to establish signal connections between the components mapped to distinct CLBs. This is the role of the switch matrix described in the following section.

3.3.2 Implementation of the Switch Matrix

There are several levels of interconnect between the CLBs that are supported within FPGAs like the XC4000 series. The first and simplest are the direct interconnects between CLBs. Short wires are used to connect adjacent CLBs in the horizontal and vertical directions. The next set of interconnects deal with the switch matrix that is illustrated in Figure 3-9. Sets of wires run horizontally and vertically between rows and columns of CLBs. At grid locations we have a programmable switch matrix (PSM). As the name suggests the switch matrix can be configured to connect a horizontal wire to a vertical wire; fan out to multiple outputs is also feasible. Thus the output from any CLB can be routed through multiple PSMs to the input of another CLB.

Within the switch matrix itself there are multiple levels of interconnect. For example one set of wires connects adjacent PSMs. These are referred to as single-length lines. Double-length lines connect every other PSM crossing two CLBs between switch matrix connections. Finally the XC4000X parts also contain quad-length lines that traverse four CLBs before passing through a buffered switch matrix. The purpose of this hierarchy of interconnects is to avoid routing signals between CLBs through too many switching points. Thus local connections use the direct interconnect or single-length lines whereas the longer wires use the double-length or quad-length lines. Finally there are long lines that run the entire length of the chip in both the horizontal and vertical directions. Through tri-state buffers within the CLBs these long lines can be configured as buses that are shared by multiple CLBs. The set of wiring resources that are available to each CLB in a XC4000X part is illustrated in Figure 3-10.

Finally, there are a few special signal networks on the chip referred to as global nets. These are low-skew signal paths that are used to distribute high fan-out signals such as clocks or reset signals. The number and availability of such global nets are dependent on the specific FPGA part.

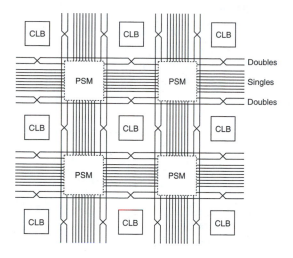

FIGURE 3-9 Programmable switch matrix (PSM)

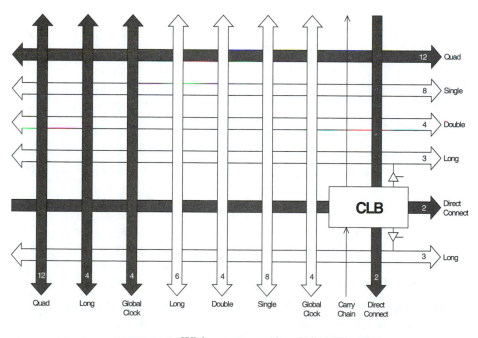

FIGURE 3-10 Wiring resources in a XC4000X CLB

3.3.3 Implementation of the IOB

The configurable block that implements I/O functionality on the chip is shown in Figure 3-11. The I_1 and I_2 signals that carry input to the FPGA can each carry the input directly from the pin or from an IOB flip-flop that can be used to capture the input data. The IOB has an additional latch that is used for the fast capture of data. In a similar fashion output signals can pass directly to the pin or can be stored in a flip-flop. The output path here also contains a multiplexor that permits two signals to share a pin enabling a higher number of effective I/Os in a design. Finally, separate clocks are provided for the input and output flip-flops.

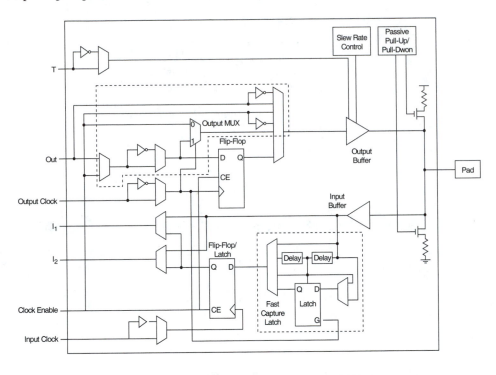

FIGURE 3-11 Implementation of the IOB

3.3.4 Configuration

Now that we understand how the CLBs, IOBs, and the PSM can implement a gate-level design we have to understand how a FPGA is configured. We have observed that each CLB is assigned some combinational functions that are implemented with the function generators. To implement the specified functions we must provide the contents of the LUTs. There are three memories for a total of 40 bits (16 + 16 + 8). Then there are various multiplexors within the CLB that among other things determine the input sources of the flip-flops, the clock edge used to trigger the flip-flops, and the inputs to the H function generator.

The interconnection between CLBs is determined by setting elements of the PSM in order to route signals. Each of these switches requires a bit of configuration memory. Depending upon the specific part there may be anywhere from several Kbits to several Mbits of configuration data. A good rule of thumb that has been proposed within the community is roughly on the order of 20 configuration bits per available user gate.

CAD tools are used to translate a VHDL description of a design into a set of bits corresponding to a configuration for the target FPGA chip. This bit stream is loaded onto the chip through a serial interface. To date configuration times have been rather slow being in the millisecond range. However we have seen the advent of recent components where chips present a memory-like interface and can be reprogrammed in tens of microseconds. In fact portions of the chip can be reprogrammed incrementally. Such capabilities raise the prospect of on-the-fly reconfiguration in an operational system rather than off-line reprogramming.

3.3.5 FPGA Design Flow

The design flow broadly refers to the sequence of activities encompassing various design tools that begin with some abstract specification of a design and ends with a configured FPGA. The design flow described in this section is that of the Xilinx Foundation Express environment and is illustrated in Figure 3-12. However most of the activities will have a counterpart in any vendors' design flow.

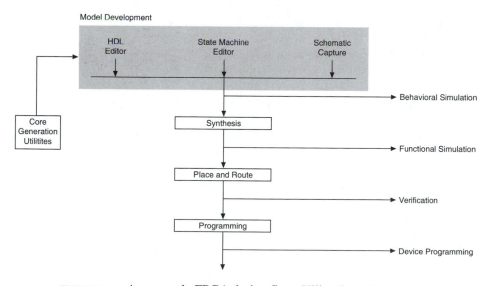

FIGURE 3-12 An example FPGA design flow: Xilinx Foundation Express

The initial description of our design may take the form of formal specification such as state diagrams, boolean expressions, or simply informal english language descriptions. Such specifications are refined through a sequence of activities to an FPGA implementation.

1. *VHDL Model*: The first step is the construction of the VHDL model. The model may be constructed by writing VHDL directly using a text editor. Modern simulators and synthesis tools will provide syntax-directed editors and facilities for insertion of language templates to make the process easier. Alternatively state machines may be described in a graphical manner and subsequently automatically translated into VHDL. Finally, traditional schematic capture is generally an available option. This step produces the VHDL source for a model that is analyzed (compiled) to an internal form while it is checked for conformance to the syntax and semantics of VHDL.

2. *Behavioral Simulation*: This VHDL model can be simulated before it is synthesized to the FPGA. The purpose of the simulation is usually to establish functional correctness. It may also be used for other tasks such as the generation of test vectors and preliminary performance evaluation.

3. *Synthesis*: The analyzed design is synthesized to a library of primitive components generally gates, flip-flops, and latches.

4. *Functional Simulation:* This synthesized design can be simulated to determine preliminary performance estimates. In Xilinx parlance this simulation is referred to as functional simulation. The timing information is obtained from known physical properties of the FPGA components. However the design still needs to be implemented in an FPGA chip so the timing is not completely accurate.

5. *Place and Route*: This design is mapped to the primitives that are used in the target chip. For example in the case of Xilinx FPGA chips the primitives are function generators and flip-flops or latches. The mapped design must now be placed, that is, each primitive must be assigned to a specific CLB. Now that the primitives have been placed, they must be connected by routing the connections through the switch matrix. Once the design is placed and routed accurate information about timing delays between parts of the circuits can be obtained. Post-placement and routing simulation is more accurate than functional simulation and is referred to as verification. The configuration bits to implement the placed and routed design are generated.

6. *Programming*: The configuration bits or *bit stream* is loaded into the target FPGA chip. The chip has now been configured to implement the desired functionality.

Although the preceding steps are drawn from the Xilinx environment, the steps are fairly generic. The design tool flow for the Xilinx foundation express are described in greater detail in the Appendix.

3.4 Chapter Summary

This chapter describes models underlying two significant applications of the VHDL language. The first application of VHDL is for the simulation of digital systems captured in VHDL models. The underlying execution model is that of discrete event simulation. A working knowledge of this execution model enables us to understand how simulators interpret VHDL programs to represent physical events and model the passage of time. Such an understanding is invaluable in debugging VHDL programs just as our familiarity with the sequential flow of C programs is the basis for debugging them. When VHDL is used for synthesis the fundamental underlying process is one of hardware inference. This process is dependent upon the hardware primitives that we have available to construct our circuits with. A closer examination of the language constructs from the point of view of inference will enable us to write VHDL models that assist the synthesis compiler. I hope that this approach, rather than diving into the language at the outset, will provide a useful mindset and an intuitive basis for the reader to learn and apply the VHDL language constructs described in subsequent chapters.

When writing code for synthesis we must remember that we are describing hardware. There is often a tendency to allow conventional programming techniques to creep into the structure and style of programs written in hardware description languages. These techniques are intended to optimize the sequential execution model of programs. They are not usually compatible with the needs of discrete event simulation nor do they promote the hardware inferencing process required of synthesis.

There are many techniques that are developed to optimize the simulation of VHDL programs. For example, knowledge of specific optimizations employed by the VHDL compiler enable us to structure our programs to speed up the simulation. However these structuring mechanisms may complicate the inferencing process. Alternatively, writing for synthesis we are motivated to expose the hardware structures which in turn could lead to longer pre-synthesis simulation times. For the most effective results, clearly we must know how the resulting VHDL models will be used. Successive chapters attempt to highlight the aspects of the language constructs that are important from this perspective.

The key attributes discussed in this chapter include:
- discrete event simulation
  - logical models
  - physical models
  - event lists and event list management
- hardware inference
  - operator inferencing
  - storage inferencing

- field programmable gate arrays
  - configurable logic
  - switching matrix
- design flow
  - behavioral simulation
  - functional simulation
  - verification
  - device programming

The following chapters fill in this gap between intuition and real tools and processes with a grounding in the major VHDL language constructs and features.

CHAPTER 4

Basic Language
Concepts: Simulation

This chapter introduces the basic language constructs of the VHDL language. Our goal in this chapter is to construct models of digital systems for the purpose of simulating their behavior. Our mindset is one where we are *describing* a physical design rather than a computation. An associated simulator is concerned with *how* the design is simulated.

VHDL has often been criticized as being overly complex and intimidating to the novice user. Although the language is extensive, a quick start towards building useful simulation models can be made by relying on a core set of language constructs. This chapter describes the language constructs provided within VHDL for describing the attributes of digital systems identified in Chapter 2, such as events, propagation delays, concurrency, and waveforms. An introduction of some concepts that extend the constructs discussed here can be found in Chapter 6; these concepts will enable the application of conventional programming constructs in building models of complex digital systems, particularly at higher levels of abstraction. Collectively these two chapters provide us with the tools necessary to model all of the attributes of digital systems described in Chapter 2.

4.1 Signals

Fundamentally, digital systems are about signals–transporting and operating on signals. We might then expect that the notion of a signal is a basic part of any language for describing digital hardware. Conventional programming languages manipulate basic objects such as variables and constants. Variables receive values through assignment statements and can be assigned new values through the course of a computation. Constants, on the other hand, may not change their values. To capture the behavior of digital signals the VHDL language introduces a new type of programming object: the signal object type.

We have seen that signals may take on one of several values such as 0, 1, or Z. Signals are analogous to the wires used to connect components of a digital circuit. Like variables, signals may also be assigned values, but differ from variables in that they have an associated *time value,* because a signal receives a value at a specific point in time. The signal retains this value until it is assigned a new value at a future point in time. The sequence of values assigned to a signal over time is the *waveform* of the signal. It is primarily this association with time–value pairs that differentiates a signal from a variable. A variable always has one current value. At any instant in time a signal may be associated with several time–value pairs, where each time–value pair represents some future value of the signal (remember we are simulating the behavior of the signal over time). Finally, note that variables may be declared to be of a specific type, such as **integer**, **real**, or **character**. In a similar manner, a signal can be declared to be of a specific type. When used in this way, a signal does not necessarily have correspondence with the wires that connect digital components. For example, we may model the output of an ALU as an integer-valued signal. This output is treated as a signal and in simulation behaves as a signal by receiving values at specific points in time. However, we do not have to concern ourselves with modeling the number of bits necessary at the output of the ALU as we would have to do if we were modeling the ALU a much lower level, for example, at the gate level. When we are building simulation models of components we often are not interested in the implementation of the ALU as much as we are interested in capturing this behavior accurately in a VHDL model. Thus we are not required to think of signals in terms of a number of bits. This behavior enables us to model systems at a higher level of abstraction than digital circuits. Such high-level simulation is useful in the early stages of the design process, where many details of the design are still being developed.

Before we can understand how to declare and operate on signals we must first cover the basic programming constructs in VHDL. We will return to discuss signal objects in greater detail later in this chapter.

4.2 Entity–Architecture

We start by addressing the issue of describing digital systems. The primary programming abstraction in VHDL is a *design entity*. Examples of design entities include a chip, board, and transistor. It is a component of a design whose behavior is to be described and simulated. Consider once again the gate-level digital circuit for a half adder shown in Figure 4-1. There are two input signals, x, and y. The circuit computes the value of two output signals, sum and carry. This half-adder circuit represents an example of a design entity.

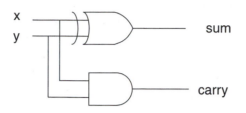

FIGURE 4-1 Half-adder circuit

How can the half-adder circuit be accurately described? Imagine that you had to describe this circuit over the telephone to a friend who was familiar with digital logic gates but was not familiar with the half adder. Your description would most likely include the input signals, the output signals, and a description of the behavior. The behavior in turn may be specified with a truth table, Boolean equations, or simply an interconnection between gates. We observe that there are two basic components to the description of any design entity, (i) the interface to the design, and (ii) the internal behavior of the design. The VHDL language provides two distinct constructs to specify the interface and internal behavior of design entities, respectively.

The external interface to this entity is specified with the **entity** declaration. For the circuit shown in Figure 4-1, the entity declaration would appear as follows:

> **entity** half_adder **is**
> **port**(x, y: **in bit**;
> sum, carry: **out bit**);
> **end entity** half_adder;

The boldface type denotes keywords that are VHDL reserved keywords. The remaining are user supplied. Just as we name programs, the label half_adder is the name given to this design entity by the programmer. Names can be composed of upper or lower case characters or digits and may include the underscore character "_", as above. However hyphens, "-", are not permitted and the first character of a user-supplied name must be a letter and the last character cannot be an underscore. The VHDL language is *case insensitive*. Thus half_adder and HALF_ADDER would refer to the same entity.

The inputs and outputs of the circuit are referred to as *ports*. The ports are special programming objects and are signals. Ports are the means by which the half adder can communicate with the external world and other circuits. Therefore, naturally, we expect ports to be signals rather than variables. Like variables in conventional programming languages, each port must be a signal that is declared to be of a specific type. In this case each port is declared to be of type **bit**, and represents a single-bit signal. A **bit** is a signal type that is defined within the VHDL language, and can take the values of 0 or 1. A **bit_vector** is a signal type composed of a vector of signals, each of type **bit**. The type **bit** and **bit_vector** are two common types of ports. In general, a port may be any one of several other VHDL data types. Common data types and operators supported by the language are described in Chapter 12.

The original VHDL language standard is referenced as the 1987 standard 1076-1987. Modifications to the language were ratified into the 1993 standard referred to as 1076-1993. This text follows the 1993 standard. Most differences introduced in VHDL'93 deal with introduction of a few new concepts, tuning the semantics of existing constructs, and refining the syntax of the major constructs. However in the interests of compatibility with legacy code we will identify differences between the VHDL'87 and VHDL'93. For example there is a difference in the syntax of the **entity** construct.

'87 vs. '93
☞

```
-- VHDL 1993

entity half_adder is
port (x, y: in bit;
sum, carry: out bit);
end entity half_adder;
```
new

```
-- VHDL 1987

entity half_adder is
port (x, y: in bit;
sum, carry: out bit);
end half_adder;
```

From our study of digital logic, we know that bits and bit vectors are fundamental signals.   From Chapter 2, we know that from the perspective of simulation we are interested in many more values of signals. For example, a signal may be uninitialized or not driven to a voltage level denoting logic 0 or logic 1 and thus be in a high-impedance state denoted by Z. Thus in practice, the types **bit** and **bit_vector** are of limited use. How many values should a signal have? The problem is that vendors began defining new signal types. For example, vendor SimVHDL Inc. defines a new type called RealSignal. All signals in a VHDL model using this company's simulator are defined to be of type RealSignal and such signals can take on, say, one of twelve values. All of the models written for this simulator cannot be used with any other simulator unless they support the type RealSignal, which in all liklihood they will not because it is not defined as part of the language. This eliminates one big hope for VHDL, namely re-use of models across vendors.

The IEEE has again and again coordinated the development of a standard type system and associated supporting implementations. The IEEE 1164 Standard has gained widespread acceptance as a standard value system. This standard defines a nine-value signal as provided in Figure 2-6. To use this value system signals would be declared to be of type std_ulogic rather than **bit**. Analogously, we would have the type std_ulogic_vector rather than **bit_vector**. Therefore, throughout the remainder of this text, all examples will utilize the IEEE 1164 standard signal and data types. The preceding entity declaration would now appear as follows:

> **entity** half_adder **is**
> **port** (x, y: **in** std_ulogic;
> sum, carry: **out** std_ulogic);
> **end entity** half_adder;

The signals appearing in a port declaration may be distinguished as input signals, output signals, or bidirectional signals. This is referred to as the *mode* of the signal. In the above example, the **in** and **out** specifications denote the mode of the signal. Bidirectional signals are of mode **inout**. Every port in the entity description must have its mode and type specified.

We see that it is relatively straightforward to write the entity descriptions of standard digital logic components. The following shows some sample circuits and their entity descriptions. Note how byte and word-wide groups of bits are specified. For example a 32-bit quantity is declared to be of the type std_ulogic_vector (31 **downto** 0). This type refers to a data item that is 32 bits long where bit 31 is the most significant bit in the word and bit 0 is the least significant bit in the word.

Example: Entity Declaration of a 4-to-1 Multiplexor

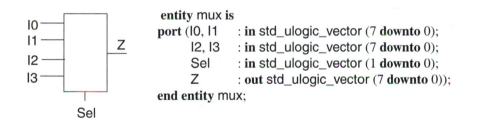

entity mux **is**
port (I0, I1   : **in** std_ulogic_vector (7 **downto** 0);
       I2, I3   : **in** std_ulogic_vector (7 **downto** 0);
       Sel   : **in** std_ulogic_vector (1 **downto** 0);
       Z   : **out** std_ulogic_vector (7 **downto** 0));
end entity mux;

Example End: Entity Declaration of a 4-to-1 Multiplexor

Example: Entity Declaration of a D Flip-Flop

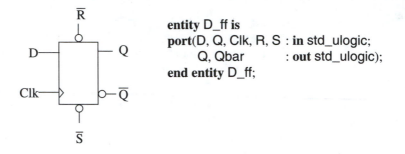

```
entity D_ff is
port(D, Q, Clk, R, S : in std_ulogic;
     Q, Qbar        : out std_ulogic);
end entity D_ff;
```

Example End: Entity Declaration of a D Flip-Flop

Example: Entity Declaration of a 32-bit ALU

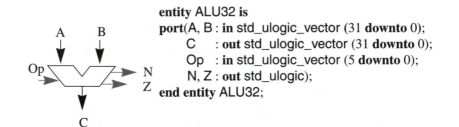

```
entity ALU32 is
port(A, B : in std_ulogic_vector (31 downto 0);
     C    : out std_ulogic_vector (31 downto 0);
     Op   : in std_ulogic_vector (5 downto 0);
     N, Z : out std_ulogic);
end entity ALU32;
```

Example End: Entity Declaration of a 32-bit ALU

From the preceding examples it is clear that design entities can occur at multiple levels of abstraction, from the gate level to large systems. In fact, it should be apparent that a design entity does not even have to represent digital hardware! The description of the interface is simply a specification of the input and output signals of the design entity.

Once the interface to the digital component or circuit has been described, it is now necessary to describe its internal behavior. The VHDL construct that enables us to specify the behavior of a design entity is the **architecture** construct. The syntax of the architecture construct is the following:

```
-- VHDL 1993                          -- VHDL 1987

architecture behavioral of half_adder is    architecture behavioral of half_adder is
-- place declarations here            -- place declarations here
begin                                 begin
-- place description of behavior here --    -- place description of behavior here --
end architecture behavioral;          end behavioral;
```

'87 vs. '93

The above construct provides for the declaration of the module named behavioral, which will contain the description of the behavior of the design entity named half_adder. Such a module is referred to as the **architecture** and is associated with the entity named in the declaration. Thus, the description of a design entity takes the form of an entity–architecture pair. The architecture description is linked to the correct entity description by providing the name of the corresponding entity in the first line of the architecture. The same rules for constructing entity names apply to architecture names.

The behavioral description provided in the architecture can take many forms. These forms differ in the levels of detail, description of events, and the degree of concurrency. The remainder of this chapter focuses on a core set of language constructs required to model the attributes of digital systems described in Chapter 2. Subsequent chapters will add constructs motivated by the need for expanding the scope and level of abstraction of the systems to be modeled.

4.3   Concurrent Statements

The operation of digital systems is inherently concurrent. Many components of a circuit can be simultaneously operating and concurrently driving distinct signals to new values. How can we describe the assignment of values to signals? We know that signal values are time–value pairs, that is, a signal is assigned a value at a specific point in time. Within VHDL signals are assigned values using *signal assignment* statements. These statements specify a new value of a signal and the time at which the signal is to acquire this value. Multiple signal assignment statements are executed concurrently in simulated time and are referred to as *concurrent signal assignment statements (CSAs)*. There are several forms of CSA statements and they are described in the following section.

4.3.1 Simple CSA

Consider a description of the behavior of the half-adder circuit shown in Figure 4-1. Recall that although VHDL manages the progression of time, we need to be able to specify events, delays, and concurrency of operation.

```
architecture concurrent_behavior of half_adder is
begin
  sum <= (x xor y) after 5 ns;
  carry <= (x and y) after 5 ns;
end architecture concurrent_behavior;
```

Just as we named entity descriptions, the label concurrent_behavior is the name given to this architecture module. The first line denotes the name of the entity that contains the description of the interface for this design entity. Each statement in the above architecture is a *signal assignment* statement with the operator "<=" denoting signal assignment. Each statement describes how the value of the output signal depends on, and is computed from, the value of the input signals. For example, the value of the sum output signal is computed as the Boolean exclusive-OR operation of the two input signals. Once the value of sum has been computed, it will not change unless the value of x or y changes. Figure 4-2 illustrates this behavior. At the current time, x = 0, y = 1, and sum = 1. At time 10, the value of y changes to 0. The new value of the sum will be (x xor y) = 0. Because there will be a propagation delay through the exclusive-OR gate, the signal sum will be assigned this value 5 ns later at time 15. This behavior is captured in the first signal assignment statement. Note that, unlike variable assignment statements, the signal assignments shown above specify both value and (relative) time.

In general, if an event (signal transition) occurs on a signal on the right-hand side of a signal assignment statement, the expression is evaluated and new values for the output signal are scheduled for some time in the future as defined by the **after** keyword. The dependency of the output signals on the input signals is captured in the two statements and **NOT** in the textual order of the program. The textual order of the statements could be reversed and the behavior of the circuit would not change. Both statements are executed concurrently with respect to simulated time to reflect the concurrency of the corresponding operations in the physical system. This is why these statements are referred to as concurrent signal assignment statements. A fundamental difference between VHDL programs and conventional programming languages is that concurrency is a natural part of the systems described in VHDL and therefore of the language itself. Note that the execution of the statements is determined by the flow of signal values, rather than textual order. Figure 4-2 shows a complete, executable half-adder description and the associated timing behavior. This description contains the most common elements used to describe a design entity.

Note the use of the **library** and **use** clauses. We can think of libraries as repositories for frequently used design entities that we wish to share. The **library** clause identifies a library that we wish to access. The name is a logical name for a library. In Figure 4-2 the

```
library IEEE;
use IEEE.std_logic_1164.all;

entity half_adder is
port (x, y: in std_ulogic;
      sum, carry : out std_ulogic);
end entity half_adder;

architecture concurrent_behavior of half_adder is
begin
sum <= (x xor y) after 5 ns;
carry <= (x and y) after 5 ns;
end architecture concurrent_behavior;
```

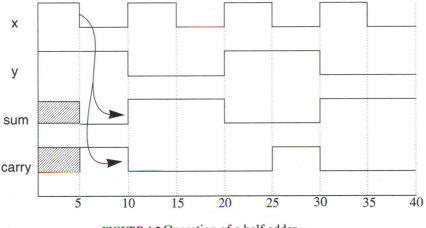

FIGURE 4-2 Operation of a half adder

library name is IEEE. In practice, this logical name will usually map to a directory on the local system. This directory will contain various design units that have been compiled. A *package* is one such design unit. A package may contain definitions of types, functions, or procedures to be shared by multiple application developers. The **use** clause determines which of the packages or other design units in a library you will be using in the current design. In the preceding example, the use clause states that in library IEEE there is a package named std_logic_1164, and that we will be able to use all of the components defined in this package. We need this package, since the definition for the type std_ulogic is in this package as it is not a part of the language definition. The VHDL models that use the IEEE 1164 value system will include the package declaration as shown. Design tool vendors typically provide the library IEEE and the std_logic_1164 package. These concepts are analogous to the use of libraries for mathematical functions and input–output in conventional programming languages. Libraries and packages are described in greater detail in Chapter 9. This example now contains the major components found in VHDL models:

declarations of existing design units in libraries that you will be using, entity description of the design unit, and the architecture description of the design unit.

The descriptions provided so far in this chapter are based on the specification of the value of the output signals as a function of the input signals. In larger and more complex designs there are usually many internal signals used to connect design components such as gates or other hardware building blocks. The values that these signals acquire can also be written using simple concurrent signal assignment statements. However, we must be able to declare and make use of signals other than those within the entity description. The gate-level description of the full adder provides an example of such a VHDL model.

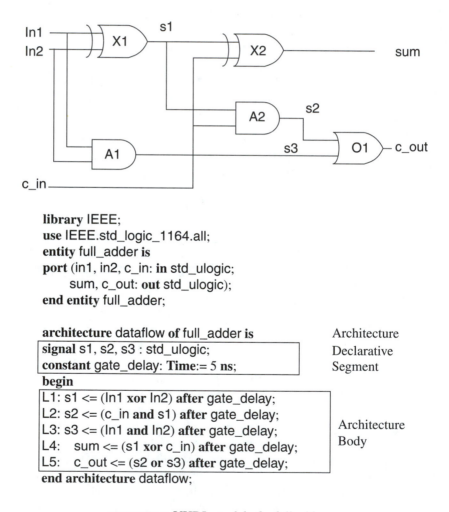

```
library IEEE;
use IEEE.std_logic_1164.all;
entity full_adder is
port (in1, in2, c_in: in std_ulogic;
      sum, c_out: out std_ulogic);
end entity full_adder;
```

```
architecture dataflow of full_adder is          Architecture
signal s1, s2, s3 : std_ulogic;                 Declarative
constant gate_delay: Time:= 5 ns;               Segment
begin
L1: s1 <= (In1 xor In2) after gate_delay;
L2: s2 <= (c_in and s1) after gate_delay;
L3: s3 <= (In1 and In2) after gate_delay;       Architecture
L4:   sum <= (s1 xor c_in) after gate_delay;    Body
L5:   c_out <= (s2 or s3) after gate_delay;
end architecture dataflow;
```

FIGURE 4-3 VHDL model of a full adder

Example: Full-Adder Model

Consider the full-adder circuit shown in Figure 4-3. We are interested in an accurate simulation of this circuit where all of the signal transitions in the gate-level realization are modeled. In addition to the ports in the entity description, we see that there are three internal signals. These signals are named and declared in the architectural description. The declarative region declares three single-bit signals: s1, s2, and s3. These signals are annotated in the circuit. Now we are ready to describe the behavior of the full adder in terms of the internal signals as well as the entity ports. Because this circuit uses two input gates, each signal is computed as a Boolean function of two other signals. The model is a simple statement of *how* each signal is computed as a function of other signals, and the propagation delay through the gate. There are two output signals and three internal signals, for a total of five signals. Accordingly, the description consists of five concurrent signal assignment statements, one for each signal.

Each signal assignment statement is given a label: L1, L2, and so on. This labeling is optional, and can be used for reference purposes. Note a new language feature in this model—the use of the **constant** object. Constants in VHDL function in a manner similar to conventional programming languages. A constant can be declared to be of a specific type, in this case of type **Time**. A constant must have a value at the start of the simulation and cannot be changed during the simulation. At this stage, it is easiest to ensure that constants are initialized as shown above. The introduction of the type **Time** is a natural consequence of simulation modeling. Any object of this type must take on the values of time such as microseconds or nanoseconds. The type **Time** is a predefined type of the language. As we know, the textual order of the statements is irrelevant to correct operation of the circuit model. Let us now consider the flow of signal values and the sequence of execution of the signal assignment statements. Figure 4-4 shows the waveforms of all of the signals in

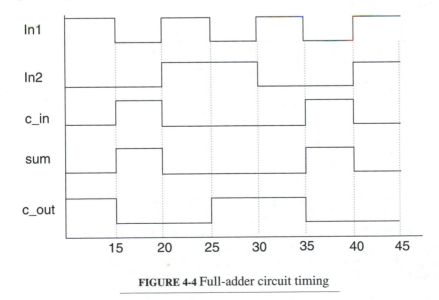

FIGURE 4-4 Full-adder circuit timing

the full-adder circuit. From the figure we see that there is an event on In1 at time 10 changing its value to 1. This causes statements L1 and L3 (from Figure 4-3) to be executed and new values to be scheduled on signals s1 and s3 5 ns later at time 15 ns. These events in turn cause statements L2 and L5 to be executed at time 20 ns and events to be scheduled on signals c_out and s2 at time 20 ns. We see that the execution of the statement L1 produced events that caused the execution of statement L5. This order of execution is maintained regardless of the textual order in which the statements appear in the program.

Note the two-stage model of time. In the first stage all statements with events occurring at the current time on signals on the right-hand side (RHS) of the signal assignment statement are evaluated. All future events that are generated from the execution of these statements are then scheduled. Time is now advanced to the time of the next event. The process is repeated. Note how the programmer specifies events, delays, and concurrency. Events are specified with signal assignment statements. Delays are specified within the signal assignment statement relative to the current time. Concurrency is specified by having a distinct signal assignment statement for each signal. The order of execution of the statements is dependent upon the flow of values (just as the case in the real circuit) and not on the textual order of the program. As long as the programmer correctly specifies how the value of each signal is computed and when it acquires this value relative to the current time, the simulator will correctly reflect the behavior of the entire circuit.

Example End: Full-Adder Model

4.3.2 Implementation of Signals

Unlike variables, signals are a new type of programming object and merit specific attention. For example we know how variables are implemented. They are simply a location in memory. If a variable is assigned a value the corresponding location in memory is written with the new value while destroying the old value. This effectively happens immediately so that if the following statement in the program uses the value of the variable it is the new value that is used. A signal is a different type of object. We naturally think of signals as having a history of values over time, for example as a waveform. If we are to preserve this intuition then the internal storage mechanism for signals must be quite different from that employed for variables.

So far we have seen that signals can be declared in the body of an architecture or in the port declaration of an entity. The form of the declaration is

signal s1 : std_ulogic := '0';

If the signal declaration included the assignment symbol (i.e., :=) followed by an expression, the value of the expression is the initial value of the signal. The initialization is not required, in which case the signal is assigned a default value as specified by the type definition. For example all boolean valued signals may be assigned FALSE initially. Signals can be declared to be one of many valid VHDL types: **integers**, **real**, **bit_vector**, and so forth.

Now consider the assignment of values to a signal. We know that signal assignment statements assign a value to a signal at a specific point in time. The simple concurrent signal assignment statements described so far in this chapter exhibit the following common structure:

sum <= (x xor y) **after** 5 **ns**;

which can be written in a more general form as

signal <= value expression **after** *time expression;*

The expression on the RHS of the signal assignment is referred to as a *waveform element*. A waveform element describes an assignment to a signal and is comprised of a *value expression* to the left of the **after** keyword and a *time expression* to the right of the keyword. The former evaluates to the new value to be assigned to the signal and the latter evaluates to the relative time at which the signal is to acquire this value. In this case the new value is computed as the exclusive-OR of the current values of the signals x and y. The value of the time expression is added to the current simulation time to determine when the signal will receive this new value. In this case the time expression is a constant value of 5 ns. With respect to the current simulation time, this time–value pair represents the future value of the signal and is referred to as a *transaction*. The underlying discrete event simulator that executes VHDL programs must keep track of all transactions that occur on a signal. The list is ordered in increasing time of the transactions.

If the evaluation of a single waveform element produces a single transaction on a signal, can we specify multiple waveform elements and, as a result, multiple transactions? For example, could we have the following?

s1 <= (x xor y) **after** 5 **ns**, (x or y) **after** 10 **ns**, (**not** x) **after** 15 **ns**;

The answer is yes! When an event occurs on either of the signals x or y, then the above statement would be executed, all three waveform elements would be evaluated, and three transactions would be generated. Note that these transactions are in increasing order of time. The events represented by these transactions must be scheduled at different points in the future, and the VHDL simulator must keep track of all of the transactions that are currently scheduled on a signal. This is achieved by maintaining an ordered list of all of the current transactions pending on a signal. This list is referred to as the *driver* for the signal. The current value of a signal is the value of the transaction at the head of the list. What is the physical interpretation of such a sequence of events? These events represent the value of the signal over time, which essentially is a waveform. This is how we can represent a signal waveform in VHDL: as a sequence of waveform elements. Therefore, within a signal assignment statement, rather than assigning a single value to the signal at some future time we can assign a waveform to this signal. This waveform is specified as a sequence of signal values and each value is specified with a single waveform element. Within the simulator these sequences of waveform elements are represented as a sequence of transactions on the driver of the signal. These transactions are referred to as the *projected output waveform*, because these events have not yet occurred in the simulation. What if the simulation attempts to add transactions that conflict with the current projected waveform? The VHDL language definition provides specific rules for adding transactions to the projected waveform of a signal. For a precise definition of the rules the reader can refer to the language reference manual (LRM) [5].

Example: Specifying Waveforms

Assume that we would like to generate the following waveform. We could do so with the signal assignment statement shown below.

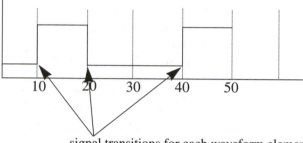

signal transitions for each waveform element

signal <= '0', '1' **after 10 ns**, '0' **after 20 ns**, '1' **after 40 ns**;

Note how each transition in the above waveform is specified as a single waveform element in the signal assignment statement. All waveform elements must be ordered in increasing time. Failure to do so will result in an error.

Example End: Specifying Waveforms

The concepts and terminology discussed so far are derived from the operation of digital circuits. In a physical circuit a wire (signal) has a driver associated with it. Over time this driver produces a waveform on that wire. If we continue to view the language constructs by analogy with the digital circuits they were intended to model, it will be easier for us to reason about the construction of models using VHDL. The constructs that manipulate signals invariably rely on waveform elements to specify input and output waveforms. Understanding this representation is key to understanding many of the VHDL programming constructs.

4.3.3 Resolved Signals

Our view of signals up to this point has been one where every signal has only one driver, that is, one signal assignment statement that is responsible for generating the waveform on that signal. We know that this is not true in practice. Shared signals occur on buses and in circuits based on wired logic. When a signal has multiple drivers, how is the value of the signal determined? In the VHDL language, this value is determined by a *resolution function*.

A resolution function examines all of the drivers on a shared signal and determines the value to be assigned to the signal. A shared signal must be of a special type: a *resolved type*. A resolved type has a resolution function associated with the type. In the preceding examples, we have been using the **std_ulogic** and **std_ulogic_vector** types for single-bit and multi-bit signals, respectively. The corresponding resolved types are **std_logic** and **std_logic_vector**. This distinction has the following consequences. In the course of the simulation, when a signal of type **std_logic** is assigned a value, the associated resolution function is automatically invoked to determine the correct value of the signal. Multiple drivers for this signal may be projecting multiple future values for this signal. The resolution function examines these drivers to return the correct value of the signal at the current time. If the signal has only one driver, then determination of the value is straightforward. However, if more than one driver exists for the signal the value that is assigned to the signal is the value determined by the resolution function. For the IEEE 1164 package, the resolution function is essentially an LUT. Provided with the signal values from two drivers, the table returns the signal value to be assigned. For example, if one source is driving the signal to 1 and a second source's output is left floating (i.e., in state **Z**), the resulting value will be 1. Alternatively, if the two sources are driving the shared signal to 1 and 0 respectively, the resulting value will be unknown or **X**. The resolution function for the **std_logic** and **std_logic_vector** types is provided by the **std_logic_1164** package. Having multiple drivers for a signal whose type is an unresolved type will result in an error. The user may define new resolved types and provide the resolution functions for their use.

We will leave resolution functions for the moment and return to them in greater detail when we deal with the creation and use of procedures and functions in Chapter 9. However, in the remainder of this book all of the examples use the IEEE 1164 resolved single-bit and multibit types, **std_logic** and **std_logic_vector**, rather than unresolved types **std_ulogic** or **std_ulogic_vector**.

Simulation Exercise 4.1: A First Simulation Model

This exercise introduces the construction and simulation of simple VHDL models. The following steps require simulator-specific commands.

Step 1. Using a text editor, create a VHDL model of the full adder shown in Figure 4-3. Do not use a word processor even though they may have an option for saving your text as an ASCII file. Some word processors place control characters in the file or may handle some characters non-uniformly, for example, left and right quotation marks. This can lead to analyzer errors (however, you could correct these errors at that time). Set the gate delays to 3 ns for the EX-OR gates and to 2 ns for all of the other gates.

Step 1 (a) Declare and reference the library IEEE and the package std_logic_1164.

Step 1 (b) Write the entity description. Use the types std_logic and std_logic_vector for the input and output signals.

Step 1 (c) Write the architecture description.

Step 2. Compile and load the model for simulation using a VHDL simulator toolset.

Step 3. Generate a waveform on each of the input signals.

Step 4. Run the simulation for 40 ns and trace (i) the input signals, (ii) the internal signals, s1, s2, and s3, and (iii) the sum and carry outputs.

Step 5. Check and list scheduled events on the internal signals and output signals.

Step 6. Pick an event on one of the input signals. Record the propagation of the effect of this event through the signal trace. Study the trace and ensure that the model is operating correctly.

Step 7. Repeat this example, only this time do not initialize one of the input signals. What does the resulting trace look like and what is the significance of the values on this uninitialized input?

End Simulation Exercise 4.1

4.3.4 Conditional Signal Assignment

The simple concurrent signal assignment statements that we have seen so far compute the value of the target signal based on Boolean expressions. The values of the signals on the RHS of the signal assignment statement are used to compute the value of the target signal. This new value is scheduled at some point in the future using the **after** keyword. Expressing values of signals in this manner is convenient for describing gate-level circuits whose behavior can be expressed with Boolean equations. However, we often find it useful to model circuits at higher levels of abstraction such as multiplexors and decoders. Modeling at this level requires a richer set of constructs.

For example, consider the physical behavior of a 4-to-1, 8-bit multiplexor shown in Figure 4-5. The value of Z is one of In0, In1, In2, or In3. The waveform that appears on one of the inputs is transferred to the output Z. The specific choice depends upon the value of the control signals S0 and S1 for which there are four possible alternatives. Each of

```
library IEEE;
use IEEE.std_logic_1164.all;
entity mux4 is
port (In0, In1, In2, In3 : in std_logic_vector (7 downto 0);
      S0, S1: in std_logic;
      Z : out std_logic_vector (7 downto 0));
end entity mux4;

architecture behavioral of mux4 is
begin
Z <= In0 after 5 ns when S0 = '0' and S1 = '0' else
     In1 after 5 ns when S0 = '0' and S1 = '1' else
     In2 after 5 ns when S0 = '1' and S1 = '0' else
     In3 after 5 ns when S0 = '1' and S1 = '1' else
     "00000000" after 5 ns;
end architecture behavioral;
```

FIGURE 4-5 Conditional signal assignment statement

these must be tested and one chosen. This behavior is captured in the conditional signal assignment statement and is illustrated for a 4-to-1, 8-bit multiplexor in Figure 4-5. The structure of the statement follows from the physical behavior of the circuit. For each of the four possible values of S0 and S1, an input waveform is specified. In this case, the waveform is comprised of a single waveform element describing the most recent signal value on that input. As pointed out in Section 4.3.2, more than one waveform element in each line of the conditional statement could have been specified, producing a waveform on the output signal Z.

In the corresponding physical circuit, an event on any one of the input signals, In0–In3, or any of the control signals, S0 or S1, may cause a change in the value of the output signal. Therefore, whenever any such event takes place the concurrent signal assignment statement is executed and all four conditions may be checked. The order of the statements is important. The expressions in the RHS are evaluated in the order that they appear. The first conditional expression that is found to be true determines the value that is transferred to the output. Therefore, we must be careful in ordering the conditional expressions on the RHS to reflect the order in which they would be evaluated in the corresponding physical system. A careful look at the example in Figure 4-5 will reveal that, in this case, only one expression can be true and therefore the order does not matter in this particular example. Finally, note that in Figure 4-5 even though there several lines of text this corresponds to only one signal assignment statement.

The effect of the priority order of the expressions is better illustrated by the example in Figure 4-6. This example represents a model of a 4-to-2 priority encoder which produces the binary encoding of the bit that is set. If more than one of the input bits has a

```
library IEEE;
use IEEE.std_logic_1164.all;
entity pr_encoder is
port (S0, S1,S2,S3: in std_logic;
      Z : out std_logic_vector (1 downto 0));
end entity pr_encoder ;

architecture behavioral of pr_encoder is
begin
Z <=    "00" after 5 ns when S0 = '1' else
        "01" after 5 ns when S1 = '1' else
        "10" after 5 ns when S2 = '1' else
        "11" after 5 ns when S3 = '1' else
     "00" after 5 ns;
end architecture behavioral;
```

FIGURE 4-6 Priority behavior of the conditional signal assignment

value of 1, then the lowest numbered input has higher priority. In this example if S0 is set then the output is 00 regardless of the state of the other input bits. The last statement sets the output value to 00 and is important because the input signals and select signals are of type std_logic. Thus each of the select signals, S0, S1, S2, and S3, can have more values than simply 0 or 1 and the conditional signal statement shown in the example does not cover all cases. There are many more conditions not covered by the statements in this example and all of these conditions are collectively covered by the last statement.

Finally, the previous forms of the conditional signal assignment statement always compute a value for the output signal whenever the any of the input signals change value. Although this is the model for combinational logic for more general modeling we may require behavior where the output signal value may remain unchanged. This behavior can be realized with the **unaffected** keyword. For example the conditional signal assignment statement may appear as follows.

'87 vs. '93

☞

```
Z <=    "00" after 5 ns when S0 = '1' else
        "01" after 5 ns when S1 = '1' else
        unaffected when S2 = '1' else
        "11" after 5 ns when S3 = '1' else
     "00" after 5 ns;
```

This statement now has the following semantics. When S2 has the value 1 and both S0 and S1 have the value 0 (remember the priority ordering!) the value of the output signal does not change. This enables the description of a richer set of responses to combinations of input signal values. As we shall see in the following chapter on synthesis this style of VHDL code really implies sequential rather than combinational logic. This feature, that is the **unaffected** keyword, is not supported in VHDL-87.

4.3.5 Selected Signal Assignment Statement

The selected signal assignment statement is very similar to the conditional signal assignment statement. The value of a signal is determined by the value of a *select expression*. For example, consider the operation of reading the value of a register from a register file with eight registers. Depending upon the value of the address, the contents of the appropriate register are selected. An example of a read-only register file with two read ports is shown in Figure 4-7.

```vhdl
library IEEE;
use IEEE.std_logic_1164.all;

entity reg_file is
port (addr1, addr2: in std_logic_vector (2 downto 0);
      reg_out_1, reg_out_2: out std_logic_vector (31 downto 0));
end entity reg_file;

architecture behavior of reg_file is
signal reg0, reg2, reg4, reg6: std_logic_vector (31 downto 0):= x"12345678";
signal reg1, reg3, reg5, reg7: std_logic_vector (31 downto 0):= x"abcdef00";
begin
with addr1 select
reg_out_1 <= reg0 after 5 ns when "000",
             reg1 after 5 ns when "001",
             reg2 after 5 ns when "010",
             reg3 after 5 ns when "011",
             reg3 after 5 ns when others;
with addr2 (1 downto 0) select
reg_out_2 <= reg0 after 5 ns when "00",
             reg1 after 5 ns when "01",
             reg2 after 5 ns when "10",
             reg3 after 5 ns when "11",
             reg3 after 5 ns when others;
end architecture behavior;
```

FIGURE 4-7 Selected signal assignment statement

This statement operates very much like a case statement in conventional languages. As a result, its semantics is somewhat distinct from conditional signal assignment statements. For example in Figure 4-7 the choices for the register addresses are not evaluated in sequence. Rather all choices are evaluated, but only one must be true. Furthermore, all of the choices that the programmer specifies must cover all of the possible values of the addresses. For example, consider the VHDL code shown in Figure 4-7. Assume that we have only four registers but both addr1 and addr2 are 3-bit addresses and therefore can address up to eight registers. The VHDL language requires you to specify the action to be taken if addr1 or addr2 takes on any of the 8 values including those between 4 and 7. This is realized with the use of the **others** clause as shown in the first selected signal assignment statement. The **others** keyword is used to conveniently state the value of the target signal over the remaining unspecified range of values and thereby cover the whole range. This is not really restrictive, because in practice we must consider what would happen in the physical system in this case. The select expression can be quite flexible and can be specified in any number of forms. For example the select expression may incorporate Boolean expressions or, as shown in the second statement in the example, a subset of bits as in addr2(1 **downto** 0). In this latter case do we still need the **when others** clause because addr2(1 **downto** 0) can only have 4 values? Yes, because addr2 is of type std_logic_vector. Therefore each bit actually can take on 9 values and addr2(1 **downto** 0) can actually have not 4 but 9^2 or 81 values!

As with simple and conditional CSAs, we must be aware of the conditions under which a selected signal assignment statement is executed. When an event occurs on a signal used in the select expression or any of the signals used in one of the choices, the statement is executed. This follows the expected behavior of the corresponding physical implementation where an event on any of the addresses or register contents could potentially change the value of the output signal. As with the conditional signal assignment statement we can use the **unaffected** clause to signify that the signal does not change value. For example, the third option in the statement may be **unaffected when** "11", rather than reg3 **after** 5 **ns when** "11". Recall that this feature is only supported in VHDL 1993.

'87 vs. '93

Note a few new statements in this example. First, we initialize the values of the registers when they are declared. In this example, the even-numbered registers are initialized with a hexadecimal value denoted by x"12345678" whereas the odd numbered registers are initialized with the hexadecimal value denoted by x"abcdef00." Note that the target is a signal of type std_logic_vector. In some older simulators the hexadecimal values must be converted to the type std_logic_vector before they can be assigned. In this case the initialization value may have to read to_stdlogicvector(x"12345678"). On the other hand, if the values were specified in binary notation explicit type conversion would not be required. The function to_stdlogicvector () is in the package std_logic_1164 and performs this type conversion operation. Although this was not necessary of the simulator we used (Active VHDL and Foundation Express), this is not necessarily the case for other simulators. Type conversion as well as other functions in support of the IEEE 1164 value system are found in the std_logic_1164 package provided by practically all CAD tool vendors. There are also other packages of functions and procedures that are provided by the vendors. Many standardization efforts are underway within the community in an effort to ensure portability of models between vendor toolsets and cooperating designers. These packages also provide similar type conversion functions often with slightly different names. Check availability of such packages within your toolset and browse through them. Packages may be located in the library IEEE. If packages you wish to use are located in another design library a new **library** clause is required to declare this library, and the **use** clause must be appropriately modified to reference this library just as shown in our examples with IEEE. The use of libraries and packages is presented in greater detail in Chapter 9.

4.4 Constructing VHDL Models Using CSAs

Armed with CSA statements, we are now ready to construct VHDL models of interesting classes of digital systems. This section provides a prescription for constructing such VHDL models. By following this approach to constructing models, we can generate an intuition about the structure of VHDL programs and the utility of the language constructs discussed so far.

In a VHDL model written using only CSA statements, the execution of a signal assignment statement is initiated by the flow of data or signal values rather than the textual order of the statements. Based on the language features we have seen thus far, a model of a digital system will be composed of an entity–architecture pair. The architecture model, in turn, will be composed of some combination of simple, conditional, and selected signal assignments statements. The architecture may also declare and use internal signals in addition to the input and output ports declared in the entity description.

The following description assumes we are writing a VHDL model of a gate-level, combinational circuit. However, the approach can certainly be applied to higher level systems using combinational building blocks such as encoders and multiplexors. The simple methodology comprises two steps: (i) the drawing of an annotated schematic, and (ii) the conversion to a VHDL description. The following procedure outlines a few simple steps to organize the information we have about the physical system prior to writing the VHDL model.

Construct_Schematic

1. Represent each component (e.g., gate) of the system to be modeled as a *delay element*. The delay element simply captures all of the delays associated with the computation represented by the component and propagation of signals through the component. For each output signal of a component associate a specific value of delay through the component for that output signal.

2. Draw a schematic interconnecting all of the components. Uniquely label each component.

3. Identify the input signals of the circuit as input ports.

4. Identify the output signals of the circuit as output ports.

5. All remaining signals are internal signals.

6. Associate a type with each input, output, and internal signal, such as std_logic or std_logic_vector.

7. Ensure that each input port, output port, and internal signal are labeled with a unique name.

An example of such a schematic is shown in Figure 4-8. Now, from this schematic, we can write a VHDL model using CSA statements. A template for the VHDL description is shown in Figure 4-9. This template can be filled in as described below in the procedure **Construct_CSA_Model**. Names used in this procedure, such as entity_name, refer to names in program template provided in Figure 4-9.

Construct_CSA_Model

1. At this point I recommend using the IEEE 1164 value system. To do so, include the following two lines at the top of your model declaration.

    library IEEE;
    use IEEE.std_logic_1164.all;

Single-bit signals can be declared to be of type std_logic whereas multi-bit quantities can be declared to be of type std_logic_vector.

2. Select a name for the entity (entity_name) and write the entity description specifying each input or output signal port, its mode, and associated type. This can be read off of the annotated schematic.

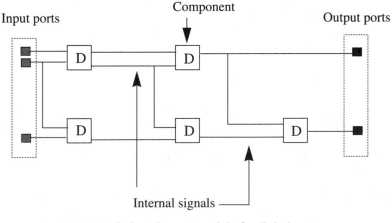

FIGURE 4-8 Delay element model of a digital system

library library-name-1, library-name-2;

use library-name-1.package-name.all;

use library-name-2.package-name.all;

entity entity_name **is**

port(*input signals* : **in** *type*;

    output signals : **out** *type*);

end entity entity_name;

architecture arch_name **of** entity_name **is**

-- declare internal signals

-- you may have multiple signals of different types

signal internal-signal-1 : *type* := *initialization*;

signal internal-signal-2 : *type* := *initialization*;

begin

-- specify value of each signal as a function of other signals

internal-signal-1 <= *simple, conditional, or selected CSA*;

internal-signal-2 <= *simple, conditional, or selected CSA*;

output-signal-1 <= *simple, conditional, or selected CSA*;

output-signal-2 <= *simple, conditional, or selected CSA*;

end architecture arch_name;

FIGURE 4-9 A template for writing VHDL models using CSAs

3. Select a name for the architecture (arch_name) and write the architecture description. Place both the entity and architecture descriptions in the same file (as we will see in Chapter 11 this is not necessary in general.)

3.1 Within the architecture description, name and declare all of the internal signals used to connect the components. The declaration states the type of each signal and its initial value. Initialization is not required, but is recommended. These declarations occur prior to the first **begin** statement in the architecture.

3.2 Each internal signal is driven by exactly one component. If this is not the case make sure the type of the signal is a resolved type such as std_logic or std_logic_vector. For each internal signal, write a CSA statement that expresses the value of this internal signal as a function of input signals for that component. Use the delay value associated with that output signal for that component. This is available from your annotated schematic.

3.3 Each output port signal is driven by the output of some internal component, that is, each output port is connected to the output of some component. For each output port signal write a concurrent signal assignment statement that expresses its value as some function of the signals that are inputs to corresponding component.

3.4 If you are using any functions or type definitions provided by a third party make sure that you have declared the appropriate library using the **library** clause and declared the use of this package via the presence of a **use** clause in your model.

If there are S signals and ports in the schematic, there will be S concurrent signal assignment statements in the VHDL model—one for each signal. This approach provides a quick way of constructing VHDL models by attempting to maintain a close correspondence with the hardware being modeled. There are many alternatives to constructing a VHDL model and the above approach represents only one method. With experience, the reader will no doubt discover many other alternatives for constructing efficient models for digital systems of interest.

Simulation Exercise 4.2: A Single-Bit ALU

Consider a simple 1-bit ALU shown in Figure 4-10 that performs the AND, OR, and ADDITION operations. The result produced at the ALU output depends on the value of signal OPCODE. Write and simulate a model of this ALU using concurrent signal assignments statements. Test each OPCODE to ensure that the model is accurate by examining the waveforms on the input and output signals. Use a gate delay of 2 ns, a delay of 6 ns through the adder, and a delay of 4 ns through the multiplexor. Remember, although the OPCODE field is 2 bits wide, there are only three valid inputs to the multiplexor.

Step 1.   Follow the steps in **Construct_Schematic**. Ensure that all of the signals including the input and output ports are defined, labeled, and their mode and types are specified.

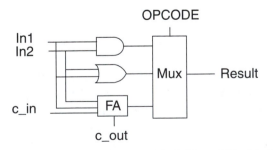

FIGURE 4-10 A single-bit ALU (FA = full adder)

Step 2. Follow the steps in **Construct_CSA_Model**. To describe the operation of the full adder, use two simple CSA statements: one each to describe the computation of the sum and carry outputs, respectively. Describe the output of the multiplexor using a conditional signal assignment statement and use the **when others** or **unaffected** clauses to account for the fact that the multiplexor has only three inputs rather than four. Call this file *alu.vhd*.

Step 3. Compile *alu.vhd*.

Step 4. Generate a sequence of inputs that you can use to verify that the model is functioning correctly.

Step 5. Open a trace window with the signals you would like to trace. Include internal signals which are signals that are not entity ports in the model.

Step 6. Run the simulation for 50 ns.

Step 7. Check the trace to determine correctness.

Step 8. Print and record the trace.

Step 9. Add new operations to the single-bit ALU, recompile, and resimulate the model. For example, you can add the exclusive-OR, subtraction, and complement operations.

End Simulation Exercise 4.2

4.5 Understanding Delays

We now have a template to help us begin to write basic VHDL models for many digital circuits. Let us examine one important aspect of these models in greater detail: propagation delays. Accurate representation of the behavior of digital circuits requires accurate modeling of delays through the various components. This section discusses the delay models available in VHDL and how they are specified. These models can be incorporated in a straightforward manner into the basic template for writing VHDL models that was described earlier. They are also used in the models that are described in Chapter 6 and the structural models that are described in Chapter 8.

4.5.1 The Inertial Delay Model

In Chapter 2 it was pointed out that digital circuits have a certain amount of inertia. For example, it takes a finite amount of time and a certain amount of energy for the output of a gate to respond to a change on the input. This implies that the change on the input has to persist for a certain period of time to ensure that the output will respond. If it does not persist long enough the input events will not be propagated to the output. This propagation delay model is referred to as the *inertial delay model* and is the default delay model for VHDL programs.

An example is shown in Figure 4-11 where a signal is applied to the input of a two-input OR gate. If the gate delay is 8 ns, any pulse on the input signal of duration less than 8 ns will not be propagated to the output. This is illustrated by waveform Out 1. However, if the gate delay is 2 ns we see that each pulse on the input waveform is of a duration greater than 2 ns and is therefore propagated to the output. Any pulse with a width of less than the propagation delay through the gate is said to be rejected. In general, the pulse widths that are actually rejected in a physical circuit are very dependent upon the physical design and manufacturing process parameters and can be difficult to determine accurately. The VHDL language uses the propagation delay through the component as the default pulse rejection width.

However, if we have a greater understanding of the properties of the components that we are modeling, VHDL supports the following specification of a value for the pulse rejection width.

sum <= **reject** 2 **ns inertial** (x xor y) **after** 5 **ns**;

In Section 4.3.2, a simple form of the waveform element was introduced as the manner in which we could specify the new value–time pair of a signal. The general form of a waveform element allows us to specify a distinct pulse rejection width (distinct from the propagation delay). Note that the expression has been preceded by the keyword **reject** and a time value has been provided. The keyword **inertial** must also be provided. Thus, in VHDL'93 we can write the general form of the simple concurrent signal assignment statement as follows.

signal <= **reject** *time-expression* **inertial** *value-expression* **after** *time-expression*;

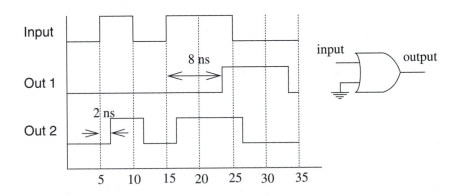

FIGURE 4-11 An example of the inertial delay model. Out 1 is the output waveform for delay = 8 ns and Out 2 is the output waveform for delay = 2 ns.

However, VHDL'87 does not support the specification of pulse rejection widths. The '87 vs. '93 delay value is utilized as the pulse rejection width. The above statement is a very general form describing the occurrence of an event on a signal. This form specifies the value of the signal, the time at which the signal is to receive this value, and the duration over which the input pulse must persist if the output is to receive this new value.

4.5.2 The Transport Delay Model

Like switching devices, signals propagate through wires at a finite rate and experience delays that are proportional to the distance. However, unlike switching devices, wires have comparatively less inertia. As a result, wires will propagate signals with very small pulse widths and we can model wires as media that will propagate any changes in signal values independent of the duration of the pulse width. In modern technologies with increasingly small feature sizes the wire delays dominate, and designs seek to minimize wire length. In these circuits wire delays are non-negligible and should be modeled to produce accurate simulations of circuit behavior. Such delays are referred to as *transport delays*. Although we naturally think of wires as elements with very little inertia there may other components that we wish to model where any event on the input must be propagated to the output. In these cases we wish to model the behavior of the component using the transport delay model. As with inertial delays, these delays can be specified by prefacing a waveform element with the keyword **transport** as follows:

sum <= **transport** (x **xor** y) **after** 5 **ns**;

In this case a pulse of any width on signal x or y can be propagated to the sum signal. We will generally not use the transport delay model for modeling components that have significant inertia. The inertial delay model is the default delay model in VHDL.

Example: Transport Delays

Up to this point, digital components have been treated as delay elements. Output signals acquire values after a specified propagation delay that we now know can be specified to be an inertial delay or a transport delay. If we wish to model delays along wires we can simply replace the wire with a delay element. The delay value is equal to the delay experienced by the signal transmission along the wire and the delay type is **transport**. Consider the half-adder circuit again redrawn to capture wire delays on the output signals, as shown in Figure 4-12. Delay elements model the delay on the sum and carry signals. Note in this example that the delay along these wires is longer than the propagation delay through the gate. From the timing diagram we see that a pulse of width 2 ns on the sum input at time 0 is propagated to signal s1 at time 2 ns. The wire delay is 4 ns. Under the inertial delay model this pulse would be rejected and would not appear on the sum output. However, we have specified the delay type to be transport. Therefore, the pulse is transmitted to the sum output after a delay of 4 ns. This signal is now delivered to the next circuit, having

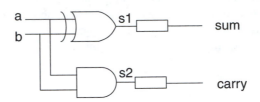

```
library IEEE;
use IEEE.std_logic_1164.all;
entity half_adder is
port(a, b: in std_logic;
       sum, carry: out std_logic);
end entity half_adder;

architecture transport_delay of half_adder is
signal s1, s2: std_logic:= '0';
begin
s1 <= (a xor b) after 2 ns;
s2 <= (a and b) after 2 ns;
sum <= transport s1 after 4 ns;
carry <= transport s2 after 4 ns;
end architecture transport_delay;
```

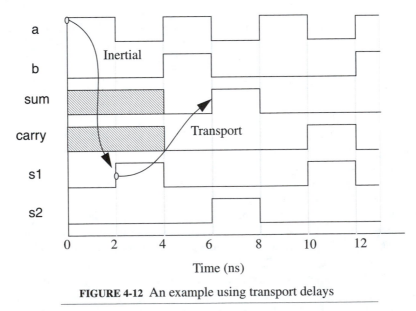

FIGURE 4-12 An example using transport delays

been delayed by an amount equal to the propagation delay through the signal wires. This approach enables the accurate modeling of wire delays although in practice it is difficult to obtain accurate estimates of the wire delay without proceeding through physical design and the layout of the circuit.

Example End: Transport Delays

The choice between the use of inertial delay or transport delay is determined by the components that are being modeled. For example, if we have a model of a board level design we may have VHDL models of the individual chips. The delay experienced by signals between chips can be modeled using the transport delay model. The procedure **Construct_Schematic** provided in Section 4.4 can be modified to include delay elements for all wire delays to be modeled. The procedure for translating this annotated schematic is simply modified to use transport delays in the CSA statements that represent wire delays.

4.5.3 Delta Delays

What happens if we do not specify a delay for the occurrence of an event on a signal? For example, the computation of the outputs for an exclusive-OR gate may be written as follows:

sum <= (x xor y);

We may chose to ignore delays when we do not know what they are or when we are interested only in creating a simulation that is functionally correct and is not concerned with the physical timing behavior. For example, consider the timing of the full-adder model shown in Figure 4-4. There is a correct ordering of events on the signals. Input events on signals In1, In2, and c_in produce events on internal signals s1, s2, and s3, which, in turn, produce events on the output signals sum and c_out. For functional correctness we must maintain this ordering even when delays remain unspecified. This is achieved within the VHDL language implementation by defining an infinitesimally small delay referred to as a *delta delay*. The above form of the signal assignment statement implicitly places an "**after** 0 **ns**" time expression following the value expression. When this is the case, the assignment to the signal is effectively assigned a delay value of Δ. Now simulation proceeds exactly as described in the earlier examples using this delay value. As the following example will demonstrate, Δ does not actually have to be assigned a numeric value but is utilized within the simulator to order events. If events with zero delay are produced at timestep T, the simulator simply organizes and processes events in time order of occurrence: events that occur Δ seconds later are followed by events occurring 2Δ seconds later, followed by events occurring 3Δ seconds later, and so on. Delta delays are simply used to enforce dependencies between events and thereby ensure correct simulation. The following example will help clarify the use of delta delays.

Example: Delta Delays

Consider the combinational logic circuit and the corresponding VHDL code shown in Figure 4-13. The model captures a behavioral description of the circuit *without* specifying any gate delays. Figure 4-14(a) illustrates the timing of the circuit when inputs are applied as shown. At time 10 ns the signal In2 makes a $1 \rightarrow 0$ transition. This causes a sequence of events in the circuit resulting in the value of Z = 0. From the accompanying VHDL code we see that the gate delays are implicitly 0 ns. Therefore, the timing diagram shows the signal Z acquiring this value at the same instant in time that In2 makes a transition. From the timing diagram it is also clear that signals s2 and s3 also make transitions at this instant in time. In reality, from the circuit diagram we know that there is a dependency between In2 and s3, and s3 and Z. These dependencies are evident from the structure of

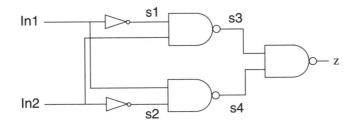

```
library IEEE;
use IEEE.std_logic_1164.all;
entity combinational is
port (In1, In2: in std_logic;
    z : out std_logic);
end entity combinational;


architecture behavior of combinational is
signal s1, s2, s3, s4: std_logic:= '0';
begin
s1 <= not In1;
s2 <= not In2;
s3 <= not (s1 and In2);
s4 <= not (s2 and In1);
z <= not (s3 and s4);
end architecture behavior;
```

FIGURE 4-13 A VHDL model with delta delays

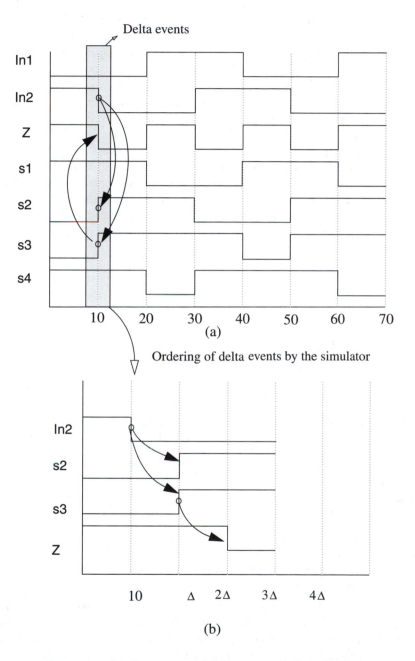

(a)

(b)

FIGURE 4-14 (a) Occurrence of delta events (b) Ordering imposed on these events within the simulator

the circuit. The event on In2 precedes and causes the transitions on s3 and s4, whereas the transition on s3 causes the transition on Z. The simulation of the circuit honors these dependencies through the logical use of delta delays. The dependencies between In2, s3, and Z are shown in Figure 4-14(b). The transition on In2 causes s3 to make a transition to 1 after Δ secs. The event on s3 causes a $1 \rightarrow 0$ event on Z after 2Δ secs. These events are referred to as delta events and are shown in Figure 4-14(b). These delta events take place within the simulator and do not appear on the external trace produced for the viewer (i.e., Figure 4-14(a)). The actual implementation of delta events is managed within the simulator by keeping track of signal values and when they are updated.

By forcing all events to take some infinitesimally small amount of time the dependencies between events can be preserved and the correct operation of the circuit maintained. Recall how a circuit is simulated. Time is advanced to that of the first event on the list. The signal is assigned this value, any new outputs computed, and the process repeated. When time is advanced by Δ, this step is referred to as a delta cycle.

Example End: Delta Delays

Simulation Exercise 4.3: Delta Delays

Repeat the simulation of the full-adder model in Simulation Exercise 4.1, but do not specify any gate delays.

Step 1. Run the simulation for 40 ns and trace input, internal, and output signals.

Step 2. Annotate the trace to identify delta events.

Step 3. Compare the trace generated here with that generated in Simulation Exercise 4.1. What are the differences?

Step 4. Modify the model to include a 2-ns wire delay for internal signals. Recompile the model.

Step 5. Simulate the model now and generate another trace. The effect of wire delays is now explicitly captured.

Step 6. Identify events that occur in this second trace that are different from those in the earlier trace.

Step 7. Create an input stimulus for one of the inputs with pulses whose duration are both shorter and longer than the gate delay. Set the value of the remaining inputs to logic 0. This is usually achieved by adjusting the simulator step time and via stimulus commands unique to the simulator that you are using.

Step 8. Generate a trace and identify pulses that are rejected by the gate models.

End Simulation Exercise 4.3

4.6 Chapter Summary

The reader should be comfortable with the following concepts that have been introduced in this chapter. A syntactic reference to common language types and operators can be found in Chapter 12.

- Entity and architecture constructs
- Concurrent signal assignment statements
  - simple concurrent signal assignment
  - conditional concurrent signal assignment
  - selected concurrent signal assignment
- Constructing models using concurrent signal assignment statements
  - modeling events, propagation delays, and concurrency
- Modeling delays
  - inertial delay
  - transport delay
  - delta delay
- Signal drivers and projected waveforms
- Shared signals, resolved types, and resolution functions
- Generating waveforms using waveform elements
- Events and transactions

The VHDL models of systems should now be beginning to take some form. The reader should be capable of constructing functionally correct models for many types of digital systems utilizing inertial, transport, or delta delay models (i.e., functional models). Now that we have seen how we may describe hardware with VHDL we can revisit these same constructs from the perspective of synthesis. Is the process of inferring the hardware from these same constructs straightforward? The complementary view of the language constructs discussed here is presented in the next chapter.

Exercises

1. A good exercise for understanding entity descriptions is to write the entity descriptions for components found in data books from component vendors, for example, the TTL data book. These entity descriptions can be compiled without the architecture descriptions and thus can be checked for syntactic correctness. Of course, we cannot say anything about the semantic correctness of such descriptions because we have not even written the architecture descriptions yet!

2. Write and simulate a VHDL model of a 2-bit comparator.

3. Sketch the output waveform produced by the following VHDL simple concurrent signal assignment statements.

   s1 <= '0' **after** 5 ns, '1' **after** 15 ns, '0' **after** 35 ns, '1' **after** 50 ns;

   s1 <= '0' **after** 20 ns, '1' **after** 25 ns, '0' **after** 50 ns;

4. Construct and test VHDL modules for generating the periodic waveforms with the structure shown in Figure 4-15.

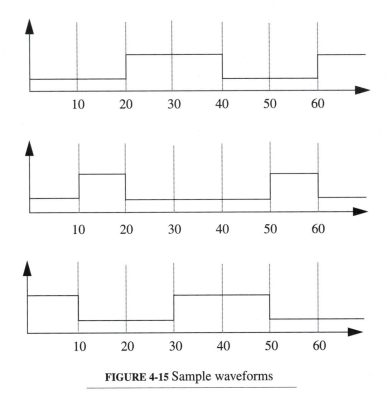

FIGURE 4-15 Sample waveforms

5. Construct a VHDL model that will accept a clock signal as input and produce the complement signal as output with a delay of 10 ns.

6. Construct a VHDL model of a circuit that will produce the set of non-overlapping clocks as output as shown below.

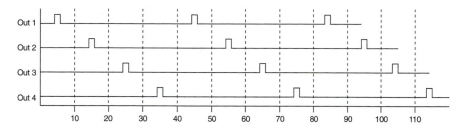

7. Write and simulate the entity–architecture description of a 3-bit decoder using the conditional signal assignment statement. Test the model with all possible combinations of inputs and plot the decoder output waveform.

8. Repeat the preceding exercise by building the decoder from basic gates. Is there any difference in the number of events generated between the simulation of this model and a model where the behavior is described using the conditional signal assignment statement? You should be able to answer this question by examining the traces in both cases over the same time interval. If your simulator permits, examine the event queues during simulation.

9. What is the difference between the hardware behaviors implied by the conditional signal assignment statement and the selected signal assignment statement? For what types of hardware structures would you use one or the other?

10. Write a VHDL model of the circuit shown below including wire delays, Use the transport delay model for the wire delays and assume a wire delay of 2 ns between components. Generate a timing diagram. Select your own gate delays. Mark events that would not have occurred under the default inertial delay model.

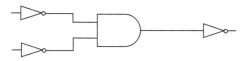

11. Why are the concepts of delta events and delta delays necessary for the correct discrete event simulation of digital circuits?

12. Write a VHDL model of the gate-level implementation of a four-input priority encoder. Do not specify any gate delays. Identify the points in trace that correspond to delta events.

13. Write and simulate a model of a 8-to-3 priority encoder circuit where the priority order of inputs is 0, 3, 4, 2, 6, 7, 5, and 1 with 0 being the highest priority input.

14. Write and simulate a VHDL model of the following circuit. Use the inertial delay model and gate delays of 2 ns/input. Use the gate level implementation of the multiplexor to determine its propagation delay.

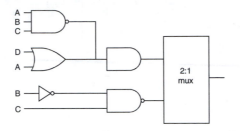

15. What delay model would you use if you were interested in functional correctness?

CHAPTER 5

Basic Language Concepts: Synthesis

Previous chapters of this book have stated that VHDL is a language for describing digital systems. Such descriptions were used to simulate digital systems. However these descriptions can also serve as the point of departure in creating digital systems. *Synthesis* is the process of analyzing a VHDL program and inferring a digital circuit that implements the behavior implied by this VHDL description. The circuit is constructed using a fixed set of hardware primitives. For example, we might have at our disposal only two input AND and OR gates and single input INVERT gates. Alternatively we may have a richer set of hardware primitives that included complex gates such EXCLUSIVE-OR and EXCLUSIVE-NOR as well as higher level components such as multiplexors and decoders. With a predefined set of building blocks synthesis compilers seek to construct efficient digital circuit implementations implied by the VHDL descriptions. The inference techniques and subsequent circuit optimizations are specific to the target hardware primitives employed. Moreover the actual circuits produced also depend on the vendor-specific synthesis compiler that is employed. The synthesis examples in this and subsequent chapters present gate-level circuits produced by Synopsys FPGA Express 3.1 targeted to the Xilinx XC4000E series of FPGAs.

This chapter is focused on the process of inferring hardware structures from concurrent signal assignment statements described in Chapter 4. For each class of signal assignment statements we show the general gate-level circuits that are inferred as well as the resulting implementation using the Xilinx 4000E series FPGA parts. Remember, when we write VHDL code we must keep in mind that we are describing hardware structures albeit at a higher level of abstraction. The presentation style here is to regard each language construct as having a hardware interpretation and to present the gate-level and FPGA schematics for that interpretation that is inferred by the FPGA Express compiler. Concurrent signal assignments statements have relatively straightforward hardware interpretations and are generally preferred from the point of view of synthesis.

5.1 A Language Directed View of Synthesis

Our goal is to understand the basic issues in the use of VHDL for synthesis. We know that the language was motivated by the desire to model digital hardware. The concurrent signal assignment statements described in Chapter 4 were presented as representations of the key behavioral and physical properties of digital circuit components. One might assume that such a hardware-oriented view of model construction would facilitate the inference of these same hardware structures from the VHDL source. The synthesis compiler should be able to transform the VHDL code into a hardware *netlist* where a netlist is a list of hardware components and their interconnections.

However, in practice it is not quite as simple. There is more than one way to write a conditional signal assignment statement to model a hardware component. The different approaches will affect the amount and structure of the synthesized hardware. For example, how many bits are required to represent the signals in a conditional expression? Can we control the number of bits used to store the value of a signal? How does the order of the components of a conditional or selected signal assignment statement affect the synthesized hardware?

The approach employed in this text is to study each of the VHDL constructs provided by the language and understand the hardware primitives that can be inferred from each of these constructs. I attempt to point out general issues in inferring hardware and opportunities for optimizing the resulting digital circuit. We can apply this understanding to larger programs comprised of many such VHDL constructs. If we understand the implications of each language construct for synthesis we can promote modeling styles that enables the synthesis process to be the most effective.

Let us examine a simple VHDL model and identify some key issues. Place yourself in the position of the synthesis compiler and consider the VHDL description shown in Figure 5-1. You are asked to generate a digital circuit that implements this description. Where do you start? You might begin by noting that we need an adder. How large should this adder be? For example, how many bits are necessary to represent the signal Z? From the model description we only know that Z is an integer. The VHDL language defines integers to be at least 32 bits. Therefore in the absence of any other information we must assume the signals are 32 bits wide. However if we know that the input operands have values that range from 0 to 15 then we can realize substantial hardware savings by explicitly providing this information in the declaration statements. Do we need one adder that is shared among the input operands or do we need several adders? This is dependent on whether the branches of the conditional are mutually exclusive or not. If they are mutually exclusive then we know that one adder with input multiplexors would be more efficient. As a designer of the circuit that implements this code you will go through the process of *infer-*

```
library IEEE;
use IEEE.std_logic_1164.all;
entity synth is
port (A, B, C, D: in integer;
      Sel : in std_logic_vector(1 downto 0);
      Z : out integer);
end entity synth;

architecture behavioral of synth is
begin
with Sel select
Z <=  A+B when "00",
      C + D when "10",
      "00000000" when others;
end architecture behavioral;
```

FIGURE 5-1 Description of a circuit to be synthesized

ence: inferring hardware primitives and their interconnection. When multiple implementation options exist you will make some choices guided by performance goals, for example, faster or smaller. It is this process that a synthesis compiler must automate.

If we can understand coding styles that make it easier to infer hardware we can aid this inference process by the manner in which we write our VHDL models. This rest of this chapter discusses these issues in the context of CSA statements.

5.2 Inference from Declarations

In programming languages declarations of variables and constants are used to allocate storage. When a variable is declared in a C or Java program the implementation of that variable is a memory location that holds the value of the variable. This value is changed by making assignments to the variable at points within the program. In a VHDL program written using CSA statements we may declare one or more signals as in the example in Figure 4-3 or Figure 5-1. How are these signals implemented in hardware? Or in other words what are the hardware structures used to store signal values? The basic hardware implementations of signals are wires, latches, and flip-flops. If we are describing a combinational circuit then signals values are carried by wires between the inputs and outputs of gate elements and the inputs and outputs of the circuits. If we are describing a sequential circuit then values are additionally stored in latches or flip-flops. The implementation of a signal as wire, latch, or flip-flop depends on how the signal is used. The manner in which synthesis compilers make this choice will become apparent from examples described later in subsequent sections.

The type of a signal, such as **integer** or std_logic is provided in the declaration. In general no additional information about the signal need be provided. This is fine for simulation. However if we want to implement the signal in a circuit we must know how many bits are necessary to represent the value of the signal. Thus the synthesis compiler must be able to infer from the declaration the number of bits required to represent a signal. Consider the example declarations shown below.

```
signal result: std_logic_vector (12 downto 0);
signal count: integer;
signal index: integer range 0 to 18;

type state_type is (state0, state1, state2, state3);
signal next_state: statetype;
```

The number of bits required for a signal can be determined implicitly or explicitly from the declaration. The signal result clearly requires 13 bits because the declaration explicitly provides this information. For bit vectors you would expect that the left-most element of the range corresponds to the most significant bit. However, the determination of the most significant bit may depend on the synthesis package. What about the signal count? It is an **integer** and the number of bits will depend on the implementation. The VHDL language reference manual specifies that the type **integer** must be at least 32 bits. If this is more than necessary the synthesis compiler will have generated more hardware than necessary in the form of wider signal paths and increased amount of hardware to process and store values carried along these signal paths. This is clearly undesirable. It is usually much easier to simply state the number of bits required when this is known. For example, if you know the range of values that the variable count will cover, this range should be explicitly specified as in the following declaration that simplifies the inference task. By declaring the range of index to be from 0 to 18 the synthesis compiler can determine that 5 bits are sufficient to represent the signal index. Even when such information is not explicitly provided more sophisticated synthesis compilers can analyze the dataflow properties of the VHDL code and often infer that a smaller number of bits will suffice for a signal. For example, if count is only used to compute the sum of two 4-bit signals then count can be implemented as a 5-bit signal. If no explicit information is provided in the declaration the compiler must work much harder to optimize the implementation, that is, determine if a smaller number of bits will actually suffice.

Compilers are conservative in the sense that they will only perform transformations that can be guaranteed to not produce incorrect answers. Thus it is difficult in general to predict when they will be able to optimize the number of bits required of a signal. Providing hints such as range declarations can go a long way towards producing smaller and often faster implementations. Note the similarities in the optimization phase of synthesis compilers and the optimizations performed by C and Pascal compilers. In the former we typically seek to minimize the amount of hardware synthesized or maximize the speed of the circuit. In the latter we typically seek to reduce the instruction count or maximize the speed by minimizing accesses to memory.

Now consider the last two declarations. Here we have an enumerated type and a signal that is declared to be of this type. The VHDL language provides a set of predefined types such as **integer, bit,** and **boolean.** Often it is convenient for us to define a new type as we have done here for **statetype**. The type declaration explicitly specifies all the values that any signal of this type can take which in this case is four distinct values. By comparison signals of type boolean can have two distinct values and signals of type integer must have at least 2^{32} distinct values. How many bits do we need to represent the signal **next_state**? As many bits as necessary to represent all of its distinct values. From the definition of the type **state_type** we see that **next_state** can take on one of four possible values. Thus we can encode the value of **next_state** into 2 bits. The value **state0** is encoded as "00" and the value of **state3** is encoded as "11". From the design of sequential circuits we know that in the case of state machines it is often desirable to control the state encoding because the specific encoding of the states can have a large impact on the quality of the circuit that is generated. Synthesis compilers will often have vendor specific mechanisms for specifying a particular encoding for such enumerated types. The number of bits required is determined by the number of possible values for the enumerated type. For example, signals or variables of type **state_type** can have four possible values and 2 bits are needed to uniquely represent all possible values of any signal declared to be on this type.

In summary by doing a bit more work in our declarations when possible we can aid the synthesis compiler. It pays to retain a hardware implementation view of signals as far as possible.

5.3 Inference From Simple CSA Statements

A simple CSA statement describes how the value of a signal is computed from one or more other signals. When the value of any of the input signals change the value of the output signal changes. This behavior corresponds to that of combinational logic and this is what the synthesis compiler will infer. The actual circuit will depend on the target hardware primitives that are available. For example let us suppose that we have at our disposal all of the standard gate-level primitives. The synthesis compiler infers logical operations from each of the VHDL signal assignment statements and utilizes the gate primitives to implement these operations. This step is referred to as *operator inferencing*. The interconnection between gates is determined by the dependencies between the signal assignment statements. The manner in which the synthesis compiler extracts these dependencies may not be obvious and there are many subtleties to the process of operator inferencing.

For example, consider the VHDL model shown in Figure 5-2. First we note that unlike the models shown in Chapter 4 there is no delay information associated with each signal assignment statement. A little thought reveals why delay information is redundant. Synthesis produces a hardware implementation from which accurate delay information is

```
library IEEE;
use IEEE.std_logic_1164.all;

entity concurrent is
port (s, t, u, w: in std_logic;
      v: out std_logic);
end entity concurrent;

architecture dataflow of concurrent is
signal s1, s2 : std_logic;
begin
L1: s1 <= s and t and u and w;
L2: s2 <= (s and t) and (u and w);
L3: v <= s1 or s2;
end architecture dataflow;
```

Synthesized Gate-Level Implementation

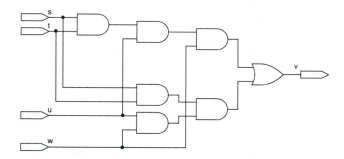

FPGA Implementation

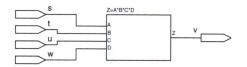

FIGURE 5-2 An example of the effect of operator precedence

available. Post-synthesis simulation will use the known delay values of the hardware components. Thus synthesis compilers will generally ignore the delay information provided in the VHDL source. Now let us focus on the statements and the circuit produced by the synthesis compiler. Each of the two signal assignment statements, L1 and L2, imply three logical AND operations. However the precedence of the operations in the second statement is clearly established through the use of parentheses whereas the precedence between the operations in the first statement is left to the synthesis compiler. Consider the gate-level description that is generated from this VHDL model and also shown in Figure 5-2. Note that statements L1 and L2 produce circuits with three two-input AND gates. Signals s1 and s2 are synthesized to wires that drive the two-input OR gate at the output of the circuit. However note the total gate delay through the three gates corresponding to the statement L1. The synthesis compiler has assumed a left-to-right precedence of the operators and thereby serialized the computation of the AND function of the four signals. An input signal experiences three gate delays through this portion of the circuit. In contrast, the use of parentheses in statement L2 explicitly identifies concurrency between two logical AND operations. Thus the implementation of the second statement exhibits more concurrency with two gates computing their outputs concurrently and subsequently driving a second gate. The total delay through the implementation of the second statement is two gate delays. The two-input OR gate implied by the last statement adds a single gate delay to both paths. Thus although the presence of three AND gates can be inferred from both statements, assumptions about operator precedence can have a significant impact on the speed of the circuit. Use parentheses where possible to control the depth of the circuit,

Now consider the implementation of this circuit in a Xilinx XC4000E chip. Note that signals s1 and s2 are intermediate signals and do not need to be available as output signals. The hardware implied by the code has a single output, v, and four input signals. The boolean equation corresponding to this function can be represented by a four-variable truth table. Recall that the configurable logic block in a Xilinx XC4000E FPGA has a pair of 16x1 LUTs that can be used to implement a four-variable truth table (refer to Section 3.3.1). This circuit can now be implemented in a single LUT as shown in Figure 5-2. Thus the circuit must be *mapped* to the available hardware primitives.

Example: A Full Adder

Let us revisit the simulation model of the gate level description of the full adder shown in Figure 5-3. This is the model from Figure 4-3 with the delay information removed. We are already familiar with the gate-level implementation of a full adder. The synthesis compiler produces a slightly different but equivalent version of the full adder and this gate level implementation is shown in Figure 5-3. Now what happens when this gate-level implementation is implemented in a Xilinx XC4000E series CLB? The result is shown in bottom part of Figure 5-3. Two LUTs are used, one each to implement the combinational functions for the sum and c_out output signals.

Example End: A Full Adder

```
library IEEE;
use IEEE.std_logic_1164.all;
entity full_adder is
port (in1, in2, c_in: in std_ulogic;
      sum, c_out: out std_ulogic);
end entity full_adder;

architecture dataflow of full_adder is
signal s1, s2, s3: std_ulogic;
begin
sum <= in1 xor in2 xor c_in;
c_out <= (in1 and c_in) or (in2 and c_in) or (in1 and in2);
end architecture dataflow;
```

Synthesized Gate-Level Implementation

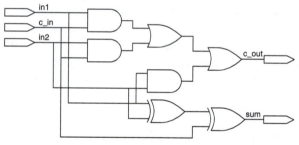

FPGA Implementation

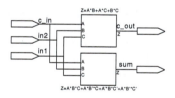

FIGURE 5-3 Synthesized full adder

Synthesis Exercise 5.1: Combinational Circuit

This exercise introduces the synthesis of a simple VHDL model constructed using concurrent signal assignment statements. The following steps require synthesis tool and vendor-specific commands. All of the synthesis exercises in this text assume that the target is an FPGA device. Tutorials for sample CAD tools are provided in the appendices.

Step 1.   Using a text editor, create a VHDL model of the full adder shown in Figure 4-3. Do not specify any gate delays.

Step 2.   Use the types std_logic and std_logic_vector for the input and output signals. Declare and reference the library IEEE and the package std_logic_1164.

Step 3.   Compile or analyze the model for the CAD toolset you are using.

Step 4.   Now prior to synthesis you must select a target set of hardware primitives for synthesis. For example, we may wish to create an implementation for the Xilinx 4010E FPGA. Using vendor-specific commands select the target device. In the process you may also select several other options such as level of effort, optimization for speed or area, and target clock frequency. For this exercise retain the default options provided by the vendor.

Step 5.   Synthesize the design.

Step 6.   Now simulate the synthesized hardware prior to placement and routing. We can start this process by generating a waveform on each of the input signals and tracing the output signals.

Step 7.   Run the simulation for 100 ns and trace (i) the input signals, (ii) the internal signals, s1, s2, and s3, and (iii) the sum and carry outputs.

Step 8.   Find the delay from the input signals to the sum and carry output signals.

Step 9.   Pick an event on one of the input signals. Record the propagation of the effect of this event through the signal trace. Study the trace and ensure that the model is operating correctly.

Step 10.   Now place and route this design on the target FPGA.

Step 11.   Simulate the placed and routed design. Compare this simulation with the post-synthesis simulation. Any obvious differences?

Step 12.   Generate a report providing the statistics the placed and routed design. These statistics will be in terms of vendor specific quantities. For example in the Xilinx Foundation tools you will be provided with the number of CLBs utilized by the design and you can also display the placed and routed design.

End Synthesis Exercise 5.1

5.4 Inference From Conditional Signal Assignment Statements

Figure 4-5 illustrated the use of a conditional signal assignment statement in the description of a 4-to-1 multiplexor. Consider a similar simpler description for single-bit signals shown in Figure 5-4.

In this model an output value is defined for the signal Z for each possible value of the input signals. When any of the inputs change value a new value of the output is re-computed. There is no need to retain the old or previous value of Z. This should sound very much like the behavior of a combinational circuit and that is indeed what the synthesis compiler infers. In fact from digital logic we know how to implement a multiplexor from basic gates. There is one other important attribute about the behavior of conditional signal assignment statements that affects the amount of hardware that is generated. Recall from Section 4.3.4 that the order of appearance of the clauses in the assignment is important. There is an implied priority order. The first condition that is true causes that statement, and only that statement, to be executed. Thus in general the synthesis compiler must generate the priority logic. The gate-level implementation that is generated for this multiplexor is shown in Figure 5-5. Note the structure of the selection logic to pick the signal value according to the order in which the statements appear in the VHDL code. For example, the input in2 is selected only if in0 and in1 are *not* selected. In the multiplexor code shown in Figure 5-4 all four conditions are mutually exclusive. Therefore in this particular application of the conditional signal assignment statement the selection logic is redundant. We

```
library IEEE;
use IEEE.std_logic_1164.all;
entity mux4 is
port (in0, in1, in2, in3: in std_logic;
      s0, s1: in std_logic;
      z: out std_logic);
end entity mux4;

architecture behavioral of mux4 is
begin
z <= in0 when s0 = '0' and s1 = '0' else
        in1 when s0 = '0' and s1 = '1' else
        in2 when s0 = '1' and s1 = '0' else
     in3 when s0 = '1' and s1 = '1' else
        '0';
end architecture behavioral;
```

FIGURE 5-4 Synthesizable model of a 4-to-1 multiplexor for single-bit signals

should note that in general the options of a conditional signal assignment statement are not mutually exclusive and the priority order implied by the textual order must be preserved in the hardware implementation. Clearly in instances where the conditions are mutually exclusive and can be determined to be so by the synthesis compiler, the optimizations by the compiler will eliminate the priority logic.

Now let us consider the implementation produced for a Xilinx XC4000E chip. From Section 3.3 we know that hardware primitives we have for implementing boolean expressions are the LUTs in each CLB in the target chip. When the description in Figure 5-4 is

Synthesized Gate-Level Implementation

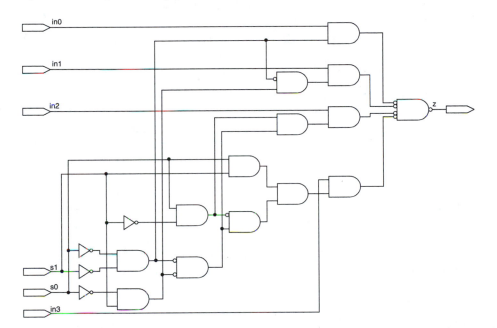

FPGA Implementation

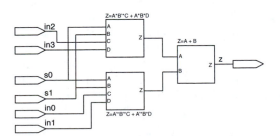

FIGURE 5-5 Hardware structure and FPGA implementation of the conditional signal assignment statement in Figure 5-4

synthesized it will produce the implementation shown in Figure 5-5. This implementation eliminates the priority logic that was synthesized with the basic gate-level implementation and produces an optimized LUT-based implementation as described below.

This circuit utilizes three LUTs. Two of these are F and G function generators (refer to Section 3.3) and the third is the H function generator. These LUTs implement the following boolean expressions:

Function Generator F: $S0\ \overline{S1}\ In2 + S0\ S1\ In3$

Function Generator G: $\overline{S0}\ \overline{S1}\ In2 + \overline{S0}\ S1\ In3$

Function Generator H: *(Output of F + Output of G)*

We see that the first LUT implements a boolean function of four variables, S0, S1, In2, and In3. It should be relatively easy to construct the truth table for this expression. Similarly we see that the second LUT implements another truth table of four variables, S0, S1, In0, and In1. Finally the last LUT simply performs the logical OR of the output of these two truth tables. With a little thought we would be sure that the behavior of this multiplexor can be described by a truth table of six variable, S0, S1, In0, In1, In2, and In3. However, to implement six-variable truth table we would need a 64x1 bit RAM. The CLBs in the target Xilinx chip have two separate 16x1 RAM modules and one additional 8x1 RAM module. As we have seen in this example the three LUTs can be combined to implement a boolean function of six variables.

Conditional assignment statements provide a natural way to construct priority encoders. However, the manner in which these encoders are written can lead to unexpected results. The following two examples address some of these issues.

Example: Priority Encoder

Consider the example of a priority encoder shown in Figure 5-6. In this example bit 0 has the highest priority followed in priority order by bits 2, 1, and 3 respectively. A conditional signal assignment statement is used because the semantics of the statement define a priority order on the sequence of options. Thus conditional signal assignment statements present a very natural construct for describing a priority circuit. The valid signal is used to determine when inputs are to be encoded. The synthesized circuit is also shown in Figure 5-6. Note how each input bit is gated by the valid signal.

Example End: Priority Encoder

```
library IEEE;
use IEEE.std_logic_1164.all;

entity priority is
port (datain : in std_logic_vector(3 downto 0);
 valid : in std_logic;
 z: out std_logic_vector(1 downto 0));

end entity priority;

architecture behavior of priority is
begin
 z <= "00" when datain (0) = '1' and valid = '1' else
      "10" when datain (2) = '1' and valid = '1'else
      "01" when datain (1) = '1' and valid = '1'else
      "11" when datain (3) = '1' and valid = '1'else
      "00";
end architecture behavior;
```

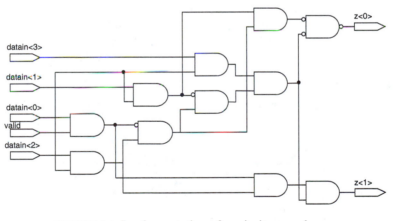

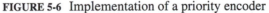

FIGURE 5-6 Implementation of a priority encoder

The options of a conditional signal assignment statement are evaluated by testing some boolean condition. In simulation we have more leeway in the type of conditions that can be tested relative to the conditions that can be tested in (synthesized) hardware. For example we can test conditions in simulation that do not have meaningful hardware counterparts. The following example illustrates this point.

Example: Synthesis of Comparison Logic

When modeling for simulation we sometimes use the don't care values to produce concise VHDL code. For example, consider another implementation of the priority encoder shown in Figure 5-7. In this implementation we are using a conditional signal assignment statement but we are describing the priority encoder in a form that we might find in a digital logic text, that is, using don't cares. In this example input 0 has the highest priority and when this bit is set the values of the remaining bits are immaterial. The

```
library IEEE;
use IEEE.std_logic_1164.all;

entity priority is
port (datain : in std_logic_vector (3 downto 0);
        valid : in std_logic;
        z: out std_logic_vector (1 downto 0));
end entity priority;

architecture behavior of priority is
begin
  z <= "00" when datain = "---1" and valid = '1' else
        "10" when datain = "-100" and valid = '1'else
        "01" when datain = "--10" and valid = '1'else
        "11" when datain = "1000" and valid = '1'else
        "00";

end architecture behavior;
```

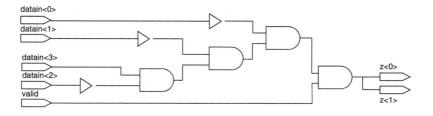

FIGURE 5-7 Another priority encoder implementation

remaining options are similarly described and the options are ordered according to the priority of the input signals. From the code we see that the priority order is bit positions 0, 2, 1, and 3. From a simulation perspective the manner in which this model is written appeals to our intuition. However from a hardware implementation perspective we have a problem. Don't care values cannot be represented in hardware and cannot be compared with a signal value of 0 or 1. A hardware implementation can only compare the values of 0 and 1. In synthesis compiles when one of the signals specified in a comparison operation uses don't care values the comparison is always assumed to return false! In the example shown in Figure 5-7 this would mean that the first three options would always return false and the output would have value of either 00 or 11. Now take a look at the synthesized hardware. What values can the output signal Z take on? Only 00 or 11!

Thus we should be careful when writing code for synthesis. Comparisons that make sense in a simulated model do not necessarily imply feasible hardware implementations and can lead to unexpected synthesis results.

Example End: Synthesis of Comparison Logic

5.5 Inference from Selected Signal Assignment Statements

In the selected signal assignment statement there is no priority ordering among the options. Consider the code for a 4-to-2 encoder shown in Figure 5-8. Encoders typically expect that only one of several input bits has value of 1 at any given time and the output is the binary-encoded position of this bit. In priority encoders more than 1 bit may have a value of 1 at any given time and the input with the highest priority, such as the highest numbered input, will take priority. The following example is simple encoder. If more than one input has a value at any time the value of result is set to XX. For synthesis this simply means that the outputs are undefined when the signal datain has any other value. This encoder is a combinational circuit that is synthesized to the implementation shown in Figure 5-8. A closer inspection of the VHDL code will reveal that the most significant bit of the result is true only when bits 3 or 2 of the input are true. This logical OR function can be implemented in one of the LUTs in a CLB. The least significant bit of the result is true when bits 2 and 4 of the input are true. This logical-OR function can be implemented by the second LUT.

```
library IEEE;
use IEEE.std_logic_1164.all;

entity encoder is
port (datain: in std_logic_vector(3 downto 0);
     result: out std_logic_vector(1 downto 0));
end entity encoder;

architecture behavioral of encoder is
begin
with datain select
result <= "00" when "0001",
              "01" when "0010",
              "10" when "0100",
              "11" when "1000",
              "XX" when others;
end architecture behavioral;
```

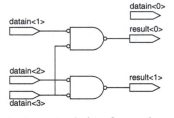

FIGURE 5-8 A 4-to-2 encoder

The keyword **unaffected** may be used for some combinations of the select expres-

'87 vs. '93   sion. For example, we might have the selected signal assignment statement written as fol-

☞   lows. VHDL'87 does not support the **unaffected** clause,

```
with datain select
result <= "00" when "0001",
              "01" when "0010",
              "10" when "0100",
              "11" when "1000",
              unaffected when others;
```

This implies that the output value does not change for this particular value of the
select expression (in this case all **other** values). In effect the output must retain its previous

value when the inputs have some range of values. Therefore a latch will be inferred by the synthesis compiler to retain the previous value of result. At the time of this writing, the **unaffected** clause is not supported for latch inference in FPGA Express 3.1.

Synthesis Exercise 5.2: A Single-Bit ALU

This exercise is the synthesis of a single-bit ALU shown in Figure 5-9. Remember, although the OPCODE field is 2-bits wide, there are only three valid inputs to the multiplexor.

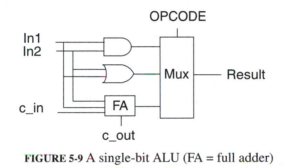

FIGURE 5-9 A single-bit ALU (FA = full adder)

Step 1. Follow the steps in Simulation Exercise 4.2 and construct a VHDL model of the single-bit ALU. Do not specify component delays. Describe the output of the multiplexor using a conditional signal assignment statement and use the **when others** clause to account for the fact that the multiplexor has only three inputs rather than four. Call this file *alu.vhd*

Step 2. Compile *alu.vhd*.

Step 3. Select a target hardware device, for example if we were using Xilinx parts we might use a XC 4010E part. You may have to make a few more vendor specific choices. Synthesize *alu.vhd*.

Step 4. Now simulate the synthesized hardware prior to placement and routing. We can start this process by generating a waveform on each of the input signals and tracing the output signals.

Step 5. Run the simulation for 40 ns and trace (i) the input signals, (ii) the internal signals, and (iii) the output Result.

Step 6. Find the delay from the input signals to the output signal.

Step 7. Now place and route this design on the target FPGA.

Step 8.   Simulate the placed and routed design and compare the trace to the previous post-synthesis simulation. Are there any differences in the timing? To what can you attribute these differences in the traces?

Step 9.   Print and record the trace.

Step 10. Add new operations to the single-bit ALU, recompile, resynthesize the model. For example, you can add the exclusive-OR, subtraction, and complement operations.

End Synthesis Exercise 5.2

5.6 Simulation Behavior vs. Synthesis Behavior

A common sequence of steps taken in design is to first develop the VHDL models and use simulation to verify the functional correctness of the model. Thereafter this model is synthesized and the synthesized model is simulated to verify the performance. One would expect that the simulation of the VHDL model and the simulation of the synthesized hardware would produce identical behavior. After all they describe the same circuit. However this is not necessarily true and it becomes important to understand the sources of this "semantic mismatch." Some common issues are identified in the following.

1. *Delay statements*: In a simulation model delays can be specified using the **after** clause in the signal assignment statements. During synthesis the delay values of the operations are derived from the synthesized implementation. This may differ from the values that the designer specified for simulation.

2. *Comparison Logic*: Comparisons maybe modeled in the simulation differently from that actually synthesized into hardware. For example consider the selected signal assignment statement used to model a priority encoder as follows.

> **with** datain **select**
> result <= "00" when "---1",
>   "01" when "--10",
>   "10" when "-100",
>   "11" when "1000",
>   **unaffected** when others;

The character "-" represents don't care value in the 1164 logic system. However, remember that digital hardware can only distinguish between ones and zeros. Comparisons to don't care, high impedance or other literals do not have meaningful hardware counterparts. Equality tests to other than 1/0 values return false for synthesis. This does not necessarily agree with the semantics for simulation where signals can actually be assigned values such as Z or U.

5.7 Synthesis Hints

1. Do not specify initial values in your declaration of signals. Most synthesis compilers will ignore them. If you wish to initialize signals to values it is advisable to do so explicitly under the control of a reset signal. Is this not how you would design the hardware anyway? The exceptions are constants which must be provided with their values within the declaration.

2. Specify the number of bits necessary for a signal explicitly in the declaration. This will avoid the allocation of much larger number of bits than necessary and therefore lead to less hardware in the form of the widths of signal paths, the number of gates necessary to process these signals, and the number of latches or flip-flops necessary to store signal values.

3. Use of the **unaffected** keyword in branches of signal assignment statements may cause latches to be inferred in the synthesized design.

4. Using don't care values to cover the **when others** case in a selected signal assignment statement can enable the synthesis compiler to optimize the logic and create a smaller circuit than if all remaining options were set to values, for example, 0000 or 1111.

5. Use parentheses to control concurrency, and therefore speed, of the synthesized circuit.

6. Use of the selected signal assignment statement will generally produce less logic because no priority among the options is implied. Alternatively this may cause us to be a bit more careful in formulating signal assignments to be in a form where we can use selected signal assignment statements.

5.8 Summary

This chapter has taken a look at the process of hardware inference from basic concurrent signal assignment statements. The VHDL language has precisely defined semantics for each of these statements, which lead to constraints on how hardware is to be inferred. Simple signal assignment statements and conditional signal assignment statements lead to the synthesis of combinational logic. This is simply because every time these statements are executed the output signal is assigned a new value. For the selected signal assignment statement the use of the **unaffected** clause (not supported in VHDL'87) can lead to instances where the statement may execute but not assign a value to the output signal. In this case the value of the output signal must be "remembered" or maintained across executions and a latch will be inferred to store the value of the output signal. The following synthesis concepts were introduced and discussed.

- inferring signal data widths from declarations
- operator inferencing from signal assignment statements
- use of parentheses to control precedence and structure of the synthesized circuit

- inference of combinational logic
- inference of latches in selected signal assignment statements
- mismatches between the behavior of the simulation of the VHDL model and the simulation of the synthesized circuit

Now we have seen how we construct VHDL descriptions from hardware, as well as how synthesis compilers interpret these same language constructs. We are now ready to move to more powerful language constructs with the attendant challenges with respect to both simulation and synthesis.

5.9 Exercises

1. Consider two 16x1 LUTs and one 4x1 LUT implemented as shown below. Show the contents of the LUTs that would implement the following boolean functions.

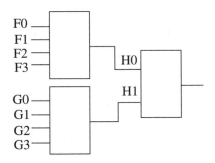

   1.1 $F = X\overline{YZ} + \overline{WU}XY$

   1.2 $F = W\overline{X} + XY + U\overline{Z}$

   1.3 $F = WXYZ + \overline{WU}$

2. Show an example of a conditional signal assignment statement where the conditional paths are not mutually exclusive. Synthesize the design and identify the priority logic in the synthesized circuit.

3. Consider the design of a circuit to sum four 3-bit words. Write this model using parentheses to control the depth of the circuit creating both minimum delay and maximum delay circuits.

4. Write and synthesize the model of a 4-bit adder subtractor that uses the interface shown below.

> **entity** add_sub **is**
> **port** (in1, in2 : **in bit_vector**(3 **downto** 0);
> result : **out bit_vector**(3 **downto** 0);
> add_or_sub : **in bit**);
> **end entity** add_sub;

5. Construct VHDL models for the following circuits. Synthesize these models and compare the gate level implementations produced by the synthesis compiler with that you would create. List the differences.

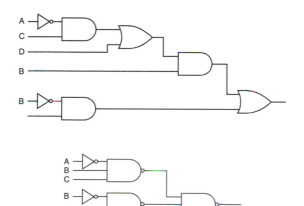

6. Model a circuit using both the conditional signal assignment statement and the selected signal assignment statement. Compare the results of synthesis.

7. Synthesize a 4-to-1 multiplexor using a conditional signal assignment statement. Now construct a multiplexor from basic gates and rewrite the model using only simple concurrent signal assignment statements. Compare the synthesis results using the two models in terms of area and speed.

8. Write and synthesize a model of a 8-to-3 priority-encoder circuit where the priority order of inputs is 0, 6, 2, 4, 3, 7, 5, and 1 with 0 being the highest priority input.

CHAPTER 6

Modeling Behavior: Simulation

This chapter expands upon the approach described so far that uses CSA statements for constructing VHDL models. In Chapter 4 digital components were modeled as delay elements and their internal behavior was described using CSA statements. Events on input signals caused events on output signals after a propagation delay. This approach works well for modeling digital systems at the gate level. However, it is difficult and often not feasible with respect to simulation time to build models of large complex systems at the gate level. We often wish to abstract or hide the details of the hardware implementation while preserving the external event behavior. To be able to write such abstract models requires language constructs more powerful than the CSA statements introduced in the last chapter.

In this chapter, we discuss more powerful constructs for describing the internal behavior of components when they cannot be simply modeled as delay elements. The basis for these descriptions is the *process* construct that enables us to use conventional programming language constructs and idioms. As a result we can model more complex behaviors than are feasible with CSA statements and are able to model systems at higher levels of abstraction.

6.1 The Process Construct

The VHDL language and modeling concepts described in Chapter 4 were derived from the operational characteristics of digital circuits, where the design is represented as a schematic of concurrently operating components. Each component is characterized by the generation of events on output signals in response to events on input signals. These output events may occur after a component-dependent propagation delay. The component behavior is expressed using a CSA statement that explicitly relates input signals, output signals, and propagation delays. Such models are convenient to construct when components correspond to gates or switch level models of transistors. However, when we wish to construct models of complex components such as CPUs, memory modules, or communication protocols, such a model of behavior can be quite limiting. The event model is still valid—externally we see that events on the input signals will eventually cause events on the output signals of the component. However, the computation of the time at which these output events will occur and the value of the output signals can be quite complex. Moreover, for modeling components such as memories, we need to retain state information within the component description over time. It is not sufficient to be able to compute the values of the output signals as a function of the values of the input signals.

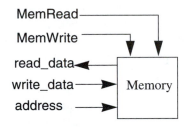

FIGURE 6-1 A model of memory

For example, consider the behavior of a simple model of a memory module as shown in Figure 6-1. The memory module is provided with address, data, and read and write control signals. Let us assume that it contains 4096, 32-bit words of memory. The value of the **MemRead** or **MemWrite** control signals determine whether the data on write_data is to be written at the address on the **address** port, or whether data is to be read from that address and provided on the output port read_data. Events on the input address, data, or control lines produce events that cause the memory model to be executed. We can also reasonably expect to know the memory access times for read and write operations and therefore know the propagation delays. However, the behavior internal to the memory module is difficult to describe using only the signal assignment statements provided in Chapter 4. How can we represent memory words? How can we address the correct word based on the values of the address lines and control signals? How can memory write operations store values to be subsequently accessed by memory read operations. The answers are easier to come by if we have access to conventional sequential programming language constructs. Memory can be implemented as an array and the address value can be used to index this array. Depending upon the value of the control signals we can decide if this array element is to be written or read. Such behavior can be realized in VHDL by using *sequential statements* via the *process* construct.

In contrast to CSA statements a process is a sequentially executed block of code. A VHDL model of a memory module equivalent to the one in Figure 6-1 is shown in Figure 6-2. This model consists of one process that is labeled **mem_process**. Process labels are delimited by colons. The structure of a process is very similar to that of programs written in a conventional block structured programming language such as Pascal. The process begins with a declarative region followed by the process body delimited by **begin** and **end** keywords. Variables and constants used within the process are declared within the declarative region. The **begin** keyword denotes the start of the computational part of the process. All of the statements in this process are executed sequentially. Data structures may include arrays and queues, and programs may use standard data types such as integers, characters, and real numbers. Unlike signals whose changes in values must be scheduled to occur at discrete points in simulated time, variable assignments take effect immediately just as in conventional programs. Variable assignment is denoted by the ":=" operator. Because all statements are executed sequentially within a process, values assigned to variables are visible to all following statements within that same process. Control flow within a process is strictly sequential altered by constructs such as **if-then-else**, or **loop** statements. In fact, we can regard the process itself as a traditional sequential program. However one of the distinguishing features of processes is that we can make assignments to signals declared external to the process. For example, consider the memory model in Figure 6-2. At the end of this process we have signal assignment statements that assign internally computed values to signals in the interface after a specified propagation delay. Thus, externally we are able to maintain the discrete event execution model: events on the memory inputs produce events on the memory outputs after a delay equal to the memory access time. However, internally we are able to develop complex models of behavior that produce these external events. *With respect to simulation time a process executes in zero time.* Delays are associated only with the assignment of values to signals.

Recall that a CSA is executed any time an event occurs on a signal in the right-hand side of the signal assignment statement. When is a process executed? In Figure 6-2, adjacent to the **process** keyword is a list of input signals to the component. This is not a parameter list. This list is referred to as the *sensitivity list.* The execution of a process is initiated whenever an event occurs on any of the signals in the sensitivity list of the process. Once started, the process executes to completion in zero (simulation) time and potentially generates a new set of events on output signals. We begin to see the similarity between a process and a CSA. In the models with CSA statements, input signals are inferred by their presence on the right-hand side of the signal assignment statement. In a process the signals can be listed in the sensitivity list. Remember that the process is only sensitive to signals placed in the sensitivity list. Thus even if an input signal changes, if this signal is not listed on the sensitivity list the process will not be executed. For all practical purposes, we can regard a process simply as a "big" CSA statement that executes concurrently with other processes and signal assignment statements. Processes are simply capable of describing more complex events than the CSA statement described in Chapter 4. *In fact, CSA statements themselves are implemented as processes!* However, they are special and do not require the **process, begin**, and **end** syntax of more complex processes.

```vhdl
library IEEE;
use IEEE.std_logic_1164.all;
use IEEE.std_logic_arith.all;
                      -- we need this package for 1164 related functions
entity memory is
port(address : in unsigned (31 downto 0); -- used unsigned for memory addresses
     write_data : in std_logic_vector (31 downto 0);
     MemWrite, MemRead : in std_logic;
     read_data : out std_logic_vector (31 downto 0));
end entity memory;

architecture behavioral of memory is
type mem_array is array(0 to 7) of std_logic_vector (31 downto 0);
                      -- define a new type, for memory arrays
begin
mem_process: process (address, write_data) is
variable data_mem : mem_array := ( -- declare a memory array
X"00000000",    --- initialize data memory
X"00000000",    --- X denotes a hexadecimal number
X"00000000",    ---
X"00000000",
X"00000000",
X"00000000",
X"00000000",
X"00000000");
variable addr :integer;

begin

-- the following type conversion function is in std_logic_arith

L1: addr := conv_integer (address (2 downto 0));
L2: if MemWrite = '1' then
L3: data_mem(addr) := write_data; -- perform a read or write operation

elsif MemRead = '1' then
read_data <= data_mem(addr) after 10 ns;
end if;
end process mem_process;
end architecture behavioral;
```

FIGURE 6-2 A behavioral description of a memory module

There are several other new language features that have made their way into this model. A new type is has been introduced in the entity description: unsigned. The definition of this type is found in the new library package declared in the model: std_logic_arith. Type unsigned is defined as a vector of bits each of type std_logic and is often used for objects such as memory addresses. The definition of the type conversion function conv_integer() is can also be found in std_logic_arith. This function is necessary for the following reason. Memory is modeled as an array of 32-bit words. This array is indexed by an integer. Therefore, the memory address that is provided as a 32-bit number of type unsigned must be converted to an integer before this array can be accessed. Of course we do not create an array with 2^{32} entries but rather eight words of memory. Therefore, the model uses only the lower 3 bits of the memory address. In this model and a few others in this text we have used other packages such as std_logic_arith. Many vendors will support various packages with many useful type conversion, arithmetic, and logic functions. These packages will be placed in various libraries. Check with your installation to determine the location and contents of available packages. This is all we need to know for the moment. We will revisit packages and libraries in greater detail in Chapter 9.

Because statements within a process are executed sequentially these statements are referred to as *sequential statements,* in contrast to the concurrent signal assignment statements that we saw in Chapter 4. As we see from Figure 6-2 sequential statements can be labeled. For example, note the labels L1, L2, and L3 in the model of Figure 6-2. The use of '87 vs. '93 labels simplifies associated descriptions as well as improves the clarity of the code. However, individual sequential statements cannot be labeled in VHDL'87. Processes can be thought of as programs that are executed within the simulation to model the behavior of a component. Thus, we have more powerful means to model the behavior of digital systems. Such models are often referred to as behavioral models, although any VHDL model using concurrent or sequential statements is a description of behavior.

Once the concepts of a process and the underlying semantics are understood, we need to know the syntax of the major programming constructs that we can use within a process. Identifiers, operators, and useful data types are provided in Chapter 12. When we first start developing models it is easier, although not the most efficient, to write models that are single processes and write models as if we were writing in C or Pascal. Based on our experience with other high-level languages, we can begin immediately describing the behavior of components using processes and start developing non-trivial simulation models. As our experience with the language grows we will become more selective and effective in how processes are used within larger models. One issue to be kept in mind is that such an approach although easier makes the process of synthesis more challenging. In general I suggest an approach that is predicated on the view that we are describing the behavior of hardware and not describing an algorithm. This will lead to more efficient models while we are climbing the learning curve. It will also naturally lead to design representations in VHDL making the job of development easier.

6.2 Programming Constructs

6.2.1 If-Then-Else and If-Then-Elsif Statements

An **if** statement is executed by evaluating a Boolean expression and conditionally executing a block of sequential statements. The structure may optionally include an **else** component. The statement may also include zero or more **elsif** branches (note the absence of the letter 'e' in **elsif**!). In this case all of the Boolean valued expressions are evaluated sequentially until the first true expression is encountered. An **if** statement is closed by the **end if** clause. A good example of the utility of the use of the **if-then-else** construct is captured in the memory model of Figure 6-2.

6.2.2 Case Statement

The behavioral model shown in Figure 6-2 utilizes a single process. Just as we had CSA statements we may also have concurrently executing processes. Consider another behavioral model of a half adder with two processes as shown in Figure 6-3. Both processes are sensitive to events on the input signals x and y. Whenever an event occurs on either x or y, both processes are activated and execute concurrently in simulation time. The second process is structured using a **case** statement. The case statement is used whenever it is necessary to select one of several branches of execution based on the value of an expression. The branches of the **case** statement must cover all possible values of the expression being tested. Of course the choices must be of the same type as that of the value produced by the expression. Each value of the case expression being tested can belong to only one branch of the case statement. The **others** clause can be used to ensure that all possible values for the case expression are covered. Although this example shows a single statement within each branch, in general the branch can be composed of a sequence of sequential statements. This example also shows that port signals are visible within a process. This means that process statements can read port values and schedule values on output ports.

The preceding example demonstrated that we are not constrained to have a single process within an architecture. In fact, we may even have a mix of processes and concurrent signal assignment statements. Furthermore, just as with selected signal assignment statements in Chapter 4 the select expression can operate on bit fields within a multi-bit signal. The following example demonstrates these features.

```
library IEEE;
use IEEE.std_logic_1164.all;
entity half_adder is
port (x, y : in std_logic;
      sum, carry : out std_logic);
end entity half_adder;

architecture behavior of half_adder is
begin
sum_proc: process(x,y) is -- this process computes the value of sum
     begin
       if (x = y) then
           sum <= '0' after 5 ns;
       else
           sum <= (x or y) after 5 ns;
       end if;
     end process sum_proc;

carry_proc: process (x,y) is -- this process computes the value of
carry
     begin
       case x is
       when '0' =>
       carry <= x after 5 ns;
       when '1' =>
       carry <= y after 5 ns;
       when others =>
       carry <= 'X' after 5 ns;
     end case;
end process carry_proc;
end architecture behavior;
```

FIGURE 6-3 A two-process half-adder model

Example: Memory Model

Figure 6-4 shows another model of a memory with four 32-bit words. There are two interesting features of this model. First rather than modeling memory as an array of values four distinct signals are used. This is clearly not scalable to larger memories and is feasible for only small memories such as a group of registers preferably organized as a register file. The second interesting feature of this model is the presence of both a process and a CSA statement in the architecture. The process mem_proc implements the initialization and

```vhdl
Library IEEE;
use IEEE.std_logic_1164.all;
use IEEE.std_logic_arith.all;

entity memory is
port (address, write_data : in std_logic_vector (7 downto 0);
        MemWrite, MemRead, clk, reset : in std_logic;
        read_data :out std_logic_vector (7 downto 0));
end entity memory;

architecture behavioral of memory is
signal dmem0,dmem1,dmem2,dmem3 : std_logic_vector (7 downto 0);
begin
mem_proc: process (clk) is
begin
if (rising_edge(clk)) then -- wait until next clock edge
if reset = '1' then              -- initialize values on reset
dmem0 <= x"00";                  -- memory locations are initialized to
dmem1 <= x"11";                  -- some random values
dmem2 <= x"22";
dmem3 <= x"33";

elsif MemWrite = '1' then -- if not reset then check for memory write
case address (1 downto 0) is
when "00" => dmem0 <= write_data;
when "01" => dmem1 <= write_data;
when "10" => dmem2 <= write_data;
when "11" => dmem3 <= write_data;
when others => dmem0 <= x"ff";
end case;
end if;
end if;
end process read_proc;

-- memory read is implemented with a conditional signal assignment
read_data <= dmem0 when address (1 downto 0) = "00" and MemRead = '1' else
             dmem1 when address (1 downto 0) = "01" and MemRead = '1' else
             dmem2 when address (1 downto 0) = "10" and MemRead = '1' else
             dmem3 when address (1 downto 0) = "11" and MemRead = '1' else
             x"00";
end architecture behavioral;
```

FIGURE 6-4 An alternative model of memory

the memory write operation. This process is sensitive to the clk signal. Whenever there is a change in the value of the clock signal the process is executed. The function rising_edge (clk) is defined in the package std_logic_1164 and is true if the signal clk has just experienced a rising edge, that is a change in value from 0 to 1. If so the reset and MemWrite signals are checked and the appropriate actions are taken, namely initialization and memory write operations respectively. This check for the rising edge prevents spurious write operations on the falling edge of clk. The write operation itself is modeled a **case** statement where the select expression is the memory address. Note that the input memory address is actually an 8-bit address. However this particular model only implements four words of memory. The select expression operates only on the least significant 2 bits of the address. Thus if a memory address is out of range the actual address computed will be (address modulo 4). We will find that being able switch on the values of bit fields within a word is a very useful capability.

Executing concurrently with this process is the memory read operation that is naturally implemented as a conditional signal assignment statement. We could have included the read operation within mem_proc by extending the **if-then-elsif** construct with a branch that checked the status of the MemRead control signal. The model would have still operated correctly although memory read operations would have been synchronous with the clk signal.

Thus we see that VHDL models can comprise of many concurrent constructs within an architecture. Each construct may be a concurrent signal assignment statement or a process.

Example End: Memory Model

6.2.3 Loop Statements

This section introduces the loop statement as well a few new VHDL operations that we have not seen before. There are two forms of the loop statement. The first form is the use of **for** loops. An example of the use of such a loop construct is shown in Figure 6-5. This example multiplies two 32-bit numbers by successively shifting the multiplicand and adding to the partial product if the corresponding bit of the multiplier is 1 [9]. The model simply implements what we have traditionally known as long multiplication using base 2 arithmetic. The model saves storage by using the lower half of the 64-bit product register to initially store the multiplier. As successive bits of the multiplier are examined, the bits in the lower half of the product register are shifted out, eventually leaving a 64-bit product. Note the use of the **&** operator representing concatenation. This operator can be used to concatenate a k_1-bit word and a k_2-bit word to produce a (k_1+k_2)-bit word. A logical shift-right operation is specified by copying the upper 63 (out of 64) bits into the lower 63 bits '87 vs. '93 of the product register and setting the most significant bit to 0 using the concatenation operator. However, when using VHDL'93 we can use the built in shift operators as provided in Chapter 12. VHDL'87 does not support these built-in operators and one approach

```vhdl
library IEEE;
use IEEE.std_logic_1164.all;
use IEEE.std_logic_arith.all;
use IEEE.std_logic_unsigned.all; -- needed for arithmetic functions

entity mult32 is
port (multiplicand, multiplier : in std_logic_vector (31 downto 0);
      product : out std_logic_vector (63 downto 0));
end entity mult32;

architecture behavioral of mult32 is
constant module_delay: Time:= 10 ns;
begin
mult_process: process(multiplicand,multiplier) is
variable product_register : std_logic_vector (63 downto 0) :=
X"0000000000000000";
variable multiplicand_register : std_logic_vector (31 downto 0):= X"00000000";

begin
multiplicand_register := multiplicand;
product_register(63 downto 0) := X"00000000" & multiplier;
--
-- repeated shift-and-add loop
--
for index in 1 to 32 loop
if product_register(0) = '1' then
product_register(63 downto 32) := product_register (63 downto 32) +
multiplicand_register(31 downto 0);
end if;
                    -- perform a right shift with zero fill
product_register (63 downto 0) := '0' & product_register (63 downto 1);
end loop;
-- write result to output port
product <= product_register after module_delay;

end process mult_process;
end architecture behavioral;
```

FIGURE 6-5 An example of the use of the loop construct

towards specifying shift operations is as illustrated in Figure 6-5. Finally, note the inclusion of the package std_logic_unsigned. In the Active VHDL distribution this package contains the definition for the "+" operator for these operand types.

There are several unique features of this form of a loop statement. Note that the loop variable index is not declared anywhere within the process! The loop index is automatically and implicitly declared by virtue of its use within the loop statement. Moreover, the loop variable index is declared locally for this loop. If a variable or signal with the name index is used elsewhere within the same process or architecture (but not in the same loop), it is treated as a distinct object. Unlike other languages the loop index cannot be assigned a value or altered in the body of the loop. Therefore, loop indices cannot be provided as parameters via a procedure call or as an input port. We see that the loop index is exactly that, a loop index, and the language prevents us from using it in any other fashion. This does make it convenient to write loops, because we do not have to worry about our choice of variable names for the loop index conflicting with names used elsewhere in the model.

Often it is necessary to continue the iteration until some condition is satisfied rather than performing a fixed number of iterations. A second form of the loop statement is the use of the **while** construct. In this form, the **for** statement is simply replaced as in the following example.

$$\begin{array}{l}\textbf{while } j < 32 \textbf{ loop}\\ \quad ...\\ \quad ...\\ j := j+1;\\ \textbf{end loop};\end{array}$$

In general the statement would appear as "**while** (*condition*) **loop**." Unlike the **for** construct, note that the loop condition may involve variables that are modified within the loop. Thus the loop can execute for a data dependent number of iterations.

6.3 More on Processes

Upon initialization all processes are executed once. Thereafter, processes are executed in a data-driven manner: activated by events on signals in the sensitivity list of the process or by waiting for the occurrence of specific events using the **wait** statement (described in Section 6.4). Remember the sensitivity list of a process is not a parameter list! This list simply identifies those signals to which the process is sensitive: when an event occurs on any one of these signals, the process is executed. This is analogous to CSA statements, which are executed whenever an event occurs on a signal on the right-hand side of a CSA. In fact CSA statements are really processes with simpler syntax. Another way of thinking about processes and sensitivity lists is by analogy with combinational logic. When any input signal changes the network of gates recomputes the value of the output signals. The values of the output signals may not change but the physical nature of the devices cause them to be recomputed. Processes can be thought of as abstractions of such circuits and this are executed when any of the signals in the sensitivity list change. In fact we when we discuss synthesis we shall see that processes can be constructed to generate combinational logic.

The fact that VHDL is a hardware description language often produces effects that may be unexpected. For example, consider successive signal assignment statements within a process. The behavior you might expect is not what is defined by the language. The following example illustrates this point.

Example: Signal Assignments within Processes

The example shown in Figure 6-6 shows two processes, proc1 and proc2, each of which executes the same sequence of operations in computing the value of the output signals res1 and res2, respectively. However, the computation of res1 uses intermediate vari-

```
library IEEE;
use IEEE.std_logic_1164.all;

entity sig_var is
port (x, y, z: in std_logic;
res1, res2 : out std_logic);
end entity sig_var;

architecture behavior of sig_var is
signal sig_s1, sig_s2 : std_logic;
begin
proc1: process (x, y, z) is -- Process 1
variable var_s1, var_s2: std_logic;
begin
L1: var_s1 := x and y;
L2: var_s2 := var_s1 xor z;
L3: res1 <= var_s1 nand var_s2;
end process;
proc2: process (x, y, z) -- Process 2
begin
L1: sig_s1 <= x and y;
L2: sig_s2 <= sig_s1 xor z;
L3: res2 <= sig_s1 nand sig_s2;
end process;
end architecture behavior;
```

FIGURE 6-6 An example of using signals in a process

ables var_s1 and var_s2 whereas the computation of the value of res2 utilizes intermediate signals sig_s1 and sig_s2. This example specifies no delays for the signal
assignment statements; therefore the delta delay model is used to order events to preserve correctness. Consider the execution of proc1. The statement L1 computes the
value of var_s1 that is used in statement L2 in the computation of the current value of
var_s2. The new values of var_s1 and var_s2 computed at the current time are used in
statement L3 to compute the value of signal res1. Now consider the execution of proc2.
Statements L1 and L2 compute new values of sig_s1 and sig_s2. These signals do not
acquire these new values until the next simulation cycle! That means the process must
run to completion using the existing values of sig_s1 and sig_s2. Thus the execution of
statement L1 will produce a future value of sig_s1 scheduled to take place 0 ns and one
delta delay into the future (see Section 4.5.3). The execution of statement L2 will use the
current value of sig_s1 and compute a new value of sig_s2 that will be assigned to
sig_s2 at 0 ns and one delta delay in the future. The computation of res2 will use the
current, and not newly computed, values of sig_s1 and sig_s2. The effect of this behavior is illustrated in Figure 6-7.

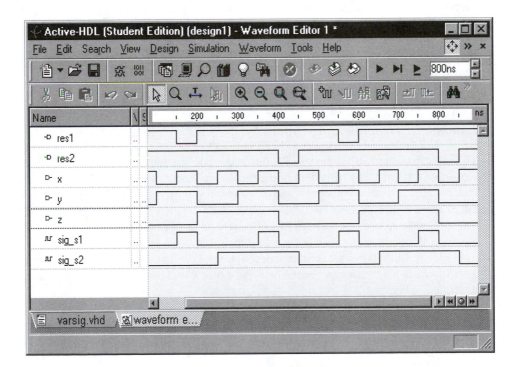

FIGURE 6-7 Illustration of the difference between signals and variables

Note that other than the use of signals vs. variables the values of res1 and res2 are computed using the same set of equations. Now observe the waveforms. They are distinct! A good rule of thumb is to keep in mind that you are modeling hardware. Objects that represent signals in the modeled system should be represented as signals. Objects that are used simply to compute values of signals can naturally use variables.

When writing a debugging VHDL program we must remember to think of these signals as hardware entities and that processes are describing a sequence of computations to determine to values that are to be assigned to signals. These assignments do not take place until the process has finished executing. On the other hand variables act just as we expect from conventional programming languages.

Example End: Signal Assignments within Processes

Another aspect of processes concerns the visibility of signals. All of the ports of the entity and the signals declared within an architecture are visible within a process, which means that they can be read or assigned values from within a process. Thus, during the course of execution a process may read or write any of the signals declared in the architecture or any of the ports on the entity. This is how processes can communicate among themselves. For example, process A may write a signal that is in the sensitivity list of Process B. This will cause Process B to execute. Process B may in turn similarly write a signal in the sensitivity list of Process A. The use of communicating processes is elaborated in the following example.

Example: Communicating Processes

This example illustrates a model of a full adder constructed from two half adders and a two-input OR gate. The behaviors of the three components are described using processes that communicate through signals and is shown in Figure 6-8. When there is an event on either input signal, process HA1 executes, creating events on internal signals s1 and s2. These signals are in the sensitivity lists of processes HA2 and O1 and therefore these processes will execute and schedule events on their outputs as necessary. Note that this style of modeling still follows the structural description of the hardware where we have one process for each hardware component of Figure 6-8. Contrast this model with the model described in Figure 4-3.

Example End: Communicating Processes

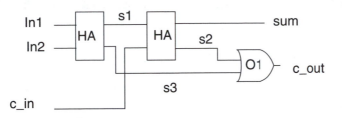

```
library IEEE;
use IEEE.std_logic_1164.all;

entity full_adder is
port (In1, c_in, In2 : in std_logic;
      sum, c_out : out std_logic);
end entity full_adder;

architecture behavioral of full_adder is
signal s1, s2, s3: std_logic;
constant delay :Time:= 5 ns;
begin
HA1: process (In1, In2) --process describing the first half adder
begin
s1 <= (In1 xor In2) after delay;
s3 <= (In1 and In2) after delay;
end process HA1;

HA2: process(s1,c_in) -- process describing the second half adder
begin
sum <= (s1 xor c_in) after delay;
s2 <= (s1 and c_in) after delay;
end process HA2;

OR1: process (s2, s3) -- process describing the two-input OR gate
begin
c_out <= (s2 or s3) after delay;
end process OR1;
end architecture behavioral;
```

FIGURE 6-8 A communicating process model of a full adder

Simulation Exercise 6.1: Combinational Shift Logic

This exercise is concerned with the construction of a combinational logic shifter. The inputs to the shift logic include a 3-bit operand specifying the shift amount, two single-bit signals identifying the direction of the shift operation—left or right—and an 8-bit operand. The output of the shift logic is the shifted 8-bit operand. These shift operations are logical shifts and therefore provide zero fill. For example, a left shift of the number 01101111 by 3 bit positions will produce the output 01111000.

Step 1. Create a text file with the entity description and the architecture description of the shift logic. Assume the delay through the shift logic is fixed at 40 ns, independent of the number of digits that are shifted. Although you can implement this behavior in many ways, for this assignment use a single process and the sequential VHDL statements to implement the behavior of the shift logic. You might find it useful to use the concatenation operator, **&,** and addressing within arrays to perform the shift operations. For example, we can perform the following assignment

dataout <= datain(4 **downto** 0) & "000";

This assignment statement will perform a left shift by three digits with zero fill. Both input and output operands are 8-bit numbers. For VHDL'93 you may use the VHDL built-in shift operators. Use the **case** statement to structure your process.

Step 2. Use the types **std_logic** and **std_logic_vector** for the input and output signals. Declare and reference the library **IEEE** and the package **std_logic_1164**.

Step 3. Create a sequence of test vectors. Each of the test vectors will specify the values of: (1) the **shiftright** and **shiftleft** single-bit control signals, (2) an 8-bit input operand, and (3) a 3-bit number that specifies the number of digits the input operand is to be shifted. Your test cases should be sufficient to ensure the model is operating correctly.

Step 4. Load the simulation model into the simulator. Set the simulator step time to be equal to the value of the propagation delay through the shift logic.

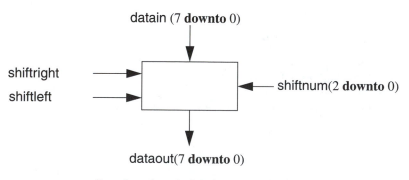

FIGURE 6-9 Interface description for a combinational logic shifter

Step 5.   Using the facilities available within the simulator, generate the input stimulus and open a trace window to view both the input stimulus and the output operand value.

Step 6.   Exercise the simulator by running the simulation long enough to cover your test cases. Verify correct operation from the trace.

Step 7.   Once you have the simulation functioning correctly, modify your model to implement circular shift operations. These operations are such that the digits that are shifted out of one end of the operand are the inputs to the other end. For example, a circular left shift of the pattern 10010111 by 3 digits will be 10111100. The circular shift operations can be implemented using the concatenation operator. In VHDL'93 the circular shift operations can be implemented with the VHDL predefined operators.

End Simulation Exercise 6.1

6.4 The Wait Statement

The execution behavior of the models presented in Chapter 4 and the behavioral models described so far in this chapter have been data-driven, where events on the input signals initiated the execution of CSA statements or processes. Signal assignment statements suspend until the next event on a signal on the RHS of the assignment statement. Processes will then suspend until the next event on a signal defined in its sensitivity list. This fits well with the behavior of combinational circuits, where a change on the input signals may cause a change in the value of the output signals. Therefore the outputs should be recomputed whenever there is a change in the value of the input signal.

However, what about modeling circuits where the outputs are computed only at specific points in time independent of events on the inputs? How do we model circuits that respond only to certain events on the input signals? For example, in synchronous sequential circuits, the clock signal determines when the outputs may change or when inputs are read. Such behavior requires us to be able to specify in a more general manner the conditions under which the circuit outputs must be recomputed. In VHDL terms, we need a more general way of specifying when a process is executed or suspended pending the occurrence of an event or events. This capability is provided by the **wait** statement.

The **wait** statements explicitly specify the conditions under which a process may resume execution after being suspended. The forms of the **wait** statement include the following.

wait for *time expression*;

wait on *signal*;

wait until *<condition>*;

wait;

The first form of the wait statement causes suspension of the process for a period of time given by the evaluation of *time expression*. This is an expression that should evaluate to a value that is of type **time**. The simplest form of this statement is as follows:

wait for 20 **ns**;

The second form causes a process to suspend execution until an event occurs on one or more signals in a group of signals. For example, we might have the following statement.

wait on clk, reset, status;

In this case, an event on any of the signals causes the process to resume execution with the first statement following the **wait** statement. The third form can specify a *<condition>* that evaluates to a Boolean value, TRUE or FALSE.

Using these wait statements processes can be used to model components that are not necessarily data driven but are driven only by certain types of events such as the rising edge of a clock signal. Many such conditions cannot be described using sensitivity lists alone. More importantly, we would often like to construct models where we need to suspend a process at multiple points within a process and not just at the beginning. Such models are made possible through the use of the **wait** statement. *Because of this behavior of* **wait** *statements a process can have a sensitivity list or use* **wait** *statements but not both!* The following examples will help further motivate the use of the **wait** statement.

Example: Positive-Edge-Triggered D Flip-Flop

The model of a positive-edge-triggered D flip-flop is a good example of the use of the wait statement. The behavior of this component is such that the D input is sampled on the rising edge of the clock and transferred to the output. Therefore, the model description must be able to specify computations of output values only at specific points on time—in this case the rising edge of the clock signal. This is done using the **wait** statement, as shown in Figure 6-10. This brings us to another very interesting feature of the language. Note the statement clk'**event** in the model shown in Figure 6-10. This statement is true if an event (i.e., signal transition) has occurred on the clk signal. The conjunction, (clk'**event and** clk = '1'), is often used to detect a rising edge on the clk signal. The signal clock is said to have an *attribute* named **event** associated with it. The predicate clk'**event** is true whenever an event has occurred on the signal clk in the most recent simulation cycle. Recall that an event is a change in the signal value. In contrast, a *transaction* occurs on a signal when a new assignment has been made to the signal, but the value may not have changed. As this example illustrates, such an attribute is very useful. The following section lists some useful attributes of VHDL objects.

The std_logic_1164 package also provides two useful functions that we could have used in lieu of the **event** attribute: rising_edge (clk) and falling_edge (clk). These functions take a signal of type std_logic as an argument and return a Boolean value denoting whether a rising edge (falling edge) occurred on the signal. The predicate clk'**event** simply denotes a change in value. Note that a single-bit signal of type std_logic can have up to 9

```
library IEEE;
use IEEE.std_logic_1164.all;
entity dff is
port (D, Clk : in std_logic;
     Q, Qbar : out std_logic);
end entity dff;

architecture behavioral of dff is
begin
output: process
begin
wait until (Clk'event and Clk = '1'); -- use the function (rising_edge(Clk)
                                      -- for true rising edge detection

   Q <= D after 5 ns;
   Qbar <= not D after 5 ns;

end process output;
end architecture behavioral;
```

FIGURE 6-10 Behavioral model of a positive-edge-triggered D flip-flop

values. Thus, if we are really looking for a rising edge from signal value 0 to 1, or a falling edge from signal value 1 to 0, it would be better to replace the test "**if** (Clk'**event and** Clk = '1')" with "**if** rising_edge(Clk)," because the former will be true even if Clk transitions from, say, X to 1.

Continuing with the description of the operation of the D flip-flop, we see that the input is sampled on the rising clock edge and the output values are scheduled after a period equal to the propagation delay through the flip-flop. The process is not executed whenever there is a change in the value of the input signal D, but rather only when there is a rising edge on the signal Clk. Thus outputs are only computed on rising clock edges just as in the operation of a physical implementation.

Example End: Positive-Edge-Triggered D Flip-Flop

The preceding example did not specify the initial values of the flip-flop. When a physical system is powered up the individual flip-flops may be initialized to some known state, but not necessarily all in the same state. In general, it is better to have some control over initial states of the flip-flops. This is usually achieved by providing such inputs as Clear or Set and Preset or Reset. Asserting the Set input forces Q = 1 and asserting the Reset input forces Q = 0. These signals override the effect of the clock signal and are active at any time, hence the characterization as asynchronous inputs as opposed to the synchronous nature of the clock signal. The following example illustrates how we can extend the previous model to include asynchronous inputs.

Example: D Flip-Flop with Asynchronous Inputs

Figure 6-11 shows a model of a D flip-flop with asynchronous reset (R) and set (S) inputs and the corresponding VHDL model. The R input overrides the S input. Both signals are active low. Therefore, to set the output Q = 0, a zero pulse is applied to the reset input while the set input is held to 1, and vice versa. During synchronous operation, both S and R must be held to 1.

```
library IEEE;
use IEEE.std_logic_1164.all;
entity asynch_dff is
port (R, S, D, Clk : in std_logic;
     Q, Qbar : out std_logic);
end entity asynch_dff;

architecture behavioral of asynch_dff is
begin
output: process (R, S, Clk) is
begin
if (R = '0') then
    Q <= '0' after 5 ns;
    Qbar <= '1' after 5 ns;
elsif S = '0' then
    Q <= '1' after 5 ns;
    Qbar <= '0' after 5 ns;
  elsif (rising_edge(Clk)) then
    Q<= D after 5 ns;
    Qbar <= (not D) after 5 ns;
end if;
end process output;
end architecture behavioral;
```

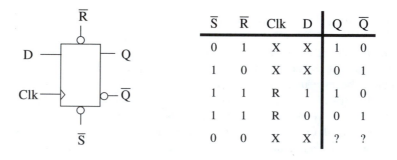

$\overline{S}$	$\overline{R}$	Clk	D	Q	$\overline{Q}$
0	1	X	X	1	0
1	0	X	X	0	1
1	1	R	1	1	0
1	1	R	0	0	1
0	0	X	X	?	?

FIGURE 6-11 D flip-flop with asynchronous set and reset inputs

Example End: D Flip-Flop with Asynchronous Inputs

Now that we have seen how to create a model for a basic unit of storage with asynchronous inputs, it is relatively straightforward to similarly create models for registers and counters. Such an example is presented next.

Example: Registers and Counters

We can construct a model of a typical 4-bit register comprised of edge-triggered D flip-flops, with asynchronous clear and enable signals. Such a model is shown in Figure 6-12. With a few modifications this example can be converted into a model of a counter. On each clock edge, rather than sampling the inputs we can simply increment the value stored in the register. The initialization step can be also changed to load a preset value into the counter rather than initializing the counter to 0.

Example End: Registers and Counters

```
library IEEE;
use IEEE.std_logic_1164.all;
entity reg4 is
port (D : in std_logic_vector (3 downto 0);
      Cl, enable, Clk: in std_logic;
      Q : out std_logic_vector (3 downto 0));
end entity reg4;

architecture behavioral of reg4 is
begin
reg_process: process (Cl, Clk) is
begin
if (Cl = '1') then
   Q <= "0000" after 5 ns;
  elsif (rising_edge(Clk)) then
  if enable = '1' then
  Q<= D after 5 ns;
  end if;
end if;
end process reg_process;
end architecture behavioral;
```

FIGURE 6-12 A 4-bit register with asynchronous inputs and enable

Example: Asynchronous Communication

Another example of the utility of wait statements is the modeling of asynchronous communication between two devices. A simple 4-phase protocol for synchronizing the transfer of data between a producer and consumer is shown in Figure 6-13. Let us assume the producer (e.g., input device such as a microphone) is providing data for a consumer device (e.g., the processor) and the transfer of each word must be synchronized. When the producer has data to be transferred the signal RQ is asserted. The consumer waits for a rising edge of the RQ signal before reading the data. The consumer then signals successful reception of the data by asserting the ACK signal. This causes the producer to de-assert RQ, which in turn results in the consumer de-asserting ACK. At this point the transaction is completed and the consumer and producer can each assert that the other has successfully completed their end of the transaction. The producer and consumer can be modeled as processes that communicate via signals. Such a model is shown in Figure 6-14. Note that signals RQ, ACK, and transmit_data are declared in the architecture and are visible within both processes. Although this example is incomplete in that the processes do not perform any interesting computations with the data, it does illustrate the use of wait statements to control asynchronous communication between processes. Moreover, it illustrates the ability to suspend the execution of a process at multiple points within the model. Because these processes execute concurrently in simulated time, they must be capable of suspending and resuming execution at multiple points within the VHDL code. Such a model is not possible using only sensitivity lists as the mechanism for initiating process execution (although other solutions to the producer–consumer problem are possible).

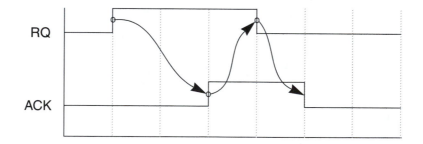

FIGURE 6-13 4-phase handshake

Example End: Asynchronous Communication

```
library IEEE;
use IEEE.std_logic_1164.all;

entity handshake is
port (input_data : in std_logic_vector(31 downto 0));
end entity handshake;

architecture behavioral of handshake is
signal transmit_data: std_logic_vector (31 downto 0);
signal RQ, ACK : std_logic;
begin
producer: process is
begin
wait until input_data'event; -- wait until input data is available
transmit_data <= input_data;     -- provide data as producer
 RQ <= '1';
wait until ACK = '1';
RQ <= '0';
wait until ACK = '0';
end process producer;

consumer: process is
variable receive_data : std_logic_vector (31 downto 0);
 begin
wait until RQ = '1';
receive_data := transmit_data; -- read data as consumer
ACK <= '1';
wait until RQ = '0';
ACK <= '0';
end process consumer;
end architecture behavioral;
```

FIGURE 6-14 A VHDL model of the behavior shown in Figure 6-13

6.5 Attributes

The example of the model of the D flip-flop introduced the idea of an attribute of a signal. Attributes can be used to formulate a query about signal to determine various types of information about the signal. For example, we have seen that the predicate **clk'event** returns true if there has been a change in the value of the signal during the last simulation cycle. This particular attribute, **event**, causes a function to be called that will return TRUE or FALSE. What other types of information can be obtained about a signal? What about obtaining information about other VHDL names such as entities or arrays? This notion of attributes appeals to our intuition as just about any object possesses attributes. For example a car has attributes of color, size, power, and cost. The notion of attributes as provided in VHDL is quite general. Some attributes are pre-defined by the language whereas user-defined attributes can be created by the programmer. In this section we will limit our presentation to commonly used pre-defined attributes.

There are five basic types of attributes pre-defined by the language. They are:

- *Function attributes*: invokes a function which returns a value.

- *Value attributes*: returns a constant value.

- *Signal attributes*: returns a signal.

- *Type attributes*: returns a type.

- *Range attributes*: returns a range.

6.5.1 Function Attributes

Attributes such as **event** that are applied to signals are referred to as *function attributes*—a function is called that returns a value. Some other useful function attributes for signals are shown in Table 6-1. For example, in addition to determining if an event has occurred on the signal we might be interested in knowing the amount of time that has elapsed since the last event occurred on the signal. This attribute is denoted using the following syntax:

clk'**last_event**

In effect, when the simulator executes this statement a function call occurs that checks this property. The function returns the time since the last event occurred on signal clk.

6.5.2 Value Attributes

A second class of pre-defined attributes is *value attributes*. As the name suggests, these attributes return constant values. For example, the memory model shown in Figure 6-2 contains the definition of a new type as follows.

type mem_array **is array**(0 **to** 7) **of** std_logic_vector (31 **downto** 0);

From Table 6-2 we have mem_array'**left** = 0, and mem_array'**ascending** = true and mem_array'**length** = 8. Another useful example is in the use of enumerated types.

TABLE 6-1 Some useful function signal attributes

Function attribute	Function
signal_name'**event**	Function returning a Boolean value signifying a change in value on this signal
signal_name'**active**	Function returning a Boolean value signifying an assignment made to this signal. This assignment may not be a new value.
signal_name'**last_event**	Function returning the time since the last event on this signal
signal_name'**last_active**	Function returning the time since the signal was last active
signal_name'**last_value**	Function returning the previous value of this signal
my_array'**length**	Function returning the length of the array my_array

TABLE 6-2 Some useful value attributes

Value attribute	Value
scalar_name'**left**	Returns the left most value of scalar_name in its defined range or values
scalar_name'**right**	Returns the right most value of scalar_name in its defined range of values
scalar_name'**high**	Returns the highest value of scalar_name in its range of values
scalar_name'**low**	Returns the lowest value of scalar_name in its range of values
scalar_name'**ascending**	Returns true if scalar_name has an ascending range of values (VHDL'93 only)
array_name'**length**	Returns the number of elements in the array array_name
array_name'**left**	The left bound of array_name
array_name'**right**	The right bound of array_name

'87 vs.'93

For example, when writing models of state machines described later in this chapter, it is useful to have the following data type defined:

type statetype **is** (state0, state1, state2, state3);

This statement defines a new datatype called statetype. Any variable or signal declared to be of this type can take on one of four values: state0, state1, state2, or state3. In this case we have statetype'left = state0 and statetype'right = state3. This is useful in behavioral models when we wish to initialize signals to values based on their types. We may not always know the range and values of the various data types nor would we really care to remember. The use of attributes makes it easy to initialize object to values without having to be concerned with the implementation. For example, on a reset operation we may simply initialize a state machine to the leftmost state of the enumerated list of possible states, that is, statetype'left. Some commonly used value attributes are shown in Table 6-2.

6.5.3 Signal Attributes

Signal attributes create new signals from the signals explicitly declared by you in VHDL models. These new signals are referred to as *implicit* signals. For example, the attribute signal_name'delayed(T) creates a new signal of the same type as signal_name, but which is delated by T. If a delay is not specified then a delta delay is inserted between the two signals.

Several such types of implicit signals can be created in VHDL as shown in Table 6-3. The 'transaction attribute creates a signal that toggle when the original signal changes value. The 'stable and 'quiet attributes are signals that provide for easy tests of the behavior of signals over periods of time.

TABLE 6-3 Some usfeul signal attributes

Signal attribute	Implicit Signal
signal_name'delayed(T)	Signal delayed by T units of time
signal_name'transaction	Signal whose value toggles when signal_name is active
signal_name'quiet(T)	True when signal_name has been quiet for T units of time
signal_name'stable(T)	True when event has not occurred on signal_name for T units of time

Keep in mind that these implicit signals are actually generated and can be used elsewhere in the model. For example, consider the simple code block shown in Figure 6-15 where signal attributes create two implicit signals. The associated entity description (not shown) has a signal data as a 4-bit input signal and the architecture produces two output signals derived from data using signal attributes. The first is a 4-bit signal delayed from data by 5 ns. The second signal corresponds to data'transaction. This implict signal toggles when ever the signal data changes value.

```
architecture behavioral of attributes is
begin
  outdelayed <= data'delayed(5 ns);
  outtransaction <= data'transaction;
end attributes;
```

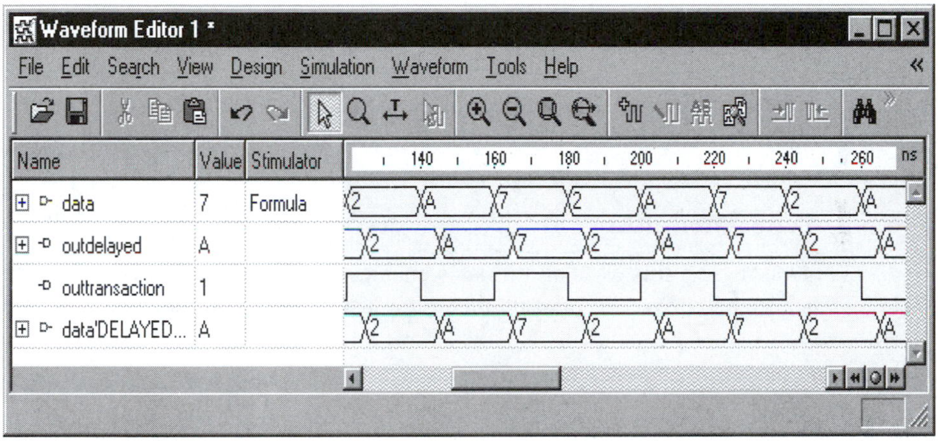

FIGURE 6-15 An example of the use of signal attributes and implicit signals

When would one use an implicit signal? Consider tests such as those shown below. If we are interested in waiting for a change in value on a signal we can simply wait for events on the 'transaction implicit signal. Furthermore, the presence of a delayed signal can be used to check for relationships between the current value of the signal and an older value of the same signal. For example, we might wish to check if the change in value has been greated than a certain amount.

wait on ReceiveData'**transaction**

if ReceiveData'**delayed (5 ns)** = ReceiveData **then**

......

6.5.4 Range Attribute

Finally, a very useful attribute of arrays is the **range** attribute. This is useful in writing loops. For example, consider a loop that scans all of the elements in an array value_array(). The index range is returned by value_array'**range**. This makes it very easy to write loops, particularly when we may not know the size of the array, as is sometimes the case when writing functions or procedures where the array size is determined when the function is called. When we do not know the array size, we can write the loop as shown below:

for i **in** value_array'**range loop**

...

my_var := value_array(i);

...

end loop;

Some specific examples of the use of the range attribute can be found in the discussion of functions and procedures in Chapter 9.

6.5.5 Type Attributes

As the name suggest this class of attributes enables queries about the type of names used in VHDL programs. We will relegate this to the list of advanced topics that are not dealt with here.

6.6 Generating Clocks and Periodic Waveforms

Because wait statements provide the programmer with explicit control over the reactivation of processes, they can be used for generating periodic waveforms as shown in the following example.

Example: Generating Periodic Waveforms

We know that in a signal assignment statement we can specify several future events. For example, we might have the following signal assignment statement:

signal <= '0', '1' **after** 10 **ns**, '0' **after** 20 **ns**, '1' **after** 40 **ns**;

The execution of this statement will create the waveform shown in Figure 6-16. Now, if we place this statement within a process and use a wait statement, we can cause the process to be executed repeatedly, producing a periodic waveform. Recall that upon initialization of the VHDL model all processes are executed. Therefore, every process is executed at least once. During initialization the first set of events shown in the above waveform will be produced. The execution of the **wait for** statement causes the process to be reactivated after 50 ns. This will cause the process to be executed again, generating events in the interval 50–100 ns. The process again suspends for 50 ns and the cycle is repeated. By altering the time durations in the statement in the above process, one can envision the generation of

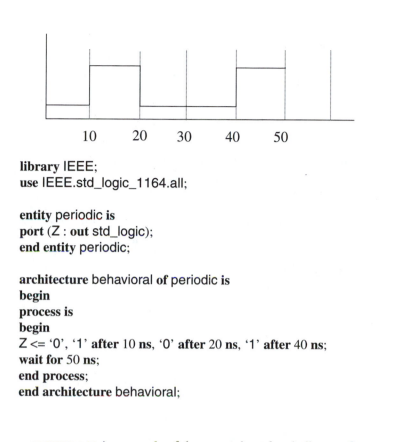

library IEEE;
use IEEE.std_logic_1164.all;

entity periodic is
port (Z : out std_logic);
end entity periodic;

architecture behavioral of periodic is
begin
process is
begin
Z <= '0', '1' after 10 ns, '0' after 20 ns, '1' after 40 ns;
wait for 50 ns;
end process;
end architecture behavioral;

FIGURE 6-16 An example of the generation of periodic waveforms

many different types of periodic waveforms. For example, if we wished to generate two-phase non-overlapping clocks we could utilize the same approach as shown in the next example.

Example End: Generating Periodic Waveforms

Example: Generating a Two-Phase Clock

An example of a model for the generation of non-overlapping clocks and reset pulses is shown in Figure 6-17. Such signals are very useful and found in the majority of circuits we will come across. The reset process is a single CSA statement and therefore we can dis-

```
library IEEE;
use IEEE.std_logic_1164.all;
entity two_phase is
port(phi1, phi2, reset : out std_logic);
end entity two_phase;

architecture behavioral of two_phase is
begin
```

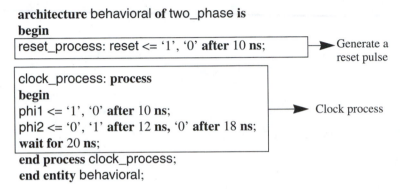

reset_process: reset <= '1', '0' after 10 ns;   → Generate a
                                                       reset pulse

```
clock_process: process
begin
phi1 <= '1', '0' after 10 ns;                        → Clock process
phi2 <= '0', '1' after 12 ns, '0' after 18 ns;
wait for 20 ns;
```

```
end process clock_process;
end entity behavioral;
```

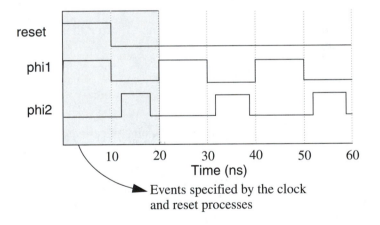

Events specified by the clock
and reset processes

FIGURE 6-17 Generation of two-phase non-overlapping clocks

pense with the **begin** and **end** statements. Recall that CSA statements are processes and we can assign them labels. Every process is executed just once, at initialization. During this initialization reset is executed, generating a pulse of width 10 ns. Because there are no input signals the reset statement is never executed again! The clock process, on the other hand, generates multiple clock edges in a 20-ns interval with each statement. Note the width of the pulses in the second clock signal: it is adjusted so as to prevent the pulses from overlapping. The **wait for** statement causes the process to be executed again 20 ns later, when each statement generates clock edges in the next 20-ns interval. This process repeats indefinitely, generating the waveforms shown in Figure 6-17. Note how CSA statements are mixed in with the process construct. This type of modeling using both concurrent and sequential statements is quite common. This is not surprising, because CSA statements are essentially processes. If we take the viewpoint that all statements in VHDL are concurrent, then processes using sequential statements can be viewed as one complex signal assignment statement. This is a useful template to have in mind when constructing behavioral models of hardware.

Example End: Generating a Two-Phase Clock

6.7 Using Signals in a Process

We can think of processes as conventional programs that can be used in VHDL simulation models to provide us with powerful techniques for the computation of events. However, the sequential nature of processes in conjunction with the use of signals within a process can produce behavior that may be unexpected. For example, consider the circuit and corresponding model and timing behavior illustrated in Figure 4-13 and Figure 4-14. Now, let us enclose the CSA statement shown in the model of Figure 4-13 in a process. This would represent a different model of operation for the following reason: the circuit being described is a combinational circuit; signal values are determined in a data-driven manner; signal assignment statements are executed only when input signal values change. Thus, the value of signal s3 is computed only when there is a transaction on signals s1 or ln2.

Now, consider the implementation using processes for which the timing is shown in Figure 6-18. When there is a change in value on either ln1 or ln2, the process is executed. By definition, a process executes to completion. All statements within a process are executed! Consider the value of signal s3 at initialization time when each process is executed. The value of this signal is undefined. Signal s4 has a value 1 because ln1 is 0. Therefore the value of s4 is 1 regardless of the value of s2. However, the value of s3 is undefined and it appears as such on the trace. Now, the process suspends and waits for an event on ln1 or ln2. It will not be executed again until 10 ns later, when a $1 \rightarrow 0$ transition occurs on ln2. From the trace in Figure 6-18 we can see that forcing the process statements to be executed in order and being sensitive only to the inputs ln1 and ln2 produces a trace very distinct from that in Figure 4-14. Although both models were intended to represent the same circuit, we have realized different behaviors. One could make a good case that the use of a process places artificial constraints on the evaluation of signal values and that the former model is indeed a more accurate reflection of the physical behavior of the circuit. In reality, if we made the process sensitive to all of the signals (i.e., including s1, s2, s3, and s4) we would find that the process model would behave exactly as the earlier model producing an identical trace. However, this is not a very intuitive description of the model. Suffice to say that when using signals within a process, one must be careful that the behavior that results is indeed what the modeler had in mind.

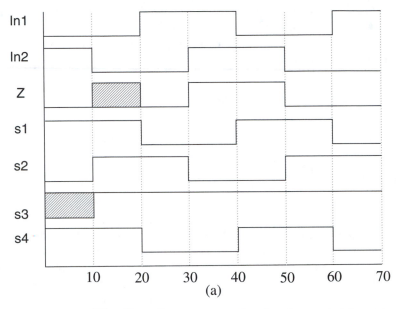

FIGURE 6-18 The effect of processes on signal assignment statements

Simulation Exercise 6.2: Use of Wait Statements

This simulation exercise provides an introduction to the use of wait statements to suspend and resume processing under programmer control. We can use such constructs to respond to asynchronous external events. Figure 6-19 shows an example of a simple interface that reads data from a device and buffers it for an output device. Let us model this interface with two processes. The first process communicates with the second via a handshaking protocol such as the one demonstrated in Figure 6-13. The second process can then drive an external device such as a display.

Step 1.   Using a text editor, construct a VHDL model for communication between an input process and an output process using the handshaking protocol captured in Figure 6-13. Assume that the input process can read only a single word at a time. The input process receives a single 32-bit word comprised of 4 bytes. This word is to be transferred to an output device whose storage layout requires reversing the byte order within the word. This reversal is performed by the input process before it is transferred to the output process, which in turn writes the value to an output port.

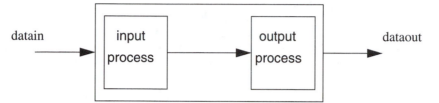

FIGURE 6-19 An example of asynchronous communication

Step 2. Use the types **std_logic** and **std_logic_vector** for input and output signals. Declare and reference the library **IEEE** and package **std_logic_1164**.

Step 3. Create a sequence of 32-bit words as test inputs.

Step 4. Compile the model and load into the simulator.

Step 5. Assign a delay of 10 ns for each handshake transition.

Step 6. Open a trace window and select the signals to be traced. Because we are dealing with 32-bit quantities, set the trace to display these signal values in hexadecimal notation. This will make it considerably easier to read the values in the trace. Such commands are simulator specific.

Step 7. Simulate for several hundred nanoseconds.

Step 8. Trace the four-phase handshake sequence of Figure 6-13.

Step 9. From the trace determine how long it takes for the input process to transfer a data item to the output process.

Step 10. Does the rate at which the input items are provided matter? What happens as we increase the frequency with which data items are presented to the input process? What is the maximum input data rate?

End Simulation Exercise 6.2

6.8 Modeling State Machines

The examples that have been discussed so far were combinational and sequential circuits in isolation. Processes that model combinational circuits are sensitive to the inputs, being activated whenever an event occurs on an input signal. In contrast, sequential circuits retain information stored in internal devices such as flip-flops and latches. The values stored in these devices are referred to as the *state* of the circuit. The values of the output signals may now be computed as functions of the internal state and values of the input signals. The values of the state variables may also change as a function of the input signals, but are generally updated at discrete points in time determined by a periodic signal such as the clock. Provided with a finite number of storage elements, the number of unique states is finite and such circuits are referred to as finite state machines.

Figure 6-20 shows a general model of a finite state machine. The circuit consists of a combinational component and a sequential component. The sequential component consists of memory elements, such as edge-triggered flip-flops, that record the state and are updated synchronously on the rising edge of the clock signal. The combinational component is comprised of logic gates that compute two Boolean functions. The *output function* computes the values of the output signals. The *next state function* computes the new values of the memory elements (i.e., the value of the next state). The state diagram is a commonly used method to capture the behavior of the state machine. From the state diagram in Figure 6-20 we know that if the machine is in state s0 and the input signal has a value of 0 then the machine transitions to state s1 while setting the value of the output signal to 1. The behavior when in state s1can be similarly described. In fact the behavior of larger state machines can be described in a similar manner—on a state by state basis. As we shall see shortly such a description leads to a very natural VHDL description.

Figure 6-20 suggests a very natural VHDL implementation using communicating concurrent processes. The combinational component can be implemented within one process. This process is sensitive to events on the input signals and changes in the state. Thus, if any of the input signals or the state variables change value this process is executed to compute new values for the output signals and the new state variables. The sequential component can be implemented within a second process. This process is sensitive to the rising edge of the clock signal. When it is executed, the state variables are updated to reflect the value of the next state computed by the combinational component. The VHDL description of such a state machine is shown in Figure 6-21. The model is structured as

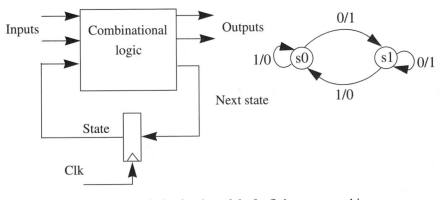

FIGURE 6-20 A behavioral model of a finite state machine

```vhdl
library IEEE;
use   IEEE.std_logic_1164.all;
entity state_machine is
port(reset, clk, x : in std_logic;
     z : out std_logic);
end entity state_machine;

architecture behavioral of state_machine is
type statetype is (state0, state1);
signal state, next_state : statetype := state0;
begin
comb_process: process (state, x) is
begin
 case state is                          -- depending upon the current state
 when state0 =>                         -- set output signals and next state
               if x = '0' then
               next_state <= state1;
               z <= '1';
         else  next_state <= state0;
               z <= '0';
         end if;
 when state1 =>
 if x = '1' then
               next_state <= state0;
               z <= '0';
         else  next_state <= state1;
               z <= '1';
         end if;
end case;
end process comb_process;

clk_process: process is
begin
wait until (rising_edge(clk)); -- wait until the rising edge
               if reset = '1' then     -- check for reset and initialize state
               state <= statetype'left;
               else    state <= next_state;
               end if;
end process clk_process;
end architecture behavioral;
```

FIGURE 6-21 Implementation of the state machine in Figure 6-20

two communicating processes, with the signals state and next_state used to communicate values between them. The structure of the process comb_process, representing the combinational component, is very intuitive. This process is constructed using a CASE statement. Each branch of the case represents one of the states and includes the output function and next-state function, as shown. The output value can be computed as a function of the current state and current input signal values. The next state can also be described as a function of the current state and current input signal values. The process clk_process updates the state variable on the rising edge of the clock. On reset, this process initializes the state machine to state state0. This process can be naturally extended to state machines comprised of a larger number of states. If we can draw the state machine diagram in the form shown in Figure 6-20 then we can describe the behavior in each state as a additional branch of the case statement in process comb_process.

There are several interesting aspects to this model. First, note the use of enumerated types for the definition of a state. The model includes the definition of a new type referred to as statetype. This type can take on the values state0 and state1. This is referred to as an *enumerated type*, because we have enumerated all possible values that a signal of this type can take: in this case exactly two distinct values, state0 and state1. This enables much more readable and intuitive VHDL code. The case statement essentially describes the state machine diagram in Figure 6-20. In the clock process, note how the initial state is initialized on reset by using attributes discussed in Section 6.5. The clause statetype'left will return the value at the leftmost value of the enumeration of the possible values for statetype. Therefore the initialization shown in the declaration is really not necessary. This is a common form of initialization and is also defined for other types in the language. The default initialization value for signals is signal_name'left. The use of such attributes during initialization provide a clean way of initializing signals without having to keep track of implementation dependent values. A simulation of this state machine would produce a trace of the behavior, as shown in Figure 6-22. Note how the state labels appear in the trace, making it easier to read. Also note that the signal next_state is changing with the input signal, whereas the signal state is not. This is because state is updated only on the rising clock edge, whereas next_state changes whenever the input signal, x, changes.

The above example could just as easily have been written as a single process whose execution is initiated by the clock edge. In this case, the computation of the next state, the output signals, and the state transition are all synchronized by the clock. Alternatively, we could construct a model where outputs are computed asynchronously with the computation of the next state. Such a model is shown in Figure 6-23. This model is constructed with three processes: one each for the output function, next-state function, and the state transition. Note how the model is constructed from the structure of the hardware: concurrency in the circuit naturally appears as multiple concurrent processes in the VHDL model. State machines wherein the output signal values are computed only as a function of the current state are referred to as Moore machines. State machines where the output values are computed as a function of both the current state and the input values are Mealy machines. It is evident that the above approaches to constructing state machines enable the construction of both Moore and Mealy machines by appropriately coding the output function.

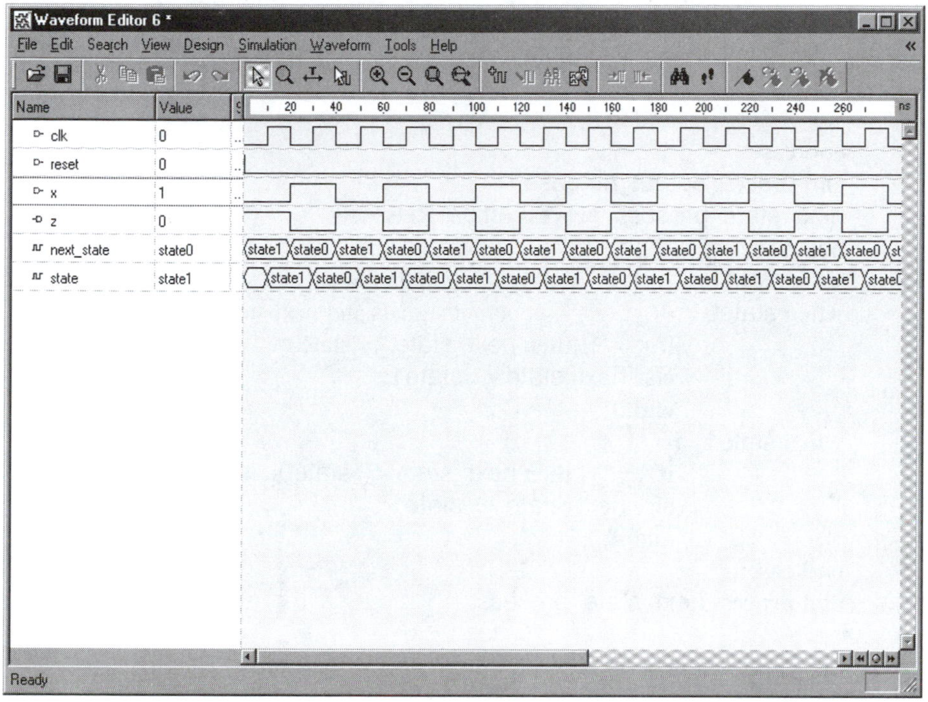

FIGURE 6-22 A trace of the operation of the state machine in Figure 6-21

```
library IEEE;
use  IEEE.std_logic_1164.all;
entity state_machine is
port(reset, clk, x : in std_logic;
     z : out std_logic);
end state_machine;

architecture behavioral of state_machine is
type statetype is (state0, state1);
signal state, next_state :statetype :=state0;
begin
output_process: process (state, x) is
begin
 case state is            -- depending upon the current state
 when state0 =>           -- set output signals and next state
            if x = '1' then z <= '0';
            else z <= '1';
            end if;
```

FIGURE 6-23 Alternative model for a finite state machine

```
            when state1 =>
                        if x = '1' then z <= '0';
                        else z <= '1';
                        end if;
            end case;
            end process output_process;
            next_state_process: process (state, x) is
            begin
             case state is                -- depending upon the current state
            when state0 =>                -- set output signals and next state
                        if x = '1' then next_state <= state0;
                        else next_state <= state1;
                        end if;
            when state1 =>
                        if x = '1' then next_state <= state0;
                        else next_state <= state1;
                        end if;
            end case;
            end process next_state_process;

            clk_process: process is
            begin
            wait until (rising_edge(clk));    -- wait until the rising edge
            if reset = '1' then   state <= statetype'left;
            else state <= next_state;
            end if;
            end process clk_process;
            end architecture behavioral;
```

FIGURE 6-23 (cont.)

6.9 Constructing VHDL Models Using Processes

A prescription for writing VHDL models using processes can now be provided. The first step is the same as that described in Section 4.4 for constructing models using CSA statements: we construct a fully annotated schematic of the system being modeled. Figure 6-24 illustrates a template for constructing such VHDL behavioral models. One approach for translating the annotated schematic to a VHDL model described in the template of Figure 6-24 is as follows:

library library-name-1, library-name-2;

use library-name-1.package-name.all;

use library-name-2.package-name.all;

entity entity_name **is**

port(*input signals* : **in** *type*;

      output signals : **out** *type*);

end entity entity_name;

architecture arch_name **of** entity_name **is**

-- declare internal signals, you may have multiple signals of
-- different types

signal *internal signals* : *type* := initialization;

begin

```
label-1: process(-- sensitivity list --) is
--- declare variables to be used in the process
variable variable_names : type:= initialization;
      begin
-- process body
end process label-1;
```
First
Process

```
label-2: process is
--- declare variables to be used in the process
variable variable_names : type:= initialization;
      begin
wait until (-- predicate--);
-- sequential statements
wait until (-- predicate--);
-- sequential statements
end process label-2;
```
Second
Process

internal-signal *or* ports <= *simple, conditional, or selected CSA*

-- other processes or CSAs

end architecture arch_name;

FIGURE 6-24 A template for a VHDL model using CSAs and processes

Construct_ Process_Model

1. At this point I recommend using the IEEE 1164 value system. To do so, include the following two lines at the top of your model declaration:

   library IEEE;
   use IEEE.std_logic_1164.**all**;

   Single-bit signals can be declared to be of type std_logic, whereas multi-bit quantities can be declared to be of type std_logic_vector. If you need arithmetic functions you may consider adding the following packages.
   use IEEE.std_logic_1164.**all**;
   use IEEE. std_logic_unsigned.**all**;

   The first package has the definitions or many arithmetic operators in objects of type std_logic. The second package is useful if we declare any objects of type unsigned. This type is useful for quantities such as memory addresses.

2. Select a name for the entity (**entity_name**) and write the entity description specifying each input and output signal port, its mode, and associated type.

3. Select a name for the architecture (**arch_name**) and write the architecture description. Place both the entity and architecture descriptions in the same file (as we will see in Chapter 11, this is not necessary in general).

   3.1 Within the architecture description name and declare all of the internal signals used to connect the components. The architecture declaration states the type of each signal, and may include initialization. The information you need is available from your fully annotated schematic.

   3.2 Each internal signal is driven by exactly one component. The computation of values on each internal signal can be described using a CSA or a process.

Using CSAs

For each internal signal select a concurrent signal assignment statement that expresses the value of this internal signal as a function of the signals that are inputs to that component. Use the value of the propagation delay through the component provided for that output signal.

Using a Process

Alternatively, if the computation of the signal values at the outputs of the component are too complex to represent using CSA statements, describe the behavior of the component with a process. One process can be used to compute the values of all of the output signals from that component.

   3.2.1 Label the process. If you are using a sensitivity list, identify the signals that will activate the process and place them in the sensitivity list.

   3.2.2 Declare variables used within the process.

3.2.3 Write the body of the process, computing the values of output signals and the relative time at which these output signals assume these values. These output signals may be internal to the architecture or may be port signals found in the entity description. If a sensitivity list is not used, specify wait statements at appropriate points in the process to specify when the process should suspend and when it should resume execution. It is an error to have both a sensitivity list and a wait statement within the process.

3.3 If there are signals that are driven by more than one source, the type of this signal must be a resolved type. This type must have a resolution function declared for use with signals of this type. For our purposes, use the IEEE 1164 types std_logic for single-bit signals and std_logic_vector for bytes, words, or multi-bit quantities. These are resolved types. Make sure you include the **library** clause and the **use** clause to include all of the definitions provided in the std_logic_1164 package.

3.4 If you are using any functions or type definitions provided by a third party, make sure that you have declared the appropriate library using the **library** clause and declared the use of this package via the presence of a **use** clause in your model.

The behavioral model will now appear structurally as shown in Figure 6-24, inclusive of both CSA and sequential statements.

Simulation Exercise 6.3: State Machines

Consider the state machine shown in Figure 6-25. This state machine has two inputs. The first is the **reset** signal, which initializes the machine to state 0. The second is a bit-serial input. The third is the clock input. The state machine is designed to recognize the sequence 101 in the input sequence and set the value of the output to 1. The value of the output remains at 1 until the state machine is reset.

Step 1. Write the VHDL model for this state machine. Use an enumerated type to represent the state (i.e., the type **statetype** as in Figure 6-23). Structure your state machine description as three processes.

Process 1: Write an output process that determines the value of the single-bit output based on the current state and the value of the single-bit input.

Process 2: Write a process that computes the next state based on the value of the input signal and the current state.

Process 3: Write a clock process that updates the state on the rising edge of the clock signal. On a **reset** pulse the state machine is reset. Otherwise the state is modified to reflect the next state.

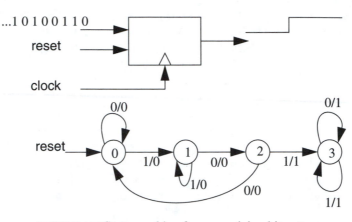

FIGURE 6-25 State machine for recognizing bit patterns

Step 2.   Within the simulator that you are using, structure the input stimulus as follows.

Apply a clock signal with a period of 20 ns.

Apply a reset signal that generates a single pulse of duration 30 ns.

Generate a random, bit-serial sequence with the pattern 101 embedded within the sequence.

Step 3.   Simulate the model long enough to detect the pattern in the input sequence.

Step 4.   Modify the model to recognize other patterns and repeat.

Step 5.   Modify the model so that after the pattern is recognized the state machine is rein-itialized to state 0. Detection of the pattern now results in a pulse on the output signal.

End Simulation Exercise 6.3

6.10 Common Programming Errors

The following are some common programming errors that are made during the learning process.

6.10.1 Common Syntax Errors

- Do not forget the semicolon at the end of a statement.
- Remember it is **elsif** and not **elseif** !

- It is an error to use **endif** instead of **end if**.

- It is an error to have a ";" after **then** in an **if-then-elsif** construct.

- Do not forget to leave a space between the number and the time base designation. For example, it should read 10 **ns** and not 10**ns**.

- Use underscore and not hyphens in label names. Thus, not half-adder but half_adder.

- Expressions on the right-hand side of an assignment statement may have binary numbers expressed as x"00000000." When we use the IEEE 1164 types, even though std_logic_vector is a vector of bit signals, they are not the same type as x"00000000." Simulators may require you to perform a type conversion operation to convert the type of this binary number to std_logic_vector before you can make this assignment. The function to_stdlogicvector(x"00000000") is available in the package std_logic_1164 that is in the library IEEE. Check the documentation for the VHDL simulator you are using. Such type mismatches will be caught by the compiler.

6.10.2 Common Run-Time Errors

- It is not uncommon to sometimes use signals when you should use variables. Signals will be updated only after the next simulation cycle. Thus, you will find that values take effect later than you expected, for example, one clock cycle later.

- If you use more than one process to drive a signal, the value of the signal may be undefined unless you use resolved types and have specified a resolution function. Make sure there is only one source (e.g., process) for a signal unless you mean to have shared signals. When using the std_logic_1164 package, use std_logic and std_logic_vector types. These are resolved types that provide an associated resolution function.

- A process should have a sensitivity list or a wait statement.

- A process cannot have both a sensitivity list and a wait statement.

- Remember that all processes will be executed once when the simulation is started. This can sometimes cause unintended side effects if your processes are not explicitly controlled by wait statements.

- Suppose you have the following sequence of statements in a process.

```
wait until rising_edge(clk);
sig_a <= sig_x and sig_y;
sig_b <= sig_a;
```

When the second statement executes sig_b will be assigned the value of sig_a from the previous execution of the process. The signal sig_b will not be assigned the value computed by the previous statement during the current execution of the process. To understand the semantics consider the synchronous hardware implementation implied by the **wait** statement where sig_a and sig_b are stored in flip-flops. The output of the flip flop holding the value of sig_a will be the input of the flip-flop corresponding to sig_b. Because there is a finite delay between from inputs to outputs of the flip-flops we see that this behavior is preserved in the semantics of the VHDL signal assignment statements.

6.11 Chapter Summary

This chapter has introduced models that use processes and the use of sequential statements. This is a generalization of the behavioral models with concurrent signal assignment statements described in Chapter 4. The concepts introduced in this chapter include.

- Processes
- Sequential statements
  - if-then-else
  - case
  - loop
- Wait statements
- Attributes
- Communicating processes
- Modeling state machines
- Using both CSA statements and processes within the same architecture description

Exercises

1. Construct a VHDL model of a parity generator for 7-bit words. The parity bit is generated to create an even number of bits in the word with a value of 1. Do not prescribe propagation delays to any of the components. Simulate the model and check for functional correctness.

2. Explain why you cannot have both a sensitivity list and wait statements within a process.

3. Construct and test a model of a negative-edge-triggered JK flip-flop.

4. Consider the construction of a register file with eight registers, where each register is 32 bits. Implement the model with two processes. One process reads the register file, while another writes the register file. You can implement the registers as signals declared within the architecture and therefore visible to each process.

5. Implement a 32-bit ALU with support for the following operations: add, sub, and, or, and complement. The ALU should also produce an output signal that is asserted when the ALU output is 0. This signal may be used to implement branch instructions in a processor datapath.

6. Show an example of VHDL code that transforms an input periodic clock signal to an output signal at half the frequency.

7. Construct a VHDL model for generating four-phase non-overlapping clock signals. Pick your own parameters for pulse width and pulse separation intervals.

8. Implement and test a 16-bit up–down counter.

9. Implement and test a VHDL model for the state machine for a traffic-light controller [4] shown in Figure 6-26.

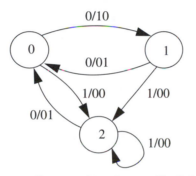

FIGURE 6-26 State machine for a traffic-light controller

10. Consider a variant of Simulation Exercise 6.3 where we are interested in the occurrence of six 1's in the bit stream. After six 1's have been detected, the output remains asserted until the state machine is reset. Construct and test this model.

11. Consider the following code sequence. At time 100 the process is activated due to an event (0 to 1) on signal x. At this time the values of signals sig_s1, sig_s2, y, and z are 0, 1, 1, and 0 respectively. What is the value of signal res2 scheduled for time 10 ns?

```
proc2: process (x, y, z) -- Process 2
begin
L1: sig_s1 <= (x and y) after 10 ns;
L2: sig_s2 <= (sig_s1 xor z) after 10 ns;
L3: res2 <= (sig_s1 nand sig_s2) after 10 ns;
end process;
```

CHAPTER 7

Modeling Behavior: Synthesis

This chapter examines the synthesis of VHDL models that contain sequential assignment statements encapsulated in the *process* construct. From the simulation perspective processes provide a powerful modeling abstraction. We can describe complex phenomena for the generation of events on digital signals and thus can develop and simulate models of digital systems at higher levels of abstraction than is feasible with only CSA statements. As a result models of complex devices such as modern microprocessors and memory systems become tractable.

However, as we increase the level of modeling abstraction, inferring hardware implementations becomes more difficult for several reasons. In general, when we construct VHDL models at higher levels of abstraction it is possible to infer multiple functionally equivalent hardware implementations and one of these implementations must be selected. Generally the inference process has more work to do. When dealing with CSA statements the relationship between signals and operators is explicitly captured in the signal assignment statements. Dataflow relationships between implementations of the operators lead to implementations of the circuit; with variables, processes, and conditional execution paths within a process these relationships are no longer necessarily explicit and must be uncovered by the synthesis compiler. As a result, optimizations to minimize the hardware or maximize circuit speed become increasingly complex and the synthesis compiler must "work harder" to generate efficient implementations. It also stands to reason that there is much to be gained by following some simple coding guidelines to ease the synthesis compiler's task.

This chapter adopts a complementary view of processes, namely from the point of view of inferring logical operators and storage, and describes some common inference mechanisms and associated coding styles.

7.1 A Language Directed View of Synthesis

When we model systems at higher levels of abstraction there is a tendency to write processes in the same manner that we write conventional programs in C or Pascal, forgetting that such coding styles are based on a model of computation that is quite different from the highly concurrent discrete event simulation model of VHDL programs. We forget that the purpose of the model is to describe hardware and not some sequential algorithm. This tends to lead to excessive logic and often long signal paths. Remember we are describing behaviors for which we must automatically generate digital logic. In general, digital hardware is inherently concurrent whereas C or Pascal programs are inherently sequential. We should keep this distinction in mind and strive to write programs that make it easy to identify concurrent activities. A good rule of thumb is to try and avoid long processes and promote concurrency within the models through the use of multiple processes and CSA statements.

To understand the problem of inferring hardware from processes it would be useful to first examine some key attributes of combinational and sequential circuits. An understanding of these attributes will go a long way towards understanding how hardware is inferred from sequential VHDL code.

Let us start with some key attributes of combinational logic circuits that do not have feedback, such as one shown in Figure 7-1. For every combination of input values the circuit computes the value of each output signal. Thus the value of an output signal is defined for *every* combination of values for the input signals. As a result the value of an output signal does not depend on its previous value and therefore the value does not have to be stored, for example in a flip-flop. Note the dependencies between gates in a combinational circuit. An intermediate signal, that is a signal that is neither an input signal or an output signal of the circuit, is assigned a value (from the output of one gate) *before* it is used to compute a new value (as the input to another gate). Because intermediate signals are defined prior to every use their value does not have to be "remembered," that is stored in latches or flip-flops. It stands to reason that if we are to write VHDL models that will produce combinational circuits after synthesis then the VHDL code must exhibit similar properties. For example every time a process is executed each output signal is assigned a value. Remember, VHDL is not a traditional programming language but rather a language for describing hardware. Specifically it describes how and when signals acquire values. Based on the preceding discussion of attributes of combinational circuits the VHDL analogy is the following. In a process if a signal of mode **out** is assigned a value for every combination of input values then the result will be combinational logic. Synthesis compilers are based on inference rules that rely on such hardware interpretations of VHDL code.

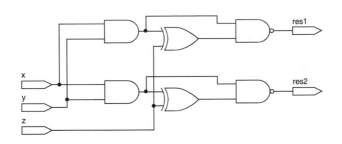

FIGURE 7-1 An example of a combinational circuit

Now consider sequential circuits. These circuits will have storage elements in the form of latches or flip-flops. Why do we need storage elements in a digital circuit? Because we often compute output signal values based on input signal values *and* values computed by the circuit at earlier points in time. These earlier values must be stored until they can be used. How does this phenomenon manifest itself in the VHDL code? Consider a process containing **if-then-else** constructs. It is possible that some execution of this process may not assign value to an output signal in the **else** part. In this case the signal must retain its previous value for potential use in the future and storage must be inferred. The next issue is whether this storage takes the form of edge triggered flip-flops, latches with enables, or flip-flops with two-phase clocking. Consider edge triggered flip-flops. These devices operate by sampling the value of an input signal on the rising or falling edge of another signal, usually the clock signal. To be able to infer flips flops from VHDL code we must be able to infer that a block of code that performs assignments of values to signals is sensitive to a clock edge. This can be achieved by identifying edge detection expressions such as "**wait until** (rising_edge(clk)". Latches are level sensitive devices and to be able to infer a latch from VHDL code we must be able to define when signal values must be preserved and under what conditions (to generate an enable signal) they are stored. These simple ideas will become concrete as we discuss specific language features and inference examples in the remainder of this chapter.

Although synthesis compilers can vary quite a bit with respect to specific inference mechanisms and optimization techniques, the preceding observations do lead to a few general principles that can be very helpful when writing VHDL code. The remainder of this chapter uses examples to describe common inferences that can be drawn from each of the language constructs used within processes. These examples can be used to guide our development of VHDL models.

7.2 Inference From Within Processes

When modeling for synthesis we must keep in mind that we are modeling hardware. We get the best results when we write statements keeping in mind we are trying to synthesize hardware. By doing do so we can generally avoid situations wherein we describe behavior

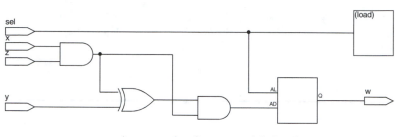

FIGURE 7-2 An example of a sequential circuit

that can be simulated but not necessarily synthesized efficiently. Thus, understanding how programming language constructs within processes imply hardware is useful in avoiding unintended redundant hardware and/or long signal paths. This section examines implications for hardware inference from the most common programming constructs used to build processes.

7.2.1 Simple Assignment Statements

Let us consider the simplest case of variable and signal assignment as shown in Figure 7-3. The example contains two processes. The first process contains a sequence of variable assignment statements whereas the second contains a sequence of signal assignment statements. Both sequences of statements exhibit data dependencies between them. These dependencies are extracted by the synthesis compiler and captured as interconnections between the operators used in the statements. The synthesized circuit follows the structure of the assignment statements. Note that the structure of the circuits for computing **res1** and **res2** are identical. This simple example illustrates a principle that is applied to any sequence of VHDL statements, namely operator inferencing and dependence analysis. Sequences of straight-line code in a process lead to the synthesis of combinational logic.

There is one other important difference between the two processes. The first process uses variable assignments whereas the second uses signal assignment statements. From Chapter 6 we know that the simulation semantics state that the values of **sig_s1** and **sig_s2** used to compute the value of **res2** in **proc2** should be the values of the signals **sig_s1** and **sig_s2** when the process in invoked and not the new values that are assigned when the process is executed. However, synthesis compilers will generally optimize this sequence to produce combinational logic and avoid latches.This is exactly what happens when the code of **proc1** is synthesized. The variable assignments are collapsed into a combinational circuit. We expect this for variable assignment statements because unlike signals, variable assignments take place immediately. Finally, note that **sig_s1** is not in the sensitivity list of the process. If there were another process writing **sig_s1** during simulation the process would not be executed. However, from the synthesized hardware we can see that any externally introduced change in the value of **sig_s1** will cause the circuit to recompute the values of its output signals. Therefore simulation semantics may not match the behavior of the synthesized circuit.

```
library IEEE;
use IEEE.std_logic_1164.all;

entity sig_var is
port (x, y, z: in std_logic;
res1, res2 : out std_logic);
end entity sig_var;

architecture behavior of sig_var is
signal sig_s1, sig_s2 : std_logic;
begin
proc1: process (x, y, z) is -- Process 1 using variables
variable var_s1, var_s2: std_logic;
begin
var_s1 := x and y;
var_s2 := var_s1 xor z;
res1 <= var_s1 nand var_s2;
end process;
proc2: process (x, y, z) -- Process 2 using signals
begin
sig_s1 <= x and y;
sig_s2 <= sig_s1 xor z;
res2 <= sig_s1 nand sig_s2;
end process;
end architecture behavior;
```

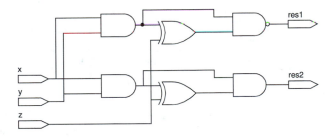

FIGURE 7-3 An example of inference from sequential assignment statements

The preceding example is quite short. However it is not hard to envision a process with a sequential block of code that is tens of statements long with data dependencies between them. Or we may have individual statements composed of many operators. The result may be a long chain of dependencies between statements. For example we may have a sequence of statements appearing as follows:

$$s1 <= .....$$
$$s2 <= ... s1 ...$$
$$s3 <= ...s2 ...$$
$$s4 <= ...s3....$$

and so on

The computation of the value of signal s4 uses the value of signal s1 through the computation of several intermediate signals. The result is long signal paths in the synthesized logic. The same principles apply to the use of variables rather than signals.

Rather than sequential blocks of code what if we have conditional blocks of code? Some output signals may or may not be assigned values depending upon the execution path. In this case the result is a sequential circuit with storage in the form of latches or flip-flops depending on how the conditions are specified. These cases are considered next.

7.2.2 If-Then-Else and If-Then-Elsif Statements

An **if** statement is executed by evaluating an expression and conditionally executing a block of sequential statements. The structure may optionally include an **else** component. The statement may also include zero or more **elsif** branches (note the absence of the letter 'e' in **elsif**). In this case all of the boolean valued expressions are evaluated sequentially until the first true expression is encountered. Let us start from the simplest program and consider this behavior from a hardware perspective. In particular let us focus on the "conditionally executing" aspect. Consider the example shown in Figure 7-4.

If the value of sel is 1 then the value of the signal w is computed as shown in the code. What if the value of sel is 0? What then should be the value of w? Clearly the current value of w should be unaltered. In hardware terms the value of a signal is unaltered or retained by storing it in a latch or flip flop. In this case a latch is inferred as shown in Figure 7-4. The combinational logic preceding the latch represents the implementation of the three expressions forming the body of the **then** clause and computes the new value of the signal w. Finally note the generation of an enable signal for the latch using the signal sel.

If we wish to avoid having latches inferred from conditional language constructs during synthesis then we need to follow one simple rule – ensure that every output signal is assigned a value on any execution of the process. For an **if-then-else** statement this means that all output signals must be assigned a value within the **then** *and* **else** parts. For nested statements such as **if-then-elsif** we must ensure that all output signals are assigned values in *every* branch. Alternatively we can assign each output signal a default value prior to the **if** statement. Assignment of default values to output signals will ensure that for every combination of input values that invokes the process each output signal is explicitly assigned a value. This behavior is exactly that of combinational logic! Thus no latches will be inferred. From the narrower perspective of the **if** statement we conclude that we must

```
library IEEE;
use IEEE.std_logic_1164.all;

entity inf_latch is
port (sel : in std_logic;
        x, y, z: in std_logic;
        w: out std_logic );
end entity inf_latch;

architecture behavior of inf_latch is
begin
process (x, y, z, sel) is
variable s1, s2: std_logic;
begin
if (sel = '1')then
s1 := x and z;
s2 := s1 xor y;
w <= s2 and s1;  -- w gets a value only conditionally
 end if;              -- hence a latch is inferred

end process;
```

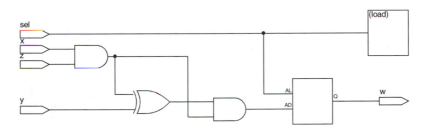

FIGURE 7-4 Synthesis of conditional expressions and latch inference

always include the **else** branch to avoid inferring a latch for this block of code. Figure 7-5 shows the example of Figure 7-4 rewritten to assign default values to the signal w. Note the absence of the latch in the synthesized logic. Any time the process is executed w will receive a value just as in the synthesized combinational logic circuit.

If we structure our code to avoid latch inferencing our focus can then shift to the efficiency of the synthesized combinational logic. Efficiency is typically measured in terms of speed and/or size. The manner in which you structure your code can have a significant impact on the logic that is generated. For example, consider the block of code and the associated synthesized logic shown in Figure 7-6. We have a logical AND operation being performed in both branches of the **if** statement. The synthesized logic shows that one two-

```
library IEEE;
use IEEE.std_logic_1164.all;

entity inf_latch is
port (sel : in std_logic;
x, y, z: in std_logic;
w: out std_logic );
end entity inf_latch;

architecture behavior of inf_latch is
begin
process (x, y, z, sel) is
variable s1, s2: std_logic;
begin
w <= '0'; -- output signal set to a default value to avoid latch inference
if (sel = '1')then
s1 := x and z; -- body generates combinational logic
s2 := s1 xor y;
w <= s2 and s1;
 end if;

end process;
end architecture behavior;
```

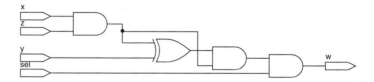

FIGURE 7-5 Avoiding latch inferencing via initialization

input AND gate has been synthesized for each branch and then a multiplexor has been synthesized to select a value from one of the two branches based on the value of the signal sel. The general principle here is that the combinational logic is generated for each branch of an **if-then-else** construct. A multiplexor is generated to select the outcome corresponding to the branch determined by the value of the sel signal.

However, by being a bit careful about how we write the code we can produce a more efficient circuit. For example, the VHDL code of Figure 7-6 is rewritten in Figure 7-7. First we note that the two branches in Figure 7-6 differ in the following way: in the second operand for the logical AND operation. The **then** part selects y as the second operand whereas the **else** part selects z. If we first select the correct operand and then perform the logical AND operation we can save a single AND gate. We can do so as follows. Use a

```
library IEEE;
use IEEE.std_logic_1164.all;

entity inference is
port (sel : in std_logic;
x, y, z: in std_logic;
w: out std_logic );
end entity inference;

architecture behavior of inference is
begin
process (x, y, z, sel) is
begin
if (sel = '1')then
w <= x and y;
 else
w <= x and z;
 end if;
end process;
end architecture behavior;
```

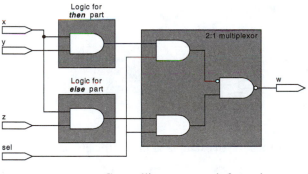

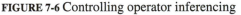

FIGURE 7-6 Controlling operator inferencing

local variable, right, to first select the values of the operators and then perform the logical AND operation. In this case we see from Figure 7-7 that the synthesized circuit is composed of the multiplexor followed by a single two-input AND gate. This corresponds to the idea of first selecting the operators (via the multiplexor) and then performing the operation (using the AND gate). In this particular example this may not seem to be a very large savings. However, consider an example where instead of the single-bit logical AND operations we have the addition of 32-bit quantities. In this case we see that the code rewritten as shown in Figure 7-7 produces one less 32-bit adder. The general principle here is to

```
library IEEE;
use IEEE.std_logic_1164.all;

entity inference is
port (sel : in std_logic;
x, y, z: in std_logic;
w: out std_logic );
end inference;

architecture behavior of inference is
begin
process (x, y, z, sel)
variable right: std_logic;
begin
if (sel = '1')then
right := y;
 else
right := z;
 end if;
w <= x and right;

end process;
end behavior;
```

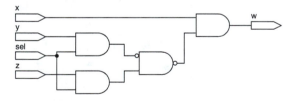

FIGURE 7-7 An example of more efficient operator inferencing

move complex or hardware intensive operations that are replicated in the **then** and **else** branches out of the **if-then-else** statement. Such coding styles help us control how much hardware is generated and are similar to the use of parentheses to control how synthesized modules are interconnected as described in Chapter 5 and illustrated in Figure 5-2.

How about multiple levels of nesting as found in **if-then-elsif** statements? The issue of inference from conditional blocks of code extend naturally to multiple levels of nesting as illustrated in the following example.

Example: Multiple Levels of Nesting

Consider the example shown in Figure 7-8. Here we see a block of code that is three levels deep. Note that in this circuit, although the signal res appears to be assigned a value in every branch, a latch is inferred. We can see why if we consider the case where all of the select signals have a value of 0. In this case the signal res is not assigned a value and thus a latch must be inferred. If we wish to avoid inferring a latch we must add an else branch at the end of the statement so that it appears as follows:

```
elsif (sel3 ='1') then
res <= x or y;
else
res <= '0';
 end if;
```

   Now the signal res is assigned a value on every execution of the process and latches can be avoided.

   When we write such nested constructs we implicitly place a priority ordering on the assignment statements. Thus we expect that the synthesized code will reflect this priority order which is indeed the case. We can see in the synthesized circuit pairs of gates in the first column. These gates reflect the computation of signal values and priority order based on the values of the signals sel1, sel2, and sel3. The three input OR gate computes the new value of the latch that contains the value of the signal res. The priority order of the inputs are controlled by gating the new signal values with priority signals computed from the values of sel1, sel2, and sel3. The highest priority is given by the case when sel1 has the value 1. In this case we see that the output from the logic corresponding to the two other branches are disabled. If sel1 is de-asserted and sel2 is asserted the logic corresponding to the last branch is disabled regardless of the value of sel3. Thus we see the synthesis compiler has created circuits that implement the computations and that are controlled by the circuits that capture the priority order implied by the written code.

Example End: Multiple Levels of Nesting

Processes can certainly become quite a bit larger than the examples shown here. If an if-then-else statement were nested in a larger block of code that was written in manner that caused a latch to be inferred then it really does not matter how the if-then-else statement is constructed with respect to making assignments to output signals. If you wish to generate combinational logic for a block of code, then you you need to avoid embedding the code in a larger block that causes latches to be inferred. The logic for generating the latch enable signals is derived from the conditional expressions. This follows our intuition because it is this expression that determines which branch of the if statement is taken and whether an output signal is to acquire a new value.

```
library IEEE;
use IEEE.std_logic_1164.all;

entity nested_if is
port (sel1, sel2, sel3 : in std_logic;
x, y, z: in std_logic;
res : out std_logic );
end nested_if;

architecture behavior of nested_if is
begin
process (x,y,z,sel1,sel2,sel3)
begin
if (sel1 = '1')then
 res <= x and y;
elsif (sel2 ='1') then
res <= y xor z;
elsif (sel3 ='1') then
res <= x or y;
 end if;
end process;
end behavior;
```

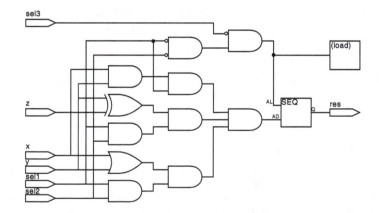

FIGURE 7-8 Synthesis with nested **if-then-elsif** statements

In Section 5.5 we discussed the issue with using don't care values in expressions when performing comparisons such as equality checks. From a hardware implementation perspective don't care values cannot be represented in hardware and cannot be compared to a signal value of 0 or 1. A hardware implementation can only compare the values of 0 and 1. For synthesis when one of the signals specified in a comparison operation uses don't care values the comparison is always assumed to return false! The synthesized hardware is based on this comparison always being false. The following example illustrates this point.

Example: Using Don't Cares in Conditional Expressions

The example code in Figure 7-9 illustrates the use if don't cares in the conditional expression. For synthesis this comparison always returns false. As a result the synthesis compiler can determine that the **then** branch is never taken. The result is that this code synthesizes to a single two-input NOR gate. This behavior may not be what the application developer intended.

```
library IEEE;
use IEEE.std_logic_1164.all;

entity sig_var is
port ( sel : in std_logic_vector (1 downto 0);
        x, y, z: in std_logic;
        w : out std_logic);
end entity sig_var;

architecture behavior of sig_var is
begin
process (x, y, z) is
begin
if (sel = "– 0") then -- the symbol "–" represents the don't care
w <= x xnor y;     -- for std_logic types
else
w <= x nor z;
end if;

end process;
end architecture behavior;
```

FIGURE 7-9 Effect of don't care values in the synthesis of comparison logic

Example End: Using Don't Cares in Conditional Expressions

We have seen several examples of how processes can be synthesized to combinational logic. The following exercise provides us with and opportunity to make our understanding a bit more concrete.

Synthesis Exercise 7.1: Basic Examples

The purpose of this simulation exercise is to establish an intuition for how signal and variable values are represented in hardware. We will use the following example architecture.

Step 1. Create the following VHDL model.

```
library IEEE;
use IEEE.std_logic_1164.all;

entity example is
port ( sel : in std_logic;
        x, y, z: in std_logic;
        w: out std_logic);
end entity example;

architecture behavior of example is
begin
process (w, x, y, z, sel) is
variable s1, s2, s3: std_logic;
begin
w <= '0'; -- set to a default value to avoid latch inference
if (sel = '1')then
s1 := x and z; -- body generates combinational logic
s2 := s1 xor y;
w <= (x and s1) or s2;
 end if;
end process;
end architecture behavior;
```

Step 2. Compile the model for the CAD toolset you are using.

Step 3. Using vendor specific commands select a target set of hardware primitives for synthesis, in our case an FPGA device. In the process you may also select several other options such as level of effort, optimization for speed or area, and target clock frequency.

Step 4. Synthesize the design.

Step 5. View the schematics of the hardware implementation. Identify the signals (wires) in the circuit that correspond to the variables s1 and s2.

Step 6. Now re-synthesize the circuit with the initialization statement for w removed. View the schematics of the synthesized design. What differences do you see?

Step 7. Now add and **else** branch to the statement in the process and in this **else** branch ensure that the signal w is assigned a value.

Step 8. Re-synthesize and view the schematics. How has the circuit changed?

Step 9. In the preceding steps, in the instances that latch has been inferred, what is the latch enable signal?

End Synthesis Exercise 7.1

7.2.3 Case Statement

The case statement is equivalent to a nested set of **if-then-elsif** constructs and similar considerations apply for synthesis. The **case** statement identifies mutually exclusive blocks of code. Recall that the language requires that only one branch of a **case** can be true and collectively the branches must cover all possible values of the select expression. The **others** clause is provided to make it easy to ensure that all possible values of the select expression are indeed covered. What type of hardware structure bears a strong resemblance to the **case** statement? Selecting one of several possible alternatives suggests a multiplexor with the values of the select expression providing the control signals for the multiplexor!

If an output signal in the process receives a value in all branches of the case then combinational logic is inferred to compute the value of that signal because each time the process is activated the output signal is guaranteed to have a new value computed. An example of this is illustrated in Figure 7-10. Note how the logic for each branch of the case is synthesized to compute a new value for the signal res. This signal value is gated with logic that is sensitive to the value of the signal sel, which is a two-bit signal because it is an integer with a range of values between 0 and 3. The logical OR of the outputs of all four branches is computed to produce the value of the output signal.

However a signal may not be assigned a value in every branch of the **case** statement. For example, the target of the **when others** clause can be **null** signifying that in this case the value of res should remain unaltered. In this instance a latch will be inferred to retain the old value of the signal res. This example is illustrated in Figure 7-11. We can avoid latch inferences by having an initialization statement prior to the case. For example suppose we were to precede the case statement in Figure 7-11 with the statement

res <= '0';

Now we would be guaranteed that every execution of the process will assign a value to the signal res and no latch will be inferred. If don't care values are used in the "**when others**" clause often synthesis compilers can use this information to optimize the generated hardware.

```
library IEEE;
use IEEE.std_logic_1164.all;

entity case_ex is
port ( sel : in integer range 0 to 3;
x, y, z: in std_logic;
res : out std_logic );
end entity case_ex;

architecture behavior of case_ex is
begin
process (x,y,z,sel) is
begin
case sel is
when 0 => res <= x and y;
when 1 => res <= y xor z;
when 2 => res <= x nand z;
when others => res <= x nor z;
end case;
end process;
end architecture behavior;
```

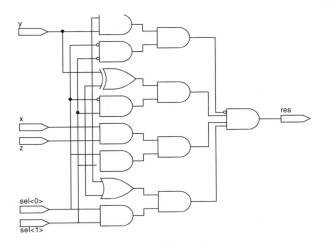

FIGURE 7-10 An example of the synthesis of the **case** statement

Any **case** statement does have an equivalent (functionally) formulation in an **if-then-elsif** form. However the latter must produce priority logic to maintain the priority order implicit in the nesting of the branches. This is not the case for the case statement. As a

```
library IEEE;
use IEEE.std_logic_1164.all;

entity case_ex is
port ( sel : in integer range 0 to 3;
x, y, z: in std_logic;
res : out std_logic );
end entity case_ex;

architecture behavior of case_ex is
begin
process (x,y,z,sel) is
begin
case sel is
when 0 => res <= x and y;
when 1 => res <= y xor z;
when 2 => res <= x nand z;
when others => null;     -- in this case the value of res remains
end case;                -- unaltered
end process;
end architecture behavior;
```

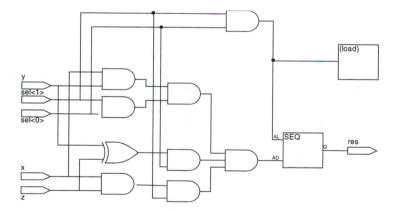

FIGURE 7-11 An example of latch inference from a **case** statement

result we would expect that the case statement is a more efficient alternative when there is no priority ordering among the alternatives.

7.2.4 Loop Statements

Although there are several constructs for iteration the **for-loop** is the most common one supported by synthesis compilers. The reason for this is as follows. At compile-time we must be able to infer the amount of hardware to be synthesized. When we use a **while-loop** it is not always possible to determine how many times the loop will be executed because the while condition may be data dependent. If this is the case then how can a fixed amount of logic be synthesized? The answer is to synthesize a state machine controller to cycle a datapath a data dependent number of times. However, the semantics of the **for-loop** simplifies the inference process. When we use a **for-loop** the maximum value of the loop index evaluates to a constant and the number of iterations is known exactly. The loop can now be replaced with an equivalent sequential block of code created by making a number of copies of the loop body with the number of copies being given by the number of iterations. For example consider the following block of code.

```
for N in 3 downto 1 loop
shift_reg (n) <= shift_reg (n-1);
end loop;
```

The preceding loop will execute three times. We can replace this loop with the following equivalent sequential code.

```
shift_reg (3) <= shift_reg (2);
shift_reg (2) <= shift_reg (1);
shift_reg (1) <= shift_reg (0);
```

This technique is referred to as *loop unrolling* and is a standard optimization technique in modern compilers for most languages. If the number of iterations are known the loop body can be unrolled by the compiler resulting in a sequential program composed of a sequence of statements such as variable assignment, signal assignment, **if-then-else**, and **case**. This sequence of statements can now be treated as any sequential code sequence in a process, several examples of which have been described earlier in this chapter.

Example: Loop Unrolling

An example of loop unrolling and synthesis is provided by the code shown in Figure 7-12. This example illustrates a model of a 4-bit shift register with a global reset to initialize the value to 0. Note that the output signal res is in the body of an **if-then** statement. We know that a latch must be inferred. The latch enable signal is normally synthesized from the predicate being tested in the **if** clause. This predicate is a call to the function rising_edge (clk). In effect this **if** statement makes the code in the **then** part conditioned on the occurrence of a rising edge on the signal clk. Therefore, rather than a latch this use

```
library IEEE;
use IEEE.std_logic_1164.all;

entity iteration is
port (clk, reset, data : in std_logic;
res : out std_logic_vector(3 downto 0));
end entity iteration;

architecture behavior of iteration is
signal shift_reg : std_logic_vector(3 downto 0);
begin
process (clk, reset, data) is
begin
if (rising_edge(clk)) then
if (reset = '1') then res <= "0000";
else
for n in 3 downto 1 loop
shift_reg(n) <= shift_reg(n-1);
end loop;
shift_reg(0) <= data;
res <= shift_reg;
end if;
end if;
end process;
end architecture behavior;
```

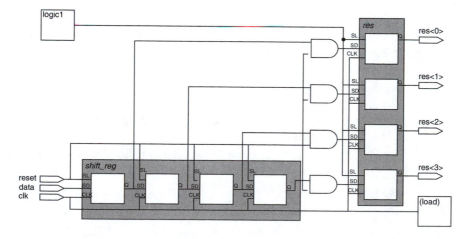

FIGURE 7-12 Loop unrolling and the synthesis of a **for-loop**

of the function **rising_edge** (clk) causes edge-triggered flip-flops to be inferred. The body of the loop will be unrolled leading to a sequence of dependent signal assignment statements each of which will result in the inference of a flip flop with the output of one connected to the input of another, The synthesized circuit is also shown in Figure 7-12 and the flip-flops corresponding to the signals **res** and **shift_reg** are identified. Note the logic synthesized for the global reset.

Example End: Loop Unrolling

Some synthesis compilers will place constraints on the type of the loop index. For example they may have to be integers or only subsets of array types. Refer to the vendor specific documentation to ensure compliance with any constraints on the loop index. In Section 7.2.1 we pointed out how dependencies can lead to long signal paths in synthesized logic. In **for-loops** these dependencies can appear across loop iterations. For example the value of a signal computed in one loop iteration can be dependent upon a value computed in the previous iteration. When the loop is unrolled we may end up with a long sequence of statements with a signal value propagating from the one of the early statements to an assignment statement near the end of the block of code. The result is a long signal path in the synthesized logic. If we formulate our VHDL models to avoid dependencies and promote concurrency we can generally create faster circuits.

Synthesis Exercise 7.2: Comparison of Modeling Approaches

This exercise enables a comparison between the use of a nested **if-then-elsif** construct and the **case** statement.

Step 1. Using a text editor create a model composed of a single process. The process implements an 8-to-1 priority encoder. The component has single-bit input signals and three single-bit output signals. The priority order of the inputs are 7, 3, 5, 2, 1, 0, 4, and 6. There is also a single bit valid input signal that when asserted will enable the output.

    Step 1 (a) Construct a model using a nested **if-then-elsif** construct. For example, the inputs would be tested in priority order.

    Step 1 (b) Construct a model of the same component using a **case** statement.

    Step 1 (c) In both models make the process sensitive to all input signals

Step 2. Use the types bit and bit_vector for the input and output signals. Because these are VHDL predefined types you avoid declaration and reference to the library IEEE and the package std_logic_1164.

Step 3. Compile or analyze the models for the CAD toolset you are using.

Step 4. Using vendor specific commands select a target set of hardware primitives for synthesis, in our case an FPGA device. In the process you may also select several other options such as level of effort, optimization for speed or area, and target clock frequency.

Step 5. Synthesize both of the designs.

Step 6. View the schematics of the hardware implementation.

> **Step 6 (a)** What differences do you see in the implementation of the **case** statement and the nested **if-then-elsif** statement?

> **Step 6 (b)** What is the reason for the differences in the logic that is synthesized? Can you relate these differences to the process of inference?

> **Step 6 (c)** What can you infer about when it would be better to use one modeling approach over the other?

Step 7. Now simulate the synthesized hardware. Depending on the vendor tools you may be able to simulate prior to placement and routing. We can start this process by generating a waveform on each of the input signals and tracing the output signals.

Step 8. Study the trace and ensure that the model is operating correctly. Find the delay from the input signals to the output signal.

Step 9. Now place and route this design on the target FPGA. Generate a report providing the statistics the placed and routed design. These statistics will be in terms of vendor specific quantities. For example in the Xilinx Foundation tools you will be provided with the number of CLBs utilized by the design and you can also display the placed and routed design.

End Synthesis Exercise 7.2

7.3 Miscellaneous Issues

The sensitivity list is very important for simulation because it determines when a process is executed. When inferring the hardware to implement a process the sensitivity list may be ignored because it is the dependencies between signals and variables that determine what the hardware computes. When a process is synthesized it naturally implements all of the signals manipulated in the process. If there are no wait statements in the process all of the signals in a process are implicitly assumed to be in the sensitivity list by the synthesis compiler. Often processes written for simulation may not include all of the signals in the sensitivity list. This will result in mismatches between pre-synthesis and post-synthesis simulation results. For example, suppose that a process uses values from three input signals, In1, In2, and In3 but the process sensitivity list only includes the signals In1 and In2. During the course of the simulation, every time there is a change in the value of the signal In1 or In2 the process is executed. However, a change in the value of In3 does not lead to the activation and execution of the process. Now let us suppose that this process is synthesized and implemented, say, in a Xilinx FPGA. Let us assume that the process was written in such a manner as to lead to a combinational logic implementation. The hardware implementation does not ignore changes in the value of the input signal In3. The behavior of the synthesized circuit may not exactly follow the behavior of the simulated circuit before synthesis. We cannot use these comparisons to validate the correctness of the synthesized circuit. To avoid such mismatches, one should include all of the signals of a process in the sensitivity list when performing simulations.

A variable that holds a temporary value may not be implemented as a wire. This appeals to our intuition in that digital logic is about signals. Variables can be thought of as the programming language objects that make our job of describing the behavior of circuits easier. They are typically used to transfer values between statements in a process. Standard compiler optimizations can collapse variable assignment statements and eliminate some intermediate variables. When it is not possible to do so then variables may be synthesized to a wire between operators, that is, gates.

In general we need to maintain an **architecture** level view of synthesis. For example, we cannot try and apply our understanding of inference rules to small blocks of code. The structure of the larger block of code within these smaller blocks reside will determine whether latches are inferred. Consider the following structure of VHDL code.

```
L1: if (s1 = '1') then
 ..
L2:   if (s2 = '1') then
            Aout <= '1';
        else
            Aout <= '0';
        end if;
end if;
 ..
 ..
```

If we were examining just statement L2 we could erroneously conclude that a latch is not inferred for the signal Aout because it garners an assignment in both branches of the conditional statement. However, L2 is nested within L1, which is conditionally executed. Therefore a latch must be inferred for Aout.

One rather subtle issue to be kept in mind is the nature of enumerated types such as std_logic. We think of a signal of type std_logic as a single bit-signal that can take on one of nine values. One of these values is a don't care value. CAD tools treat this value as exactly that, a value; it is not treated as don't care value as is used in logic minimization. One important consequence of this is in comparisons. In our logic courses a comparison to a don't care value is always regarded as true and we create digital logic that reflects the fact that the actual value of this signal is inconsequential. In synthesis tools where this value of std_logic signals is treated as a value and not a condition such optimizations are not possible. Comparisons to don't care values are defined to always return false because there is no hardware or physical analog to a don't care value. We are caught in this situation because these enumerated types provide powerful simulation modeling paradigms and we are using the same types for synthesis. This has led to definition of packages such as Numeric_std in support of the IEEE 1164 value system for synthesis.

Even in simulation we are often faced with the problem of modeling the computation of output values that are also used elsewhere in the same circuit. This creates a problem in determining the type of the output signal because it is also being read. This problem and a solution is illustrated in the following example.

Example: Buffer and Inout Entity Modes

Consider the following code sequence that is embedded in a process that is written to generate combinational logic, that is every path through the process will make assignments to Aout and Bout.

$$\text{Aout} <= \text{In1 \textbf{and} In2};$$
$$\text{Bout} <= \text{Aout \textbf{xor} In3};$$

Aout is being driven as an output signal and is also being read internally as part of the computation of other output signals. In order to facilitate this modeling style, VHDL provides the **port** signal modes **buffer** or **inout**. The former permits signals in the interface to serve as outputs and be read internally. The latter identifies bidirectional signals. When we begin to construct hierarchical models (Chapter 8) then we need ensure that **port** types in entities are compatible up and down the hierarchy. This can be tedious to keep track of. An alternative is to use variables internally to compute the values of the output signals and then make single assignment at the end of the process. In this case the preceding code sequence could be rewritten as follows:

$$\text{VarAout} := \text{In1 \textbf{and} In2};$$
$$\text{Bout} <= \text{VarAout \textbf{xor} In3};$$
$$\text{Aout} <= \text{VarAout};$$

As long the preceding block is not in a conditional block of code then the two versions are equivalent.

Example End: Buffer and Inout Entity Modes

7.4 Inference Using Signals vs. Variables

Signals correspond to hardware objects. Thus signals are synthesized into wires or storage devices such as latches and flip-flops. Variables are programming objects that are used (typically) to compute the values of signals. The dependencies between variables are used for the purpose of propagating values in the computation of some signal value. Thus you do not expect all variables to be synthesized into hardware, but in some instances they may be represented in hardware. The following example will illustrate these crucial differences.

Figure 7-13 provides a simple example with two **if** statements, labeled L1 and L2, within the same process. Statement L1 contains two signal assignment statements. The value of the signal sig_s1 is an input to the computation of the new value of signal v. Because both assignment statements are in a conditional branch, latches are inferred for both signals. The computation of the value of v uses the old value of sig_s1 that is contained in the latch. When executing, the existing value of sig_s1 must be used in the computation of the new value of signal v. This is reflected in the structure of the synthesized hardware as identified in Figure 7-13. Now consider the second block of code in the example. Here we have only one signal assignment statement that uses the *current* value computed for the variable var_s1 in the following signal assignment statement. The structure of this part of the synthesized circuit that does not include a latch is also identified in Figure 7-13. We might regard the value of the variable var_s1 as being synthesized into a wire, specifically the wire connecting the output of the AND gate to the input of the XOR gate. Finally we see that a 2-to-1 multiplexor has been synthesized to select the new value of v computed by one of the blocks of code. The selection is based on the value of the signal sel. In summary we see that the new value of v is stored in a latch and this value is computed from one of two possible sources. One source requires uses an existing value of sig_s1 whereas another uses the current value of var_s1.

It would appear that every execution path through the process would set the value of v. Why then is a latch inferred for v? Why do we not see a combinational circuit for the computation of v? The answer is because the signal sel is of type std_logic, and it may take on values other than '0' or '1'. Therefore not every execution path through the process will set the value of v and hence a latch is inferred.

Latches may also be inferred for variables under certain conditions. An example is shown in Figure 7-14. The presence of the **wait** statement and the clock expression causes a flip-flop to be inferred for the signal res. However note the variable var_s2. This variable is used before it is defined. This inference follows from the semantics of the process. Variables in processes retain their values across invocations. Therefore a flip-flop is inferred when a variable is used before it is defined. Subsequent computations to determine the value of var_s2 forms the input to this flip-flop. This is again a condition wherein there is some execution sequence, namely the first, that does not compute the value of a variable or signal.

```
library IEEE;
use IEEE.std_logic_1164.all;

entity sig_var is
port (sel : in std_logic;
x, y, z: in std_logic;
v, w: out std_logic );
end entity sig_var;

architecture behavior of sig_var is
signal sig_s1 : std_logic;
begin
process (x, y, z, sel)
variable var_s1: std_logic;
begin
L1: if (sel = '1')then          latch inferred for sig_s1
sig_s1 <= x and z;
v <= sig_s1 xor y;
end if;

L2: if (sel = '0') then          no latch inferred for var_s1
var_s1 := x and z;
v <= var_s1 xor y;
end if;
end process;
end architecture behavior;
```

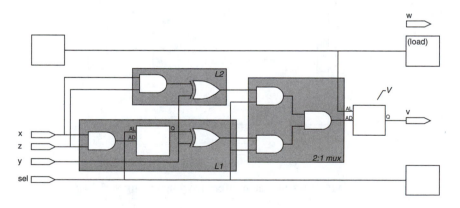

FIGURE 7-13 Inference from signals vs. variables

```
library IEEE;
use IEEE.std_logic_1164.all;

entity sig_var is
port (clk, x, y, z: in std_logic;
res : out std_logic);
end sig_var;

architecture behavior of sig_var is
begin
process
variable var_s1, var_s2 :std_logic;
begin
wait until (rising_edge(clk));
var_s1 := x nand var_s2;
var_s2 := var_s1 xor y;
res <= var_s1 xor var_s2;
end process;
end behavior;
```

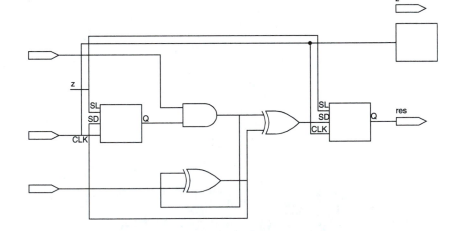

FIGURE 7-14 Latch inference when using variables

7.5 Latch vs. Flip-Flop Inference

Generally **if**, **case**, **wait**, conditional signal assignment statements, and selected signal assignment statements can be used to infer latches because they describe programming constructs where code is conditionally executed. If the conditional part is specified as level detection, for example as in

> **if** (sel = '1') **then.**

latches are inferred. However if the conditional expression represents edge detection, for example as in

> **if** (rising_edge (clk)) **then.**

edge-triggered flip-flops are inferred. The conditional expression may also take the form

> **if** (clk'**event and** clk = '1') **then.**

The preceding expression may not detect a 0 to 1 transition on the signal clk if it is of type std_logic. For example, the expression could also detect a transition from X to 1. For true rising edge detection one must also know that an event occurred on the signal and the previous value of the signal was 0. The VHDL language provides a signal attribute known as **last_value**. Thus clk'**last_value** will return the previous value of clk and can be tested to ensure a 0 to 1 transition. Although this works fine in simulation this attribute is not supported in synthesis tools. The reason for this is that it is a function that has nothing to do with the physical implementation of the circuit but rather is only concerned with enabling the accurate simulation modeling of the behavior of the circuit. Simulators can record the last value of a signal for the purposes of mimicing true rising edge detection. However, if we are to synthesize a physical device that operates on a rising edge of a signal we realize that clk'**last_value** has no appropriate physical analog. Rather we must recognize edge detection expressions and select the right flip-flop, namely positive- or negative-edge triggered, from our target library. The simplest approach to inferring edge-triggered flip-flops is to use the functions rising_edge (clk) and falling_edge (clk) in conditional expressions.

The use of level sensitive conditional expressions or edge detection expressions should be guided by the parts available in our target library. For example, if latches are not available then the synthesis tools may try to create a latch by synthesizing the gate level equivalents. This can complicate timing analysis and render the circuit much more difficult to debug. The choice of coding style should be guided by the building blocks that we have to operate with. The Xilinx XC4000 series FPGAs support both edge-triggered and level-sensitive devices.

Finally, there is the issue of using asynchronous or synchronous clear and set signals. This is a function of the parts that are available within the library you are using. Synthesis compilers will generally synthesize the logic that determines the set and preset signals from the conditional expressions such as those used in the **if** statements. If the target set of parts that used by the synthesis compiler does not have asynchronous clear or set signals then an error message will be generated when the design is optimized for the specific target architecture in question. For example find and state what the primitives are for the Virtex and XC4000 parts. This issue is illustrated in the following example:

Example: Flip-Flop Inferencing with Asynchronous Reset

Consider the example of flip-flop inferencing shown in Figure 7-15. The figure shows the model of a 4-bit synchronous counter. The counter model is captured in an edge-triggered section of code. Therefore all of the signals in this section of code will be implemented with flip-flops. However, pay attention to the value of the variable var_count. This variable needs to retain its value between invocations of the process because it stores the current count value. We know that process variables retain their values between invocations. The variable var_count is also used before it is defined. Therefore flip-flops are also inferred for this variable too. The synthesized circuit is shown in Figure 7-16. The circuit includes one adder module to compute the new count value. One of the inputs of the adder is hardwired to the value 0001. The second input is the value of var_count from a set of four flip-flops. Finally we have four flip-flops at the output to hold the value of res. The additional logic supports reset and initialization.

```
library IEEE;
use IEEE.std_logic_1164.all;
use IEEE.std_logic_arith.all;

entity counter is
port (clk, reset : in std_logic;
res : out unsigned (3 downto 0));
end entity counter;

architecture behavior of counter is
begin
process (clk, reset)
variable var_count : unsigned (3 downto 0);
begin
if (rising_edge (clk)) then
if (reset = '1') then res <= "0000";
else
var_count := var_count + 1;
end if;
res <= var_count;
end if;
end process;
end architecture behavior;
```

FIGURE 7-15 Flip-flop inference from a model of a synchronous counter

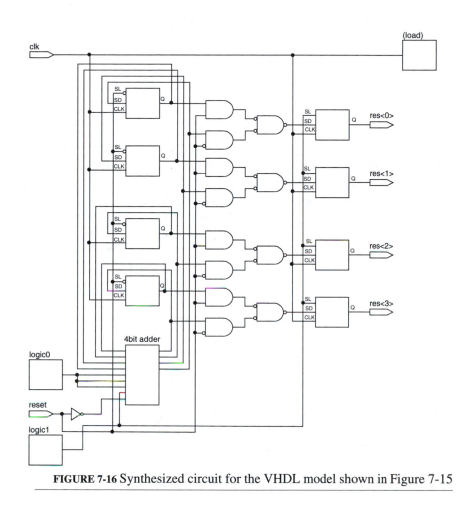

FIGURE 7-16 Synthesized circuit for the VHDL model shown in Figure 7-15

Example End: Flip-Flop Inferencing with Asynchronous Reset

7.6 The Wait Statement

Recall from Chapter 2 that the inclusion of the **wait** statement in VHDL is motivated by the need to model circuits wherein events happen at specific points in time such as the occurrence of a clock edge. This captured in the following form of the wait statement

    wait until *condition*;

where *condition* is a boolean expression that is true when a clock edge arrives. Example forms include:

> **wait until** (clk'**event** and clk = '1');
>
> **wait until** (rising_edge (clk);
>
> **wait until** (falling_edge (clk);

From a synthesis perspective a **wait** statement implies synchronous logic. The functions rising_edge () and falling_edge () are defined in the std_logic_1164 library. Some synthesis compilers will place restrictions on the types of expressions that can be in a **wait** statement. Common usages are shown in the preceding paragraph. The **wait** statement is motivated by synchronous logic and we can gain some insight into the synthesis process by considering the operation of synchronous circuits. Consider circuits where signal values are stored in edge-triggered flip-flops and their values are updated in the clock edge, say by a rising edge. Therefore all signals whose values are controlled by the **wait** statement will be synthesized into flip-flops whose update will take place on the clock edge as defined by the *condition*, that is rising or falling.

Only one **wait** statement is permitted in a process and it must be the first statement in the process. Therefore if we use an edge-detection expression in the **wait** statement a flip-flop will be inferred for every signal in the process. This may not be what we wish to create. For example, we may wish to create latches or flips-flops for only some signals with larger blocks of combinational circuitry. In such cases it is preferable to use an **if-then-endif** statement. Using an **if-then-endif** statement with an edge detection expression limits flip-flop inference to signals assigned in the body of the **then** statement rather than affecting all signals in a process. The remaining statements in the process can lead to the synthesis of combinational logic. Such usage provides us with some guidelines on when to use an **if** statement rather than a **wait** statement. Thus if we wish to be able synthesize portions of our processes into combinational logic the use of **if-then-elsif** or **if-then-endif** statements provided us with the requisite flexibility.

Example: Wait Statement vs. If-Then Statements

Consider the example code shown in Figure 7-17. The **wait** statement controls the body of the process. Therefore flip-flops are inferred for all signals in the process as shown in the synthesized circuit. Let us suppose that we are actually modeling a system where we really only care about controlling the assignment to Bout with a clock edge and that assignments to Aout can actually be asynchronous and implemented in combinational logic. In this case we have needlessly generated flips flops for Aout. Figure 7-18 shows the same code rewritten where the assignment to Bout is controlled by the clock edge and the assignment to Aout is asynchronous. From the synthesized logic we see that no flip-flops are inferred for the signal Aout. Note that the structure of the assignment statement for Aout is identical in both code examples. It is just that in one case it is controlled by an edge-detection

```
library IEEE;
use IEEE.std_logic_1164.all;
entity edge is
port(reset, clk, x : in std_logic;
Aout, Bout : out integer range 0 to 3);
end entity edge;

architecture behavioral of edge is
begin
 process
begin
wait until (rising_edge(clk));
if reset = '1' then
Aout <= 1;
else
Aout <= 3;
end if;
Bout <= 0;
end process;
end architecture behavioral;
```

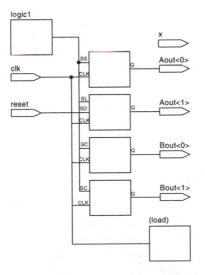

FIGURE 7-17 An example of synthesis with the **wait** statement

```
library IEEE;
use IEEE.std_logic_1164.all;
entity edge is
port(reset, clk, x : in std_logic;
Aout, Bout : out integer range 0 to 3);
end entity edge;

architecture behavioral of edge is
begin
 process (reset, clk) is
begin
if reset = '1' then
Aout <= 1;
else
Aout <= 3;
end if;
if (rising_edge(clk)) then
Bout <= 0;
end if;
end process;
end architecture behavioral;
```

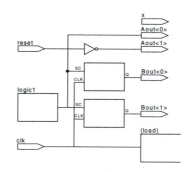

FIGURE 7-18 Using the if statement

expression whereas in the other case it is not. This example illustrates the point that if we are describing computations that really correspond to combinational logic we can avoid unnecessary flip-flops by carefully structuring our code. In general the use of edge-detection expressions with **if** statements is a bit more flexible in that it gives us better control over when flip-flops are (needlessly) inferred.

Example End: Wait Statement vs. If-Then Statements

Consider the following pair of statements that are controlled by a **wait** statement.

wait until rising_edge (clk);
sig_a <= sig_x **and** sig_y;
sig_b <= sig_a **xor** sig_c;

What is the value of sig_a used in the computation of sig_b? Is it the value computed in the previous line or the value held in the flip-flop? The synthesized circuit will create flip-flops for both sig_a and sig_b. However the input of the sig_b flip-flop will be the logical AND of sig_c and the output of the sig_a flip-flop that holds the *previous* value of sig_a. Note that this is consistent with the simulation semantics of this pair of statements. We might also observe that the simulation semantics are consistent with a hardware implementation of the preceding code sequence.

However, if the preceding signal assignment statements were included in a process rather than the body of a wait statement then flip-flops may not be inferred. For example, consider the following block of code:

process (x, y, z)
begin
L1: s1 <= x **xor** y;
L2: s2 <= s1 **or** z;
L3: w <= s1 **nor** s2;
end process;

In this case the sequential semantics of the process enable the synthesis compiler to optimize the implementation and produce a gate-level netlist. In this case we see that the semantics of the simulation may not match that of the synthesized circuit.

What about the use of variables in a process that is controlled by a **wait** statement? Are flip-flops also inferred for variables? Remember that, unlike signals as discussed earlier, variables assignments take effect immediately. Thus variable assignment statements are usually collapsed into combinational logic unless a variable is used before it is defined. The following example clarifies this point.

Example: Variables Controlled by a Wait Statement

A simple example of a variable controlled by a **wait** statement is shown in Figure 7-19. In this example the sequence of variable assignments is collapsed into a combinational logic shown in the figure with variables effectively synthesized into wires. However let the first statement be modified as follows:

$$a\_var := (x \text{ or } y) \text{ nor } b\_var;$$

```
library IEEE;
use IEEE.std_logic_1164.all;
entity sigvar is
port(y,z, x,clk : in std_logic;
    res: out std_logic);
end entity sigvar;

architecture behavioral of sigvar is
begin
 process is
variable a_var, b_var : std_logic;
begin
wait until (rising_edge(clk));
 a_var := x or y;
b_var := a_var nor z;
res <= b_var xor y;
end process;
end architecture behavioral;
```

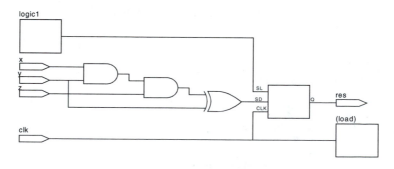

FIGURE 7-19 An example of variables controlled by a **wait** statement

In this case the variable b_var is used before it has been defined and a flip-flop will be inferred for b_var.

Example End: Variables Controlled by a Wait Statement

We expect that it is the level-sensitive or edge-sensitive expressions within the conditional part of the code that determine whether latches or flip-flops are inferred. However some synthesis compilers may still infer flip-flops from **wait** statements regardless of whether the conditional expression is level or edge sensitive.

Synthesis Exercise 7.3: Inferring State Elements

This exercise addresses the development of models that contain combinational logic in conjunction with state elements that are updated on the rising edge of a clock signal. Consider the following computation to be implemented by a circuit.

Aout = In1 **and** In2 **xor** In3;
MyState = In1 **or** In2 **and** MyState;

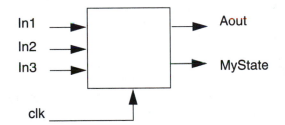

Both Aout and MyState are outputs and clearly MyState must be implemented with state elements.

Step 1. Create a VHDL model for the above computation with the following characteristics.

> **Step 1 (a)** All signals are single-bit signals and are of type std_logic.

> **Step 1 (b)** Use a single process with a **wait** statement that is sensitive to the rising edge of the clock.

Step 2. Compile the model for the CAD toolset you are using.

Step 3. Using vendor-specific commands select a target set of hardware primitives for synthesis, in our case an FPGA device. In the process you may also select several other options such as level of effort, optimization for speed or area, and target clock frequency.

Step 4.   Synthesize the design.

Step 5.   Examine the schematic and note the number of state elements that have been generated.

Step 6.   Simulate the design. Generate a trace of the output signal Aout. From the reporting facility within the CAD tool determine the maximum rate at which this circuit can be clocked and set a the period of clk to be well within this limit.

Step 7.   Now modify the design as a follows.

Step 7 (a)   Now have a single process with a sensitivity list rather than the **wait** statement. Make the process sensitive to the clk signal.

Step 7 (b)   Structure your process with statements computing the value of Aout and a single **if-then-end if** statement for computing the value of MyState. Do not structure an **else** branch!

Step 7 (c)   The conditional test in the **if** clause should check if rising_edge(clk) is true to test for the rising edge on the signal clk.

Step 8.   Now re-synthesize the design and examine the resulting schematic.

Step 9.   What differences are apparent from the implementation of the first model? What about the number of state elements?

Step 10.   Study the report for the model and determine the maximum speed of operation. Set the period of clk to be well within this limit and simulate the design. Generate a trace of the output signal Aout.

Step 11.   Now construct a model with a single process and no **wait** statements. However, include all of the input signals in the process sensitivity list. Perform a pre-synthesis simulation of this model as follows.

Step 11 (a)   From the preceding steps we know how fast the circuits for the two preceding models can be clocked.

Step 11 (b)   Open a trace window to view the operation of this simulation model.

Step 11 (c)   Modify the inputs stimulus so that the inputs In1, In2, and In3 change values at a rate faster than these clock rates. Set the period of clk to be equal to that of the earlier models (either one). The goal is to make the inputs change values more than once in a single clock cycle.

Step 11 (d)   Simulate the model, generate a trace, and record the behavior of Aout.

Step 12.   Compare the behavior of Aout in the previous step with the behavior of Aout captured in the traces of the post-synthesis simulations of the preceding two models, namely, one using **wait** statements and one using a sensitivity list with only the clk signal.

Step 12 (a)   Although both models represent the same circuit why are there differences?

Step 12 (b)   Which of the traces would you say is more accurate?

Step 12 (c) What is a viable solution to avoiding such mismatches between pre-synthesis and post-synthesis simulation?

End Synthesis Exercise 7.3

7.7 Synthesis of State Machines

In Section 6.8 we discussed the basic modeling approaches for state machines. We can generalize the basic organization discussed in that section to a state machine implementation shown in Figure 7-20. This figure identifies Mealy outputs as well as Moore outputs. The former is computed as function of the inputs and the current state. The latter are computed as a function of the current state or may correspond to elements of the current state. This model is sufficiently general to capture all of the state machines that we would be interested in studying.

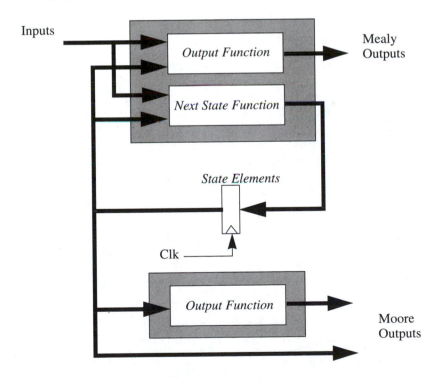

FIGURE 7-20 A Mealy/Moore state machine

One of the first issues with the synthesis of state machines is the manner in which the state elements are encoded. On the surface this is strictly a function of the number of states. For example, if the state machine has eight states then three bits are required to provide a unique representation for each state. However, how are the individual states numbered? For example, which state is numbered six? Which state is numbered seven? From digital design we know that the actual numbering can significantly affect the quality of the synthesized hardware. Three common state encodings are shown in Table 7-1. The first column identifies the state. Each successive column provides an alternative encoding of that state. The sequential and Gray code encodings are the most compact in the number of flip-flops used. However, the impact on the speed and area are not obvious. The one hot encoding uses one flip-flop to uniquely identify each state. Clearly this implementation uses the most flip-flops but the next state equations are relatively simple to deduce and the implementation tends to be somewhat less complex. Synthesis tools will often permit custom encodings of states permitting the designers to specify the state encodings. For example, the VHDL models in Section 6.8 defined a new type as

type statetype **is** (state0, state1, state2, state3),

where signals can now be defined as,

signal state, next_state :statetype;

The designer may be able to designate that **state0** is encoded a 0001, **state1** is encoded as 1000, and so on. We would be inclined to use this capability if we had knowledge of the structure of the problem and the manner in which the encodings would affect the implementation. In the absence of such knowledge we would forgo an explicit enumeration of the state encodings whereas synthesis compilers will provide for a selection of several options such as one hot encodings or Gray code encodings. The synthesis compilers will also incorporate optimizations that seek to select the optimal encodings of states, where optimal is typically defined with respect to speed and/or area.

TABLE 7-1 Example State Encodings

State	Sequential	Gray Code	One Hot
0	000	000	00000001
1	001	001	00000010
2	010	011	00000100
3	011	010	00001000
4	100	110	00010000
5	101	111	00100000
6	110	101	01000000
7	111	100	10000000

Example: State Machine Synthesis

If we are not careful with our coding style we may produce unnecessary flip-flops in the next state or output logic. Consider the example shown in Figure 7-21. This state machine

```
library IEEE;
use IEEE.std_logic_1164.all;
entity state_machine is
port(reset, clk, x : in std_logic;
      res : out std_logic);
end entity state_machine;

architecture behavioral of state_machine is
type statetype is (state0, state1);
signal state, next_state : statetype ;
begin
 process is
begin
wait until (rising_edge(clk)); -- wait until the rising edge
if reset = '1' then
res <= '0'; -- check for reset and initialize state
state <= statetype'left;
else
case state is -- depending upon the current state
when state0 => -- set output signals and next state
if x = '0' then
state <= state1;
res <= '1';
else state <= state0;
res <= '0';
end if;
when state1 =>
if x = '1' then
state <= state0;
res <= '0';
else state <= state1;
res <= '1';
end if;
end case;
end if;
end process;

end architecture behavioral;
```

FIGURE 7-21 An example of inferring extra flip-flops in state machine synthesis

is the same as that shown in Figure 6-21 but rewritten to utilize just one process. The model has an synchronous reset signal. The edge-triggered portion of the code includes the output function as well as the next state function. This is a Mealy machine where the output signal **res** is a function of the current state as well as the input signal **x**. Flip-flops will be inferred for all signals in the edged-triggered section of the code that includes the whole process due to the presence of the **wait** statement. The synthesized circuit is shown in Figure 7-23. Note that this circuit infers flip-flops for both the signal **state** as well as the output signal **res**. Alternatively, consider the model shown in Figure 7-22. When this model is synthesized flip-flops will be inferred only for the signal **state**. The signal **res** is assigned a value through any execution of the first process and therefore combinational logic is inferred. By paying close attention to the structure of the code we can avoid unnecessary inferences of flip-flops and produce a more efficient implementation.

Example End: State Machine Synthesis

Finally, how do we deal with initial values and avoid the state elements being set in an illegal state on power up? There are two options. One is to explicitly include external reset signals in your design as shown in the examples in this chapter. A second approach is to utilize vendor specified mechanisms to ensure that all state elements are set or reset on power up.

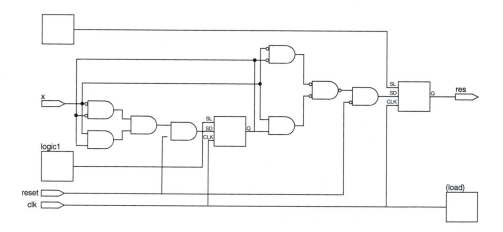

FIGURE 7-23 Synthesized circuit for Figure 7-21

```vhdl
library IEEE;
use   IEEE.std_logic_1164.all;
entity state_machine is
port (reset, clk, x : in std_logic;
res : out std_logic);
end entity state_machine;

architecture behavioral of state_machine is
type statetype is (state0, state1);
signal state, next_state : statetype;
begin
process (state, x) is
begin
 case state is                              -- depending upon the current state
 when state0 =>                             -- set output signals and next state
                if x = '0' then
                next_state <= state1;
                res <= '1';
        else    next_state <= state0;
                res <= '0';
        end if;
when state1 =>
if x = '1' then
                next_state <= state0;
                res <= '0';
        else    next_state <= state1;
                res <= '1';
        end if;
end case;
end process;

clk_process: process is
begin
wait until (rising_edge(clk); -- wait until the rising edge
            if reset = '1' then       -- check for reset and initialize state
            state <= statetype'left;
            else    state <= next_state;
            end if;
end process clk_process;
end architecturebehavioral;
```

FIGURE 7-22 State machine model rewritten to avoid inferring flip-flops for the signal res

Synthesis Exercise 7.4:

Consider the state machine from Simulation Exercise 6.3 shown in Figure 7-24. This state machine has three inputs. The first is the **reset** signal, which initializes the machine to state 0. The second is a bit-serial input, and the third is the clock input. The state machine is designed to recognize the sequence 101 in the input sequence and set the value of the output to 1. The value of the output remains at 1 until the state machine is reset.

Step 1. Write the VHDL model for this state machine. Use an enumerated type to represent the state (i.e., the type **statetype**). Structure your state machine description as three processes.

Process 1: Write an output process that determines the value of the single-bit output based on the current state and the value of the single-bit input.

Process 2: Write a process that computes the next state based on the value of the input signal and the current state.

Process 3: Write a clock process that updates the state on the rising edge of the clock signal. On a **reset** pulse the state machine is reset. Otherwise the state is modified to reflect the next state.

Step 2. Use the types **std_logic** and **std_logic_vector** for the input and output signals. Declare and reference the library **IEEE** and the package **std_logic_1164**.

Step 3. Compile or analyze the models for the CAD toolset you are using.

Step 4. Using vendor-specific commands select a target set of hardware primitives for synthesis, in our case an FPGA device. In the process you may also select several other options such as level of effort, optimization for speed or area, and target clock frequency.

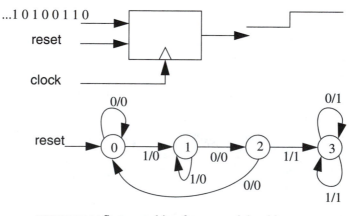

FIGURE 7-24 State machine for recognizing bit patterns

Step 5.   Synthesize the designs and view the schematic. You should be able to identify structural components as captured in Figure 7-20.

Step 6.   Simulate the design. Depending on the vendor tools you are using you may be able to simulate prior to placement and routing of the design. Structure the input stimulus as follows.

   Step 6 (a)   Apply a clock signal with a period of 20 ns.

   Step 6 (b)   Apply a reset signal that generates a single pulse of duration 30 ns.

   Step 6 (c)   Generate a random, bit-serial sequence with the pattern 101 embedded within the sequence.

   Step 6 (d)   Verify correct operation.

   Step 6 (e)   From vendor-supplied timing analysis tools what is the projected clock rate at which this circuit can execute?

Step 7.   Now modify the model such that the entire state machine is implemented as a single process.

Step 8.   Re-synthesize and view the schematic of the synthesized design. What differences do you see in this second implementation?

Step 9.   Generate and compare reports for each design with respect to area and speed.

End Synthesis Exercise 7.4

7.8 Simulation vs. Synthesis

A common sequence of steps taken in design is to first develop the VHDL models and use simulation to verify the functional correctness of the model. Thereafter this model is synthesized and the synthesized model is simulated to verify the performance. One would expect that the simulation of the VHDL model and the simulation of the synthesized hardware would produce identical behavior. After all they describe the same circuit. However this is not necessarily true and it becomes important to understand the sources of this "semantic mismatch." Some common issues are identified below.

1. *Incomplete sensitivity list*: One can write processes where the sensitivity list includes only a few of the signals that are manipulated in the process. Thus during functional simulation processes are executed only when there are events on these signals. However if the synthesis process produces combinational logic for a process then this logic will respond to events on *any* of the input signals. This is the nature of combinational logic. Synthesis compilers will expect the process to be sensitive to all of the signals

that are manipulated in a process. As a result the behavior of the synthesized hardware will not follow exactly the simulate behavior of the process. For example, consider the following code:

```
process (sel) is
begin
if (sel = '1' and En = '0') then
A <= 1;
else
A <= '0';
end if;
end process;
```

During simulation, events on signal En will not cause the process to execute. For example if sel = 1 and at some later point in time the value of En changes to 1 the process will not execute. However after synthesis the resulting combinational logic will be sensitive to events on signal En. Synthesis compilers may in fact ignore the sensitivity list of the process or provide warnings if the sensitivity list is incomplete.

2. *Sequential signal assignments in a process*: Imagine the following sequence of signal assignment statements in a process.

```
process(x, y, z)
begin
L1: s1 <= x xor y;
L2: s2 <= s1 or z;
L3: w <= s1 nor s2;
end process;
```

Let x, y, and z be input signals that are declared as ports in the corresponding **entity** and let s1 and s2 be signals declared in the architecture. The simulation semantics state that the values of s1 and s2 used in statement L3 should be the values of the signals s1 and s2 when the process in invoked and not the new values that are assigned when the process is executed. However synthesis compilers will generally optimize this sequence to produce combinational logic and avoid latches.

3. *Delay statements*: When we have user specified delays in simulation, these delays may not match the actual delays that result in the synthesized circuit.

4. *Simulation Overhead*: The behavior captured in conditional and selected signal assignment statements have equivalent representations using the **process** construct (see Section 6.1). The former are always active and generally have more simulation overhead but are better for synthesis. Remember that in general optimizations for simulation may be at odds with synthesis.

5. *Speed*: Use of variables will lead to faster simulation. This follows form the need to maintain and manipulate the driver data structure for each signal. However the use of processes obscures concurrency within a process and may reduce the effectiveness of the inference mechanisms.

7.9 Synthesis Hints

The following are some general hints when writing VHDL models for synthesis:

1. The **while-loop** statement is generally not supported for synthesis because the loop range must be statically determined in order to generate a fixed amount of logic.

2. All **for** loop indices must have statically determinable loop ranges.

3. If you wish to avoid having a latch inferred for a signal in a process then every execution path through the process must assign a value for that signal.

4. If you use variables in a process before they are defined a latch will be inferred for that variable.

5. Do not specify initial values in your declaration of signals. Most synthesis compilers will ignore them. If you wish to initialize signals to values it is advisable to do so explicitly under the control of a reset signal. The exceptions are constants that must be provided with their values within the declaration. Keep a hardware, and not programming language, view of the process.

6. Include all signals in a process in the sensitivity list of the process to avoid pre-synthesis and post-synthesis simulation mismatches.

7. To ensure that combinational logic is generated from a process or CSA statements (conditional or selected) every possible execution path through the code must determine all output values. In this case there is no need to retain values across executions of the process and therefore no need to infer storage.

8. Keep in mind that the code should "imply" hardware structures. Avoid purely algorithmic descriptions of hardware. This will assist the synthesis compiler's inference process.

9. To avoid the inference of latches, make sure that default values are assigned to signals before a conditional block of code, for example the use of **case** or **if-then-end if** statements.

10. For variables or signals assigned within a **for-loop** a default value must be assigned before the **for** loop to avoid latch inference.

11. Avoid programming as in C or Java where we try and exploit the sequentiality of the code. This will lead to long signal paths. Attempt to minimize dependencies between statements and try and promote concurrency.

12. Using don't care values to cover the **when others** case in a case statement can enable the synthesis compiler to optimize the logic and create a smaller circuit than if all remaining options were set to values such as 0000 or 1111.

13. If possible specify data ranges explicitly in the declarations. This will avoid larger default sizes for signals leading to narrower datapaths and reduced logic.

14. Minimize signal assignment statements within a process and use variables.

15. Use **if-then** statements to infer flip-flops rather than **wait** statements. The advantage is that combinational logic and sequential logic can be modeled within the same process. If you use a **wait** statement it must be the first statement in the process and the only **wait** statement in the process. Therefore latches or flip-flops are inferred for every signal assigned a value in that process. On the other hand if we only have small block of code sensitive to a clock edge then that block of code can be encapsulated within an **if** statement and cause flip-flops to be inferred for its signals. The rest of the process can be synthesized to combinational logic. Thus using clock edge detection expressions within an **if** statement rather than a **wait** statement will enable combinational and sequential logic to co-exist within a process.

16. Do not use don't care symbols in comparisons. Although this will work fine for simulation there is no hardware equivalent and such comparisons are defined to always return false. A little thought reveals that this will significantly alter the behavior of the code. For example, the code that is executed when the condition is true is now never executed and is effectively removed by the compiler.

17. Check vendor specific constraints on the permitted types and range of the **for-loop** index.

18. Move common complex operations out of the branches of **if-then-else** statements and place them after the conditional code. This will generally lead to less hardware.

19. Using a **case** statement rather than an **if-then-elsif** construct will produce less logic since priority logic will have to be generated for the latter.

20. The choice of level-sensitive conditional expressions vs. edge-detection expressions should be guided by the parts available in our target library. For example, if latches are not available then the synthesis tools may try to create a latch by synthesizing the gate-level equivalents. This can complicate timing analysis and render the circuit much more difficult to debug. The choice of coding style should be guided by the building blocks that we have to operate with. For example in the Xilinx XC4000 series FPGAs we can find support for both edge-triggered and level-sensitive devices so this choice is not as crucial.

7.10 Chapter Summary

This chapter focused on the synthesis of hardware from sequential statements encapsulated in processes. The style of the discussion was to present general principles that can be used by application developers in writing VHDL code so that their expectations were consistent with the results of synthesis. Individual synthesis compilers differ in the specific optimizations but there are some general inference principles that are common across most synthesis compilers. The discussion in this chapter attempted to provide an intuition for these principles. Specifically, the following topics were covered:

* inference from sequential statements
    * simple assignment statements
    * **if-then-else** and **if-then-elsif**
    * **case** statement
    * **loop** statement
* latch inference vs. flip-flop inference
* effect of using variables vs. signals
* optimizations
    * avoiding latch inference
    * reducing the amount of inferred hardware
    * sharing hardware across conditional branches
* using **wait** statements vs. **if-then-else** statements
* synthesis of state machines
    * initialization
    * Mealy vs. Moore machines

Now we can move from language statements into other aspects of the language that deal with global issues such as hierarchy, abstraction, modularity, and input/output. These presentations concurrently deal with simulation and synthesis issues.

Exercises

1. Which of the following blocks of code will generate a latch upon synthesis? Provide a brief explanation for your answer.

   1.1

   ```
   proc1: process (x, y, z) is
   variable var_s1, var_s2: std_logic;
   begin
   var_s1 := var_s2 and y;
   var_s2 := var_s1 xor z;
   res1 <= var_s1 nand var_s2; -- res is a port
   end process;
   ```

   1.2

   ```
   process (x,y,z, a, b, c)
   begin
   if (a = '1')then
    res <= x and y;
   elsif (b ='1') then
   res <= y xor z;
   elsif (c ='0') then
   res <= x or y;
    end if;
   end process;
   end behavior;
   ```

   1.3

   ```
   process (x, y, z, sel) is
   begin
   if (sel = "– 0") then -- the symbol "–" represents the don't care
   w <= x xnor y;        -- for std_logic types
   end if;
   v <= (x and y) and z;
   end process;
   ```

2. The following piece of VHDL code will exhibit mismatches between the functional simulation and the simulation of the synthesized hardware. Why? Modify the VHDL code to avoid this mismatch.

```
process ( x, y) is
variable a_var, b_var : std_logic;
begin
wait until (rising_edge(clk));
 a_var := x or y;
b_var := a_var nor z;
res <= b_var xor y;
end process;
```

3. Synthesize a VHDL model of a 4-bit loadable counter that can be initialized to any value. The counter should be equipped with a load enable, and a reset to 0.

4. Synthesize and test the VHDL model for the following state machine for a traffic-light controller [4]. Ensure that flip-flops are inferred only for the state elements, that is only two flip-flops will be inferred for this model.

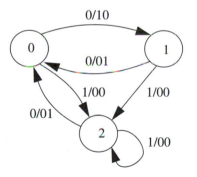

5. Synthesize and test a base 10 counter, that is, the counter should count to 10 and then roll over to 0. Use vendor specific tools to estimate area and speed of the resulting design.

6. Synthesize and test a 4-input priority encoder where the priority order is input 3, 2, 1, and 0 with 3 being the highest priority. Include a Valid input signal where the outputs are valid only when the Valid = '1'.

7. Create a state machine to recognize the string 1011 in a bit serial stream. When this string is recognized a pulse should be generated on the output signal Present. The resulting VHDL model should synthesis to a circuit with one positive-edge-triggered flip-flop. Place and map this circuit onto an FPGA chip. Use the reporting facilities of the CAD tools you are using to determine the fastest rate at which this circuit will run.

CHAPTER 8

Modeling Structure

Our model of a digital system remains that of an interconnected set of components. The preceding chapters described how the behavior of each component could be specified in VHDL. Informally, the behavior of each component is specified as the set of output events that occur in response to input events. Behavioral descriptions of a component may be specified using CSA statements. When this is infeasible due to the complexity of the event generation models the behavioral models of each component are specified using one or more processes and sequential statements. A third approach to describing a system is simply in terms of the interconnection of its components. Rather than focusing on what each component does we are concerned with simply describing how components are connected. Behavioral models of each component are already assumed to exist in the local working directory or in the library known the VHDL simulator. Such a description is referred to as a *structural model*. Such models may describe only the structure of a system, without regard to the operation of individual components.

Several motivations drive the need for structural models. They enable the definition of a precise interface for the sharing of model components between developers within an organization. Structural models also facilitate the use of hierarchy and abstraction in modeling complex digital systems. As we will see at the end of this chapter, structural models are easily integrated with models that use processes and CSA statements providing a powerful modeling approach for complex digital systems. This chapter discusses the basic principles governing the specification and construction of structural models in VHDL.

8.1 Describing Structure

A common means of conveying structural descriptions is through block diagrams. Components represented by blocks are interconnected by lines representing signals. In Chapter 4, models of a full adder using CSA statements were described. These models provide a description of "what" the system does, namely computes the value of and assigns signals values at certain points in time relative to the current time. Instead of employing such a model suppose we wish to describe the circuit as being constructed from two half adders under the assumption that we already understand the behavior of a half adder. Such a design is shown in Figure 8-1. In understanding how such a design may be described in VHDL, imagine conveying this schematic over the telephone (no faxes!) to a friend who has no knowledge of full-adder circuits. You would like to have them correctly reproduce the schematic as you describe it. You can also think of describing this schematic across the table to someone without showing them the diagram or taking a pen to paper yourself. Do not use your fingers or hands to point and use only verbal guidelines! When we think of conveying descriptions in these terms we see that we need precise and unambiguous ways to describe structure.

We might convey such a description as follows. First, we must describe the inputs and outputs to the full adder. This is not too difficult to convey verbally. We can easily state the type and mode of the input–output signals, for example, whether they are single-bit signals, input signals, or output signals. This information constitutes the corresponding entity description. Now imagine describing the interconnection of the components over the telephone. You would probably first list the components you need: two half adders and a two-input OR gate. Conveying such a list of components verbally is also not difficult, but now comes the tricky part. How do you describe the interconnection of these components unambiguously? In order to do so you must first be able to distinguish between components of the same type. For example, in Figure 8-1(a), the half adders must be distinguished by assigning them unique labels, such as H1 and H2. The signals that will be used to connect these components are also similarly labeled. For example, we may label them s1, s2, and s3. Additional annotations that we need are the labels for the ports in a half adder and the ports in an OR gate. Such detailed annotations are necessary so that we can refer to them unambiguously, such as the sum output port of half-adder H1 or the sum output port of half-adder H2. We have now completed the schematic annotation to a point where the circuit can be described in a manner that allows the person at the other end of the telephone to draw it correctly. For example, the interconnection between H1 and H2 can be described by stating that the sum output of H1 is connected to signal s1, and the x input of H2 is connected to signal s1. Implicitly we have stated that the sum output of H1 is connected to the x input of H2 using signal s1. We have done this indirectly by describing connections between the ports and signal s1. There is an analogy with the physical process of constructing this circuit. If you were wiring this circuit on a protoboard in the laboratory you would actually use signal wires to connect components. Once all of the components and their input and output ports are labeled we see that we can describe this circuit in a manner that will allow the person to correctly build the circuit.

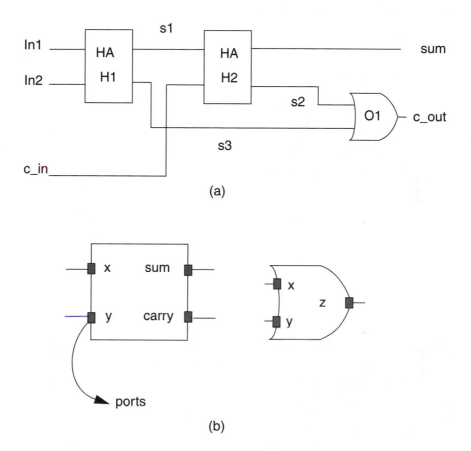

FIGURE 8-1 (a) Full-adder circuit (b) Interface description of the half-adder and OR-gate components

Based on the above example we can identify a number of features that a formal, VHDL structural description might possess: (i) the ability to define the list of components, (ii) the definition of a set of signals to be used to interconnect these components, (iii) the ability to uniquely label, and therefore distinguish, between multiple copies of the same component, and (iv) the ability to specify how signals are connected to ports. The VHDL syntax that realizes these features in an architecture description is shown in Figure 8-2.

The component declaration includes a list of the components being used and the input and output signals of each component; or, in VHDL terminology, the input and output ports of the component. This component declaration essentially states that this architecture will be using components named half_adder and or_2 gate, but so far has not stated how many of each type of component will be used. The declaration of the compo-

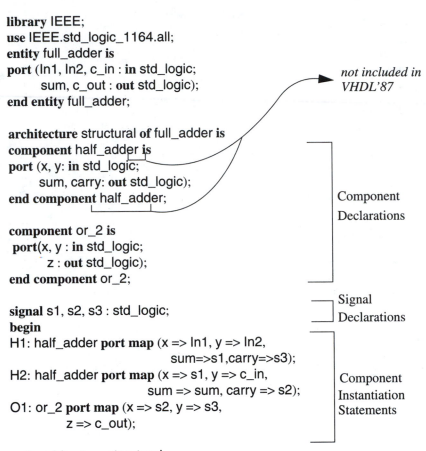

```
library IEEE;
use IEEE.std_logic_1164.all;
entity full_adder is
port (In1, In2, c_in : in std_logic;
      sum, c_out : out std_logic);
end entity full_adder;

architecture structural of full_adder is
component half_adder is
port (x, y: in std_logic;
      sum, carry: out std_logic);
end component half_adder;

component or_2 is
 port(x, y : in std_logic;
      z : out std_logic);
end component or_2;

signal s1, s2, s3 : std_logic;
begin
H1: half_adder port map (x => In1, y => In2,
                    sum=>s1,carry=>s3);
H2: half_adder port map (x => s1, y => c_in,
                    sum => sum, carry => s2);
O1: or_2 port map (x => s2, y => s3,
        z => c_out);

end architecture structural;
```

not included in VHDL'87

Component Declarations

Signal Declarations

Component Instantiation Statements

FIGURE 8-2 Structural model of a full adder

nents is followed by the declaration of all of the signals that will be used to interconnect the components. These signals would correspond to the set of signal wires you might use in the laboratory. From a programming languages point of view we note similarities with the manner in which we construct Pascal or C programs. In a Pascal program we declare the variables and data structures that we will use (e.g., arrays) and their types before we actually use them. In a VHDL structural model as shown in Figure 8-2, we declare all of the components and signals that we will use before we describe how they are interconnected. Collectively, the component and signal declarations complete the declarative part '87 vs. '93 of the **architecture** construct. This is analogous to the parts list that you would have if you were to build this circuit in the laboratory. One syntactic note: in VHDL'87 the syntax of the component declarations are a bit different as identified in the Figure 8-2. Now all that remains is the process of actually "wiring" the components together. This is provided in the **architecture** body that follows the declarative part, and is delimited by the **begin** and **end** statements.

Consider the first statement in the architecture body. Let us go back to our analogy of wiring the circuit on a protoboard in the laboratory. We must first acquire the components, label them, and lay them out on the board. Each component must then be connected to other components or circuit inputs using the signal wires. Each line in the architecture body provides this information for each component. This is a component *instantiation statement*.

Recall that processes and assignment statements can be labeled. Components are similarly labeled. The first word, H1, is the label of a half-adder component. This is followed by the **port map** ( ) construct. This construct states how the input and output ports of H1 are connected to other signals and ports. The first argument of the port map construct simply states that the x input port of H1 is connected to the In1 port of the entity full_adder. The third argument states that the sum output port of H1 is connected to the s1 signal. The port map constructs in the remaining two component instantiation statements can be similarly interpreted. Note that both components have identical input port names. This is not a problem since the name is associated with a specific component which is unambiguously labeled, namely H1 and O1. When we instantiate a component it is as if we were peering at the circuit through a keyhole and could see only one component at a time. We must completely describe the connections of all of the ports of each component before we can describe those of the next component. A close examination will reveal that the interconnection of the schematic in Figure 8-1(a) is completely specified in the structural description of Figure 8-2.

Finally, one other important feature of this model should be noted. The behavioral models of each component are assumed to be provided elsewhere, that is, there are entity–architecture pairs describing a half adder. The simulators and synthesis compilers must be able to find these models, which is achieved by matching the names provided in the models. For example, the structural model shown in Figure 8-2 states that a half-adder description, whose entity is labeled half_adder, is to be used. The simulator can find these models in the working directory, a library, or in some directory contained in the search path that the user defines in the CAD tools. Note that there are no implications on the type of model used to describe the operation of the half adder. This behavioral model could comprise CSA statements, or use processes and sequential statements, or itself be a structural model describing a half adder as the interconnection of gate level behavioral models. Such hierarchies are very useful and are discussed in greater detail later in this chapter.

Example: Structural Model of a State Machine

Consider a bit-serial adder shown in Figure 8-3. Two operands are applied serially, bit by bit, to the two inputs. On successive clock cycles, the combinational logic component computes the sum and carry values for each bit position. The D flip-flop stores the carry bit between additions of successive bits and is initialized to 0. As successive bits are added the corresponding bits of the output value are produced serially on the output signal. The state machine diagram is shown below the circuit. As described in Section 6.8, we can develop this as a behavioral model of a state machine that implements the state diagram shown in the figure. In this example we show the structural model of the state machine implementation. We have redrawn this circuit in the manner shown in Chapter 6 with a combinational logic component and a sequential logic component. The corresponding VHDL structural model is shown in Figure 8-4. Note the use of the **open** clause for component labeled **D1**. The signal qbar at the output of the flip-flop is not used. The **port map**() clause in the component instantiation statement expresses this by setting the signal to **open**. The hardware analogy is that of an output pin on a chip that remains uncon-

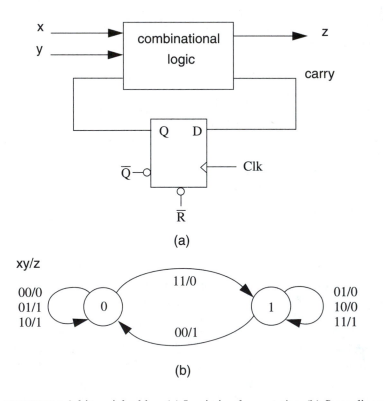

FIGURE 8-3 A bit-serial adder: (a) Logic implementation (b) State diagram

```vhdl
library IEEE;
use IEEE.std_logic_1164.all;
entity serial_adder is
port (x, y, clk, reset : in std_logic;
        z : out std_logic);
end entity serial_adder;

architecture structural of serial_adder is
--
-- declare the components that we will be using
--
component comb is
 port (x, y, c_in : in std_logic;
        z, carry : out std_logic);
end component comb;
component dff is
port (clk, reset, d : in std_logic;
        q, qbar : out std_logic);
end component dff;
signal s1, s2 :std_logic;
begin
--
-- describe the component interconnection
--
C1: comb port map (x => x, y => y, c_in => s1, z =>z, carry => s2);
D1: dff port map(clk => clk, reset =>reset, d=> s2, q=>s1,
                    qbar => open);
end architecture structural;
```

FIGURE 8-4 VHDL structural model of the bit-serial adder

nected. Also note the first item in port map for C1 — x =>x. Initially it may appear that this port map is ambiguous because it may not be obvious which x is which. In fact the parameter to the left of the => operator refers to a port on the component. The parameter to the right of the => operator refers to signal in the architecture or an entity port. The component has only one port named x and the architecture and entity ports have only one signal named x; thus there is no ambiguity. Part of the rationale for permitting such syntactic arrangements follows from the need to reuse models developed by distinct users. We have no idea what another designer might name their ports. Thus we cannot rely on the fact that all port names will be distinct. Imagine what would happen if we required everyone to use distinct port names. Every time there is a name conflict a significant amount of error-prone effort will be required to rename ports and signals throughout large complex models. The syntax and scope rules for names used in the port maps ensure that the use of the same port names in distinct components does not pose a problem thereby making it easier to share component models.

Example End: Structural Model of a State Machine

8.2 Constructing Structural VHDL Models

We are now ready to provide a prescription for constructing structural VHDL models. As with behavioral models, this simple methodology comprises two steps: (i) the drawing of an annotated schematic, and (ii) the conversion to a VHDL model.

Construct_Structural_Schematic

1. Ensure that you have a behavioral or structural description of each component in the system being modeled. This means that you have a correct, working entity–architecture description of each component. Using the entity descriptions, create a block for each component with the input and output ports labeled.

2. Connect each port of each component to the port of another entity, or to an input or output port of the system being modeled.

3. Label each component with a unique identifier: H1, U2, and so on.

4. Label each internal signal with a unique signal name and associate a type with this signal, for example, std_logic_vector. Make sure the signals and ports that are connected are of the same type.

5. Label each system input port and output port and define its mode and type.

This annotated schematic can be transcribed into a structural VHDL model. Figure 8-5 illustrates a template for writing structural models in VHDL. One approach to filling in this template is described in the following procedure. This procedure relies on the availability of the annotated schematic.

Construct_Structural_Model

1. At this point we recommend using the IEEE 1164 value system. To do so include the following two lines at the top of your model declaration.

> **library** IEEE;
> **use** IEEE.std_logic_1164.all;

library library-name-1, library-name-2;

use library-name-1.package-name.all;

use library-name-2.package-name.all;

entity entity_name **is**
port(*input signals* : **in** *type*;
        output signals : **out** *type*);
end entity entity_name;

architecture arch_name **of** entity_name **is**

> *-- declare components used*

component component1_name **is**
port(*input signals* : **in** *type*;
        output signals : **out** *type*);
end component component1_name;

component component2_name **is**
port(*input signals* : **in** *type*;
        output signals : **out** *type*);
end component component2_name;

> *-- declare all signals used to connect the components*

signal *internal signals* : *type* := *initialization*;

begin

> *-- label each component and connect its ports to signals or entity ports*

Label1: component1-name **port map** (port=> signal,.....);

Label2: component2-name **port map** (port => signal,.....);

end architecture arch_name;

FIGURE 8-5 Structural model template

Single-bit signals can be declared to be of type std_logic whereas multibit quantities can be declared to be of type std_logic_vector.

2. Select a name for the entity (entity_name) representing the system being modeled and write the entity description. Specify each input and output signal port, its mode, and associated type.

3. Select a name for the architecture (`arch_name`) and write the architecture description as follows.

   3.1 Construct one component declaration for each unique component that will be used in the model. A component declaration can be easily constructed from the component's entity description. The name used in the component declaration must be the same name used for the entity in the existing entity-architecture model of this component. This is how the simulator can find the model for the corresponding components when it is time to simulate the model.

   3.2 Within the declarative region of the architecture description—before the **begin** statement—list the component declarations.

   3.3 Following the component declarations name and declare all of the internal signals used to connect the components. These signal names are shown on your schematic. The declaration states the type of each signal and may also provide an initial value.

   3.4 Now we can start writing the architecture body. For each block in your schematic write a component instantiation statement using the **port map** () construct. The component label is derived from the schematic. The **port map** () construct will have as many entries as there are ports on the component. Each element of the port map construct has the form

      port-signal => (internal signal or entity-port)

   Each port of the component is connected to an internal signal or to a port of the top-level entity. Remember, the mode and type of the port of the component must match that of the internal signal or entity port that is connected to the component port.

4. Some signals may be driven from more than one source. If this is the case then this signal is a shared signal and its type must be a resolved type. We can either define a new resolved type and its associated resolution function (as described in Chapter 9) or simply use the IEEE 1164 data types `std_logic` and `std_logic_vector`, which are resolved types.

It should be apparent that the process of generating a structural VHDL model from a schematic is a mechanical process. Thus it is not surprising that modern CAD tools can generate such structural models automatically from designs diagrams created with schematic capture tools available in modern CAD environments.

Simulation Exercise 8.1: A Structural Model

The goal of this exercise is to introduce the reader to the construction, testing, and simulation of a simple structural model.

Step 1.   Create a text file with the structural model of the full adder shown in Figure 8-2. Let us refer to this file as *full-adder.vhd*.

Step 2.   Create a text file with the model of the half adder shown in Figure 4-2. Let us refer to this file as *half-adder.vhd*. Ensure that the entity name for the half adder in this file is the same as the name you have used for the half-adder component declaration in the full-adder structural model. Remember the environment must have some way of being able to find and use the components that you need when you simulate the model of the full adder. Just as in the laboratory, components names are used for the purpose. In fact the file names can be different as long as you consistently name architectures (arch_name), entities (entity_name), and components (component_name).

We use this approach to naming because it is intuitive. Designs must be described in terms of lower level design units. File names are an artifact of the computer system we are using. When we compile an entity named E1 in a file called *homework1.vhd*, we will see that compiled unit names will be based on the label E1 rather than *homework1.vhd*. This will enable compilation of higher level structural models to find relevant files based on the component names and not the filenames that they are stored in. More detail on the programming mechanics can be found in Chapter 11.

Step 3.   Create a text file with a model of a two-input OR gate. Let us refer to this file as *or2.vhd*. Use a gate delay of 5 ns. Again make sure that the entity name is the same as the component name for the two-input OR gate model declared in the model of the full adder.

Step 4.   Compile the files *or2.vhd, half-adder.vhd*, and *full-adder.vhd* in this order.

Step 5.   Load the simulation model into the simulator.

Step 6.   Open a trace window with the signals you would like to trace. Include internal signals which are signals that are not entity ports in the model.

Step 7.   Generate a test case. Apply the stimulus corresponding to the test case to the inputs. Run the simulation for one time step. Examine the output to ensure it is correct.

Step 8.   Run the simulation for 50 ns.

Step 9.   Check the behavior of the circuit and note the timing on the internal signals with respect to the component delays.

End Simulation Exercise 8.1

8.3 Hierarchy, Abstraction, and Accuracy

The structural model of the full adder shown in Figure 8-2 presumes the presence of models of the half adder. Although this model could be any one of the behavioral models described in Chapter 4 or Chapter 6, the model could also be a structural model itself as shown in Figure 8-6. Thus, we have a hierarchy of models. This hierarchy can be graphically depicted as shown in Figure 8-7. Each box in the figure denotes a VHDL model: an entity–architecture pair. The architecture component of each pair may in turn reference other entity–architecture pairs. At the lowest level of the hierarchy exist architectures composed of behavioral rather than structural models of the components.

A few interesting observations can be made about the model shown in Figure 8-6. We see that structural models simply describe interconnections. They do not describe any form of behavior. There are no descriptions of how output events are computed in response to input events. How can the simulation be performed? When the structural model is loaded into the simulator, a simulation model is internally created by replacing the components by their behavioral descriptions. If the description of a component is also a structural description (as is the case in the model of Figure 8-2 using the architecture of the half-adder model in Figure 8-6), then the process is repeated for structural models at each level of the hierarchy. This process is continued until all components of the hierarchy have been replaced by behavioral descriptions. The levels of the hierarchy correspond to different levels of detail or *abstraction*. This process is referred to as *flattening* of the hierarchy. After the hierarchy has been flattened we have a discrete event model that can be simulated. From this point of view, we see that structural models are a way of managing large, complex designs. A modern design may have several million to tens of millions of gates. It is infeasible to build a single, flat, simulation model at the level of individual gates to test and evaluate the complete design. This may be due to the amount of simulation time

```
architecture structural of half_adder is
component xor2 is
 port (x, y : in std_logic;
       z : out std_logic);
end component xor2;
component and2 is
port (x, y : in std_logic;
       z : out std_logic);
end component and2;
begin
EX1: xor2 port map (x => x, y => y, z => sum);
OR1: and2 port map (x=> x, y=> y, z=> carry);
end architecture structural;
```

FIGURE 8-6 Structural model of a half adder

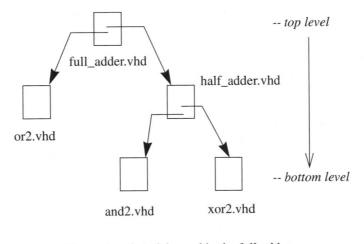

FIGURE 8-7 Hierarchy of models used in the full adder

required or the amount of memory required for such a detailed model. Thus, we may chose to approximate this gate-level behavior by constructing less-accurate models. For example, we have seen that a state machine may be described at the gate level, or via a process level description (as in Figure 6-20). The latter model is said to be at a higher level of abstraction. The ability to work at multiple levels of abstraction is required to manage large complex designs. For example:

1. We may have a library of VHDL models of distinct components, such as those derived from the manufacturer's component data book. These models have been developed, debugged, and tested. You can construct a model of a circuit by simply using these components. The only model you will have to write is a structural model. You also have to know the component entity description so that you correctly declare the component you are using. This is akin to using a library of mathematical functions in C or Pascal.

2. After three weeks, you might have a new and improved model of a half adder that you would like to use. You can test and debug this model in isolation. Then simply replace the old model with this new model. The need to recompile any dependent design entities is determined by the rules described in Chapter 11.

Finally, we note that the simulation time is directly impacted by the level at which we construct simulation models. Consider the behavioral model of the half adder described in Chapter 6, Figure 6-3. Events on input signals produce events on output signals. In contrast, when we flatten the hierarchy of Figure 8-2, events on input signals will produce events on outputs of the gates within the half adders and eventually propagate to the output signals as events. The more detailed the model, the larger the number of events we must expect the model to generate. The larger the number of events generated by the model the greater the simulation time. As a result, more accurate models will take a significantly longer time to simulate. Generally, the closer we are to making implementation decisions, the more accurate we wish the simulation to be and hence more time is invested in simulation.

Because the full-adder model depends upon the existence of models for the half-adder and two-input OR gate components, it follows that these models must be analyzed before the model for the full adder is analyzed. Once all of the models have been analyzed what happens if we make changes to only some design units? Must we recompile all of the design units each time we make a change to any one? If not, what dependencies between design units must we respect? These issues are discussed in Chapter 11.

Simulation Exercise 8.2: Construction of an 8-bit ALU

The goal of this exercise is to introduce trade-offs in building models at different levels of abstraction and trading accuracy for simulation speed.

Step 1. Start with the model of a single-bit ALU as given in Simulation Exercise 4.2. This model is constructed with CSA statements. Replace this model with one that replaces all of the CSA statements in the architecture body with sequential assignment statements and a single process. The process should be sensitive to events on input signals x, y, and c_in. The process should use variables to compute the value of the ALU output. The last statement in the process should be a signal assignment statement assigning the ALU output value to the signal result. Use a delay of 10 ns through the ALU.

Step 2. Analyze, simulate, and test this model and ensure that all three operations (AND, OR, and ADD) operate correctly.

Step 3. Construct a VHDL structural model of a 4-bit ALU. Use the single-bit ALU as a building block. Use a ripple carry implementation to propagate the carry between single-bit ALUs. Remember to compile the single-bit model before you compile the 4-bit model.

Step 4. Construct an 8-bit ALU using the 4-bit ALU as a building block. Use a ripple carry implementation to propagate the carry signal. Remember to compile the single-bit model before you analyze the 8-bit model.

Step 5. Based on your construction, what is the propagation delay though the 8-bit adder?

Step 6. Open a trace window with the signals you would like to trace. In this case, you will need to trace only the input and output signals to test the model.

Step 7. Generate a test case for each ALU instruction. Apply the stimulus for a test case to the inputs. Run the simulation for a period equal to at least the delay through the 8-bit adder. Examine the output values to ensure it is correct.

Step 8. Print the trace.

Step 9. Rewrite the 8-bit model as a behavioral model rather than a structural model. In this case there is no hierarchy of components. Use a single process and the following hints.

> **Step 9 (a)** Inputs, outputs, and internal variables are all now 8-bit vectors of type std_logic_vector (use the IEEE 1164 value system.)
>
> **Step 9 (b)** Make use of variables to compute intermediate results.
>
> **Step 9 (c)** Use the **case** statement to decode the opcode.
>
> **Step 9 (d)** Do not forget to set the value of the output carry signal.
>
> **Step 9 (e)** The propagation delay should be set to the delay through the hierarchical 8-bit model.

Step 10. Test the new model. You should be able to use the same inputs to test this model as you used for the hierarchical model.

Step 11. Generate a trace for the single-level model demonstrating that the model functions correctly.

Step 12. Qualitatively compare the two models with respect to the difference in the number events that occur in the flattened hierarchical model and the single-level model in response to a new set of inputs.

End Simulation Exercise 8.2

8.4 Generics

What if we would like to use the latest semiconductor technology that produces lower delays for our components? Suppose gate delays have now dropped from 5 ns to 1 ns. How do we keep our models current? We can run through them with a text editor and change all of the gate delays but this is clearly undesirable. The right answer is to be able to construct parameterized models rather than have hard coded delays. The actual value of the gate delay is determined at simulation time by the value that is provided to the model. Having parameterized models makes it possible to construct standardized libraries of models that can be shared. The issue to be addressed in creating parameterized models is the accommodation of hierarchical models composed of many components organized in multiple levels whose relative delays are not independent but rather maintain a fixed relationship. The VHDL language provides the ability to construct such parameterized models using concept of *generics*.

Figure 8-8 illustrates a parameterized behavioral model of a two-input exclusive-OR gate. The propagation delay in this model is parameterized by the constant gate_delay. The default (or initialized value) value of gate_delay is set to 2 ns. This is the value of delay that will be used in simulation models such as that shown in Figure 8-6, unless a different value is specified. A new value of gate_delay can be specified at the time the model is used, as shown in Figure 8-9. This version of the half adder will make use of exclusive-OR gates that exhibit a propagation delay of 6 ns through the use of the **generic map**() construct. Note the absence of the ';' after the **generic map**() construct!

The xor2 model is now quite general. Rather than manually editing and updating the delay values in the VHDL text, we can specify the value we must use when the component is instantiated. Considering the thousands of digital system components that are available, manually modifying each model when we wish to change its attributes can be quite tedious, inefficient, and error prone.

```
library IEEE;
use IEEE.std_logic_1164.all;

entity xor2 is
generic (gate_delay : Time:= 2 ns);
port (In1, In2 : in std_logic;
      z : out std_logic);
end entity xor2;

architecture behavioral of xor2 is
begin
z <= (In1 xor In2) after gate_delay;
end architecture behavioral;
```

FIGURE 8-8 An example of the use of generics

8.4.1 Specifying Generic Values

The example in Figure 8-9 illustrates how the value of a generic constant can be specified using the **generic map**() construct when the component is instantiated. Alternatively, the value can be specified when the component is declared. For example, in Figure 8-8 the component declaration of xor2 includes a declaration of the generic parameters. This statement can be modified to appear as follows.

```
generic (gate_delay: Time:= 6 ns);
```

```
architecture generic_delay of half_adder is
component xor2 is
generic (gate_delay: Time); -- new value may be specified here instead
port (x, y : in std_logic;      -- of using a generic map() construct
      z : out std_logic);
end component xor2;
component and2 is
generic (gate_delay: Time);
port (x, y : in std_logic;
      z : out std_logic);
end component and2 ;
begin
EX1: xor2 generic map (gate_delay => 6 ns)
          port map(x => x, y => y, z => sum);
A1: and2 generic map (gate_delay => 3 ns)
          port map(x=> x, y=> y, z=> carry);
end architecture generic_delay;
```

FIGURE 8-9 Use of generics in constructing parameterized models

Therefore, we observe that within a structural model there are at least two ways in which the values of generic constants of lower-level components can be specified: (i) in the component declaration, and (ii) in the component instantiation statement using the **generic map()** construct. If both are specified, then the value provided by the **generic map()** takes precedence. If neither is specified, then the default value defined in the model is used.

The values of these generics can be passed down through multiple levels of the hierarchy. For example, suppose that the full-adder model shown in Figure 8-2 defines the value of gate_delay for all lower level modules. In this case, the half-adder module may be modified to appear as shown in Figure 8-10.

Within the half adder the default gate delay is set to 3 ns. This is the value of gate_delay that is normally passed into the lower level models for xor2 and and2. However, if the full-adder description uses **generic maps** to provide a new value of the gate delay to the half-adder models that are instantiated in the structural description shown in Figure 8-2, then these values take precedence and will flow down to the gate-level models. This process is depicted graphically in Figure 8-11. From the figure it is evident that by changing the value of gate_delay in the full-adder model, the gate-level VHDL models for xor2 and and2 will utilize this value of the gate delay in the simulation. Although the

```
library IEEE;
use IEEE.std_logic_1164.all;

entity half_adder is
generic (gate_delay:Time:= 3 ns);
port (a, b : in std_logic;
       sum, carry : out std_logic);
end entity half_adder;

architecture generic_delay2 of half_adder is
component xor2 is
generic (gate_delay: Time);
 port (x,y : in std_logic;
        z : out std_logic);
end component xor2;

component and2 is
generic (gate_delay: Time);
port (x, y : in std_logic;
       z : out std_logic);
end component and2;

begin
EX1: xor2 generic map (gate_delay => gate_delay)
          port map(x => x, y => y, z => sum);
A1: and2 generic map (gate_delay => gate_delay)
         port map(x=> x, y=> y, z=> carry);
end architecture generic_delay2;
```

FIGURE 8-10 Passing values of generics through multiple levels of the hierarchy

models are written with default gate delay values of 2 ns, the new value overrides this default value.

8.4.2 Some Rules about Using Generics

The terminology is quite appropriate: the use of generics enables us to write *generic* models whose behavior in a particular simulation is determined by the value of the generic parameters. Generics appear very much like ports. They are a part of the interface specification of the component. However, unlike ports, they do not have a physical inter-

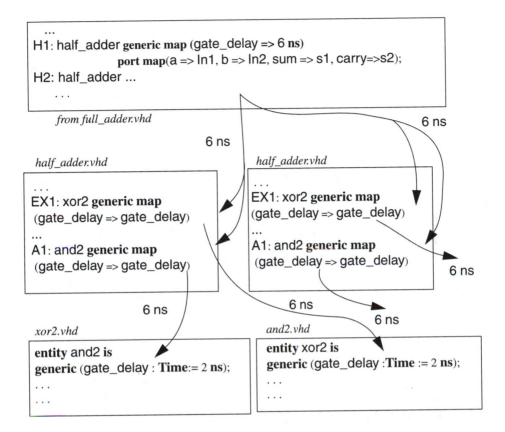

FIGURE 8-11 Parameter passing through the hierarchy using generics

pretation. They are more a means of conveying information through the design hierarchy, thereby enabling component designs to be parameterized. Generics are constant objects. Therefore, they cannot be written, but only read. The values of generic parameters must be computable at the time the simulator is loaded with the VHDL model. Therefore, we may include expressions in the value of a generic parameter. However, the value of this expression must be computable at the time the simulator is loaded. Finally, we must be careful about the precedence of the values of generic objects, as described in the preceding sections.

The use of generics is not limited to the specification of delays. In fact the most powerful uses of generics deal with physical attributes other than delays. The following examples further illustrates this power of constructing parameterized models.

Example: N-Input OR Gate

One class of generic gate-level models is one where the number of inputs can be parameterized. Therefore we can have just one VHDL model of an N-input gate. We can produce a 2-, 3-, or 6-input gate model by setting the value of a generic parameter. This example is shown in Figure 8-12. When this OR-gate model is used in a VHDL model, the generic parameter n must be mapped to the required number of inputs using the **generic map** () construct in a higher level structural model. We see how such models are constructed. The VHDL code uses a loop to perform the gate operation in a bit serial fashion. The generic parameter defines the loop index and therefore the number of bits at the gate input. The bit serial nature of the model decouples the computation from a fixed bit width.

If we were using several OR gates in a structural model, we would have one instantiation statement for each model. Each instantiation statement could include the following statement for different values of n: **generic map** (n=>3). In this statement the value 3 would be replaced by the number of inputs for that particular gate. Note that there is only one VHDL model but we can use it to instantiate multiple gates of different input widths. The conventional programming language analogy would be that of using functions where the arguments determine the computation performed by the function.

```
library IEEE;
use IEEE.std_logic_1164.all;
entity generic_or is
generic (n: positive:=2);
port (in1 : in std_logic_vector ((n-1) downto 0);
    z : out std_logic);
end entity generic_or;

architecture behavioral of generic_or is
begin
process (in1) is
variable sum : std_logic:= '0';
begin
sum := '0'; -- on an input signal transition sum must be reset to 0
for i in 0 to (n-1) loop
sum := sum or in1(i);
end loop;
z <= sum;
end process;
end architecture behavioral;
```

FIGURE 8-12 An example of a parameterized gate model

Example End: N-Input OR Gate

Example: N-Bit Register

Another example of the use of generics is a parameterized model of an N-bit register. Generics may be used to configure the model in a specific instance to be of a fixed number of bits. Let us consider a register comprised of D flip-flops with asynchronous reset and load enable signals. The model is shown in Figure 8-13. The operation of the register (process) is sensitive to the occurrence of an event on the **reset** or **clk** signals. The size of the register is determined when this model is instantiated by a higher level model. The default value is a 2-bit register. Note the predefined type we have used for the generic parameter, namely, **positive**. This type is defined in VHDL to be a subtype of an integer with a range starting from 1 rather than 0. This forces the generic parameter to have a value of at least 1 and it cannot be less than 1. There can be no registers with 0 bits, which certainly makes sense. In general, when we are parameterizing physical quantities is usually the case that a value of 0 or negative values do not make sense. In these instances it is natural to use the type positive.

```vhdl
library IEEE;
use IEEE.std_logic_1164.all;
entity generic_reg is
generic (n: positive:=2);
port ( clk, reset, enable : in std_logic;
        d : in std_logic_vector (n-1 downto 0);
        q : out std_logic_vector (n-1 downto 0));
end entity generic_reg;

architecture behavioral of generic_reg is
begin
reg_process: process (clk, reset) is
begin
 if reset = '1' then
    q <= (others => '0');
   elsif (rising_edge(clk)) then
    if enable = '1' then
       q <= d;
   end if;
  end if;
 end process reg_process;
 end architecture behavioral;
```

FIGURE 8-13 An example of a parameterized model of an N-bit register

Note how the value of q is set using the **"others"** construct. Because q is a vector of bits, this statement provides a concise approach to specifying the values of all the bits in a vector when they are equal. A trace of the operation of this 2-bit register in the presence of various waveforms on the input signals is also shown in Figure 8-14.

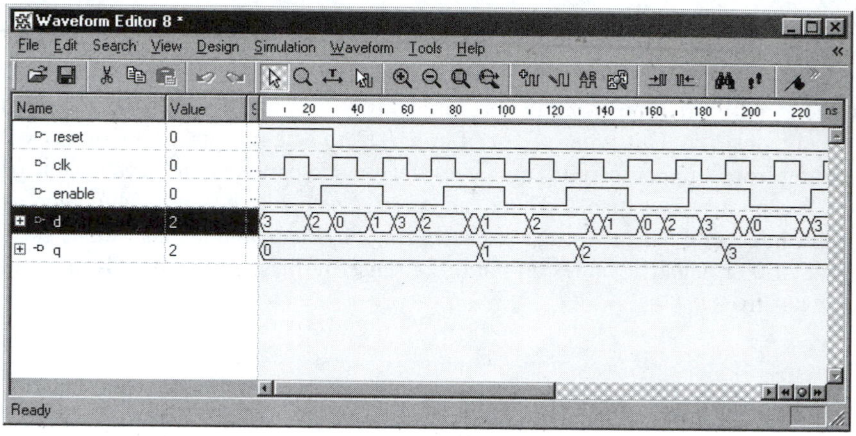

FIGURE 8-14 Trace of the operation of a 2-bit register

Example End: N-bit Register

Simulation Exercise 8.3: Use of Generics

This exercise illustrates the utility of the use of generics for parameter passing in structural models.

Step 1.   Start with the model of a single-bit ALU that is written using CSAs from Simulation Exercise 4.2. Modify this model to include a generic parameter to specify the gate delay. Set the default gate delay to 3 ns. Use 2 ns for the delay through the multiplexor.

Step 2.   Compile, simulate, and test this model and ensure that all three operations (AND, OR, and ADD) are correctly computed using this value of gate delay.

Step 3. Construct a VHDL structural model of a 2-bit ALU. Use the single-bit ALU as a building block. Use a ripple carry implementation to propagate the carry between single-bit ALUs. Remember to analyze (compile) the single-bit model before you analyze (compile) the 2-bit model.

Step 4. Use the **generic map** construct in the structural model of the 2-bit ALU to set the value of the gate delay 4 ns.

Step 5. Compile, simulate, and verify the functionality of this model.

Step 6. Open a trace window with the signals you would like to trace. In this case, you will need to only trace the input and output signals to test the model.

Step 7. Note how easy it is to modify the values of the gate delay at the top level, re-compile and simulate. Now change the model to use a generic n-input AND gate. The model can be modified as follows:

Step 7 (a) Create a model of a generic n-input AND gate to follow the model shown in Figure 8-12. Compile, simulate and test this model in isolation. Make sure it is in the same working directory as the rest of your model.

Step 7 (b) Modify the single-bit ALU model to declare the generic AND model as a component and specify a default value of 3 for the number of inputs to the AND gate.

Step 7 (c) In the model of the single-bit ALU replace the CSA describing the operation of the AND gate with a component instantiation statement for the generic AND model. This instantiation statement should also include a **generic map** statement providing the number of gate inputs as a parameter.

Step 7 (d) Because the default value of the number of inputs to the AND gate is 3, you must pass parameters correctly for this model to function.

Step 8. Compile and test your model. Trace the input and output signals to determine that the model functions correctly.

Step 9. Experiment with other possibilities. For example, you can use a generic model of an OR gate as well. This model is shown in Figure 8-12.

End Simulation Exercise 8.3

8.5 Component Instantiation and Synthesis

Up until this point the discussion in this chapter focused on the construction of structural models for the purpose of simulation. What are the implications, if any, of the structural style of modeling for synthesis? The specification of structural models does not by itself pose any fundamental issues for synthesis. The use of structural models is primarily a means for managing the complexity of a design in a manner that promotes the easy reuse of components. Before we can do anything with a structural model, for example simulation, the hierarchy must be flattened. The flattened model contains no structural descriptions but rather a number of interconnect components—entity-architecture pairs. This flattened model can now be simulated or placed and routed depending upon whether we have compiled or synthesized the individual components. However, the ability to instantiate specific components enables us to use previously synthesized and optimized implementations of common components that are provided by vendors or other design groups within an organization.

We have seen how VHDL models can be synthesized, placed, and routed in FPGAs. It is clear that there are many possible avenues for improving a synthesized design. For example we might structure the VHDL code in a manner that enables the synthesis compiler to produce better quality circuits where better quality typically refers to smaller or faster. The place and route tools may produce designs that are not as efficient as ones that we could perhaps realize manually if we had the time, energy, and someone paid us enough to optimize the placement and routing manually! However, the vendors may indeed take the time to develop highly optimized implementations of key components such as adders/subtractors, shift registers, counters, multiplexors, and ALUs. Often using proprietary tools and manual input very fast or very compact implementations of standard digital components as well as higher level architectural components such as queues and stacks are created. These components are provided in libraries to the users for use in larger systems.

For example consider the design or a simple 8-bit integer datapath that will be used as a programmable controller. This datapath is comprised of an adder/subtractor, four 8-bit registers, several multiplexors, 8-bit to 16-bit sign extension unit, and 1K 16-bit words of memory. We wish to construct a synthesizeable version of this datapath. If we already have optimized implementations for the 8-bit adder/subtractor and the memory in the vendor library we only need to write descriptions of two components, namely the register file and the sign extension unit. We can then write one structural model that instantiates all of these components. This structural model can then be synthesized. The re-use of existing components reduces the design time and often leads to implementations that are more efficient than we ourselves have time to generate. In fact, for sufficiently complex components, such as encryption modules, such placed and routed designs represent key intellectual property and such models are often for sale by third party design houses.

Many vendors will provide CAD tools that serve as "core generators" for common digital components. The idea is that a series of dialog boxes will enable you to select and then configure the component of your choice. The CAD tool will then generate a synthesizeable model of this component and a corresponding VHDL model that can be used for simulation. This is certainly more time efficient than writing your own. Furthermore the CAD tools generally do a good job of producing models that will generate highly optimized implementations for the target vendor FPGA devices. The VHDL modeling approach to using such a priori generated components is through component instantiation.

Example: Core Generation

The LogiBLOX module generator can be found within the Xilinx Foundation tools. This tool can be used to generate FPGA implementations of common components that can then be instantiated in a design. When the LogiBLOX module is invoked the dialog box shown in Figure 8-15 is produced. The pull-down menu in the upper center of the dialog box can

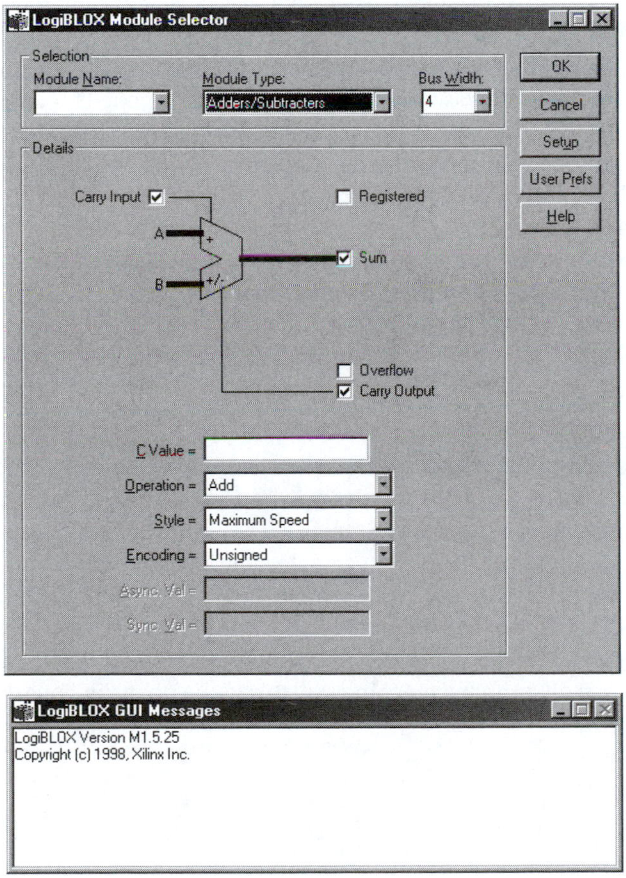

FIGURE 8-15 LogiBLOX module generator interface

be used to select from a variety of component types. The figure shows an adder/subtractor as the selected component. The user can select whether there is a carry in signal and whether carry out and overflow signals are to be generated. The bit width is also configurable. The options button leads to a dialog box where the user can select the vendor, target device, as well as options such as the generation of VHDL code for the model that can be used for functional simulation. At the bottom of the window are pull-down menus where the user can select the metric to be optimized such as area or speed. Once these options are selected the module generator creates an adder/subtractor module as well as an interface file shown in Figure 8-16. The user can simply cut-and-paste the component declaration into the architecture body of the VHDL model. The component instantiation statement is also provided. We need to simply replace the string "instance_name" with the name we wish to give this instance of the adder/subtractor and then specify the signals in our model that are to be connected to the inputs and outputs of this newly generated adder/subtractor. The LogiBLOX module generator has created the appropriate files in the working directory. Thus when our higher level structural VHDL model is analyzed and synthesized the tools can find the appropriate files.

One can expect that as time goes by the vendor-supplied module generators will only continue to grow in the number of components that are supported. This approach is not limited to synthesis. Component generators can also generator VHDL code for simulation. For example the LogiBLOX module generator will also generate VHDL code for the module that can be used for simulation-based studies. Such graphical interfaces for generating simulatable or synthesizeable VHDL code are becoming commonplace and may be found within the specific CAD tool suite you are using as well as be available from third party CAD tool vendors.

Example End: Core Generation

In addition to the generation of component implementations optimized for a specific target FPGA, there are other reasons why we may wish to instantiate existing special library components within a VHDL model. The most common reason is access to special components within the FPGA. For example, consider the case where your design requires a clock at a specific frequency, for example 15 Hz. FPGA chips typically will provide on chip oscillators that can be configured to provide clocks at one of several frequencies. By instantiating an oscillator component in your design the CAD tools can place and route the appropriate signals from the on-chip oscillator to the points in your design that need it.

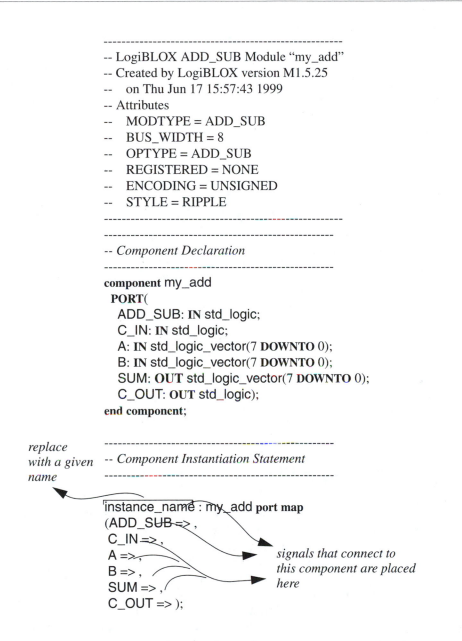

```
-------------------------------------------------------
-- LogiBLOX ADD_SUB Module "my_add"
-- Created by LogiBLOX version M1.5.25
--    on Thu Jun 17 15:57:43 1999
-- Attributes
--    MODTYPE = ADD_SUB
--    BUS_WIDTH = 8
--    OPTYPE = ADD_SUB
--    REGISTERED = NONE
--    ENCODING = UNSIGNED
--    STYLE = RIPPLE
-------------------------------------------------------
-------------------------------------------------------
-- Component Declaration
-------------------------------------------------------
component my_add
 PORT(
   ADD_SUB: IN std_logic;
   C_IN: IN std_logic;
   A: IN std_logic_vector(7 DOWNTO 0);
   B: IN std_logic_vector(7 DOWNTO 0);
   SUM: OUT std_logic_vector(7 DOWNTO 0);
   C_OUT: OUT std_logic);
end component;
```

replace with a given name

```
-------------------------------------------------------
-- Component Instantiation Statement
-------------------------------------------------------
instance_name : my_add port map
(ADD_SUB => ,
 C_IN => ,
 A => ,
 B => ,
 SUM => ,
 C_OUT => );
```

signals that connect to this component are placed here

FIGURE 8-16 Example of LogiBLOX generation

Example: Instantiation of an Oscillator

The Xilinx XC4000 chips have an on-chip oscillator that can provide signals generated from an 8-MHz clock. The user has access to 8-MHz, 500-KHz, 16-KHz, 490-Hz, and 15-Hz signals. This particular oscillator should not be expected to provide very timing tight tolerances (in fact they are rather loose!). To use this oscillator we simply declare the following component:

```
component OSC4 is
port (  F8M : out std_logic;
        F500k : out std_logic;
        F15 : out std_logic);
end component OSC4
```

Now the component can be instantiated in a design with the appropriate signals connected to internal signals of the design. If you only need a 15-Hz clock then you need only declare the component with one argument. The operator name is overloaded (see Chapter 9). Now a component instantiation statement can be used to connect this 15-Hz clock signal, namely F15 to any signal in the design.

Associated with the use of clocks is the availability of global low-skew lines in the FPGA chips to facilitate the distribution of global signals such as clocks across the chip. These low-skew signal paths can be accessed via global buffers or BUFG components. The component declaration is as follows:

```
component BUFG is
port (  I : in std_logic;
        O : out std_logic;);
end component BUGF;
```

We can instantiate this component and connect the input of this component to the output of the OSC4 component. The output of the BUFG component can then be mapped to the clock signal local to the VHDL model. When this design is placed and routed in the FPGA chip the clock signals will be distributed via the global lines. Any component that has this clock signal as an input has access from any portion of the chip to this signal because the clock is distributed throughout the chip via a low-skew global signal distribution network. Although this example shows how you can distribute the clock signal the BUFG components can be used to distribute any global signal. Such global buffers are generally scarce resources and should be used sparingly.

Figure 8-17 shows the use of the OSC4 and BUFG components in a design of a circuit that creates two clock signals. The OSC4 component is instantiated and the 15-Hz output is connected to one global buffer, namely a BUFG component. This clock signal is also inverted and connected to a second BUFG component. Thus this entity generates two global clock signals. The outputs of the BUFG components are connected to the output

```vhdl
library IEEE;
use IEEE.std_logic_1164.all;

entity my_clocks is
port (phi1, phi2: out std_logic);
end entity my_clocks;

architecture behavioral of my_clocks is
component OSC4 is -- we will use the on chip oscillator
port (F8M : out std_logic; -- 8-Mhz clock
F500k : out std_logic;    -- 500-Khz clock
F15 : out std_logic);     -- 15-Hz clock
end component OSC4;

component BUFG is      -- global buffer connection to low skew lines
port (I : in std_logic;
     O : out std_logic);
end component BUFG;

signal local_F15, local_phi2 : std_logic; -- local signals
begin
O1: osc4 port map(F15 =>local_F15); -- instantiate the oscillator
B1: bufg port map (I => local_F15, O => phi1); -- instantiate the two global buffers
B2: bufg port map (I => local_phi2, O => phi2);

local_phi2 <= not local_F15; -- phi2 is the complement of phi1

end architecture behavioral;
```

FIGURE 8-17 An example of instantiating predefined components

ports of the my_clocks entity. When this model is placed and routed the BUFG components will be placed on the global buffers in the FPGA and the phi1 and phi2 signals will
be available on the output signals from these buffers, which are globally distributed on the
chip. We will instantiate this entity, my_clocks, in a larger design to provide the phi1 and
phi2 clock signals. When this larger design is placed and routed the phi1 and phi2 signals
will be available from the global signals on the chip. Although this example is Xilinx specific, generally vendors will supply similar pre-defined components for such chip specific
functions.

Example End: Instantiation of an Oscillator

When designing logic that has sequential components such as flip-flops we are concerned with ensuring that the circuits are initialized to a correct state. When we use flip-flops with asynchronous clear and set inputs this can be achieved by driving these inputs on power up. FPGA vendors such as Xilinx provide global reset signals on chip (GSR) that can be accessed to initialize all flip-flops on the chip. The manner in which this facility can be accessed is described in the following example.

Example: Using Global Set Reset

The Xilinx XC4000XL components provide global set/reset signal that is distributed througout the chip to the set/reset inputs of the flip-flops. Each flip can be configured to use set or reset functionality, but not both. When using the Xilinx Foundation Express CAD environment, the manner in which we can gain access to this functionality from within VHDL models is by instantiating the STARTUP component and connecting the GSR input to a reset signal used in your design. An example is illustrated in Figure 8-18.

We have a simple block of code encapsulated in a process whose execution is controlled by a **wait** statement. Flip-flops are inferred for all signals in the process by virtue of being conditioned by the **wait** statement. Now a reset signal is checked to initialize the values of all of the flip-flops. Because this single signal is being used to reset all of the flip-flops we would like for this to be connected to a low-skew on-chip signal that is distributed globally to all flip-flops. This is achieved at the VHDL level by specifying the connection of the reset signal to the GSR input of the STARTUP symbol. During synthesis the placement and routing of signals will ensure that the reset signal will be connected to global set/reset signal that is present on the chip.

A few observations can be made about the use of the GSR net. Certainly a viable option is for the reset signal to be routed around the chip using the regular routing resources. However having a special signal that is routed around the chip to all of the set/ reset inputs of the flip-flops has some advantages. Because this implementation is custom the signal path can be made a low-skew path. Further, by not using the regular routing resources we prevent the distribution of reset from interacting/interfering with the routing of the remaining signals in the design. This improves the degree of freedom present to route the remainder of the design. Finally, this example illustrates how global set/reset behavior can be explicitly realized by the designer. Modern synthesis compilers do go through the process of GSR inferencing where the compiler attempts to automatically infer the presence of a GSR signal and simply use it transparent to the user.

Example End: Using Global Set/Reset

It should be apparent now that from the point of view of writing models a component instantiation statement is on par with a CSA statement or a process construct. The body of an architecture may be comprised of all three types of statements and they individually

```vhdl
library IEEE;
use IEEE.std_logic_1164.all;

entity startup_exm is
port ( clk, reset,x, y, z: in std_logic;
w : out std_logic);
end startup_exm;

architecture behavior of startup_exm is
component STARTUP is          -- declare the STARTUP component
port (GSR : in std_logic);
end component STARTUP;
signal s1, s2 : std_logic;
begin
U1: STARTUP port map(GSR => reset); -- instantiate the STARTUP component
process is
begin
wait until (rising_edge(clk));
if (reset = '1') then                 -- this is the reset signal that should be driving
w <= '0';                             -- preset or clear inputs
s1 <= '0';                            -- a flip-flop is inferred for each of these signals
s2 <= '0';
else
L1: s1 <= x xor y;
L2: s2 <= s1 or z;
L3: w <= s1 nor s2;
end if;
nd process;
end architecture behavior;
```

FIGURE 8-18 Implementing global set/reset functionality

model concurrent activities. The declaration part of the **architecture** construct may now include declarations of signals as well as components. Thus we see that the term structural models does not imply that we can only describe the digital system or circuit as an interconnected set of components, We can mix component instantiation statements with signal assignment statements and processes. A template for a general VHDL model is illustrated in Figure 8-19.

library library-name-1, library-name-2;
use library-name-1.package-name.all;
use library-name-2.package-name.all;

entity entity_name **is**
port(input signals : **in** *type*;
    output signals : **out** *type*);
end entity entity_name;

architecture arch_name **of** entity_name **is**

    -- declare components used

component component1_name

port(input signals : **in** *type*;

    output signals : **out** *type*);

end component;

 component component2_name

port(input signals : **in** *type*;

    output signals : **out** *type*);

end component;

    -- declare all signals used to connect the components

signal internal signals : type := initialization;

begin

    -- label each component and connect its ports to signals or other ports

Label1: component1-name **port map** (port=> signal,.....);
Label2: component2-name **port map** (port => signal,.....);

      -- we can include behavioral modeling statements that execute
      -- concurrently
concurrent signal assignment statement-1;
concurrent signal assignment statement-2;
process-1: ..
process-2:..

end architecture arch_name;

FIGURE 8-19 Component instantiation in behavioral models

Synthesis Exercise 8.4:

The synthesis and simulation of a structural model follows a sequence of steps similar to that encountered in functional simulation. In this exercise we will use the same model as in Simulation Exercise 8.1 and synthesize the hierarchical model of the full adder. Using the same model will highlight similarities as well as differences between functional simulation and synthesis of structural models.

Step 1. Create a text file with the structural model of the full adder shown in Figure 8-2. Let us refer to this file as *full-adder.vhd*.

Step 2. Create a text file with the model of the half adder shown in Figure 4-2. Let us refer to this file as *half-adder.vhd*. Ensure that the entity name for the half adder in this file is the same as the name you have used for the half-adder component declaration in the full-adder structural model. Remember the environment must have some way of being able to find and use the components that you need when you synthesize the model of the full adder. The same considerations apply here as in step 2 of Simulation Exercise 8.1.

Step 3. Create a text file with a model of a 2-input OR gate. Let us refer to this file as *or2.vhd*. Again make sure that the entity name is the same as the component name for the 2-input OR gate model declared in the model of the full adder. Unlike the simulation model in Simulation Exercise 8.1 you will not include gate delays in the model description.

Step 4. Synthesize *or2.vhd, half-adder.vhd*, and *full-adder.vhd* in this order.

Step 5. Now you can simulate the full-adder model.

Step 6. Open a trace window with the signals you would like to trace.

Step 7. Generate a test case. Apply the stimulus corresponding to the test case to the inputs. Run the simulation for one time step. Examine the output to ensure it is correct.

Step 8. Run the simulation for 50 ns.

Step 9. Using the reporting facility available in your CAD tools determine the input to output delay of the synthesized circuit. What is the maximum clock rate at which this circuit can operate?

Step 10. View the schematic of the synthesized circuit. Can you recognize the half adder components.

Step 11. For comparison purposes create a VHDL model of a full adder shown in Figure 4-3. This is a flat as opposed to hierarchical model. Compare the structure and the resulting speed and area characteristics of the synthesized circuits of the two models.

End Synthesis Exercise 8.4

8.6 The Generate Statement

In the preceding sections the construction of structural models was based on instantiation the components in a design. Each component instantiation statement described how the component inputs and outputs were connected to other signals in the design. As a result if we create designs with a large number of components we write a large number of component instantiation statements. Apart from the obvious time investment opportunities increase for errors.

Suppose the design we are describing has a very regular structure. It would be very economical to be able to describe this structure and let the language or CAD tools worry about the detailed list of component instantiation statements. For example, the construction of a 32-bit register from D flip-flops can be easily described more compactly that having to write 32 component instantiation statements. The VHDL language provides such descriptive power in the form of the **generate** statement. The choice of terminology is intentional and descriptive. Let us start with the simple example of a 32-bit register. Then we will proceed to a more complex example.

Example: N-bit Register

Let us assume the availability of a model of a 1-bit D flip-flop named dff. Using this component we wish to construct an 4-bit register. A straightforward model constructed using the techniques described earlier in this chapter is shown in Figure 8-20. The model is composed of four component instantiation statements—one for each flip-flop that is used to construct the register.

The **generate** statement can be used to describe such a model more compactly. For example, note the arguments for the signals din and qout in the architecture body. In each statement the value increases by one. In conventional programming languages we do not add two arrays by having one assignment for each pair of elements; instead, we write a loop. The **generate** statement can be used to perform the same function. The example in Figure 8-20 is rewritten using the **generate** statement and is shown in Figure 8-21.

The structure is very similar to that of a loop. In addition the model uses a generic parameter to set the bit width resulting is a very general, configurable register model. Each iteration through the loop effectively creates one of the component instantiation statements in Figure 8-20.

Example End: N-bit Register

The majority of structures one will typically encounter will not be as regular as registers. Rather a large portion of the design may be regular with a few components that warrant special treatment. Moreover the individual components are not likely to be independent of the other components as individual register bits are. There may be depen-

```
library IEEE;
use IEEE.std_logic_1164.all;

entity dregister is
port ( din : in std_logic_vector(3 downto 0);
       qout : out std_logic_vector(3 downto 0);
       clk : in std_logic);
end entity dregisters;

architecture behavioral of dregister is
component dff is
port ( d, clk : in std_logic;
       q : out std_logic);
end component dff;

begin
       bit0: dff port map( d=>din(0), q=>qout(0), clk=>clk);
       bit1: dff port map( d=>din(1), q=>qout(1), clk=>clk);
       bit2: dff port map( d=>din(2), q=>qout(2), clk=>clk);
       bit3: dff port map( d=>din(3), q=>qout(3), clk=>clk);
end architecture dregister;
```

FIGURE 8-20 Creating an N-bit register using the component instantiation statements

dencies between components in the form of input/output signals. For example, consider the case of an 8-bit adder. For a ripple carry adder, full adders used in adjacent bit positions are connected by the carry signals between them. Models for such circuits employ the **generate** statement for portions of the design and can rely on general component instantiation statements for the remaining components. The following example will illustrate this point.

Example: N-bit ALU

This example illustrates the use of the generate statement for the construction of a multibit ALU. Let us assume that we have a model of a single bit ALU described in Simulation Exercise 4.2 and shown in Figure 4-10 and the name of this model is one_bit. This model can perform single-bit addition, logical AND, and logical OR on a pair of bits. The actual operation is selected by the opcode input signal. Our goal is to construct a multibit model using the generate statement. We arrive at the VHDL model as follows.

```
library IEEE;
use IEEE.std_logic_1164.all;

entity dregister is
generic (width : natural:=16); -- default width of the register is 16
port ( din : in std_logic_vector(width-1 downto 0);
       qout : out std_logic_vector(width-1 downto 0);
       clk : in std_logic);
end entity dregisters;

architecture behavioral of dregister is
component dff is
port ( d, clk : in std_logic;
       q : out std_logic);
end component dff;

begin
       dreg: for i in d'range generate
       reg: dff port map( d=>din(i), q=>qout(i), clk=>clk);
       end generate;
end architecture dregister;
```

FIGURE 8-21 The model in Figure 8-20 rewritten using the generate statement

The ALU model will use ripple carry for addition. In this case the ALUs at bit positions 0 and 7 differ in their external interconnects from the ALUs in bit positions 1 through 6. Consider an ALU in any of the positions 1 through 6. For any such ALU, i, it will receive a carry input from ALU i-1 and will generate a carry signal for ALU i+1. The inputs will be drawn from entity inputs i and the outputs will produce values for entity output bit i. The ALU at bit position 0 differs in that the carry input will be from the entity carry input. The ALU in bit position 7 similarly differs in that the carry that is generated must be connected to the carry output of the entity. Thus, we can use a generate statement to instantiate ALUs in bit positions 1 through 6 whereas the ALUs in bit positions 0 and 7 will be instantiated separately.

Note the need to provide separate **generic map** statements. Finally, to connect the individual carry signals a local array of signals, carry_vector, is declared. From the code it is clear that declaring these signals as an array is necessary to be able to the write the **generate** statement.

Example End: N-bit ALU

In the example shown in Figure 8-22 you will notice that all of the statements are labeled. The language requires all component instantiation statements to be labeled as well as all **generate** statements. Note that the labels by themselves have no active role. Thus the label a2to6 could just as easily have been GTech. However in general, the use of meaningful labels and names is of course encouraged. Further, as you might expect generate statements can be nested.

From the preceding examples we can uncover a few general principles to help guide us in the use of the **generate** statement when we have arrays of components that we wish to instantiate.

- Structure the array of components indexed by i, j, an so on.

- Declare, as necessary, signal vectors local to the architecture to interconnect the components.

- Determine which range of components that can be encapsulated within a generate statement.

- Write one component instantiation statement for each of the remaining components.

In trying to determine how to correctly index the components and signal vectors it is useful to think of sequential program loops whose loop bodies process array data structures. Exercising care is necessary because unconnected ports on a component are not necessarily reported by the compiler. The resulting design can easily lead to errorneous results because these unconnected signals are simply modeled as unconnected signals in the target design. This can lead to the propagation of undefined signal values through the design as well as the computation of incorrect signal values.

8.7 Configurations

We have seen that there are many different ways in which to model the operation of a digital circuit utilizing behavioral and structural models. Approaches to the construction of behavioral models may differ in the use of concurrent and/or sequential statements. Structural models may employ multiple levels of abstraction and each component within a structural model may, in turn, be described as a behavioral or structural model. Consider the structural model of the full adder shown in Figure 8-2. Assume that two alternate architectures exist for the half-adder components. Design–1 is a behavioral model, as specified in Figure 4-2. Design–2 is a structural model, as specified in Figure 8-6. When the full-adder model shown in Figure 8-2 is compiled and simulated, which architecture for the half adder should be used? You would like to configure your simulation model to be able to use one or the other. The VHDL language provides *configurations* for explicitly associating an architecture description with each component in a structural model. This process of association is referred to as *binding* an instance of the component (in this example, the half adder) to an architecture. In the absence of any programmer-supplied configuration information, *default* binding rules apply.

```vhdl
library IEEE;
use IEEE.std_logic_1164.all;

entity multi_bit_generate is
generic(   gate_delay:time:= 1 ns;
              width:natural:=8); -- the default is a 8-bit ALU
port(  in1 : in std_logic_vector(width-1 downto 0);
       in2 : in std_logic_vector(width-1 downto 0);
       result : out std_logic_vector(width-1 downto 0);
       opcode : in std_logic_vector(1 downto 0);
       cin : in std_logic;
       cout : out std_logic);
end multi_bit_generate;

architecture behavioral of multi_bit_generate is
component one_bit is -- declare the single bit ALU
generic (gate_delay:time);
port ( in1, in2, cin : in std_logic;
       result, cout : out std_logic;
       opcode: in std_logic_vector (1 downto 0));
end component one_bit;

signal carry_vector: std_logic_vector(6 downto 0); -- the set of signals for the
                                                    -- ripple carry
begin
a0:  one_bit generic map (gate_delay) -- instantiate ALU for bit position 0
port map (in1=>in1(0), in2=>in2(0), result=>result(0), =>cin, opcode=>opcode,
     cout=>carry_vector(0));

a2to6: for i in 1 to width-2 generate  -- generate instantiations for bit positions 2-6
     a1: one_bit  generic map (gate_delay)
     port map(in1=>in1(i), in2=> in2(i), cin=>carry_vector(i-1),
          result=>result(i), cout=>carry_vector(i),opcode=>opcode);
end generate;

a7: one_bit generic map (gate_delay) -- instantiate ALU for bit position 7
     port map (in1=>in1(width-1), in2=>in2(width-1), result=> result(width-1),
cin=>carry_vector(width-2), opcode=>opcode, cout=>cout);
end architecturebehavioral;
```

FIGURE 8-22 Generating a multi-bit ALU

The notion of configurations is graphically illustrated in Figure 8-23. A design will have a single entity that describes how this design interfaces to its environment. The implementation is captured in the corresponding architecture that may instantiate several components. For each of these components there are multiple possible implementations and each implementation is captured in an entity-architecture pair. In fact all of these alternative implementations will have identical entity descriptions but distinct architecture descriptions. To construct a simulation configurations are used to specify a specific entity-architecture for each component that is instantiated in the top level model.

Rather than jump right into the syntax and semantics of configurations we are better served if we can at first generate an intuition about the nature of configurations. What better way to do this than by examples?

Example: Component Binding

As an example of binding architectures to components, consider the structural model of a state machine for bit-serial addition shown in Figure 8-4. The component C1 implements the combinational logic portion of the state machine. There may be alternative implementations of the gate-level design of C1 corresponding to alternative designs for high speed,

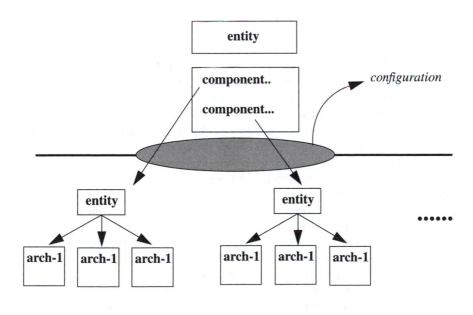

FIGURE 8-23 The role of configurations

low power, parts from different vendors, or even simply a behavioral model written for simulation. One of these alternative models must be *bound* to the component C1 for simulation. The configuration construct in VHDL specifies one, and only one, such binding.

Note that we are concerned only with binding the combinational logic component with an architecture and are not concerned with configuring the entity description of C1. This is because the interface does not change and therefore all alternative architectures for C1 will share an identical entity description. In fact the entity description is identical to the component declaration for C1. It is the implementation of C1 that may change and this is captured in an architecture for C1.

Example End: Component Binding

Notice how easy it is to analyze different implementations. We simply change the configuration, compile, and simulate. Configurations also make it easy to share designs. When newer component models become available we can bind the new architecture to the component by editing the configuration information and compile and simulate. We do not have to modify the VHDL structural model.

There are two ways in which configuration information can be provided: *configuration specification* and *configuration declaration*. But first, let us state the default binding rules that have been in effect for the examples in this chapter and explain how the VHDL tools find the architectures for the components in a structural model when no configuration information is provided.

8.7.1 Default Binding Rules

The structural model is simply a description of a schematic. Revisiting our analogy with the construction of a circuit on a protoboard, we now have to build the operational circuit. Assume that each component can be realized with a single chip from one of many vendors. We can think of the configurations as describing the chips we need to obtain and place on the board: one for each component. What if no configuration information was provided? How would we know what chip to use for each component and where to get them from? Clearly, we expect some rules for doing so. For example, we might first look around the lab bench for chips with the same names as the components. If we could not find them we might then look in the "usual" cabinet where all chips are stored, again looking for chips with the same names as the component names. Such rules are analogous to the default binding rules in VHDL.

If no configuration information is provided as in the preceding examples then a default architecture may be found as follows: if the entity name is the same as the component name, then this entity is bound to the component. For example, for the structural model in Figure 8-4, no configuration information is provided. The language rules enable a search for entities with the same names, in this case, comb and dff. These may be found in the working directory, in which case the architectures associated with these entities are used. However, what if there are multiple architectures for the entity, such as for comb, as shown in Figure 8-24? In this case, the last compiled architecture for entity comb is used. Now the environment can construct a complete simulation model. Using the default rules, we see that by using component names that are the same as the entity names we can avoid writing configurations. This is what we have managed to do up to this point in this chapter. Using the same names for components and their entities also improves the readability of the code.

However, if no such entity with the same name is visible to the VHDL environment, then the binding is said to be deferred, that is, no binding takes place now, but information will be forthcoming later, as described in the following sections. This is akin to going ahead with wiring the rest of the circuit and hoping your partner comes up with the right chips before you are ready to run the experiment!

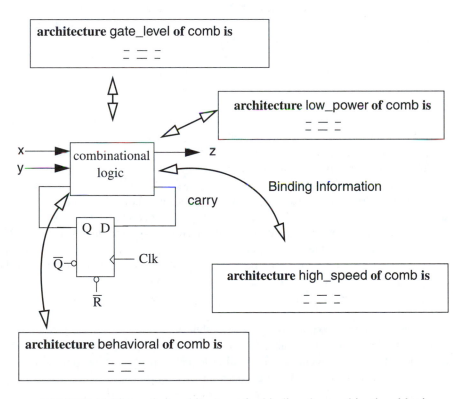

FIGURE 8-24 Alternative architectures for binding the combinational logic component of a state machine

8.7.2 Configuration Specification

Configuration specifications are used in the architecture body to identify the relationships between the components and the entity–architecture pairs to be used to model each component. Continuing with our laboratory analogy, consider how we might specify the chips to be used for a component that we have declared. We might specify the chip name and location, for example, in the box labeled half adders in the gray cabinet. How can we similarly define the exact location of an entity–architecture pair? We can do so by naming the design library within which it is located and the name of the design unit within which they are stored. The syntax is shown in Figure 8-25.

For the first half-adder component we state that the entity description can be found in the library WORK. Libraries are generally implemented as directories in most systems. The library WORK is a special library and is usually the default working directory. Because an entity can have multiple architectures, the name of the architecture to be used for this entity can be specified within parentheses. Notice that for the second half adder, the configuration specification uses a different architecture. If only an entity and no architecture is specified, then the last compiled architecture for that entity is used. All components of the same type need not use the same architecture, or even the same entity! The configuration of the two-input OR gate deserves special attention. In this case, we have chosen to use an entity with a name different from the component. Therefore we have to provide additional information. For example, if you were simply given a new chip named lpo2, you would need to know which pins corresponded to inputs and which corresponded to outputs before you could use this in place of the or_2 component. This information is provided as part of the configuration statement, as shown in Figure 8-25 via a **port map** () construct. We are using an entity named lpo2 that has been compiled into a library named POWER. The corresponding architecture that we will use is named behavioral and can be found in the same library. Similar arguments hold for any generic parameters.

Thus, we see that we can specify any type of binding as long as the ports and arguments match up. We do not even need to use the same names. However, just as wiring up a circuit becomes a bit more involved, so does the writing and management of the models. The readability of the code is particularly important as the sizes of the models grow and the choice of names does become important. If we keep the same names for the entities and the components that are bound to them, then we can rely on default rules for configuring the simulation models and no **port map** clause is required in the configuration statement.

There is some economy of expression that we can employ if all of the half_adder components in the circuit use the same entity-architecture pair. In this case the two component instantiation statements corresponding to H1 and H2 can be replaced by a single component instantiation statement as follows:

for all: half_adder **use entity** WORK.half_adder (behavioral);

```
library IEEE;
library POWER; -- a new library
use IEEE.std_logic_1164.all;
entity full_adder is
port (In1, In2, c_in : in std_logic;
      sum, c_out : out std_logic);
end entity full_adder;

architecture structural of full_adder is
component half_adder is
port (x, y : in std_logic;
      sum, carry : out std_logic);
end component half_adder;

component or_2 is
generic (gate_delay : Time:= 2 ns);
 port (x, y : in std_logic;
       z : out std_logic);
end component or_2;
signal s1, s2, s3 : std_logic;
--
-- configuration specification
--
for H1: half_adder use entity WORK.half_adder (behavioral);
for H2: half_adder use entity WORK.half_adder (structural);
for O1: or_2 use entity POWER.lpo2 (behavioral)
generic map(gate_delay => gate_delay)
port map (I1 => x, I2 => y, Z=>z);

begin      -- component instantiation statements
H1: half_adder port map (x =>In1, y => In2,
                              sum => s1, carry=> s2);
H2: half_adder port map (x => s1, y => c_in,
                              sum => sum, carry => s2);
O1: or_2 port map(x => s2, y => s3, z => c_out);

end architecture structural;
```

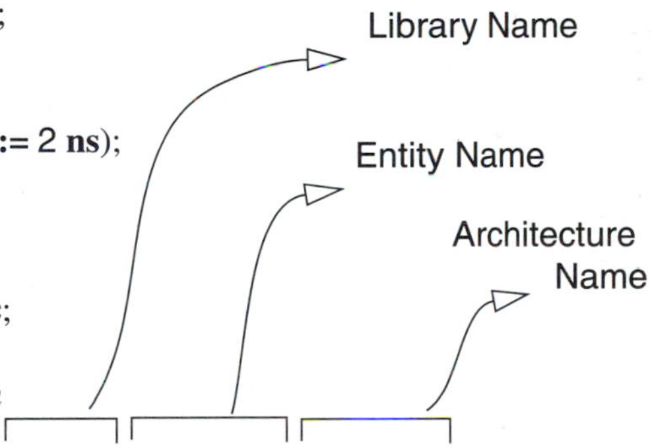

Library Name

Entity Name

Architecture Name

FIGURE 8-25 An example of using configuration specifications for the structural model of a full adder

We can think of configuration specifications as syntactic representations of what we might ask for verbally if we were wiring up the circuit on a protoboard. For example, the preceding configuration statement can be thought of as stating "for all of the half adder components use the same chip XYZ". Machine readable representations of such statements must necessarily follow a precise syntax and have clear semantics associated with the statements.

Finally we note that configuration specifications are not always supported for synthesis. In this case the default binding rules apply.

8.7.3 Configuration Declaration

The configuration specification is part of the architecture and must be placed within the architecture body. Modification of our choice of models to implement a component requires editing the architecture and recompiling the model. A configuration declaration enables us to provide the same configuration information, but as a separate design unit and, if desired, in a separate file. In the same way that entities and architectures are design units, so are configuration declarations. Suppose we take all of the configuration information provided in the architecture in Figure 8-25, name it, and refer to it by its name. This unit is a configuration declaration and is a distinct design unit. An example of the configuration information in Figure 8-25 provided as a configuration declaration, is shown in Figure 8-26.

```
configuration Config_A of full_adder is   -- name the configuration
                                           -- for the entity
    for structural    -- name of the architecture being configured
    for H1: half_adder use entity WORK.half_adder (behavioral);
    end for;
    --
    for H2: half_adder use entity WORK.half_adder (structural);
    end for;
    --
    for O1: or_2 use entity POWER.lpo2 (behavioral)
    generic map(gate_delay => gate_delay)
    port map (I1 => a, I2 => b, Z=>c);
    end for;
    --
    end for;
    end configuration Config_A;
```

FIGURE 8-26 A configuration declaration for the structural model of the full adder in Figure 8-25

Like other design units, we name configuration declarations as shown on the first line. In addition, the entity that is to utilize this configuration information is also named. Note that this declaration looks very similar to an architecture declaration. The second line identifies the name of the specific architecture of this entity that is being configured. For example, there could be another structural model of the full adder placed in an architecture labeled Structural_B. We must be able to distinguish between alternative architectures unambiguously and do so by referring to the unique architecture labels.

A close examination of the syntax will reveal that the **for** statements are terminated by **end for** clauses. Although the above declaration deals only with one level of the hierarchy, configuration declarations can be written to span a complete design hierarchy with nested **for...end for** constructs to bind components at all levels of the hierarchy. It is also apparent that we can have different configurations for the full adder. For example, we might have a Config_B and a Config_C. Each configuration could use a different set of components or models for the half adder and two-input OR gate components. We might be motivated to take this approach to study the implementation with different technologies, for example, low-power versus high-speed implementations.

There are several other advanced topics in the area of binding components to architectures, such as direct instantiation, incremental binding, and binding to configurations rather than an entity–architecture pair. These topics can be found in any advanced book on VHDL. The key issue to be understood here is that configurations are the language mechanism that is provided to specify a particular implementation when a myriad of alternative models are available for the constituent components. The use of configurations is motivated in part by the need to be able to re-use models and share models among developers. This implies that it should be easy to selectively replace individual components of large simulation models and configurations are the VHDL solution to this problem.

Simulation Exercise 8.5: Use of Configurations

This exercise will emphasize the need and importance of configurations. The exercise builds on Simulation Exercise 8.2, which produced two distinct models of an 8-bit adder. The first model was a structural model hierarchically built from smaller size ALUs, and the second was a behavioral model constructed using processes.

Step 1.   Construct a 16-bit ALU from two 8-bit ALUs using ripple carry. Use the entity description of the 8-bit ALU developed in Simulation Exercise 8.2.

Step 2.   Include in the model a configuration specification such as the one shown in Figure 8-25, to specify the name of the architecture of the 8-bit model that you wish to use. Start with the hierarchical 8-bit model. All of the models that are used in building this 8-bit ALU are assumed to have been compiled into your working directory. Make sure the library WORK is set to your current working directory.

Step 3.   Compile the 16-bit ALU. Test the model and ensure that it is functioning cor-
           rectly.

Step 4.   Now modify the configuration specification to use the behavioral model of the 8-
           bit ALU. This should require editing one line (in fact one word) of your VHDL
           model—the line in your configuration specification.

Step 5.   Test this model and ensure that it is working. Note the ease with which it is possi-
           ble to "plug" in different models of subcomponents of the 16-bit ALU.

Step 6.   List some of the differences between the two models that you have constructed.

End Simulation Exercise 8.5

8.8 Common Programming Errors

The following are some common programming errors.

*   Modifying the model of a component and forgetting to reanalyze the component model
    prior to reuse.

*   Generics can have their values defined at three places: within the model, in a compo-
    nent instantiation statement using the **generic map()** construct, and within an architec-
    ture in a component declaration. Changing the value of the generics in one place may
    not have the intended effect due to precedence of the other declarations. The actual
    value of the generic parameter may not be what you expect.

*   When using default bindings of components, the name, type, and mode of each signal
    in the component declaration must exactly match that of the entity, otherwise an error
    will result.

*   Inheriting a generic value by way of default intializations in the component declara-
    tions in the higher level may lead to unexpected values of the generic parameters. A
    clear idea of how generic values are propagated through the hierarchy is necessary to
    ensure that the acquired values of the generic parameters corresponds to the intended
    values.

*   When instantiating components a signal in a component may be overlooked. This does
    not necessarily lead to compiler errors and the signal is modeled as unconnected in the
    design. The result can be incorrectly computed values or undefined signals propagating
    through the design.

8.9   Chapter Summary

The focus of this chapter has been on the ability to specify hierarchical models of digital systems *ignoring* how the internal behavior of components may be specified. Internal behavior can be described using language features described in Chapter 4 and Chapter 6. An important aspect of the construction of hierarchical models is the ability to construct parameterized behavioral models and to be able to determine values of parameters by passing information down this hierarchy. This is facilitated by the **generic** construct and enables the construction of libraries of models that can be shared by designers. Finally, given such a library of alternative models for a component, the specification of the particular models to be used in the construction of a model is provided by **configuration** construct.

The concepts covered in this chapter include:

- Structural models
    - component declaration
    - component instantiation
- Construction of hierarchical models
    - abstraction
    - trade-offs between accuracy and simulation speed
- Generics
    - specifying generic values
    - constructing parameterized models
- Component instantiation for synthesis
    - use of core generators
    - instantiating and using device specific, vendor supplied components
- Configurations
    - component binding
    - default binding rules
    - configuration specification
    - configuration declaration

We now have command of the basic constructs for creating VHDL models of digital systems. The following chapters address remaining issues in support of these basic constructs to provide a complete set of modeling tools.

Exercises

1. Complete the structural model of the bit-serial adder shown in Figure 8-4 by constructing a model for the two components. You must complete the design of the combinational logic component. Compile, simulate, and test the model.

2. Consider the detailed hierarchical model of an 8-bit ALU constructed in Simulation Exercise 8.2. Now consider a single-level, behavioral model of the 8-bit ALU constructed using a single process and 8-bit data types. Compare the two models and comment on the simulation accuracy, simulation time, and functionality.

3. You are part of a software group developing algorithms for processing speech signals for a new digital signal processing chip. To test your software your options are to construct (i) a detailed hierarchical model of the chip composed of gate-level models at the lowest level of the hierarchy or (ii) a behavioral-level model of the chip that can implement the algorithms that you wish to use. Your goal is to produce correct code for a number of algorithms prior to detailed testing on a hardware prototype. How would you evaluate these choices and what are the trade-offs in picking one approach over the other?

4. Construct and test a structural model of the circuit shown below. Note that there are many different ways in which to do this. You might consider each gate a component or groups of gates as a component represented by the Boolean function that is computed by this gates.

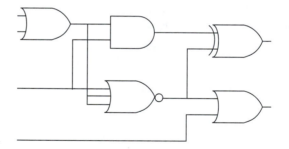

5. Consider the circuit shown below. Construct a structural model comprised of two components: a generic N-input AND gate and a two-input OR gate. By passing the appropriate generic value we can instantiate the same basic AND gate component as a two-input or three-input AND gate.

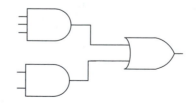

6. In problem 5 use generics to set default gate delays for the components. Now instantiate each AND gate with different gate delays using the **generic map** construct.

7. Modify the generic model of an N-bit register shown in Figure 8-13 to operate as counter that is initialized to a preset value.

8. Compare the use of configuration specifications and configuration declarations. When is one or the other advantageous?

9. Implement the structural model of a full adder using configuration specifications as shown in Figure 8-25. Use a simple model of the two-input OR gate rather than the one shown in the figure. You can omit the configuration statement for the OR gate and use the default binding for this component. Use two different architectures for the half-adder components.

CHAPTER 9

Sub-Programs, Packages, and Libraries

With any large body of software we need mechanisms for structuring programs, reusing software modules, and otherwise managing design complexity. In conventional languages, these mechanisms have been available to us for some time. The VHDL language, however, also provides support for such mechanisms through the definition and use of procedures and functions for encapsulating commonly used operations, and the concepts of packages and libraries for sharing large bodies of code.

However, hardware description languages possess several attributes that do not have counterparts in conventional programming languages. For example, the presence of the **signal** class of objects and the notion of simulation time are very different abstractions from those we normally use. The VHDL models may be used for the discrete event simulation of physical systems or to generate an implementation of the physical system described by the model. Collectively these features generate considerations that do not arise in conventional programming languages. For example, can **wait** statements be used in a procedure? How are signals passed as parameters to procedures and modified? How are procedures synthesized? Can functions operate on signals? The essential issues governing the use of functions and procedures are initially discussed in this chapter.

Related groups of functions and procedures can be aggregated into a module that can be shared across many different VHDL models. Such a module is referred to as a *package*. In addition to the definitions of procedures and functions, packages may contain user-defined data types and constants. Packages in turn can be placed in *libraries*. Libraries are repositories for design units in general, and packages are one type of design unit. Other design units are entities, architectures, and configurations. Collectively, procedures, functions, packages, and libraries provide facilities for creating and maintaining modular and reusable VHDL programs.

Functions and procedures are a means for structuring VHDL programs. Thus, from the perspective of synthesis I do not view these constructs as being special from the point of view of inferring hardware. Rather, the concepts conveyed in Chapter 5 and Chapter 7 are fundamental to the use of the language for synthesis. The synthesis considerations discussed here really follow from those basic language concepts—we just need to interpret them in the context of the semantics of function calls and procedure calls. From this perspective packages and libraries can be viewed as repositories for functions, procedure calls, and data types. Thus, rather than provide a separate chapter for this subject, synthesis considerations are treated along with the discussion of the use sub-programs and packages for simulation.

9.1 Essentials of Functions

As in traditional programming languages, functions are used to compute a value based on the values of the input parameters. An example of a function declaration is:

function rising_edge (**signal** clock: **in** std_logic) **return boolean**;

The function definition provides a function name, specification of the input parameters, and the type of the result. Functions return values that are computed using the input parameters. Therefore, we would expect that the parameter values are used, but not changed within the function. This notion is captured in the **mode** of the parameter. Parameters of mode **in** can only be read. Functions cannot modify parameter values (procedures can) and therefore functions do not have any parameters of mode **out**. Because the mode of all function parameters is **in**, we do not have to specify the mode of a parameter. A discussion of other possible modes is presented with a discussion of procedures in Section 9.2.

Consider the structure of a function as shown in Figure 9-1. The function has a name (rising_edge) and a set of parameters. The parameters in the function definition are referred to as *formal* parameters. Formal parameters can be thought of as placeholders that describe the type of object that will be passed into the function. When the function is actually called in a VHDL module, the arguments in the call are referred to as *actual* parameters. For example, the above function may be called in the following manner:

rising_edge (enable);

In this case, the actual parameter is the signal enable, and takes the place of the formal parameter clock in the body of the function. The type of the formal and actual parameters must match—except for formal parameters, which are constants. In this case, the actual parameter may be a variable, signal, constant, or an expression. When no class is specified, the default class of the parameter is constant. Wait statements are not permitted in functions. Thus, functions execute in zero simulation time. It follows that wait statements cannot exist in any procedures called by a function (although procedures are

```
function rising_edge (signal clock: std_logic) return boolean is
--
--declarative region: declare variables local to the function
--
begin
--
-- body
--
return (value)
end function rising_edge;
```

FIGURE 9-1 Structure of a function

allowed to have wait statements). Furthermore, parameters are restricted to be of mode **in**, and therefore functions cannot modify the input parameters. Thus, signals passed into functions cannot be assigned values. This behavior is consistent with the conventional definition of functions.

VHDL'93 supports two distinct types of functions: pure functions and impure functions. The former are functions that always return the same value when called with the same parameter values. Such functions conform to what we normally regard as the mathematical definition of a function. Impure functions on the other hand can return different values when called with the same parameter values at different times. This is possible because functions may have visibility over signals that are not in the parameter list, for example, ports of the encompassing entity. Pure functions occur commonly as type conversion and resolution functions. In this chapter our discussion is restricted to only pure functions.

'87 vs. '93

Example: Detection of Signal Events

Often we find it useful to perform simple tests on signals to determine if certain events have taken place. For example, the detection of a rising edge is common in the modeling of sequential circuits. Figure 9-2 shows the VHDL model of a positive-edge-triggered D flip-flop from Figure 6-10. The only difference is the inclusion of a function for testing for the rising edge, rather than having the function code in the body of the VHDL description. Note the placement of the function in the declarative portion of the architecture. Normally this region is used to declare signals and constants used in the body of the architecture. Therefore, we might expect that we can also declare functions (or procedures) that are used in the architecture too. This is indeed the case. The function could have also been declared in the declarative region of the process that called the function (i.e., between the keywords **process** and **begin**.) The question is whether you wish to have the function be

```
library IEEE;
use IEEE.std_logic_1164.all;
entity dff is
port (D, Clk : in std_logic;
      Q, Qbar : out std_logic);
end entity dff;

architecture behavioral of dff is
function rising_edge (signal clock : std_logic) return boolean is
variable edge : boolean:= FALSE;
begin
edge := (clock = '1' and clock'event);
return (edge);
end function rising_edge;

begin
output: process is
begin
wait until (rising_edge(Clk));

    Q <= D after 5 ns;
    Qbar <= not D after 5 ns;

end process output;
end architecture behavioral;
```

FIGURE 9-2 An example of the use of functions

visible to, and therefore callable from, all processes in the architecture body, or visible to just one process. In practice, we would much rather place related functions and procedures in packages: a type of design unit described later in this chapter.

Example End: Detection of Signal Events

9.1.1 Type Conversion Functions

Type conversion is another common instance of the use of functions. The model of the memory module in Section 6.1 represented memory as a one-dimensional array. This array is indexed by an integer. However, memory addresses are provided as an n-bit binary address. We find that we need to convert this bit vector representing the memory address to an integer used to index this array representing memory. In other instances we may want to use models of components developed by others. We would most likely use their models by instantiating their components as part of a larger structural model. For example, suppose we are designing an ALU and wish to incorporate a multiplier developed by a colleague. We do not need to understand the internal operation of the multiplier but we do need to know the input and output signals and their types so that we may correctly interface to the multiplier. Let us say that he has used signals of type **bit** and **bit_vector** whereas you have been using signals of type std_logic and std_logic_vector. Type conversion functions will be necessary for interoperability if we do not wish to invest in the time to convert their models to use the IEEE 1164 types.

Example: Type Conversion

Consider the VHDL type **bit_vector** and the IEEE 1164 type std_logic_vector. We may wish to make assignments from a variable of one type to a variable of the other type. For example, consider conversion of a signal of type **bit_vector** to std_logic_vector. We can use the function to_stdlogicvector() that is provided in the package std_logic_1164.vhd (more on packages in Section 9.4). This function takes as an argument an object of type **bit_vector** and returns a value of type std_logic_vector. Conversely we may wish to convert from std_logic_vector to **bit_vector**. An example of the implementation of this function is shown in Figure 9-3. Recall that each element in a std_logic_vector is of type std_logic and each element in a **bit_vector** is of type **bit**. The function simply scans the vector and converts each element of the input std_logic_vector to a **bit_vector** element. The type **bit** may take on values 0 and 1, whereas the type std_logic may take on one of nine values. Note the declaration of the variable outvalue. The function declaration does not provide the size of the number of bits in the argument. This is set when the formal parameter is associated with the actual parameter at the time the function is called. In this case, how can we declare the size of

```
function to_bitvector (svalue : std_logic_vector) return bit_vector is
variable outvalue : bit_vector (svalue'length-1 downto 0);
begin
for i in svalue'range loop -- scan all elements of the array
case svalue (i) is
when '0' => outvalue (i) := '0';
when '1' => outvalue (i) := '1';
when others => outvalue (i) := '0';
end case;
end loop;
return outvalue;
end function to_bitvector;
```

FIGURE 9-3 An example of a type conversion function

any local variable that is to have the same number of bits as the input parameter? The answer is: by using attributes. As discussed in Section 6.5, arrays have an attribute named **length**. The value of svalue'**length** is the length of the array. By using unconstrained arrays in the definition of the function, we can realize a flexible function implementation where the actual size of the parameters are determined when the actual parameters are bound to formal parameters, which occurs when the function is called.

There are many ways in which to perform such type conversions, and Figure 9-3 shows but one of them. By examining commercial packages such as std_logic_arith.vhd and std_logic_1164.vhd we will find many such conversion functions. Examples include conversion from std_logic_vector to **integer** and vice-versa. Check the libraries that come with the installation of your VHDL simulator and tools. You will find many packages and it is useful to browse through them and study the procedures and functions that are contained within them.

Example End: Type Conversion

9.1.2 Resolution Functions

Resolution functions comprise a special class of functions. Recall from Chapter 6 that the resolved type is a signal that may have multiple drivers. This occurs quite often in digital systems. For example, consider a high-level model of a computer system shown in Figure 9-4. The CPU, memory, and some peripherals such as a disk and other I/O devices must exchange data. It is quite expensive to have a dedicated interconnect between every pair of communicating devices. Furthermore, all of the devices do not necessarily have to communicate at the same time. A common architecture is to have these devices communicate over a shared set of signals called a bus. In the VHDL model of such an architecture, the shared bus could be a signal datatype and several components may make assignments to the shared signal during the course of a simulation. The physical analogy of such assignments is that of multiple physical drivers placing values on this bus at different points in time.

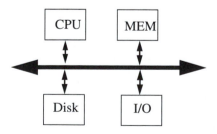

FIGURE 9-4 A simple model of a computer

Circuits that implement wired logic are another example of instances where a signal can have multiple drivers. The design is such that the final signal value represents a logical operation such as a boolean AND. The following example illustrates the need for shared signals.

Example: Programmable Array Logic

Switches are often used to implement logic gates as shown in Figure 9-5. The switches are turned on by a 0 value on the control input. A pull-up circuit normally drives the output signal to a logic high or 1 value. When a switch is turned on it pulls the output signal down to a logic low or 0 value. Thus in order for the output to be at a logic 1 value all of the switches must be off. If any one of the switches is turned on the output signal is pulled to a logic 0. This behavior is the logic AND function. Now imagine describing the behavior of this circuit in VHDL. We can conceive of an architecture description wherein the output signal is declared in the architecture. The operation of each switch might be described by a process that is sensitive to the value of its control input signal and drives the output signal accordingly. Thus each process will drive the output signal. The actual value of the signal is determined by checking if any of the processes are driving the signal to a logic 0. The function that checks all of the values being driven by each process is the resolution function. In this case the resolution function returns a value of 0 for the signal if any of the processes attempt to drive the signal to a value of 0.

In general, the VHDL model should be capable of handling more general cases. For example, we should be able to describe other ways to pick the value of the shared signal when multiple drivers tried to schedule values on the shared signal at the same point in simulation time.

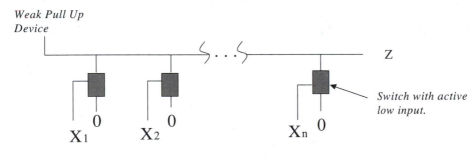

Any Xn=0 turns switch on producing Z=0.

FIGURE 9-5 An example of wired AND logic

Example End: Programmable Array Logic

To correctly simulate circuits such as those described in the preceding example we must be able to unambiguously state the value of the signal at any point in time. The value must be *resolved* based on the values scheduled by the multiple drivers of the signal. The algorithm for resolving the issue of the signal value at any time is captured in the *resolution function*. One can think of the resolution function as examining all of the scheduled values on the bus for that time and determining the value of the signal. For example, the value could be a logical OR of all of the signals or the maximum value.

The shared signal must be declared as a *resolved type*, which means that there is a resolution function associated with all signals of this type. This function should accurately reflect the behavior of the physical system being modeled. During the course of a simulation when any signal of this type is to be assigned a value, the resolution function is invoked. This function examines the values on all drivers for that signal and computes the correct signal value as defined by the resolution function. The resolution function must be an associative operation so that the order in which the multiple signal drivers values are examined does not affect the resolved value of the signal. For example, a logical OR operation on a set of values of type **bit** is an associative operation. The logical AND function as well as maximum and minimum value functions are associative operations. Throughout this text we have used the signal type **std_logic**: a resolved type defined by the IEEE 1164 standard. The following example from the implementation of the IEEE 1164 standard illustrates how resolved types can be declared and how resolution functions can be defined.

Example: Resolved Types in the IEEE 1164 Standard

Let us examine the definition and use of the resolved type **std_logic** from an implementation of the IEEE 1164 standard. Figure 9-6 shows an example of the declaration and use of resolved types taken from an implementation of the IEEE 1164 standard, **std_logic_1164.vhd**, that is provided with just about any VHDL toolset. This implementation of the standard first defines a new type: **std_ulogic**. A signal of this type takes on nine values, as defined in Figure 9-6 and as described in Section 2.5. This type is referred to as an enumerated type, because the list of values of an object of this type are explicitly enumerated. However, any signal declared to be of this type can support only a single driver. Therefore, we wish to define a new signal type that can take on all of the values of **std_ulogic**, but can also support multiple drivers. This is done on the following line by creating the (sub) type **std_logic**.

Consider the structure of this declaration. It looks very much like any other declaration except for two items. A *sub-type* simply means that the declared signal can take on a range of values that is a sub-range of the original or *base* type. Secondly, the type provides the name of a *resolution function* that is associated with all objects declared to be of this type. In this case it is the function named **resolved**. What this definition means is the following: whenever a signal of type **std_logic** is to be assigned a value, there may be multiple drivers associated with this signal. The values from these multiple drivers are passed to the resolution function, which determines the value to be assigned to the signal. For example, consider the case where a single-bit bus is being driven to a logic 1 by one driver while being left in a high-impedance state or **Z** by another driver. The value of the signal

```
type std_ulogic is ('U', -- Uninitialized
                    'X', -- Forcing Unknown
                    '0', -- Forcing 0
                    '1', -- Forcing 1
                    'Z', -- High Impedance
                    'W', -- Weak Unknown
                    'L', -- Weak 0
                    'H', -- Weak 1
                    '-'  -- Don't care
                    );

function resolved (s : std_ulogic_vector) return std_ulogic;

sub-type std_logic is resolved std_ulogic;
```

FIGURE 9-6 An example of the declaration of resolved signals

should be a logic 1. The resolution function must be capable of making this determination and of handling more than two drivers.

One simple approach to implementing a resolution function is to build a table. The row and column indices correspond to the signal values from two drivers. The table entry corresponds to the value that would be produced if these two drivers were attempting to drive a signal to these two values. For example, the entry in a table at location $(Z,1)$ would be 1. Now, if we had a set of drivers, we could compute the final value by resolving the values of all drivers in a pairwise manner, hence the requirement for associativity. The structure of the table used by an implementation of the IEEE 1164 standard to resolve the values of a pair signals of type std_logic is shown in Table 9-1. For example, two driver values of Z and W will yield a signal value of W.

TABLE 9-1 Table for Resolving the Values of a Pair of Signals of Type std_logic

	U	X	0	1	Z	W	L	H	-
U	U	U	U	U	U	U	U	U	U
X	U	X	X	X	X	X	X	X	X
0	U	X	0	X	0	0	0	0	X
1	U	X	X	1	1	1	1	1	X
Z	U	X	0	1	Z	W	L	H	X
W	U	X	0	1	W	W	W	W	X
L	U	X	0	1	L	W	L	W	X
H	U	X	0	1	H	W	W	H	X
-	U	X	X	X	X	X	X	X	X

Example End: Resolved Types in the IEEE 1164 Standard

Example: Using Resolution Functions

Let us consider another example of the implementation of resolution functions. Consider a system with multi-chip modules (MCM): these are chip carriers that can support multiple semiconductor die on a single substrate and within a single package. Suppose that we have multiple die placed on a single MCM, as shown in Figure 9-7. Assume that for this MCM module to be functional all of the die must be functional. This means that when one die has failed, the module is considered defective. Periodically self-test circuitry in the die (or even in the MCM substrate!) will locally run diagnostics to test the individual die to ensure that they remain functional. There is a single global error signal that is driven by an output of the self-test circuitry within each die. This global signal performs the logical OR of all of the single-bit diagnostic results from the individual die. If this global error signal is asserted, then at least one bad die exists on the MCM and the complete package is considered to be faulty. Because there are multiple drivers, this global signal must be of a resolved type. An example of the VHDL code that may be used to implement this signal type is shown in Figure 9-8.

In this model, we assume that the behavior of each chip is captured with a process. Each of the processes may place a value of 0 or 1 on the shared signal error_bus. If at least one driver forces error_bus to 1, we would like the value of error_bus to remain 1. This behavior is captured in the resolution function shown in Figure 9-8.

The function wire_or receives as input an array of values. The loop simply scans this array looking for the first 1. One very interesting feature about this function is that the parameter is an unconstrained array. This means that we have not specified the number of elements that will be passed to the function. Can we pass an array of 32 elements? What about 64 elements? The answer is yes to both. The size of the input parameter will be determined at the time the function is called. In this case we do not know how many signal drivers may exist. The use of unconstrained arrays in this manner is quite common. This body of the function simplifies the process of resolving signal values. The base type of

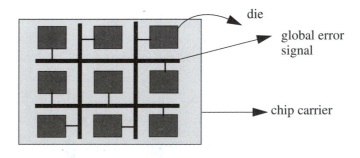

FIGURE 9-7 Structure of a multi-chip module with multiple die

```
library IEEE;
use IEEE.std_logic_1164.all;

entity mcm is -- an empty entity description
end entity mcm;

architecture behavioral of mcm is
function wire_or (sbus :std_ulogic_vector) return std_ulogic;
begin
for i in sbus'range loop -- this loop implements a logical OR across all signals
 if sbus(i) = '1' then
return '1';
end if;
end loop;
return '0';
end function wire_or;

sub-type wire_or_logic is wire_or std_ulogic; -- declare the new resolved type
signal error_bus : wire_or_logic; -- this signal is global to all processes
begin
Chip1: process is
begin
-- ..
error_bus <= '1' after 2 ns;
-- ..
end process Chip1;
Chip2: process is
begin
-- ..
error_bus <= '0' after 2 ns;
-- ..
end process Chip2;
end architecture behavioral;
```

There could be many more processes like this, e.g., corresponding to each di.e.

FIGURE 9-8 An example of the use of resolution functions

wire_or_logic is std_ulogic. Thus, any signal of type wire_or_logic can actually take on values other than 1 or 0. However, the resolution function shown here reflects a classical 0/1 view of single-bit signals and ignores these other values. A more realistic and robust approach would account for all possible combination of signal values.

Example End: Using Resolution Functions

Synthesis issues for functions arise from an understanding of the VHDL hardware inference mechanisms in the context of the semantics of function calls. These issues are discussed in the following section.

9.1.3 Synthesis Considerations

To understand the synthesis of functions let us examine the semantics of functions in the context of what we know of synthesis from Chapter 7. Functions are used in VHDL expressions as placeholders for the values computed by the functions. For example we might have an assignment statement of the form

p_bit <= odd_parity (x);

where p_bit is of type std_logic and x is of type std_logic_vector. Functions are typically found in expressions and compute the values of signals and variables. They do not exist independent of such expressions, unlike procedures. All parameters of a function are of mode **in** and there are no parameters of mode **out**. Each time this assignment statement is executed the function odd_parity() is called with a std_logic_vector type operand as the parameter. When a function is called all local variables declared within the function are initialized and the function is executed computing the value of the function that is returned to the calling process. The next time the function is called this process is repeated. The key observation is that the local variables in a function do not retain values between functions calls. Thus the behavior is one wherein each time the function is called the output value is computed as a function of its input values. This sounds suspiciously like the behavior of a combinational logic circuit and that is exactly what we obtain! In fact we can think of the VHDL model being rewritten with the function code being placed in-line in the main program. The following example illustrates this point.

Example: Synthesis of Functions

Figure 9-9 illustrates an example of the synthesis of functions. In this example the functions ones() is used to count the number of bits that are set in the input vector data. The body the of process is a single statement where the function appears in the right hand side of the expression. During the process of synthesis can imagine that the function body is placed in the process and the loop is unrolled to reveal the statements in the following order:

if data(0) = '1' **then** count := count + 1;
end if;
if data(1) = '1' **then** count := count + 1;
end if;
..and so on.

```vhdl
library IEEE;
use IEEE.std_logic_1164.all;
 entity func is
 port (data : in std_logic_vector(7 downto 0);
        count: out integer range 0 to 7);
 end entity func;

 architecture behavioral of func is
 function ones (signal data : std_logic_vector) return integer is
 variable count : integer range 0 to 7;
 begin
 for i in data'range loop
 if (data(i) = '1') then -- check if the bit is 1
        count := count +1; -- keep counting the number of bits set
 end if;
 end loop;
 return (count);
 end function ones;

 begin
check: process is
 begin
count <= ones(data);
 end process check;
 end architecture behavioral;
```

FIGURE 9-9 An example of the synthesis of functions

This code is now synthesized as described in Chapter 7. With the dependencies between successive statements we would expect the synthesized structure to exhibit many dependencies. In fact we would expect to see seven levels of logic corresponding the unrolled loop statements and this is what the synthesis compiler will see. A simpler example that exhibits the same structure is the calculation of the parity of a bit vector. Replace the inner loop code of the function with the statement

parity := parity xor data(i);

and return the value parity to the calling program. If there are an odd number of 1's in data the value of parity will be 1. When this circuit is now synthesized you will see a circuit with seven two-input exclusive-OR gates organized to compute the pairwise exclusive-OR of all of the input bits of data. The delay from input to output is seven gate delays. (Refer to Exercise 5 at the end of this chapter for more on this subject.)

Example End: Synthesis of Functions

The second class of sub-programs are procedures. A distinguishing feature of procedures is that they can modify input parameters. In this case we must consider how signals are passed and handled. The essential issues in getting started with writing and using procedures are addressed in the next section.

9.2 Essentials of Procedures

Procedures are sub-programs that can modify one or more of the input parameters. The following procedure declaration illustrates the procedure call interface.

procedure read_v1d (**variable** fname: **in text**; v : **out** std_logic_vector);

This is a procedure to read data from a file where fname is a file parameter. The first characteristic we might notice is that parameters may be of mode **out**. Just as parameters of mode **in** must be read and cannot be written, parameters of mode **out** cannot be read and used in a procedure but can only be written by the procedure. We may also have parameters of mode **inout**. As with functions, the type of the formal parameters in a procedure declaration must match the type of the actual parameters that are used when the procedure is called. If the class of the procedure parameter is not explicitly declared, then parameters of mode **in** are assumed to be of class **constant**, whereas the parameters of mode **out** or **inout** are assumed to be of class **variable**. Variables declared within a procedure are initialized on each call to the procedure and their values do not persist across invocations of the procedure.

Example: Interface to Memory

Let us consider a VHDL model for a simple processor where we have two components: a CPU and memory. The behavioral model of the CPU must be able to read and write locations from memory. These operations are common candidates for implementation as procedures. We will create two procedures: one to read and one to write memory locations. We will assume the memory model and associated signals as shown in Figure 6-1, with the addition of one additional signal from memory that signifies the completion of a memory operation. These procedures are shown in Figure 9-10. Both procedures should manipulate the signals shown in the memory interface in Figure 6-1. There are a number of interesting features shown here. Note the presence of **wait** statements within the procedure. Thus, a process can suspend inside a procedure. Furthermore, signals can be assigned values within a procedure. This raises the issue of how signals are passed into a procedure, and this issue is dealt with in Section 9.2.1. Signals that are modified within the procedure are declared to be of mode **out**. For example, see signal R in procedure mread() in Figure 9-10.

```
library IEEE;
use IEEE.std_logic_1164.all;
entity CPU is
port (write_data : out std_logic_vector (31 downto 0); -- data from memory
      ADDR :out std_logic_vector (2 downto 0); -- CPU generated address
      MemRead, MemWrite: out std_logic; -- read and write control signals from CPU
      read_data : in std_logic_vector(31 downto 0); -- data to memory
      S : in std_logic);
end entity CPU;

architecture behavioral of CPU is
procedure mread (address : in std_logic_vector (2 downto 0);
                 signal R : out std_logic;
                 signal S : in std_logic;
                 signal ADDR: out std_logic_vector (2 downto 0);
                 signal data : out std_logic_vector (31 downto 0)) is
begin
ADDR <= address;
R<= '1';
wait until S = '1';
data <= read_data;
R<= '0';
end procedure mread;

procedure mwrite (address : in std_logic_vector (2 downto 0);
                  signal data : in std_logic_vector (31 downto 0);
                  signal ADDR : out std_logic_vector (2 downto 0);
                  signal W : out std_logic;
                  signal DO : out std_logic_vector (31 downto 0)) is
begin
ADDR <= address;
DO<= data;
W<= '1';
wait until S = '1';
W <= '0';
end procedure mwrite;
--
-- any signal declarations for the architecture here
--
```

FIGURE 9-10 An example of the use of procedures

```
begin
--
-- CPU behavioral description here
--
process is
begin
--
-- behavioral description
--
end process;

process is
begin
--
-- behavioral description
--
end process;
end architecture behavioral;
```

FIGURE 9-10 (continued)

The body of the architecture description is likely to include processes within which the procedure calls can be made. Alternatively, the procedures could have been declared within the declarative region of the process: just before the **begin** statement and after the **process** statement. Just as processes can declare and use variables that are local to the process, processes may also declare and use procedures within a process. However, in this case they would be visible only within that process.

Example End: Interface to Memory

9.2.1 Using Procedures

Signals cannot be declared within procedures. However, signals can be passed into procedures as parameters. Due to visibility rules, procedures can make assignments to signals that are not explicitly declared in the parameter list. For example, procedures declared within a process can make assignments to signals corresponding to the ports of the encompassing entity. This is possible because the ports are visible to the process. The procedure is said to have side effects, because it has an effect on a signal that is not declared in the parameter list. This is poor programming practice, because it makes it difficult to reason about the models (e.g., when debugging) and understand their behavior. Clarity and understanding of the code is enhanced if parameters are passed explicitly rather than relying on side effects. If the class of a parameter is not declared, and the mode is **out** or **inout**, then the class defaults to that of a **variable**. If the mode is **in**, the class of the parameter defaults to a **constant**.

Procedures can also be placed in the declarative region of a process. We know that processes cannot have a sensitivity list and also have wait statements in the body of the process. Therefore, when we use procedures, it follows that a process that calls a procedure with a **wait** statement cannot have a sensitivity list.

9.2.2 Concurrent and Sequential Procedure Calls

Depending on how procedures are used, we can distinguish between concurrent and sequential procedure calls. Remember the CSA statements from Section 4.3.1? Each statement represented the assignment of a value to a signal, and this assignment occurred in simulated time concurrently with the execution of the other concurrent signal assignment statements and processes. Concurrent procedure calls can be viewed similarly. The procedure is invoked in the body of an architecture concurrently with other concurrent procedures, CSA statements, or processes. The procedure is invoked when there is an event on a signal that is an input parameter to the procedure. It follows that if we use a concurrent procedure, the parameter list cannot include a variable (in VHDL'87), because variables '87 vs. '93 cannot exist outside of a process. However, VHDL'93 supports shared variables, but we ☞ consider shared variables to be advanced features not discussed here. In contrast, sequential procedure calls are those where the procedure is invoked within the body of a process. In this case, the invocation of the procedure is determined by the sequence of execution of statements within the process—just like in a conventional program. The following example should help solidify our understanding of the differences between concurrent and sequential procedure calls.

Example: Concurrent and Sequential Procedure Calls

Figure 9-11 illustrates an example of a concurrent procedure call. The structural model of a bit-serial adder from Figure 8-4 has been rewritten such that the D flip-flop component instantiation statement has been replaced by a procedure. The procedure is invoked concurrently with the component comb whenever there are events on the signals that are declared to be of mode **in**. Thus, events on the clk, reset, or d inputs will cause this procedure to be invoked. From the procedure body we see that the output is modified only on the rising edge of the clk signal.

This structure does appeal to our understanding of VHDL programs. Consider what would happen in the model in the example of Figure 8-4. When this model is simulated, let us assume that the component dff would be replaced by a behavioral model similar to the one shown in Figure 6-10. We see that the procedure effectively implements the same behavior. Note how the parameter list explicitly associates the formal and actual parameters rather than having this association made by virtue of the position in the call. The sig-

```vhdl
library IEEE;
use IEEE.std_logic_1164.all;
entity serial_adder is
port (a, b, clk, reset : in std_logic;
      z : out std_logic);
end entity serial_adder;

architecture structural of serial_adder is
component comb is
 port (a, b, c_in : in std_logic;
       z, carry : out std_logic);
end component comb;

procedure dff(signal d, clk, reset : in std_logic;
                    signal q, qbar : out std_logic) is
begin
 if (reset = '0') then
    q <= '0' after 5 ns;
    qbar <= '1' after 5 ns;
   elsif (rising_edge(clk)) then
   q <= d after 5 ns;
   qbar <= (not d) after 5 ns;
 end if;
end procedure dff;

signal s1, s2 : std_logic;

begin
C1: comb port map (a => a, b => b, c_in => s1, z =>z, carry => s2);
--
-- concurrent procedure call
--
dff(clk => clk, reset =>reset, d=> s2, q=>s1, qbar =>open);
end architecture structural;
```

FIGURE 9-11 An example of a concurrent procedure call

nal qbar is associated with the keyword **open** in the procedure call. This is akin to leaving a pin of a device (dff) unconnected.

Figure 9-12 shows the equivalent implementation as a sequential procedure call. The procedure is encased in a process with an explicit **wait** statement. Note the structure of the **wait** statement. If an event occurs on any of the signals in the list, the process will be exe-

```vhdl
library IEEE;
use IEEE.std_logic_1164.all;
entity serial_adder is
port (a, b, clk, reset : in std_logic;
      z : out std_logic);
end entity serial_adder;

architecture structural of serial_adder is
component comb is
 port (a, b, c_in : in std_logic;
       z, carry : out std_logic);
end component comb;
procedure dff(signal d, clk, reset : in std_logic;
                    signal q, qbar : out std_logic) is
begin
 if (reset = '0') then
    q <= '0' after 5 ns;
    qbar <= '1' after 5 ns;
   elsif (clk'event and clk = '1') then
   q <= d after 5 ns;
   qbar <= (not d) after 5 ns;
 end if;
end dff;
signal s1, s2 : std_logic;
begin
C1: comb port map (a => a, b => b, c_in => s1, z =>z, carry => s2);
process
begin
 dff(clk => clk, reset =>reset, d=> s2, q=> s1, qbar => open);
wait on clk, reset, s2;
end process;
end architectural structural;
```

FIGURE 9-12 An example of a sequential procedure call

cuted, which in this case will cause the procedure dff() to be called. This procedure call model is equivalent to the model shown in Figure 9-11.

Example End: Sequential and Concurrent Procedure Calls

9.2.3 Synthesis Considerations

Basic issues concerning synthesis and procedures follow from thinking of procedures being in-lined in the code, that is, the procedure call is replaced with the procedure code. For example consider a procedure called from within a process as follows:

```
process is
begin
    ..
    ..
    my_procedure(sig1, sig2);
    ..
    ..
end process;
```

The procedure call my_procedure(sig1, sig2) can be replaced by the sequential code body of the procedure. Synthesis considerations are now as that discussed for processes as in Chapter 7. This view of synthesis for procedures is not entirely unexpected because procedures are essentially mechanisms for structuring code and do not contribute any new language features from which hardware must be inferred. In-lining "flattens" hierarchically structured code and is now amenable to the application of the basic hardware inferencing mechanisms (discussed in Chapter 7).

Like functions, local variables in a procedure do not retain values across procedure calls and therefore will synthesize to wires and not latches. However, signals that are of mode **out** in a procedure may infer latches depending on the context within which the procedure call resides. For example if a procedure resides in a conditional block of code such as that controlled by a **wait** statement, latches will be inferred for the output signals of the procedure.

Synthesis compilers generally limit each sequential block of code to one **wait** statement. Typically such a **wait** statement will appear in the process. In this case the body of procedures called from this process cannot contain any **wait** statements. The problem is that in general it is not always possible to predict how a procedure will be used. As a result **wait** statements are generally not supported in procedures for synthesis. If we wish to model synchronous logic within a procedure we can use the **if** statement and clock-level or clock-edge-detection expressions. Concurrent procedure calls appearing in an architecture can effectively be replaced by an equivalent process prior to synthesis.

Example: Synthesis of Procedures

Figure 9-13 shows an example of the use of procedures to compute the parity of an 8-bit vector. The parity bit is computed as the exclusive-OR of all of the bits in the word. This computation is encapsulated in a procedure declared in the architecture. A single line in body of the architecture implements a concurrent procedure call. The synthesized netlist consists of seven two-input exclusive-OR gates forming the pairwise exclusive-OR operation on the eight bits. The total delay through the implementation is seven gate delays.

```vhdl
library IEEE;
use IEEE.std_logic_1164.all;
 entity proc_call is
 port (data : in std_logic_vector(7 downto 0);
      count : out std_logic);
 end entity proc_call;

 architecture behavioral of proc_call is
 procedure ones (signal data : in std_logic_vector; signal count : out std_logic) is
 variable parity : std_logic;
 begin
 for i in data'range loop
 parity := parity xor data(i);
 end loop;
 count <= parity;
 end procedure ones;

 begin
 ones(data, count); -- concurrent procedure call
 end architecture behavioral;
```

FIGURE 9-13 An example of the synthesis of procedures

Example End: Synthesis of Procedures

9.3 Sub-Program and Operator Overloading

A very useful feature of the VHDL language is the ability to *overload* the sub-program name. For example, there are several models and implementations of a D flip-flop. We saw a few examples in Section 6.4. Imagine we were to write behavioral models of sequential circuits that included D flip-flops. We might be using procedures such as the one shown in Figure 9-11 to model the behavior of a D flip-flop. If we wished to incorporate models that had asynchronous set and clear signals, we might write another procedure with a different name, say **asynch_dff()**. What if we wish to have procedures that would operate on signal arguments of type **bit_vector** rather than **std_logic_vector**? We would write distinct procedures to incorporate models with these types and behaviors. By accommodating various possibilities of argument types and flip-flop behavior we might have to write many different procedures while keeping track of the names to distinguish them.

It would be very helpful to be able to use a single name for all procedures describing the behavior of various types of D flip-flops. We would like to call dff() with the right parameters and let the compiler determine which procedure to use based on the number and type of arguments. For example, consider the two procedure calls:

dff(clk, d, q, qbar)

dff(clk, d, q, qbar, reset, clear)

From the arguments, we can see that we are referring to two different procedures, one that utilizes asynchronous reset and clear inputs and one that does not (e.g., corresponding to Figure 6-10 and Figure 6-11, respectively). From the type and number of arguments we can tell which procedure we meant to use. This process is referred to as overloading subprogram names or simply *subprogram overloading*. When we create such a set of procedures or functions with overloaded names, we would probably place them in a package (see Section 9.4) and make the package contents visible via the **use** clause. If we examine the contents of some of the packages shown in Appendix F, we will see examples of overloaded functions and sub-programs. For example, note that in **std_logic_1164.vhd** the boolean functions **and**, **or**, and so on have been defined for the type **std_logic**.

Similarly, the operators such as "*", and "+" have been defined for certain predefined types of the language such as integers. What if we wish to perform such operations on other data types that we may create? We can overload these operators by providing definitions of "*" and "+" for these new data types. CAD tool vendors typically distribute packages that contain definitions of operators and sub-programs for various operations on data types that are not predefined for the language. For example, the **std_logic_arith.vhd** package distributed by CAD tool vendors provides definitions for various operators over the **std_logic** and **std_logic_vector** types. Two examples of overloading the definitions of "*" and "+" operators taken from this package are:

function "*" (arg1, arg2: std_logic_vector) **return** std_logic_vector;
function "+" (arg1, arg2 :signed) **return** signed;

This means that if the contents of this package is included in a model via the **use** clause, then statements such as

s1 <= s1 + s2;

are valid, where all three signals are of type std_logic. Otherwise, the "+" operation is not defined for objects of type std_logic and this statement would be in error.

Procedures and functions are necessary constructs for building reusable blocks of VHDL code, for hiding design complexity, and for managing large complex designs. As we have seen in this section, they are also a means for enriching the language to easily handle new data types by encapsulating the definitions of common operations and operators over these data types. Even with a small number of new data types, the need to overload all of the common operators can generate quite a large number of functions. Furthermore, when we think of overloading subprogram names we can generate quite a few additional procedures and/or functions. Packages are a mechanism for structuring, organizing, and using such user-defined types and sub-programs. These concepts are discussed next.

9.4 Essentials of Packages

As we acquire larger groups of functions and procedures within the models that we construct, we must consider how they will be used. We can use text editors and manually insert these functions into the VHDL models as we use them. This is a rather tedious process at best, especially when the models we construct grow large. A better approach would be to group logically related sets of functions and procedures into a module that can be easily shared among distinct designs and people. *Packages* are a means for doing so within the VHDL language.

Packages provide for the organization of type definitions, functions, and procedures so that they can be shared across distinct VHDL programs. To gain an intuition for the constructs used in building packages, it is instructive to consider how we try to reuse code modules across projects. When we are working on large class projects we attempt to make the most efficient use of our time by reusing functions or procedures that we may have written for older programs, have found available for free somewhere on the Internet, or garnered from friends. For example, imagine that you have painstakingly put together a package that contains useful functions, procedures, and data types to help designers build simulation models of common computer architectures. This package may include definitions of new types for registers, instructions, and memories, as well as procedures for reading and/or writing memories, procedures for performing logical shift operations, and functions for type conversion operations. After months of tedious development you are now interested in promoting its use among fellow VHDL developers. How might you communicate the contents of this package in convincing them of its utility? What would developers want or need to know to determine if they could benefit from using the contents of your package? At the very least we would need to have a list of the functions and procedures and what they do, for example, what values are computed and returned for each procedure, and what parameters must be passed to perform these computations. This information forms the basis of the *package declaration*. It forms the interface or specification of the services that your package provides. When we write C or VHDL programs we must declare the variables or signals that we using: their type and possibly initial values. Similarly, when we write packages we must declare their contents. It is just that their contents are now more complex objects, such as functions, procedures, and data types. The package declaration is the means by which users declare what is available for use by VHDL programs. In the same sense that a hardware design unit possesses an external interface to communicate with other components, the package declaration defines the interface to other VHDL design units.

The easiest way to understand packages is by example, so let us examine a package that provides a new data type and a set of functions that operate on that data type. Throughout this text, the examples have declared and used the package std_logic 1164.vhd. Now let us look inside this package to see how the type is declared and how functions and declarations are used. Figure 9-14 shows a portion of the package declaration of an implementation of the IEEE 1164 package distributed with the vast majority of the VHDL environments. The listing of the package declaration is provided in Appendix F.3. We know that the basic VHDL type **bit** can take on only values 0 and 1 and therefore is inadequate to represent most real systems. By using the concept of enumerated types (see Chapter 12) a new type, std_ulogic, is defined as shown in Figure 9-14. Now a signal can be declared to be of this type:

signal *example_signal* : std_ulogic: = 'U';

The signal *example_signal* can now be assigned any one of the nine values defined above rather than the two values 0 and 1. The package also declares a resolved type, std_logic, which is a sub-type of std_ulogic. This declaration simply states that in the course of the simulation when a signal of type std_logic is assigned a value, the resolution function **resolved** will be invoked to determine the correct value of a signal from the multiple drivers associated with the signal. However, we do have a problem in that all of the predefined logical functions, such as AND, OR, and XOR, operate on signals of type **bit,** which is predefined by the language. These logic functions must be redefined for signals of the above type. Some of these functions are shown in Figure 9-14. The declaration of all of the functions provided in this package can be found in Appendix F.3. If we are constructing a package that uses types, procedures, or functions from another package, then access to this package from our VHDL program must be provided via **library** and **use** clauses.

Now that we have defined what is in the package, we must provide the VHDL code that implements these functions and procedures. This implementation is contained in the *package body*. The package body is essentially a listing of the implementations of the procedures and functions declared in the package declaration. The body is structured as follows:

package body my_package **is**
--
-- *type definitions, functions, and procedures*
--
end package body my_package;

package std_logic_1164 **is**

-- logic state system (unresolved)

----

type std_ulogic **is** ('U', *-- Uninitialized*

'X', *-- Forcing Unknown*

'0', *-- Forcing 0*

'1', *-- Forcing 1*

'Z', *-- High Impedance*

'W', *-- Weak Unknown*

'L', *-- Weak 0*

'H', *-- Weak 1*

'-' *-- Don't care*

);

type std_ulogic_vector **is array** (**natural range** <>) **of** std_ulogic;

function resolved (s : std_ulogic_vector) **return** std_ulogic;
sub-type std_logic **is** resolved std_ulogic;

type std_logic_vector **is array** (**natural range** <>) **of** std_logic;

function "and" (l, r : std_logic_vector) **return** std_logic_vector;
function "and" (l, r : std_ulogic_vector) **return** std_ulogic_vector;

--

--..<rest of the package definition, for example other function and
-- ..procedure interfaces>

--

end package std_logic_1164;

FIGURE 9-14 Examples from the package declaration of an implementation
of the IEEE 1164 standard

Once we have these packages how do we use them? They are typically compiled and
placed in *libraries* and referenced within VHDL design units via the **use** clause. All of
the examples in this text have utilized the package std_logic_1164.vhd, which is in the
library named IEEE. The essential properties of libraries are discussed next.

9.5 Essentials of Libraries

Each design unit—entity, architecture, configuration, package declaration, and package body—is analyzed (compiled) and placed in a *design library*. Libraries are generally implemented as directories and are referenced by a logical name. In the implementation of the VHDL environment, this logical name maps to a physical path to the corresponding directory and this mapping is maintained by the host implementation. However, just like variables and signals, before we can use a design library we must declare the library we are using by specifying the library's logical name. This is done in the VHDL program using the library clause that has the following syntax:

    library *logical-library-name-1*, *logical-library-name-2*,...;

In VHDL, the libraries STD and WORK are implicitly declared. Therefore user programs do not need to declare these libraries. The former contains standard packages provided with VHDL distributions. The latter refers to the working directory that can be set within the VHDL environment you are using. Refer to your CAD tool documentation on how this can be done. However, if a program were to access functions in a design unit that was stored in a library with the logical name IEEE, then this library must be declared at the start of the program. Most, if not all, vendors provide an implementation of the library IEEE with packages such as std_logic_1164.vhd, as well as other mathematics and miscellaneous packages.

Once a library has been declared all of the functions, procedures, and type declarations of a package in this library can be made accessible to a VHDL model through the **use** clause. For example, the following statements appear prior to the entity declaration in all of the examples in this text:

    library IEEE;

    use IEEE.std_logic_1164.**all**;

When these declarations appear just before the **entity** design unit they are referred to as the *context clause*. The second statement in the above context clause makes *all* of the type definitions, functions, and procedures defined in the package std_logic_1164.vhd visible to the VHDL model. It is as if all of the declarations had been physically placed within the declarative part of a process that uses them. A second form of the **use** clause can be used when only a specific item, such as a function called my_func, in the package is to be made visible.

    use IEEE.std_logic_1164.my_func;

The **use** clause can be appear in the declarative part of any design unit. Collectively the **library** and **use** clauses establish the set of design units that are visible to the VHDL analyzer as it is trying to analyze and compile a specific VHDL design unit.

When we first start writing VHDL programs we tend to think of single entity–architecture pairs when constructing models. We probably organize our files in the same fashion with one entity description and the associated architecture description in the same file.

When this file is analyzed, the **library** and **use** clauses determine which libraries and packages within those libraries are candidates for finding functions, procedures, and user-defined types that are referenced within the model being compiled. However, these clauses apply only to the immediate entity–architecture pair! *Visibility must be established for other design units separately!*

There are three primary design units—entities, package declarations, and configuration declarations. The context clause applies to the following primary design unit. If we start having multiple design units within the same physical file, then each primary design unit must be preceded by the **library** and **use** clauses necessary to establish the visibility to the required packages. For example, let us assume that the VHDL models shown in Figure 9-2 and Figure 9-8 are physically in the same file. The statements

library IEEE;

use IEEE.std_logic_1164.**all**;

must appear at the beginning of *each* model, that is, prior to the **entity** descriptions. We cannot assume that because we have these statements at the top of the file, they are valid for all design units in the same file. In this case if we neglected to precede each model with the preceding statements, the VHDL analyzer would return with an error on the use of the type std_logic in the subsequent models because this is not a predefined type within the language, but rather is defined in the package std_logic_1164.

Simulation Exercise 9.1: Packages and Libraries

This exercise concerns creating and using a simple package the development of a VHDL simulation model.

Step 1.   Using a text editor create a package with the following characteristics.

Step 1 (a)   Include several procedures for simulating a D flip-flop. You can start with the basic procedure given in Section 6.4 and modify this to produce procedures for the following:

– arguments of type **bit** and std_logic

– arguments of type **bit_vector** and std_logic_vector (these are registers)

– use of reset and clear functions for different types of arguments

Step 2.   Analyze and test each of the procedures separately before committing them to placement within the package.

Step 3.   Define a new type designed to represent a 32-bit register. This is simply a 32-bit object of the type std_logic_vector.

type register32 **is** std_logic_vector (31 **downto** 0);

Step 4.   Propose and implement one or two other types of objects that you may expect to find in a model of a CPU or memory system.

Step 5.   Create a library named MYLIB. This operation is usually simulator specific.

Step 6.   Compile the package into the library MYLIB. Your CAD tool documentation should provide guidelines on compiling design units into a library.

Step 7.   Write a VHDL model of a bit-serial adder using signals of type **bit** and adopting the structure shown in Figure 9-11. The model must declare the library MYLIB provide access to your package via the **use** clause.

Step 8.   Test the model of the bit-serial adder to ensure that it is functioning correctly.

Step 9.   Modify the model to use signals of type std_logic. Nothing else should have to change including the structure of the procedure call. By virtue of the argument type in the procedure call, the correct procedure in the package that you have written will be used.

Step 10.   Modify the **use** clause to limit the visibility to one procedure in the package. Repeat your simulation experiments. You might have multiple instances of the **use** clause to provide visibility to each of the procedures you wish to utilize.

Step 11.   Repeat the experiment to use other models of the D flip-flop that include signals such as reset and clear.

End Simulation Exercise 9.1

9.6 Chapter Summary

Designs can become large and complex. We need constructs that can help us manage this complexity and enhance sharing of common design units. This chapter has addressed the essential issues governing the construction and use of sub-programs: functions and procedures. Commonly used sub-programs can be organized into packages and placed in design libraries for subsequent reuse and sharing across distinct VHDL models. Synthesis issues were discussed in the context of the semantics of function and procedure calls. The concepts introduced in this chapter include the following:

- Functions
    - type conversion functions
    - resolution functions
    - synthesis issues
- Procedures
    - concurrent procedure calls
    - sequential procedure calls
    - synthesis issues

- Subprogram overloading
  - subprogram name
  - operator overloading
- Visibility rules
- Packages
  - package declaration
  - package body
- Libraries
  - relationships between design units and libraries
  - managing the scope and visibility of package contents

We are now armed with constructs for hiding complexity and sharing and reusing VHDL code modules.

Exercises

1. Create a package with functions–procedures for performing various shift operations and increment and decrement operations on **bit_vector** elements and std_logic_vector elements. Place the package declaration and package body in distinct files and analyze them separately. Remember to declare and use the library IEEE and the package std_logic_1164.vhd.

2. Consider a VHDL type that can take on the values (0, 1, X, U). The values X and U correspond to the values unknown and uninitialized respectively. Define a resolved type that takes on these values and write and test a resolution function for this resolved type.

3. Write and test a set of procedures for performing arithmetic left and right shifts on vectors of type std_logic_vector.

4. Write and test a resolution function that operates on elements of type std_logic_vector and returns the largest value.

5. Consider the example function shown in Figure 9-9. Modify this function to compute the parity of a std_logic_vector. The value of the parity bit is set if the number of 1's in the value of data is odd. This can be done with the exclusive-OR operation. You will need to change several things in the function besides the loop body. For example the type returned by the function and the type of signal that receives the function value. Verify the correctness of the function via simulation. Now synthesize the VHDL model and examine the structure of the synthesized circuit. What is the total delay expressed in gate delays for this circuit. Can you explain how or why the inference mechanisms may have produced such a structure?

6. Write and test functions that can perform type conversion between multi-bit quantities of type std_logic_vector and integers.

7. Using a concurrent procedure looks very much like using a component in a hierarchically structured design. What is the difference between using a concurrent procedure and constructing a structural design?

8. Create a design library My_Lib and place a package in this library. You might create a package of your own or simply "borrow" any one of a number of existing packages that come with VHDL environments. Analyze this package into this library. The creation of this library with the logical name My_Lib will involve simulator specific operations. Ensure that you have correctly implemented this library by using elements of this package in a VHDL model analyzed into your working library, WORK.

CHAPTER 10

Basic I/O

Thus far, we have written VHDL programs that manipulate three classes of programming objects: variables, signals, and constants. We adhere to certain rules when using these objects. For example, if we were to use a variable in our program, we would give it a name such as Index, and we first declare the type of Index using a declaration statement. The range of values that the program can legally assign to Index, and the operations that can be performed on Index are determined by its type. For example, if Index is an integer, we may perform integer arithmetic using Index, and the range of values that it may take depends on the number of bits used to represent an integer: 16, 32, and so forth. In an analogous fashion, the use of I/O functions necessitates the introduction of the *file* type that permits us to declare file objects.

Files are special and serve as the interface between the VHDL programs and the host environment. They are manipulated in a manner very different from variables or signals, hence the need for a distinct object type. As you might expect, there are special operations that are performed only on files: reading and writing files. This chapter discusses how file objects are created, read, written, and used within VHDL simulations. File input and output cannot be synthesized. I/O operations as described here refer to interaction with the host environment and not the I/O pins of an FPGA chip. A very useful example of the application of file I/O is the construction of testbenches—VHDL programs for testing VHDL models. The testbench reads test inputs from a file, applies them to the VHDL model under test, and records model outputs for analysis. The notion of a testbench follows directly from the testing of chips and boards and provides a structured approach for validating designs captured in VHDL simulation models.

10.1 Basic I/O Operations

As with variable, signal, and constant objects, before we can use a file object we must give it a name and declare its type. What determines the type of a file? A natural expectation is that the type of a file is determined by the information provided in the file. For example if a file contained a sequence of integers we might naturally think of this file as being of type integer. As users we tend to create files with all types of information, for example, strings, real numbers, and std_logic_vectors. To create and access information from these files we would like a way to state the type of information contained in these files and have functions for reading and writing this information. This chapter focuses on file I/O mechanisms in VHDL'93. File I/O in VHDL'87 is quite different and is explicitly marked in the text.

Based on our experiences with I/O in conventional programming languages and the preceding discussion we can identify the following basic operations that we need for reading and writing files:

- Declaration of a file and its type

- Opening and closing a file of a specified type

- Reading and writing from a file

    We now consider each of these steps and conclude this section with some examples.

10.1.1 File Declarations

If we want to declare a file we also wish to make sure that the host environment can correctly interpret the format of the data stored in the file. This is achieved by first declaring the type of a file as follows:

type TEXT **is file of string**;

type INTF **is file of integer**;

    The first declaration defines a *file type* that can store ASCII data. Files of this type contain human readable text. The second declaration defines a file type that can store a sequence of integers. Files of this type are stored in binary form and are machine readable but not human readable. Both **string** and **integer** are predefined types of the language and their definition can be found in the package STANDARD. In general, file types can describe sequences of more complicated data structures however we restrict ourselves to the essentials of the language and therefore the relatively simpler cases of predefined data types.

    Now we can declare a file object as being of a particular file type as follows:

file Integer_File : INTF;

file Input_File : TEXT;

Note that the file type TEXT is also a predefined type in the package TEXTIO that is typically distributed with all VHDL environments and is described in Section 10.2. We can think of Integer_File and Input_File as pointers to files that contain sequences of integers and characters respectively. When VHDL procedures are used to read and write from these files the file type enables the procedures to correctly interpret the values being read from the files.

10.1.2 Opening and Closing Files

Once we have declared files of a specific type we must open these files prior to use and close these files prior to termination of the program. In conventional programming languages I/O operations involve calls to initialization procedures to open files *prior* to reading or writing data. Other procedures must also be called prior to closing files. For example, the C language provides the fopen() function call that returns a pointer to a file. The fclose() function call is provided to close the file and make sure the last updates have been written out to the file on disk (because they may still be cached in memory). In between calls to these two procedures, a file can be read or written. In VHDL'93 the following procedures are provided for opening and closing files.

> **procedure** FILE_OPEN (**file** file_handle : FILE_TYPE;
>
> File_Name : **in** STRING;
>
> Open_Kind: **in** FILE_OPEN_KIND := READ_MODE);
>
> **procedure** FILE_OPEN (File_Status: **out** FILE_OPEN_STATUS;
>
> **file** file_handle : FILE_TYPE;
>
> File_Name : **in** STRING;
>
> Open_Kind : **in** FILE_OPEN_KIND := READ_MODE);
>
> **procedure** FILE_CLOSE (**file** f : FILE_TYPE);

Consider the first procedure. The first argument is the file pointer that used in the VHDL program, for example in the read and write procedures to be discussed in Section 10.1.3. The second argument is the name of the file that will read or written. For example you might have a file named *input_file.txt* in your working directory. The third argument describes how this file is to be used, that is the mode of the file. A file can be opened in three modes—READ_MODE, WRITE_MODE, and APPEND_MODE. The default mode is READ_MODE. The second procedure is the same as the first with the addition of a new parameter, File_Status. This parameter has a value returned by the procedure that may have one of four values:

OPEN_OK – file open operation was successful

STATUS_ERROR – attempted to open an already open file

NAME_ERROR – file not found

MODE_ERROR – file cannot be opened in this mode

The File_Status variable is an enumerated type whose value can be checked to make sure that the FILE_OPEN call was successful. Finally the FILE_CLOSE procedure closes the file. An implicit call to FILE_CLOSE exists and is called when execution terminates. Thus you do not have to explicitly make the FILE_CLOSE call. As a matter of fact we can even avoid making the FILE_OPEN call by providing the same information in the file declaration as illustrated in the following example.

Example: Explicit vs. Implicit File Open

The following template of code is typically found in a processes that use files. In the file open call the name of the file can include a path in you local machine hierarchy.

```
type IntegerFileType is file of integer; -- declare a file type in the
--                                       -- architecture declarative region
process is - a template for a process
file datain :IntegerFileType; -- declare file handle
variable fstatus :File_open_status; -- declare file status variable
--
-- other misc declarations
--
begin
file_open(fstatus, dataout,"myfile.txt", read_mode);
--
-- body of process: reading and writing files and
-- performing computations
--
end process; -- termination implicitly causes a call to FILE_CLOSE
```

Files can be implicitly opened by providing the necessary information in the file declaration as follows. There is no explicit FILE_OPEN call.

> **type** IntegerFileType **is file of integer**; *-- declare a file type in the*
>
> **--** *-- architecture declarative region*
> **process is -** *a template for a process*
> **file** datain:IntegerFileType **open** read_mode **is** "myfile.txt"; *-- declare file han-*

dle

> **--**
> *-- other misc declarations*
> **--**
> **begin**
> **--**
> *-- body of process: reading and writing files and*
> *-- performing computations*
> **--**
> **end process**; *-- termination implicitly causes a call to* FILE_CLOSE

Example End: Explicit vs. Implicit File Open

10.1.3 Reading and Writing Files

Now that we can declare files of a certain type and open and close these files prior to and after their use, we need procedures and functions to read and write files of the declared type. What are these I/O procedures and how are they used? The arguments of these functions include a pointer to the file and the variables to be written or read. Most other programming languages provide equivalent functions to be used in a similar manner. In principle, the VHDL language operates in much the same way with a few important differences. The standard VHDL procedures made available by the definition of the language are as follows:

> **procedure** READ (**file** file_handle : FILE_TYPE; value : **out** type);
>
> **procedure** WRITE (**file** file_handle : FILE_TYPE; value : **in** type);
>
> **function** ENDFILE (**file** file_handle : FILE_TYPE) **return boolean**;

The above I/O procedures are implicitly declared following a file type declaration. This means that you do not have to declare these procedures prior to their use. Whereas the procedures **READ** and **WRITE** are used for I/O operations, the **ENDFILE** function is used to test for the end of file when reading from files. Most VHDL simulators will support a set of procedures for reading and writing various data types: **character, integer,**

real, and so on. Refer to your simulator documentation for more details on the available I/O procedures for reading and writing different data types. The standard package TEXTIO provides procedures for reading and writing files of type TEXT. More information on the package TEXTIO is provided in Section 10.2.

Although this book focuses on the basic features of the language, advanced topics covering I/O can be found in several excellent books [2,10].

'87 vs. '93

☞ 10.1.4 VHDL 1987 I/O

File type declarations within VHDL'87 are the same as in VHDL'93. However the file declarations that provide pointers to files are different and incorporate the functionality of the FILE_OPEN procedure in VHDL'93. The VHDL'87 file declarations will appear as follows:

    File infile : intf **is in** "inputdata.txt";

    File outfile : INTF **is out** "outputdata.txt";

Note the case of the file type INTF : VHDL is case insensitive so both statemenst refer to the same filetype. The object infile can be regarded as a pointer to a file to be opened for input. The name of the file is inputdata.txt. Because the file is open for input, the access mode of the file is said to be of type **in**. The default location of this file is the current working directory. Similarly, the object outfile is declared as a pointer to a file named outputdata.txt. The access mode for this latter file is declared to be of type **out** and can only be written. When VHDL was revised in 1993 changes were introduced in the input and output operations. In contrast to VHDL'87, file declarations in VHDL'93 appear as shown below:

    File infile : text **open** read_mode **is** "inputdata.txt";

    File outfile : text **open** write_mode **is** "outputdata.txt";

The file objects infile and outfile can be used by VHDL procedures to read and write the files inputdata.txt and outputdata.txt, respectively, using the **read**() and **write**() procedures as defined in Section 10.1.3.

    procedure READ (**file** file_handle : FILE_TYPE; value : **out** type);

    procedure WRITE (**file** file_handle : FILE_TYPE; value : **in** type);

    function ENDFILE (**file** file_handle : FILE_TYPE) **return boolean**;

We see that the syntax of these procedures is essentially the same in VHDL'93. Finally, note that in VHDL'87 there are no explicit FILE_OPEN and FILE_CLOSE procedures. These operations are performed implicitly during the file declarations as shown earlier in this section.

Example: Basic Binary File I/O

The code in Figure 10-1 shows an example of basic binary file output. We wish to write a file with integer values. Therefore a file type IntegerFileType is declared and a file pointer, dataout, is declared as a pointer to a file of this type. Now we are ready to write to this file. Initialization is performed in the body of the process by opening the file "myfile.txt" in mode write_mode. The text following the file open procedure is a simple loop that generates a sequence of integer values to be written to the file. The code block ends rather artificially with the process suspended by the **wait** statement. To read the file "myfile.txt" we can imagine another VHDL model with a block of code that looks exactly like the above **for-loop** but with the write(dataout, count) procedure replaced by a read(dataout, myinteger[i]) so that the sequence of values can be read into an integer array myinteger[]. The mode of the FILE_OPEN() procedure would also have to be read_mode rather than write_mode.

```
entity io93 is -- this entity is empty
end entity io93;

architecture behavioral of io93 is
begin
process is
type IntegerFileType is file of integer; -- file declarations
file dataout :IntegerFileType;
variable count : integer:= 0;
variable fstatus: FILE_OPEN_STATUS;

begin
file_open(fstatus, dataout,"myfile.txt", write_mode); -- open the file
for j in 1 to 8 loop
write(dataout,count); -- some random values to write to the file
count := count+2;
end loop;
wait; -- an artificial way to stop the process
end process;
end achitecture behavioral;
```

FIGURE 10-1 Basic binary file I/O

Example End: Basic Binary File I/O

The language supports reading and writing from files of the predefined types of the language. If you wish to read or write other types not defined by the language you must write your own I/O procedures built on these basic procedures. It is common to do so and encapsulate these procedures and any new type definitions in a package. In fact vendors will often supply a set if procedures and functions for reading and writing specific data types. Check the vendor documentation for more specific information.

One common approach to input/output for the predefined types of the language is the use of the TEXTIO package, which is described in the following section.

10.2 The Package TEXTIO

The package TEXTIO is a standard package supported by all VHDL simulators. Recall that packages can be thought of as a library or repository of predefined types, variables, signals, constants, functions, and procedures. The TEXTIO package provides a standard set of file types, data types, and I/O functions. In general, when you use a package in a VHDL model, you must declare the package to be used. The declaration will state the library (system directory) that serves as the location of the package. The TEXTIO package is in the library STD, which is implicitly declared. This means that unlike other libraries, you do not have to declare the use of STD as we do with the library IEEE. However, usage of the package contents must be declared via the **use** clause as shown in the preceding examples.

The package TEXTIO defines a standard file type called TEXT and provides the procedures for reading and writing the predefined types of the language, such as **bit**, **integer**, and **character**. These are shown in the package definition provided in Appendix F. For example, the text object type and file handles for std_input and std_output are provided. From Appendix F we see that **read** () and **write** () procedures are defined for several data types. Normally, we expect that each data type will have a distinct procedure for reading and writing the type to a file. For example, we could have read_string () and read_bit_vector (). However, given the large number of data types, we see that this quickly becomes a rather tedious exercise in naming procedures. Instead, it is convenient for all of the procedures that perform the same function, such as **read**(), to have the same name, and permit the actual argument to identify the correct implementation: **read** () and **write** () are overloaded procedure names. We do not have to remember the exact name of the procedure to read and write elements of type **bit_vector** or **string**. We simply use the procedures **read** () and **write** (), and, depending on whether the argument is a **bit_vector** or **string** the appropriate implementation is invoked. We see that **read** () and **write** () procedures are available for the predefined types **bit**, **bit_vector**, **character**, and **string**.

The use of the TEXTIO package is based on the following view of I/O operations. Imagine a buffer that exists between the file you wish to read and the VHDL program. Think of this buffer as type of "staging area" and in our discussion let us refer to this buffer as buf. The **read**() and **write**() procedures access and operate on **buf** reading the values of program variables from buf or writing the values of program variables into buf. The **readline**() and **writeline**() procedures move the contents of buf to and from files. These procedures are defined in the package TEXTIO that is contained in the library STD. There are two "special" buffers call input and output that are predefined in the package

TEXTIO. These buffers are mapped to the std_input and std_output of the host environment that usually is the console window of the VHDL simulator. This reading from and writing to input and output respectively will read from and print to the simulator console window. Let us look at an example of the use of the TEXTIO package.

Example: Use of the TEXTIO Package

Figure 10-2 illustrates and example of the use of the TEXTIO package. The pointer outfile is declared to point to a file of type text. Again note that VHDL is not case sensitive and therefore text, Text, and TEXT are all identical. Statement L1 writes the text string "This

```
use STD.Textio.all;
entity formatted_io is -- this entity is empty
end formatted_io;

architecture behavioral of formatted_io is
begin
process is
file outfile :text; -- declare the file to be a text file
variable fstatus :File_open_status;
variable count: integer := 5;
variable value : bit_vector(3 downto 0):= X"6";
variable buf: line; -- this is the buffer between the program and the file

begin

file_open(fstatus, outfile,"myfile.txt", write_mode); -- open the file for writing
L1: write(buf, "This is an example of formatted IO");
L2: writeline(outfile, buf); -- this procedure writes the buffer to a line in the file
L3: write(buf, "The First Parameter is =");
L4: write(buf, count); -- this procedure writes to the next location in the buffer
L5: write(buf, ' ');
L6: write(buf, "The Second Parameter is = ");
L7: write(buf, value);
L8: writeline(outfile, buf);
L9: write(buf, "...and so on");
L10: writeline(outfile, buf);
L11: file_close(outfile); -- flush the buffer to the file
wait;
end process;
end architecture behavioral;
```

FIGURE 10-2 File I/O with the TEXTIO package

is an example of formatted IO" to the buffer buf. Statement L2 then writes the buffer to the file causing this text string to appear on a line in the output file. The next sequence of writes in statements L3 through L7 are written in the buffer and when statement L8 is executed the contents of writes in L3 through L7 will appear on the same line. When viewed with a text editor the output file will appear as follows:

> This is an example of formatted IO
> The First Parameter is = 5 The Second Parameter is = 0110
> ...and so on

A few items are worth noting. The variable buf can be accessed only via the **read** () and **write** () procedures. This is because buf is of type line that is a special type referred to as an **access** type. An access type is very similar to a pointer in C or Pascal. While providing powerful programming flexibility we are more concerned here with the hardware modeling aspects of VHDL. Therefore other than its use in file I/O, we will not deal with access types any further. Statements L4 and L7 each write a distinct data type to buf. The **write** procedures are overloaded and support the predefined types (as are the read procedures). Writing **bit_vector** and **integer** types with the TEXTIO package creates files that are human readable. The file_close() procedure call will ensure that all writes to file are complete. In general it is not necessary to call this procedure explicitly. This procedure will be called implicitly when the process terminates. However the process in Figure 10-2 suspends indefinitely on the **wait** statement. Again this is an artifact of the contrived nature of this example. In general if you know your simulation will terminate file_close() will be called on program termination.

Finally, if we were to replace the variable outfile with the variable output in all of the **writeline**() procedure calls then the text output would be printed to std_output rather than the file myfile.txt. Usually std_output is the simulator console.

Example End: Use of the TEXTIO Package

The preceding example uses the **write**() procedures on the predefined types of the language. What about types such as std_logic_vectors? To use the TEXTIO package with any of these types we need to convert these types to characters for writing into the buffer buf. An example of writing and using type conversion functions in a package is illustrated in the following example.

Example: Basic Text I/O Operations

Suppose that we wish to read and write signal values of the type std_logic_vector. This example illustrates how we can develop I/O procedures to read and write signal values based on available elementary character I/O operations that are provided by VHDL. If we can provide these new procedures in a package, we can then use these procedures in our VHDL models and hide the fact that we are using character I/O. This is exactly what most VHDL environments do by providing a set of functions in the package **TEXTIO** to read various data types. Note that we do need the **use** clause so that the contents of the **TEXTIO** package is visible to the VHDL programs.

Figure 10-3 shows a package with two procedures. The first procedure is for reading a bit vector of type std_logic_vector and the second is for writing a bit vector of type

```
library IEEE;
use IEEE.std_logic_1164.all;
use STD.textio.all;

package classio is
procedure read_v1d (variable f: in text; v : out std_logic_vector);
procedure write_v1d (variable f:out text; v : in std_logic_vector);
end package classio;

package body classio is
procedure read_v1d (variable f:in text; v : out std_logic_vector) is
variable buf: line;
variable c : character;

begin
readline(f, buf);
for i in v'range loop
read(buf, c);
case c is
  when 'X' => v (i) := 'X';
  when 'U' => v (i) := 'U';
  when 'Z' => v (i) := 'Z';
  when '0' => v (i) := '0';
  when '1' => v (i) := '1';
  when '-' => v (i) := '-';
  when 'W' => v (i) := 'W';
  when 'L' => v (i) := 'L';
  when 'H' => v (i) := 'H';
  when others => v (i) := '0';
end case;
end loop;
end procedure read_v1d;
```

FIGURE 10-3 An example of using character I/O to read and write single-bit vectors

```
procedure write_v1d (variable f: out text; v : in std_logic_vector) is
variable buf: line;
variable c : character;

begin
for i in v'range loop
case v(i) is
when 'X' => write(buf, 'X');
 when 'U' => write(buf, 'U');
 when 'Z' => write(buf, 'Z');
 when '0' => write(buf, character'('0'));
 when '1' => write(buf, character'('1'));
 when '-' => write(buf, '-');
 when 'W' => write(buf, 'W');
 when 'L' => write(buf, 'L');
 when 'H' => write(buf, 'H');
 when others => write(buf, character'('0'));
end case;
end loop;
writeline (f, buf);
end procedure write_v1d;
end package body classio;
```

FIGURE 10-3 (continued)

std_logic_vector. Each procedure requires a file pointer as an argument. Each procedure also accepts as a parameter a variable v of type std_logic_vector. We can use the same procedures for reading and writing bit vectors of differing precision. Note how each procedure works. In the read procedure a complete line is read into the buffer buf using the **readline**() VHDL procedure call. Once the complete vector is read into buf, this buffer is scanned to test for the value of each digit in the vector and to set the value of each output digit accordingly using the **case** statement. Finally, note that the loop scanning the input vector executes a number of times that is determined by the **'range** attribute of the vector being read. An analogous procedure is used for writing bit vectors of type std_logic_vector out to a file. Because we are dealing with text-based I/O in this example, when writing the bit values 0 and 1, they must be first converted to characters as shown in write_v1d() in the figure. This is necessary so that the implementation may distinguish between the value of 0 and 1 and its corresponding ASCII character representation. By using the basic read and write procedures provided by VHDL, we are now able to read and write single-bit vectors of the type std_logic_vector. This package can be compiled into a library or simply into the local working directory that is accessed via the logical name WORK.

Example End: Basic Text Input/Output Operations

We can similarly construct procedures for reading and writing other data types from files. Generally, rather than the user developing these procedures, the CAD tool vendor will provide a comprehensive set of input/output functions for reading and writing various data types. The package described in Figure 10-3 can be used within VHDL model for reading std_logic_vector values from file and using them internally, or for writing generated std_logic_vectors to a file for later analysis. A simple template for using the package *classio.vhd* is described in the example that follows.

Example: Using the Classio Package

An example of how the procedures and the package shown in Figure 10-3 might be used is shown in the example code in Figure 10-4. This example simply reads 16-bit vectors from infile.txt and writes them out to the file outfile.txt. Note that by changing the resolution of

```vhdl
library IEEE;
use IEEE.std_logic_1164.all;
use STD.textio.all;
use Work.classio.all; -- the package classio has been compiled into
                      -- the working directory
entity checking is
end checking; -- the entity is an empty entity

architecture behavioral of checking is
begin
process is
-- use implicit file open
--
file infile : TEXT open read_mode is "infile.txt";
file outfile : TEXT open write_mode is "outfile.txt";
variable check : std_logic_vector (15 downto 0) := x"0008";

begin
-- copy the input file contents to the output file
while not (endfile (infile)) loop
read_v1d (infile, check);
write_v1d (outfile, check);
end loop;
file_close(outfile); -- flush buffers to output file
wait; -- artificial wait for this example
end process;
end architecture behavioral;
```

FIGURE 10-4 An example of the use of the package *classio.vhd*

the variable **check** to 32 bits, the same procedures can be used for reading and writing 32-bit vectors. This is because the loop in the read/write procedures that scans the vectors is parameterized by the range of the vector as opposed to a fixed value. The simple test program is written using a **wait** statement to ensure that the simulation progresses. Remember that, in general, processes are executed once, when the simulation is initialized. Thereafter, processes are executed only if they are invoked by events. Events may occur in a sensitivity list or via the use of **wait** statements. In general, you will probably be performing I/O operations within some process that will be invoked due to some simulation events and therefore the use of the **wait** statement in the above example should be regarded as somewhat artificial.

Example End: Using the Classio Package

We have now covered the essentials of binary and text file I/O. The next section will focus on the use of file I/O as part if the important process of testing and validation of VHDL models.

Simulation Exercise 10.1: Basic I/O

This exercise introduces the student to the basic steps involved in reading and writing text files, covering the following concepts: (i) declaring, and opening files, (ii) initialization of data structures from files, and (iii) recording simulation results in file.

Step 1. Create a text file, *memory.vhd*, with the model of a memory module from Figure 6-2. The succeeding steps will modify this model to initialize the memory to encoded values read from a file.

Step 2. Create the file *classio.vhd* shown in Figure 10-3. This is a package. Compile this package into your working directory. The simulator you are using should have the default library **WORK** set to this directory.

Step 3. Edit *memory.vhd* to enable references to the package *classio.vhd* by placing the following clause at the beginning of the file.

use WORK.classio.all;

Step 4. Create a text file *infile.txt*. This file will include the contents of memory. Each line should be a 32-bit vector of type **std_logic_vector**, and there should one word per line. For the model we are using, the file should have eight words.

Step 5. Add a single-bit signal, **reset**, as an input signal to the entity description. This signal is of mode **in** and of type **std_logic**. A pulse on this signal will indicate that the memory contents are to be initialized from a file.

Step 6. Add a separate process to the model to read eight 32-bit values from a file and initialize the contents of memory to these values.

Step 6 (a)   Label this process ioproc.

Step 6 (b)   Have the first line in the process be a **wait** statement, causing the process to wait for a rising edge on the signal reset. Examples of the detection of rising edges on signals can be found in the D flip-flop examples in Chapter 6.

Step 6 (c)   Use the functions in the package classio in writing the body of the process. The process body reads and initializes the contents of memory from the input file. The model in Figure 10-4 can be used as an example of how a **while** loop can be used for this purpose.

Step 7.   The modified memory model is now complete. Compile the model into the working directory.

Step 8.   Test the model as follows.

Step 8 (a)   Create a sequence of test inputs to the model. For the reset signal we must supply a single pulse. For the remaining inputs, supply a sequence of addresses starting from 0 and through memory address 7. The memory read control signal must be asserted.

Step 8 (b)   Select the signals to be traced. Trace all of the signals in the entity description.

Step 8 (c)   Apply the stimulus as generated in Step 8 (a). Observe the trace.

Step 8 (d)   After eight memory read operations the values read from memory should be identical to the values initialized from the file.

Step 9.   Modify the model to use an output file *outfile.txt*. Now generate a sequence of read and write operations to memory using the external stimulus capabilities of the simulator you are using.

Step 10.   Now modify the model to log all memory operations to the output file. For each read and write operation, the model records the value and address in *outfile.txt*.

Step 11.   Verify that the contents of *outfile.txt* agree with the test sequence that you generated in Step 9.

Step 12.   Modify the memory model so that data types used are **bit** and **bit_vector** rather than std_logic and std_logic_vector. For example, memory would be an array of words of type **bit_vector**. Now we can use the I/O functions in the package TEXTIO. These functions are shown in Appendix F. Modify the model to use the I/O functions from this package.

Step 13.   Rerun the model using the TEXTIO package rather than the classio package. I/O procedures are available for all of the predefined types of the language, for example, strings. Modify the **use** clause accordingly. Remember, std_logic and std_logic_vector are not predefined types of the language. They are defined by the package std_logic_1164!

End Simulation Exercise 10.1

The examples we have seen up to this point have had the filenames specified in the file declarations or file open procedures. As with conventional languages it is desirable to be able to specify the filename and thereby avoid recompiling the simulation model each time we change the input file.

Example: Filenames as Inputs

We would like to be able to read a character string corresponding to the filename from the simulator console. Fortunately for us the TEXTIO package defines file handles for std_input and std_output as input and output, respectively. The following process code block can be used to read a file name from the simulator console assuming that the simulator console is mapped to std_input.

```
process is
variable buf : line;
variable fname : string(1 to 10);
begin
--
-- prompt and read filename from standard input
--
write(output, "Enter Filename: ");
readline(input,buf);
read(buf, fname);
--
-- process code
--
end process;
```

The variable fname can now be used in the file_open procedure.

Example End: Filenames as Inputs

Now that we have the ability to perform file input/output what else can we do other than the obvious? The following section describes a very important process central to digital design, namely testing and validation of VHDL models. File I/O is routinely used in this process.

10.3 Testbenches in VHDL

Much of the motivation for simulation is to be able to test designs prior to construction and use of the circuit. To motivate a testing methodology we might consider the physical analogy. How would we test an electronic component such as a silicon chip that implements some digital circuit? Intuitively, we would like to provide a set of inputs and check the observed output values against the corresponding correct set of output values. The chip can be placed in a specialized piece of equipment, referred to as a test frame, that allows us to apply an electrical stimulus to the inputs and examine the values of the outputs using a logic analyzer. By cycling through possible input sequences, we could analyze the corresponding output sequences to determine if the component was functioning correctly.

When developing VHDL models, we find ourselves in a similar situation. We construct a VHDL simulation model of some digital system component such as an encoder for audio signals. How do we test this model to ensure that (i) the model is operating as designed, and (ii) the design itself is correct? Verifying a design via simulation is certainly more cost-effective than testing a fabricated part and then determining that it has a design error that must be fixed. If our VHDL model is sufficiently detailed, then thorough testing in simulation significantly reduces the chances of errors, minimizes costly design rework, and reduces the time to get the product to the marketplace.

Most simulators provide commands to apply stimulus to the input ports of a design entity. By tracing and viewing the resulting values of the signals on the output ports, we can determine whether the model is operating correctly. However, by recognizing that VHDL provides powerful programming language abstractions for describing the operation of digital systems a more structured approach toward testing VHDL models can be realized. The test frame described for placing and testing chips is itself a digital system and we should be able to describe the operation of the tester in VHDL! The logical behavior of the tester is simple to understand. The model generates sequences of inputs and reads the outputs of the module being tested. This behavior is captured in the notion of a *testbench* and is illustrated in Figure 10-5.

In this figure, one VHDL module (*tester.vhd*) generates the stimulus to be applied. A second VHDL module (*model.vhd*) is the model being tested. Finally, a third module (*testbench.vhd*) is a structural VHDL model that describes the interconnections between the tester and the model under test. This model describes how the ports of the tester are connected to ports of the model. The simulation progresses with the tester applying a stimulus to the model and reading and recording the responses. The sequences of input values to be applied to the input ports of the model under test can be read from a file, or they can be generated in VHDL. For example, clock signals, reset pulses, and other types of periodic waveforms can be generated using approaches described in Section 6.6. The results returned from the VHDL model can be checked by the tester against a known correct set of output values and errors can be flagged. When testing large systems with a potential of

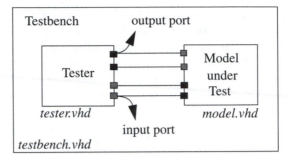

FIGURE 10-5 The structure of a testbench

millions of test vectors, automation of this process is a very productive enterprise. The construction of testbenches is best illustrated with an example.

Example: Writing a Testbench

Let us assume we wish to write a testbench to test the VHDL model of the positive-edge-triggered D flip-flop developed in Chapter 6 and shown in Figure 10-6. In order to test this model, we must generate a clock signal and a sequence of values on the D input signals. We must also test the Set (S) and Reset (R) operations. A sample test pattern for the clock and input (D) is shown in Figure 10-7. The D input is sampled at the rising edge of the clock producing the output waveforms shown in the figure. The Set (S) input and Reset (R) inputs can be tested by applying a test vector where either S or R or both are asserted and then reading the value of the flip-flop outputs after a delay equal to the propagation delays of the signals through the flip-flop.

   An example of a tester module that generates the clock signal and applies a set of test vectors to the D flip-flop model is shown in Figure 10-8. Note that the example I/O package shown in Figure 10-3 is compiled into the library WORK. Consider the structure of the tester module. The process named clk_process generates a clock signal with a period of 20 ns. This process executes concurrently with the io_process. This latter process reads test vectors from file *infile.txt*. Each test vector is five bits long. The first three bits correspond to input values for R, S, and D. The last two bits are the corresponding correct values of Q and Qbar. Collectively these five values constitute one test vector. The input test vector values are applied to the flip-flop model at 20 ns intervals—the rising edge of the clock. From the correct timing behavior shown in Figure 10-7 we can generate a set of

```
library IEEE;
use IEEE.std_logic_1164.all;

entity asynch_dff is
port (R, S, D, Clk : in std_logic;
    Q, Qbar : out std_logic);
end entity asynch_dff;

architecture behavioral of asynch_dff is
 begin
output: process (R, S, Clk) is
 begin
if (R = '0') then
    Q <= '0' after 5 ns;
    Qbar <= '1' after 5 ns;
 elsif S = '0' then
    Q <= '1' after 5 ns;
    Qbar <= '0' after 5 ns;
  elsif (rising_edge(Clk)) then
    Q <= D after 5 ns;
    Qbar <= ( not D) after 5 ns;
end if;
end process output;
end architecture behavioral;
```

FIGURE 10-6 Behavioral model of a positive-edge-triggered D flip-flop

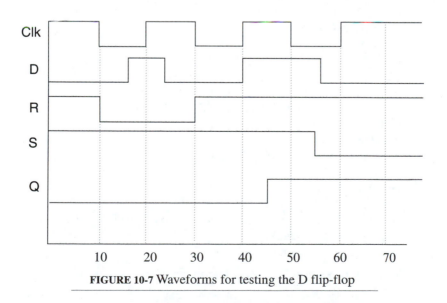

FIGURE 10-7 Waveforms for testing the D flip-flop

```vhdl
library IEEE;
use IEEE.std_logic_1164.all;
use STD.textio.all;
use WORK.classio.all; -- declare the I/O package

entity srtester is              -- this is the module generating the tests
port (R, S, D, Clk : out std_logic;
     Q, Qbar : in std_logic);
end entity srtester;

architecture behavioral of srtester is
begin
clk_process: process  is -- generates the clock waveform with
begin                            -- period of 20 ns
Clk<= '1', '0' after 10 ns, '1' after 20 ns, '0' after 30 ns;
wait for 40 ns;
end process clk_process;

io_process: process is -- this process performs the test
file infile : TEXT open read_mode is "infile.txt";        -- functions
file outfile : TEXT open write_mode is "outfile.txt";
variable buf : line;
variable msg : string(1 to 20) := "This vector failed! ";
variable check : std_logic_vector (4 downto 0);
begin
while not (endfile (infile)) loop   -- loop through all test vectors in
read_v1d (infile, check);          -- the file
R <= check(4);
S <= check(3);
D <= check(2);
wait for 20 ns;                    -- wait for outputs to be available after applying
                                   -- the stimulus
if (Q /= check (1) or (Qbar /= check(0))) then -- error check
write (buf, msg);
writeline (outfile, buf);
write_v1d (outfile, check);
end if;
end loop;
file_close(outfile); -- flush contents to file
wait;      -- this wait statement is important to allow the simulation to halt!
end process io_process;
end architecture behavioral;
```

FIGURE 10-8 Behavioral description of the tester module

test vectors by looking at the values of the inputs on each rising edge (i.e., at time 20 ns, 40 ns, and so on). This can give rise to the following test vectors in file *infile.txt*.

```
11001   -- initial vector
01101
11110
10010
10011   -- illegal case
```

Each vector is applied at 20 ns intervals to coincide with the rising edge of the clock. The last test vector corresponds to an illegal case, because both Q and Qbar cannot be asserted at the same time. Therefore this test vector will fail and an error message will be logged to the output file *outfile.txt*. This example also shows that failure of a test vector may not be due to an incorrect model but an incorrect test vector. In fact running these test vectors as given will also generate an error for the first vector because at this time the values of Q and Qbar are undefined or U. We should build flip-flop models with global reset to a known state. The generation of test vectors in general is a computationally intensive and non-trivial task. Once the stimulus is applied, the process waits for 20 ns. By this time the flip-flop outputs become stable (see Figure 10-6). At this time, the outputs are read and compared to known correct values that were read from the input file. If there is any discrepancy in these values, the corresponding test vector is flagged by writing out an error message to an output file along with the test vector. After all the test vectors have been read and applied, the output file contains the list of test vectors for which the model failed.

The top-level module for our testbench is a structural model for specifying the connections between the tester and the model under test and is shown in Figure 10-9. Note the use of configuration specifications to explicitly state which VHDL architectures are to be used for the design entities srtester and asynch_dff. In general, there could have been more than one architecture that we could have used. The configuration specification states that the architecture labeled behavioral is to be used for each entity. The configuration also states that these architectures can be found in the working directory denoted by the library WORK. If no configuration specification had been provided, default rules would apply and the last compiled architecture for entities srtester and asynch_dff would have been used.

When testing combinational circuits there may be no clock or periodic signal. In this case the tester module can be written without having to be concerned about synchronizing with a periodic signal. The module can apply the input vectors, wait for a period equal to the propagation delay of the longest path through the circuit, and then read the output signal values of the module under test.

Example End: Writing a Testbench

```
library IEEE;
use IEEE.std_logic_1164.all;
use WORK.classio.all; -- declare the I/O package

entity srbench is    -- the entity interface is empty
end srbench;

architecture behavioral of srbench is
component asynch_dff is
port (R, S, D, Clk : in std_logic;
      Q, Qbar : out std_logic);
end component asynch_dff;

component srtester is
port (R, S, D, Clk : out std_logic;
      Q, Qbar : in std_logic);
end component srtester;
--
-- configuration specification
--
for T1:srtester use entity WORK.srtester (behavioral);
for M1: asynch_dff use entity WORK.asynch_dff (behavioral);

signal s_r, s_s, s_d, s_q, s_qb, s_clk : std_logic;

begin
T1: srtester port map (R=>s_r, S=>s_s, D=>s_d, Q=>s_q, Qbar=>s_qb,
                       Clk => s_clk);
M1: asynch_dff port map (R=>s_r, S=>s_s, D=>s_d, Q=>s_q,
                         Qbar=>s_qb, Clk => s_clk);
end behavioral;
```

FIGURE 10-9 Structural description of the testbench module

10.4 ASSERT Statement

In the prior example, the testbench model recorded errors or failures to pass a test vector by writing the failed test vector and a brief message to the file outfile.txt. Alternatively, we could use the **assert** statement. The **assert** statement is a general mechanism for detecting and reporting incorrect conditions during a simulation. We can use this statement for detecting failed test vectors, as shown in Figure 10-10. This statement would replace the **if** statement in the srtester module in Figure 10-8 that checks the output signal values and causes error messages to be written to a file. If we use the **assert** statement, rather than having an error message and the offending test vector being written to a file, the message regarding a violation and the string provided with the **report** clause would be sent to the simulation output. For example, the contents of the simulator console when executing the example testbench in Figure 10-9 is shown in Figure 10-10. This is the output from the Active VHDL simulator.

Note the absence of a semicolon after the report clause. This output is generally the simulator console window unless you have redirected this to a file. The designer can report messages at one of several predefined severity levels: NOTE, WARNING, ERROR, and FAILURE. This provides a clean mechanism for the designer to classify the levels of information conveyed during simulation. For example, the NOTE category can be used to provide information about the progress of the simulation whereas a severity level of ERROR may cause the simulation to be aborted.

> **assert** Q = check(1) **and** Qbar = check(0)
> **report** "Test Vector Failed"
> **severity error**;

Example of Simulator Console Output

> Selected Top-Level: srbench (behavioral)
> : ERROR : Test Vector Failed
> : Time: 20 ns, Iteration: 0, Instance: /T1.
> : ERROR : Test Vector Failed
> : Time: 100 ns, Iteration: 0, Instance: /T1.

FIGURE 10-10 An example of the use of the **assert** statement in the testbench shown in Figure 10-8 and the resulting message printed in the simulator console

10.5 A Testbench Template

We are now ready to outline a few basic steps toward constructing a testbench for testing a VHDL model. It should be clear from the above examples that the testbench is a structural model with two components: a tester and the model under test. This is not the only way to structure a testbench, but is intuitive, common, and simple to construct.

The model under test may be a behavioral or structural VHDL model of a digital system. The tester is usually a behavioral model written using the constructs described in Chapter 6. Typical segments of VHDL code that we may find in tester modules include (i)

processes to generate waveforms, (ii) VHDL statements to read test vectors from input files and apply them to the model under test, and (iii) VHDL statements to record the outputs that are produced by the model under test in response to the test vectors. A template for such a top-level structural model is shown in Figure 10-11. A step-by-step description for the construction of such a testbench model is the same as that for creating structural models as described in Chapter 8.

Recall from Chapter 6 that we can mix concurrent and sequential statements (via processes) in the architecture description of a circuit. Rather than have distinct models for

```
library Lib1;    -- declare any libraries that will be needed
library Lib2;
use Lib1.package_name.all; -- declare the packages that will be used
use Lib2.package_name.all; -- in these libraries

entity test_bench_name is

port( input signals : in type;
      output signals : out type);

end entity test_bench_name;

architecture arch_name of test_bench_name is

-- declare tester and model components
component tester_name is
port ( input signals : in type;
       output signals : out type);
end component tester_name;

 component model_name is
port( input signals : in type;
      output signals : out type);
end component model_name;

-- declare all signals used to connect the  tester and model

signal internal signals : type := initialization;

begin

-- label each component and connect it's ports to signals or other ports

T1: tester-name port map (port=> signal1,.....);

M1: model-name port map (port => signal2,.....);

end arch_name;
```

FIGURE 10-11 A testbench model template

the testbench module, tester module, and the model under test, the tester VHDL code may be directly included the testbench architecture. The component instantiation statement T1 in Figure 10-9 can be replaced by the tester code. If we took this approach we would have only two code modules: the testbench and the model under test.

The models we are dealing with here are relatively small. We can see that as models become more complex the number and size of the test vectors could become very large. For example, consider a circuit that processes 32-bit data according to a 16-bit operation code. At the very least, this circuit will have 48 inputs. A naive testing approach would attempt to test all possible input combinations. The total number of possible combinations of input values (assuming only 0 and 1 values) is 2^{48}! Even if we could perform each test in a nanosecond it would still take on the order of thousands of years to finish the test suite. Furthermore, the number of inputs in modern chips and systems is considerably higher. In reality, the number of input combinations that must be tested can be pared considerably and many computational as well as design techniques have been implemented to further reduce the cost of testing. Even so, it is apparent that the generation of test vectors can be a very complex process in its own right. To facilitate sharing of test vectors among groups (e.g., the people generating them and the designers using them), standards are often defined for the specification of these vectors.

Finally, remember that often input or output functions are expected to be executed only once, such as in loading memory in a processor datapath model. If the I/O code is placed in part of a process that is executed repetitively, array out of bounds errors can occur.

Simulation Exercise 10.2: Constructing Testbenches

This exercise familiarizes the student with the basic steps involved in constructing and executing a testbench for testing and validating a VHDL model. Basic concepts covered include (i) generating a stimulus for a model under test, (ii) reading test vectors from a file and applying them to the VHDL model under test, and (iii) recording failed test vectors and generating error messages for examination.

Step 1. Using a text editor, create the files *dff.vhd*, *srtester.vhd*, and *testbench.vhd* shown in Figure 10-6, Figure 10-8, and Figure 10-9, respectively. These files should be in your working directory. Compile each file.

Step 2. Create the file *classio.vhd* shown in Figure 10-3. This is a package. Compile this package into your working directory. The simulator you are using should have the default library **WORK** set to this directory.

Step 3. Create a text file named *infile.txt*. This file contents should appear as follows:
```
11001
01101
11110
10010
```

This file represents a set of test vectors to be applied to the model *dff.vhd*. The first three bits (left to right) represent test inputs for the R, S, and D inputs respectively. The last two inputs represent the corresponding correct values for Q and Qbar, respectively.

Step 4. Create the empty text file *outfile.txt*.

Step 5. Run the simulation long enough to apply the test vectors.

Step 6. Examine the output file *outfile.txt* for any error messages. How many error message should appear, if any, for the above sequence of test vectors?

Step 7. Modify some of the test vectors in *infile.txt*. Rerun the simulation and study the input and output files to determine if the model is functioning correctly.

Step 8. Modify the tester module as follows: consider the **if** statement in *srtester.vhd* that compares the output of the D flip-flop with the test vector and writes *outfile.txt*. Replace this statement with an ASSERT statement as follows.

> **assert** Q = check(1) **and** Qbar = check(0)
> **report** "Test Vector Failed"
> **severity error**;

Step 9. Rerun the simulation. Any previous error messages should appear as an assertion violation accompanied by the error message being printed on the simulator command line rather than being directed to the file *outfile.txt*.

End Simulation Exercise 10.2

10.6 Chapter Summary

This chapter has presented the basic concepts for reading and writing files. One common application of file I/O was developed: writing testbenches for testing VHDL simulation models. The exercises stressed basic binary and text I/O from files, and construction of functions for reading and writing other data types. This concepts covered in this chapter include the following:

- Files, file types, and file declarations.

- Basic operations for reading and writing text and binary files.

- Creation and use of procedures for reading and writing other data types to files.

- Construction and operation of testbenches.

Armed with an understanding of the basic issues of file I/O we can proceed to ask the right questions to determine the I/O functions that are supported within any commercial simulator. This includes declaring and using any general I/O packages that may be publicly available, such as the TEXTIO package, or creating a new package as required to read and write application specific data types.

Exercises

1. Write and test a model for a 16-bit shift register that is initialized to a value read from a file.

2. In models of complex components such as memories in modern processors, accesses to memory must follow certain restrictions. For example, you generally cannot write to the area of memory that stores program instructions. Modify the memory model used in Simulation Exercise 10.1 to include an **assert** statement with a severity level of NOTE. Use this statement to produce a message whenever a particular memory location is written. Compile and test the model.

3. What are some of the advantages to using the idea of testbenches rather than testing your model by providing stimuli to the entity input using the facilities in a simulator?

4. Consider a testbench for a combinational circuit such as the single-bit ALU described in Simulation Exercise 4.2. Write a VHDL model for this circuit. Develop a testbench to test the model. Verify the functionality of the ALU using this testbench.

5. Modify the D flip-flop model shown in Figure 10-6 to include the use of an **assert** statement to check for conditions when both the Set and Reset inputs are asserted.

6. Write a testbench and test a model for an 8-bit counter. Use **bit** and **bit_vector** types. Therefore you can use the procedures in the package TEXTIO to read test vectors from a file.

7. Consider the memory model of Figure 6.2. Modify this model to load memory from a file. Test this model by writing a testbench that prints accesses each memory location and compares the value to the original value in the file used to load memory.

8. Modify the testbench model of Figure 10-8 as follows.

   - The printed output should be formatted as follows:

   The test vector has failed. The model value of Q = 0 and the value of Qbar = 1
   The input vector is 11011

   - The printed output should be printed to a file and should appear as shown above.

   - The problem is printing the values of Q and Qbar since they are of type std_logic. You can do so by using the case statement shown in Figure 10-3 in procedure write_v1d(). Because Q and Qbar are single-bit signals the **for-loop** is not necessary.

CHAPTER 11   Programming Mechanics

Up until this point the text has focused on the VHDL language and the construction of simulation and synthesis models. Using these models, CAD tool environments support activities such as simulation, synthesis, and FPGA device programming. These activities are structured around a set of concepts defined within the language and a set of conventions defined by CAD tool vendors. We refer to this body of knowledge as the *programming mechanics.* For example, for C or Pascal programs we must be able to identify default libraries, program units that must be linked, and set the directory paths to be searched for missing program units.

This chapter covers the mechanics of organizing, building, simulating, and synthesizing VHDL models. Understanding the programming mechanics is useful in debugging and reasoning about model behavior as well as quickly coming up to speed in being able to productively use VHDL-based CAD environments. This chapter tries to give the reader an intuitive grounding in the practical aspects of VHDL environments and hopefully eases the transition into their proficient use and avoids some of the frustrations that often accompany navigation through seemingly complex set of inter-related CAD tools. We first focus on the practical aspects of simulation followed by a discussion of the synthesis-related concepts and conventions. The discussion strives to remain independent of specific CAD environments by focusing on issues common to all CAD environments. In this regard I hope to convey a sense of being able to "ask the right questions" when attempting to navigate through a new CAD environment.

11.1 Terminology and Directory Structure

You will have noticed that much of the terminology used within the language has a hardware flavor, for example, signals, entities, and architecture. This way of thinking about VHDL designs continues through the design environment. The basic unit of VHDL programming is a *design unit*. A design unit is a component of a VHDL design and is one of:

• Entity

• Architecture

• Configuration

• Package Declaration

• Package Body

The entity, configuration declarations, and package declarations are primary design units. Primary design units are characterized by not being dependent upon other design units. The remaining are secondary design units. Design units are contained in *design files,* which contain the VHDL source for the individual design units. A single design file may contain the source for one or more design units. For example, imagine we were developing a VHDL model of an 8-bit adder. As newcomers to VHDL our natural inclination is to place the **entity** and associated **architecture** code in the same file. This seems only natural. Alternatively, we could place the **entity** description and the **architecture** description in two separate files. When design entities are compiled or synthesized CAD environments will create many intermediate files. The filenames are constructed from the names given to the design entities and the not from the filenames. For example, suppose we created a file called *foo.vhd* within which we place an **entity** named my_adder. When *foo.vhd* is compiled intermediate files created will have names derived from my_adder. This is to be expected since it is the design unit names and not the file names that link hierarchical models (see Chapter 8).

The compiled design units are placed in a *design library*. Design libraries are typically implemented as directories in most computing environments. A design library is identified by a logical name. This logical name is used to reference the library in a VHDL program using the **library** clause. The relationships of all of the components are illustrated in Figure 11-1. For the moment think of the "analyzer" as the compiler. A better description will be provided in the following section. The figure shows the libraries with logical names WORK, STD, and IEEE. The library WORK is the current working library. If a user package is referenced in a user design unit, the compiled package must be placed in a designated library. The default library for the placement of the compiled package is the library WORK.

An arbitrary number of libraries can exist and a given design can reference design units in one or more of these libraries as needed. Libraries may have been created by the designer or there may be libraries created by the VHDL tools vendor. There are two spe-

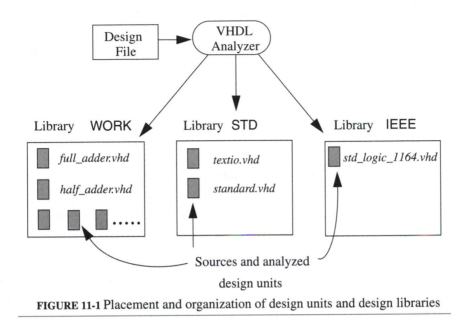

FIGURE 11-1 Placement and organization of design units and design libraries

cial libraries that exist in all VHDL environments. These are the libraries STD and WORK. Recall that a library is implemented as a directory. The STD library contains the compiled descriptions of two packages, STANDARD and TEXTIO. The STANDARD package contains the definitions of the predefined types and functions of the language. For example, the definitions of **integer**, **real**, and **bit_vector** types and functions for operations on these types are defined in the package STANDARD. The TEXTIO package contains the predefined types, functions, and procedures for reading and writing from files using text-based I/O. The library WORK corresponds to your working directory. Analyzed design files are placed in the working directory. The logical names STD and WORK are defined by the system implementation. This means that if you wish to use packages that are available in these libraries, you can do so via the **use** clause. You do not need to declare these libraries using the **library** clause as we do with the library IEEE. Typically, each design tool vendor will provide initialization files that assigns directory path names to STD and WORK when you first invoke the VHDL environment. If there are other libraries present that you wish to use in your VHDL programs, you must decide on a logical name to reference this library. This logical name then must be setup in the host environment to point to the physical directory that will contain the packages that constitute the library. Check your simulator documentation for details.

11.2 Simulation Mechanics

Here we are concerned with simulation of VHDL models, often prior to synthesis. In fact these simulation models may not even be synthesizeable! For example, we may include file I/O or multiple **wait** statements within a process.

Just as we have compilation, linking, and loading of C or Java programs, the major concepts in programming mechanics for simulation can be identified as *analysis, elaboration, initialization,* and *simulation.*

11.2.1 Analyzing VHDL Programs

Analyzing VHDL programs is synonymous with compiling VHDL programs. The two terms are often used interchangeably. In some CAD tool environment you will find menu items labeled Analyze whereas others may use the term Compile for the same purpose. Consider the conventional process of compiling and executing a Pascal program. We start with a text file containing the program. This program may reference functions or procedures found in other program modules, such as function libraries created by the user, or system libraries that are a part of the programming environment. For example, procedures to read and write files as well as many mathematical functions are provided by the system libraries whereas the user may have created a library of functions for manipulating data such as strings or image data. Common programming environments provide rules for referencing these libraries, and for compiling and linking independently compiled program modules to create a single executable program image. Similar conventions exist for compiling and linking distinct VHDL modules into a single image that can be used for simulation. The structure of the programming units and the concepts that govern their compilation and linking are similar to those governing conventional programming languages. Design files containing design units are *analyzed* to produce a form that can be used by a simulator. The *VHDL analyzer* performs the customary syntactic checks and compilation to a form executable by a VHDL simulator. This process is analogous to the process of compilation of conventional programs such as Pascal.

With respect to analyzing VHDL programs, we must be concerned with the order in which design units are analyzed because of dependencies between them. Throughout the examples in this text, entities and architectures were maintained in the same file for convenience. This is not strictly necessary. Design units can be in independent files and analyzed separately. Now if we make a change to one file what then is the order in which a large set of design entities must be analyzed? What dependencies between design units must we be aware of?

We can generate an intuition about compilation order by remembering that VHDL is a hardware description language. Consider the architecture of the structural model of a full adder reproduced from Figure 8-2 and shown here in Figure 11-2. In order to build the circuit shown we must have first "built," so to speak, the half-adder circuits and the two-input OR gate. Analogously, we must first have analyzed these design entities before we can analyze the architecture named structural. In general, for hierarchically structured mod-

```
architecture structural of full_adder is
component half_adder is
port (a, b : in std_logic;
       sum, carry : out std_logic);
end component half_adder;

component or_2 is
 port (a, b : in std_logic;
        c : out std_logic);
end component or_2;

signal s1, s2, s3 : std_logic;

begin
H1: half_adder port map (a => In1, b => In2, sum => s1, carry=> s3);
H2: half_adder port map (a => s1, b => c_in, sum => sum, carry => s2);
O1: or_2 port map (a => s2, b => s3, c => c_out);

end architecture structural;
```

FIGURE 11-2 Structural model of a full adder

els, we must remember to analyze hierarchical descriptions in a bottom-up fashion, starting from models at the lowest level in the hierarchy and proceeding to higher levels.

When we make changes to a design, we must consider dependencies between design units in determining which ones must be re-analyzed. Once again let us pursue the hardware analogy. Suppose we describe a board-level design by the interconnection of the component chips and the chip interfaces. If we now decide to replace one of the chips with a new chip with a different interface then we must take a closer look at the design and re-analyze it to make sure it is still functionally and electrically correct. On the other hand if we replace a chip with a newer, cheaper version, but one that maintains the same interface, we really do not have to perform any analysis and the design should remain correct. Similar relationships carry over to the relationships between VHDL design units. Consider the structural model in Figure 11-2. This model depends on the availability of an entity named half_adder. If that entity description is changed (as in changing the chip interface) then the full_adder model that *depends* on it must be re-analyzed. Thus, if any entity description is changed then *all* architectures that depend on that entity description must be re-analyzed. For similar reasons, if a package declaration is changed, then any design unit (entity, architecture) that depends on that package must be re-analyzed. This chain of dependencies may pass through multiple design units.

However, suppose all of the entity descriptions and architecture descriptions are in separate files. What if we now change the architecture and not the entity description? Continuing with the natural hardware analogy, consider the architecture in Figure 11-2. Suppose we wish to change this architecture to use some new, detailed two-input OR gate component model named fast_OR2. The half-adder model is not affected, nor is the entity description of the full adder that happens to be in a separate file. We simply need to (i) declare the component fast_OR2, (ii) change the component instantiation statement O1 to reflect the use of this new component, and (iii) re-analyze the architecture structural. Alternatively, suppose that the architecture of the half adder has changed but the entity description of the half adder remains the same. In this case, we simply re-analyze the architecture of the half adder. We do not need to re-analyze the full-adder model! From our hardware analogy, it is as if we had wired up the full-adder circuit and simply swapped out the half-adder chip for another one. As long as the entity description of the half adder has not changed, the changes in the architecture of the half adder are not visible to the full adder at this time. When the full-adder model is loaded into a simulator then the later architecture for the half adder will be used.

At this point in our VHDL modeling experience we may be inclined to organize our models with entity and architecture descriptions in the same physical file. Therefore, even if we only change the architecture description when we re-analyze the file the entity description is also re-analyzed and thus appears to have changed! All models that use this entity now have to be re-analyzed! This is because the environment determines if a design unit has changed by looking at the time stamp of the files created by the analyzer. If we reanalyze an entity description, even if we have not changed the interface the creation time of the analyzed files will have changed. The VHDL environment must operate on the assumption that the entity description has changed. We now cannot simulate any model that uses this entity without re-analyzing it.

In summary, analyze design units in a bottom-up fashion. When changes are made to entities or package declarations, all design units that depend on these units must be re-analyzed. If changes to the architecture or package bodies are made, then only these units need be re-analyzed. If only the architectures are to be analyzed, ensure that they are in separate files from the associated entity description to avoid unnecessarily propagating changes throughout the design hierarchy.

11.2.2 Elaboration of VHDL Programs

We have seen that structural models are a means for managing large designs. Before a design can be simulated, it must first be flattened into a description of the system that can be simulated. We know that a CSA statement is a process. Now we see that flattening a design essentially produces a large number of processes that communicate via signals. These signals are referred to as *nets*. It is easy to think of a combinational circuit as a set of nets. Consider the gate level circuit shown in Figure 11-3. The signals s1, s2, s3, s4, s5, s6, and z, correspond to nets. A *netlist* is a data structure that describes all of the components connected to each net. Many industry standard formats exist for describing a netlist so that designs may be transferred easily between various design tools. This process of

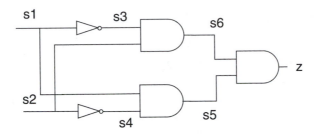

FIGURE 11-3 Netlists in a circuit

flattening a hierarchical description of a design is done during the phase of *elaboration* of the VHDL model. The elaboration produces a netlist of processes. Other functions are also carried out during elaboration and the overall process is composed of the following steps:

1. *Elaboration of the Design Hierarchy:* This step includes flattening the hierarchy. In doing so, components must be associated with the architecture that is to be used to describe their behavior. This may be specified through a configuration or through the default choice of the architecture for an entity. Flattening the hierarchy produces a netlist of processes where each process describes the behavior of each component at the lowest level of the hierarchy.

2. *Elaboration of the Declarations*: Recall that generic parameters must be constants and their values must be known prior to simulation. These values are determined and checked in this step. The declarations are also checked for type consistency and initialization of signals and variables. The language has many rules that govern the initialization of signals and variables. These checks are completed in this step.

3. *Storage Allocation*: Storage is allocated for variables, signal drivers, constants, and other program objects.

4. *Initialization*: All signals and variables are initialized in this step, either to user specified values such as those provided in declarations or to default values.

11.2.3 Initialization of VHDL Programs

Prior to simulation two important actions take place. First, all signals (nets) are initialized to their default or explicitly initialized values. Second, all processes are executed until they are suspended explicitly by the use of wait statements or implicitly by the use of a sensitivity list. This execution may also produce values for signals. Simulation time is set to 0 ns, and the model is ready to be begin simulation.

11.2.4 Simulation Of VHDL Programs

Simulation proceeds as a discrete event simulation of the design. This is achieved by evaluating the values of all signals. If an event has occurred on any signal (i.e., net), all of the processes affected by that signal are executed, possibly generating future events on other nets. The events are conceptually managed as an event list organized according to the time stamp of the event as described in Chapter 3.

Let us consider what actually happens when a structural model such as the one shown in Figure 11-2 is simulated. We might first create a file with this model. Let us call this file *structural.vhd*. The models for the half adder and the two-input OR gate may be created in two other files, say *ha.vhd* and *OR2.vhd*. We now know that the order of compilation is important. The latter two files are first analyzed. Independent of the file names, the compiled design units will be identified by their entity and architecture labels.

The process of simulation utilizes a number of concepts that are realized in various simulators in different ways. Some of the common steps that you can expect to encounter are the following:

Initialization

The simulator environment must maintain information about various design units involved in simulation such as the location of libraries. We know that libraries are logical names for directories. Most simulators need access to information about the libraries that you plan to use (such as IEEE), the location of your working design library (WORK), and the location of the library containing the standard packages expected with the VHDL distribution (STD). This information is usually created and maintained in initialization files by the simulation environment. On some simulators it may be necessary to set them explicitly by editing the initialization files created at installation time. If the VHDL analyzer returns errors relating to the absence of key libraries it is most likely a result of the lack of definition of the physical location of the logical libraries.

Loading the Model

For the example in Figure 11-2, the compilation will produce a design unit named full_adder. Simulators will provide facilities for loading a model. When the design unit full_adder is loaded into a simulator, the working directory (WORK), IEEE, STD, and any other libraries that you may have declared will be searched for any compiled design units with the labels half_adder and or_2. The order in which these libraries are searched is important, because you do not want to inadvertently use a design entity of the same name in another library. This order of search is simulator specific although it is not uncommon for the order to be based on that in which they are listed in the initialization files. Usually you would want the library WORK to be the first in the search order.

In this example, because no configuration is explicitly provided, the simulator will look for a design unit with the same name as the component and an architecture associated with *that* component. In our example, the system would look for an entity named half_adder. Because no other information is provided, the names, types, and modes of all of the signals provided in the component declaration must exactly match that in the entity declaration. Recall that if you use the **port map** and **configuration** statements, this will not be necessary.

Simulation Setup

Now that the model is loaded, we may want to generate test cases and provide stimulus to the model to determine if the model is indeed operating correctly. Generally, most simulators will provide for ways in which to specify a waveform on an input port of the entity being loaded. There will also be facilities for forcing signals to a certain value. Signal initialization, especially on input ports, is a necessary prelude to simulation. If we have constructed a model with a testbench format, then we may not need to do so. However, if we load a model such as the full adder into the simulator we will need to provide a stimulus to each of the inputs and examine the output signals to determine if the model is correct.

Example: Generating an Input Stimulus

Figure 11-4 shows an example of the stimulator dialog box from the **Active-HDL** simulator. A waveform is specified on the input signal c_in by specifying the following formula:

$$1\ 0,\ 0\ 10\ \text{ns},\ 1\ 40\ \text{ns}\ \text{-r}\ 60\ \text{ns}$$

The formula can be interpreted as follows. Each pair of numbers specifies a value and a time. The preceding formula states that the signal has the value 1 at time 0 ns, the value 0 at time 10 ns, and the value 1 at time 40 ns. The pattern repeats 60 ns later. By denoting this waveform as a clock pattern, as simulation time progresses the waveform

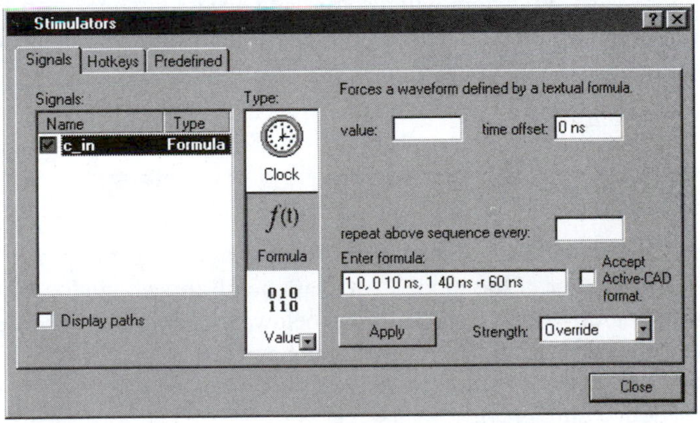

FIGURE 11-4 An example of creating stimulus on an input signal

will be applied repeatedly until it is changed by the user. From the dialog box we can see that other options are available such as forcing a signal to a value and the ability to toggle the value of the signal using a "hot key," or defining clocks.

Example End: Generating an Input Stimulus

Another aspect of simulation is the notion of a simulator *step time*. Typically, you can advance simulation time in units called steps. For example, you might pick the step time as 10 ns. Running the simulation for 10 steps is analogous to running it for 100 ns. Simulators will provide facilities for setting the value of the step size. Step time can be important because often the input stimulus to a model being tested is applied for a period equal to the step time. For example, suppose you would like to create the following waveform on an input signal named reset: 0 1 0 0. The signal reset should be driven to logic 0 for some duration and then logic 1 for some duration, and so on. For how long is reset driven to each value? The duration is generally equal to the simulator step time. If it is necessary to have a pulse of a specific width on reset, then the step time should be adjusted accordingly. More recently simulators have been moving away from the notions of step time and deal with physical timing values.

Execution and Tracing

We are finally ready to execute the model and trace the values of signals. Typically, execution can be initiated by a run or step command. The former starts a simulation for a fixed period of time or a fixed number of simulator steps. The latter steps through a single simulation cycle. Typically the values of all signals can be displayed in a trace window. *Remember: you cannot trace variables, only signals!* You can set break points and look at the value of the variables via simulator commands. However, variables do not exhibit time-dependent behavior in the same manner as signals and therefore cannot be traced in that fashion. Most simulators will also provide access to simulation statistics such as the number of events executed. This can provide useful insight into the behavior of the models as well as aid in debugging them.

Example: Signal Traces

All simulators provide some facility for tracing signals so that we may actively monitor the internal behavior of the model. An example of a trace window from the Active-HDL simulator for a full-adder model is shown below. By examining specific points on the trace we can determine if the model is functioning correctly.

Example End: Signal Traces

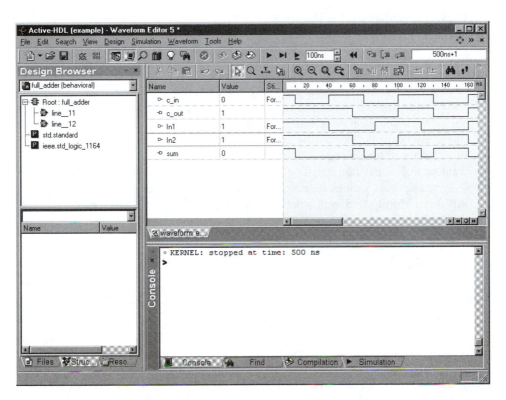

FIGURE 11-5 An example of a signal trace

11.3 Synthesis Mechanics

We now describe typical steps in the synthesis of VHDL programs for execution in FPGAs. The specific steps we describe here are drawn from activities encountered for design with Xilinx FPGA devices. However, in this section, the discussion is focused on the level of generic steps that one would encounter in most synthesis environments.

11.3.1 Analysis

Analysis precedes both the simulation and synthesis of VHDL models. The set of VHDL constructs supported for synthesis is contained in the set that is supported for simulation. Thus there is little to add over and above that provided in Section 11.2.1.

11.3.2 Synthesis of a Design

The analyzed design is synthesized to a library of components, typically gates, latches, or flip-flops. Hierarchical designs are synthesized in a bottom up fashion, that is lower level components are synthesized before higher level components. Once the design is synthesized we have a gate-level netlist. This gate-level netlist can now be simulated. Delays for the individual components are available as part of the descriptions of the component libraries. Timing accurate simulation is not possible at this point because the actual timing characteristics is determined by the physical placement of this design within the FPGA chip. However, the functional simulation that is possible at this point is quite a bit more accurate than simulation based on user specified delays. Throughout this book the results of synthesis from various language constructs have been shown with the examples so I will forgo additional examples here. See Chapter 5, Chapter 7, and Chapter 8 for specific examples.

11.3.3 Mapping a Design

Now that we have a gate-level netlist the next step is to map this design onto the FPGA. From Chapter 3 we know the primitive hardware elements that are available in a Xilinx XC4000 chip, namely look-up tables and positive-edge-triggered flip-flops are organized as a two-dimensional array of CLBs. The netlist from synthesis is composed of gates, latches, and flip-flops. It is necessary to assign configurable logic blocks to netlist primitives. This is the process of *mapping* a design. For example gates will be assigned to look-up tables as illustrated in Figure 3-8. This process effectively translates the gate-level netlist produced by the synthesis compiler into a netlist of FPGA primitive hardware components. Each element of this new netlist corresponds to a hardware primitive in the FPGA chip. An example of a netlist and the corresponding mapped design is shown in Figure 11-6. It follows that the netlist produced by synthesis compiler will produce distinct netlists for different chips following the mapping process.

11.3.4 Place and Route

The mapped design produces identifies the set of FPGA hardware primitives and their interconnection. The next step is to assign each of the components in the netlist to a equivalent physical primitives on the FPGA chip. Once this assignment or *placement* is made the interconnections between components in the netlist must be made within the chip. This will require *routing* signals through the switch matrix and other interconnect resources available on the FPGA chip. The placed and routed design from Figure 11-6 is shown in Figure 11-7. This layout was generated from Xilinx Foundation Express. Only a portion of the chip that contains the placed design is shown in this figure. We can see that there are three look-up tables that are hosted in one CLB. The IOBs that host the input and output signals are also shown placed in IOBs on the periphery of the chip and in the vicinity of the synthesized logic. The routed signals are not shown in this figure although the source and destinations of the internal signals is quite clear.

Synthesized Gate Level Implementation

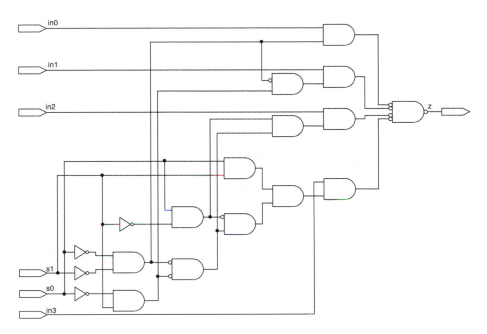

Mapped FPGA Implementation

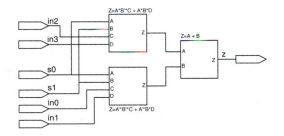

FIGURE 11-6 An example of mapping a design

After place and route the design can be simulated to validate the design. At this point timing is more accurate because the propagation delays along routed signals and through CLBs can be more accurately estimated. This is particularly important for designs that are operating under tight timing tolerances.

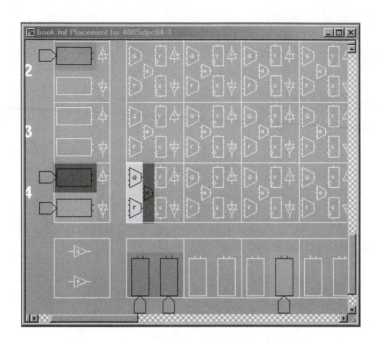

FIGURE 11-7 Placed and routed design from Figure 11-6.

11.3.5 Bit Generation

After the place and route step the CLBs on the chip must be configured to implement the behavior of the netlist components that have been mapped to them. This is achieved by determining the values of configuration bits that are described in Section 3.3.4. Additional configuration bits must be set to realize the routing between configurable logic blocks. This is the process of *bit generation*. Now when these configuration bits are loaded into the FPGA the chip will have been customized to implement the design.

11.3.6 Programming

CAD vendors will typically provide tools to download configurations onto FPGA chips residing on development boards. Some tools integrate this step into the high-level tools whereas others may require a command line interface to what amounts to a device driver. In either case the chip is now programmed and ready to run.

11.4 Chapter Summary

Traditionally, CAD tools have been large, complex aggregations of tools such as simulators, schematic capture tools, and layout editors. Although one can have a thorough knowledge of VHDL or VLSI design, and this knowledge may enable one to understand the concepts underlying the use of these tools, it also appears to be necessary to have some experience in the state of the practice to be able to use these tools successfully with minimal aggravation. This experience is often unrelated to design. This has often been referred to as "knowledge of the third kind." From a learning perspective, that situation is changing with the advent of low-cost, relatively easy to use point tools such as VHDL environments for PCs. Because these are focused on VHDL, we can make use of them without having to navigate through the maze of complex CAD environments. However, there are still conventions, concepts, and state-of-the-practice notions that are acquired through experience. It is difficult to provide concrete actions, because these are dependent on the VHDL toolset and its command set. However, we can introduce the common steps, concepts, and operations that will be encountered in the use of almost any simulator. Understanding how environments are structured and how these structures are related to language concepts, is necessary for productive application to VHDL modeling. This chapter has attempted to provide an intuition about the practical aspects of VHDL environments and hopefully ease the transition into proficient use. Often considerable frustration can be avoided by simply knowing what questions to ask and what to expect. This chapter, coupled with detailed tutorials for specific VHDL environments provided in the Appendices, will hopefully bring the reader closer to that goal.

The concepts covered in this chapter include the following.

- Basic design units
  - entity
  - architecture
  - configuration
  - package declaration
  - package body
- Analyzing VHDL programs
  - order of analysis of design units
- Elaboration
  - elaboration of the design hierarchy
  - elaboration of the declarations
  - storage allocation
  - initialization
- Initialization of VHDL programs
- Simulation

- Synthesis of a design
  - gate-level netlist generation
- Mapping
  - netlist translation
- Place and route
  - placement within configurable logic blocks
  - routing between configurable logic blocks hosting computations
- Bit generation
- Device Programming

These concepts are embedded within VHDL environments although user interfaces increasingly hide the majority of these steps from direct manipulation by users.

CHAPTER 12

Identifiers, Data Types, and Operators

The VHDL language provides a rich array of data types and operators along with rules that govern their use. The goal of this chapter is to provide the reader with ready access to the syntax and semantics of commonly used data types and operators. This chapter is intended to serve more as a guide when writing your first VHDL programs rather than as a comprehensive language reference source. The more advanced language features are not referenced here but can be found in a variety of excellent books on the VHDL language or the VHDL Language Reference Manual (LRM). Familiarity with common programming language concepts and idioms is assumed.

12.1 Identifiers

Identifiers are used as variable, signal, or constant names as well as names of design units such as entities, architectures, and packages. A basic identifier is a sequence of characters that may be upper or lower case, the digits 0–9, or the underscore ("_") character. The VHDL language is not case sensitive. The first character must be a letter and the last character must not be "_". Therefore Select, ALU_in and Mem_data are valid identifiers, whereas 12Select, _start, and out_ are not valid identifiers. Such identifiers are known as *basic identifiers*.

12.2 Data Objects

'87 vs. '93 In VHDL'87 there are three classes of objects: signals, variables, and constants. In ☞ VHDL'93 files are introduced as a fourth class of object. In VHDL'87 file types represent a subset of a variable object type. The range of values that can be assigned to a signal, variable, or constant object is determined by its type.

A signal is an object that holds the current and possibly future values of the object. In keeping with our view of VHDL as a language used to describe hardware, signals are typically thought of as representing wires. They occur as inputs and outputs in port descriptions, as signals in structural descriptions, and as signals in architectures. The signal declarations take the following form:

signal *signal_name*: *signal_type*:= *initial_value*;

Examples include:

signal status : std_logic:= '0';

signal data : std_logic_vector (31 **downto** 0);

Recall that signals differ from variables in that signals are scheduled to receive values at some point in time by the simulator. Variables are assigned during execution of the assignment statement. At any given time, multiple values may be scheduled at distinct points in the future for a signal. In contrast, a variable can be assigned only one value at any point in time. As a result, the implementation of signal objects must maintain a history of values and therefore require more storage and exact higher execution time overhead than variables.

Variables can be assigned a single value of a specific type. For example, an integer variable can be assigned a value in a range that is implementation dependent. A variable of type real can be assigned real numbers. Variables are essentially equivalent to their conventional programming language counterparts and are used for computations within procedures, functions, and processes. The declaration has the following form:

variable *variable_name*: *variable_type* := *initial_value*;

Examples include:

variable address: **bit_vector**(15 **downto** 0) := x"0000";

variable Found, Done: **boolean** := FALSE;

variable index: **integer range** 0 **to** 10:=0;

The last declaration states that the variable index is an integer that is restricted to values between 0 and 10 and is initialized to the value 0.

Constants must be declared and initialized at the start of the simulation and cannot be changed during the course of the simulation. Constants can be any valid VHDL type. The declaration has the following form:

constant *constant_name*: *constant_type* := *initial_value*;

Examples include the following:

constant Gate_Delay: Time:= 2 ns;

constant Base_Address: integer:= 100;

The first declaration states that the constant is of type **time**. This is a type unique to hardware description languages. Just as an integer variable can be assigned only integer values, the values assigned to the constant Gate_Delay must be of type time, such as 5 ns, 10 ms, or 3 s. In the above example, Gate_delay is initialized to 10 ns.

12.3 Data Types

The type of a signal, variable, or constant object specifies the range of values it may take and the set of operations that can be performed on it. The VHDL language supports a standard set of type definitions as well as enabling the definition of new types by the user.

12.3.1 The Standard Data Types

The standard type definitions are provided in the package **STANDARD** (see Appendix F.1) and include the types listed in Table 12-1. Note the definitions of **bit** and **bit_vector** types. From Chapter 2 we know that a simple 0/1 value system is not rich enough to describe the behavior of single-bit signals. This is why the community has moved towards standardization of a value system that multiple vendors can use. Such a standard is the IEEE 1164 value system, which is defined using enumerated types.

12.3.2 Enumerated Types

Although the standard types are useful for constructing a wide variety of models, they fall short in many situations. We know that single-bit signals may be in states that cannot be represented by 0/1 values. For example, signal values may be unknown, or signals may left

TABLE 12-1 Standard Data Types Provided within VHDL

Type	Range of Values	Example Declaration
Integer	Implementation defined	**signal** index: **integer**:= 0;
Real	Implementation defined	**variable** val: **real**:= 1.0;
Boolean	(TRUE, FALSE)	**variable** test: **boolean**:=TRUE;
Character	Defined in package STANDARD	**variable** term: **character**:= '@';
Bit	0, 1	**signal** In1: **bit**:= '0';
Bit_vector	Array with each element of type bit	**variable** PC: **bit_vector**(31 **downto** 0)
Time	Implementation defined	**variable** delay: **time**:= 25 **ns**;
String	Array with each element of type character	**variable** name : **string**(1 **to** 10) := "model name";
Natural	0 to the maximum integer value in the implementation	**variable** index: **natural**:= 0;
Positive	1 to the maximum integer value in the implementation	**variable** index: **positive**:= 1;

floating. The language does support the definition of new language types by the programmer and the ability to provide functions for operating on data that is of this type. For example consider the following definition of a single bit:

```
type std_ulogic is (' U' -- uninitialized
                    'X' -- forcing unknown
                    '0' -- forcing 0
                    '1' -- forcing 1
                    'Z' -- high impedance
                    'W' -- weak unknown
                    'L' -- weak 0
                    'H' -- weak 1
                    '-' -- don't care
                    );
```

Now, assume we declare a signal to be of this type:

```
signal carry: std_ulogic : = 'U';
```

The signal carry can now be assigned any one of the values defined above. Note that operations such as AND, OR, and "+/-" must be redefined for this data type. The type definitions and the associated operator and logical function definitions can be provided in a package that is referenced by your model. The above type definition is a standard defined by the IEEE and the associated package is referred to as the IEEE Standard Logic 1164 package (see Appendix F.3). This package is gaining popularity for two reasons. It provides a type definition for signals that is more realistic for real circuits. Furthermore, use of the same value system makes it easier for designers to share models, increasing interoperability, and consequently reducing model cost.

The above type definition is referred to as an *enumerated type.* The definition explicitly enumerates all possible values that a variable or signal of this type can assume. Another example of where enumerated types come in handy is the following:

> **type** instr_opcode **is** ('add', 'sub', 'xor', 'nor', 'beq', 'lw', 'sw');

An instruction set simulation of a processor may have a large case statement with the following test:

> **case** opcode **is**

> **when** beq =>

Each branch of the **case** statement may call a procedure to simulate the execution of that particular instruction. Such type declarations can be made and placed in a package or in the declarative region of the **process**. For an example of the definition, declaration, and use of a type definition for memory in a simulation model of a simple processor, see the example code in Figure 6-2.

12.3.3 Array Types

Arrays of bit-valued signals are common in digital systems. An array is a group of elements, all of the same type. For example, a word is an array of bits and memory is an array of words. A common practice is to define groups of interesting digital objects as a new type. For example:

> **type** byte **is array** (7 **downto** 0) **of bit**;

> **type** word **is array** (31 **downto** 0) **of bit**;

> **type** memory **is array** (0 **to** 4095) **of** word;

Now that we have created these new types, we can declare variables, signals, and constants to be of these types.

> **signal** program_counter : word;= x"00000000";

> **variable** data_memory : memory;

The use of type definitions in this manner enables us to define elements that we use when designing digital systems. For example, the preceding declarations demonstrate how we could define new types for words, registers, and memories. These new types make writing VHDL models more intuitive as well as easier to comprehend.

12.3.4 Physical Types

Physical types are motivated by the need to represent physical quantities such a time, voltage, or current. The values of a physical type are defined to be a measure such as seconds, volts, or amperes. The VHDL language provides one predefined physical type: **time**. The definition of the type **time** can be found in the package STANDARD. The definition from this package is reproduced below.

type time **is range** *<implementation dependent>*
units
fs;   -- femtoseconds
ps = 1000 fs;   -- picoseconds
ns = 1000 ps;   -- nanoseconds
us = 1000 ns;   -- microseconds
ms = 1000 us;   -- milliseconds
s = 1000 ms;   -- seconds
min = 60 s;   -- minutes
hr = 60 min;   -- hours
end units;

The first unit is referred to as the base unit and is the smallest unit of time. All of the other units can be defined in terms of any of the units defined earlier. For example, they all could have been defined in terms of femtoseconds. We can see how it is possible to define other physical types such as distance, power, or current. For example, we might define a type power as follows:

type power **is range** 1 to 1000000
units
uw;   -- base unit is microwatts
mw = 1000 uw;   -- milliwatts
w = 1000 mw;   -- watts
kw = 1000000 mw   -- kilowatts
mgw = 1000 kw;   -- megawatts
end units;

Note how kilowatts are defined in terms of milliwatts rather than watts. Now we can declare signals or variables to be of this type and assign or compute values of this type.

variable chip_power: power:= 120 mw;

The above declaration creates a variable of type power and whose value will be in the units defined above for variables of type power. When we are modeling physical systems it is very useful to have the ability to define physical types and the units that can be used to express their values. We might use such types to execute simulations that estimate the power dissipation over the course of execution of a component. This capability merits an example.

Example: Use of Physical Types

Consider the example code shown in Figure 12-1. Let us assume that we are using the definition of the type **power** as shown earlier in this section and that this definition is placed in a package named **my_pkg** that is compiled into the local working directory. The code template shown in Figure 12-1 illustrates how one might use physical types. In this case each time the circuit modeled by the code is executed the power dissipated is increased. This value may be written to a file, or as shown above written to a port. Thus higher level components in a hierarchy may use this computed value or simply drive a signal trace for viewing purposes.

Example End: Use of Physical Types

```
library IEEE;
use IEEE.std_logic_1164.all;
use Work.my_pkg.all;

entity example_power is
port(clk : in std_logic;
outpower : out power);
end entity example_power;

architecture behavioral of example_power is

begin
process
variable my_power: power:= 1 uw;

begin
wait until (rising_edge(clk));
--
-- miscelleneous modeling code here
--
my_power := my_power + 100 uw;
outpower <= my_power;
 end process;
end behavioral;
```

FIGURE 12-1 An example of the use of physical types

12.4 Operators

Operators are used in expressions involving signal, variable, or constant object types. The **VHDL'93** following are the sets of operators as defined in the VHDL language [5]. Note that the shift operations are new in VHDL'93. The miscellaneous operators include **abs** for the computation of the absolute value, and ****** for exponentiation. The latter can be applied to any integer or real signal, variable, or constant.

logical operators	**and**	**or**	**nand**	**nor**	**xor**	**xnor**
relational operators	**=**	**/=**	**<**	**<=**	**>**	**>=**
shift operators	**sll**	**srl**	**sla**	**sra**	**rol**	**ror**
addition operators	**+**	**–**	**&**			
unary operators	**+**	**–**				
multiplying operators	*****	**/**	**mod**	**rem**		
miscellaneous operators	******	**abs**	**not**			

The classes of operators shown are listed in increasing order of precedence from top to bottom. Operators with higher precedence are applied to their operands first. All of the operators within the same class are of the same precedence and are applied to operands in textual order—left to right. The use of parentheses can be used to define explicitly the order of precedence. In general, the operands of these operators must be of the same type, whereas the type of the permissible operands may be limited. Tables 12–2 to 12–5 provide information from the VHDL Reference Manual and define the permissible operand types.

TABLE 12-2 Operator–Operand Relationships

Operator	Operand Type	Result Type
=	Any type	Boolean
/=	Any type	Boolean
<, >, <=, >=	Scalar or discrete array types	Boolean

VHDL'93

The shift operators are defined in Table 12-3. These operators are new in VHDL'93, and are particularly useful in describing operations in models of computer architecture components. Some examples of the application of these shift operators are provided in Table 12-4.

TABLE 12-3 Shift Operators   '87 vs. '93

Operator	Operation	Left Operand Type	Right Operand Type	Result Type
sll	Logical left shift	Any one dimensional array type whose element type is **bit** or **Boolean**	**integer**	Left operand type
srl	Logical right shift	"	"	"
sla	Arithmetic left shift	"	"	"
sra	Arithmetic right shift	"	"	"
rol	Rotate left logical	"	"	"
ror	Rotate right logical	"	"	"

TABLE 12-4 Examples of the Application of the Shift Operators

Example Expression	Result Operand Value
value <= "10010011" sll 2	"01001100"
value <= "10010011 sra 2	"11100100"
value <= "10010011" ror-3 (i.e., rotate left)	"10011100"
value <= "10010011" srl-2	"01001100"

The addition, subtraction, and concatenation operators are described in Table 12-5. The first two are self-explanatory.

TABLE 12-5 Addition and Subtraction Operators

Operator	Operation	Left Operand Type	Right Operand Type	Result Type
+ or -	Addition/subtraction	Numeric type	Same type	Same type
&	Concatenation	Array or element type	Array or element type	Same array type

The concatenation operator composes operands. For example, we might have:

result(31 **downto** 0) <= '0000' **&** jump (27 **downto** 0);

The upper 4 bits of result will be cleared and the remaining 28 bits will be set to the value of the 28 least significant bits of jump.

The unary operators are described in Table 12-6.

TABLE 12-6 Unary Operators

Operator	Operation	Operand Type	Result Type
+/-	Identity/negation	Numeric type	Same type

Finally, some remaining numerical operators are illustrated in Table 12-7.

TABLE 12-7 Numerical Operators

Operator	Operation	Left Operand Type	Right Operand Type	Result Type
* or /	Multiplication or division	Integer or floating point type	Same type	Same type
mod or rem	Modulus/remainder	Integer type	Same type	Same type

12.5 Chapter Summary

This chapter has provided a brief overview of the common objects, types, and operators in the VHDL language. I have taken the approach of focusing on the unique aspects of the VHDL language throughout most of the text while assuming that language features such as types, identifiers, and objects are familiar concepts to the reader and a handy reference is all that is necessary as a prelude to writing useful models. This chapter is intended to fill that role and will be only as useful as the previous chapters have been successful in providing an intuitive way of thinking about, constructing, and using VHDL models. Familiarity at this level can lead to the next level in using the more powerful (and complex) features of the language.

Synthesis Hints: Beginner's Reference

Several of the preceding chapters have addressed issues facing the synthesis of digital circuits from VHDL models. The goal here is to provide the beginning user with a point of reference for common inference issues. This appendix organizes and summarizes many of the observations into a handy beginner's reference.

A.1 Some Useful Hints and Observations

A.1.1 Initialization

1. Do not specify initial values in your declaration of signals. Most synthesis compilers will ignore them. If you wish to initialize signals to values it is advisable to do so explicitly under the control of a reset signal. Is this not how you would design the hardware anyway? The exceptions are constants that must be provided with their values within the declaration.

2. Specify the number of bits necessary for a signal explicitly in the declaration. This will avoid the allocation of much larger number of bits than necessary and therefore lead to less hardware in the form of the widths of signal paths, the number of gates necessary to process these signals, and the number of latches or flip-flops necessary to store signal values.

A.1.2 Inferring Storage

3. Generally edge-detection expressions will cause flip-flops rather than latches to be inferred. Otherwise latches will be inferred.

4. If you wish to avoid having a latch inferred for a signal in a process then every execution path through the process must assign a value for that signal.

5. If you use variables in a process before they are defined a latch will be inferred for that variable.

6. To avoid the inference of latches, make sure that default values are assigned to signals before a conditional block of code, for example the use of **case** or **if-then-endif** statements.

7. For variables or signals assigned within a **for-loop** a default value must be assigned before the **for-loop** to avoid latch inference.

8. To ensure that combinational logic is generated from a process or CSA statements (conditional or selected) every possible execution path through the code must determine all output values. In this case there is no need to retain values across executions of a process and therefore no need to infer storage.

9. Use of the **unaffected** keyword in branches of signal assignment statements may cause latches to be inferred in the synthesized design. Note this keyword is VHDL 1993 only.

10. Use **if-then** statements to infer flip-flops rather than **wait** statements. The advantage is that combinational logic and sequential logic can be modeled within the same process. If you use a **wait** statement it must be the first statement in the process and the only **wait** statement in the process. Therefore latches or flip-flops are inferred for every signal assigned a value in that process. On the other hand if we only have a small block of code sensitive to a clock edge then that block of code can be encapsulated within an **if** statement and cause flip-flops to be inferred for its signals. The rest of the process can be synthesized to combinational logic. Thus using clock edge detection expressions within an **if** statement rather than a **wait** statement will enable combinational and sequential logic to co-exist within a process.

A.1.3 Optimizations

11. Avoid programming as in C or Java where we try and exploit the sequentiality of the code. This will lead to long signal paths. Attempt to minimize dependencies between statements and try and promote concurrency.

12. Using don't care values to cover the **when others** case in a case statement or selected signal assignment statement can enable the synthesis compiler to optimize the logic and create a smaller circuit than if all remaining options were set to values such as 0000 or 1111.

13. Move common complex operations out of the branches of **if-then-else** statements and place them after the conditional code. This will generally lead to less hardware.

14. Using a **case** statement rather than an **if-then-elsif** construct will produce less logic because priority logic will have to be generated for the latter.

15. Use parentheses in simple CSA statements to control the depth of the circuit. Thus you can exercise some control over operator concurrency in, and therefore speed of, the synthesized circuit

16. Use of the selected signal assignment statement will generally produce less logic than conditional signal assignment statements because no priority among the options is implied. This observation often leads us to attempt to formulate signal assignments to be in a form where we can use selected signal assignment statements.

17. The **for-loop** is synthesized by first unrolling the loop. Loop carried dependencies, where computations in one iteration are dependent on computations in another iteration, can lead to long signal paths.

18. Minimize signal assignment statements within a process and use variables.

A.1.4 Potpourri

19. Do not use don't care symbols in comparisons. Although this will work fine for simulation there is no hardware equivalent and such comparisons are defined to always return false. A little thought reveals that this will significantly alter the behavior of the code. For example, the code that is executed when the condition is true is now never executed and is effectively removed by the compiler.

20. Check vendor specific constraints on the permitted types and range of the **for-loop** index.

21. Keep in mind that the code should "imply" hardware structures. Avoid purely algorithmic descriptions of hardware. This will assist the synthesis compiler's inference process.

22. All loop indices must have statically determinable loop ranges.

23. The **while-loop** statement is generally not supported for synthesis because the loop range must be statically determined in order to generate a fixed amount of logic.

24. The choice of level-sensitive conditional expressions vs. edge-detection expressions in your VHDL code should be guided by the parts available in our target library. For example, if latches are not available then the synthesis tools may try to create a latch by synthesizing the gate-level equivalents. This can complicate timing analysis and render the circuit much more difficult to debug. The choice of coding style should be guided by the building blocks that we have to operate with. For example we find in the Xilinx XC4000 series FPGAs support for both edge-triggered and level-sensitive devices so this choice is not as crucial.

A.1.5 Consistency with Pre-Synthesis Functional Simulation

25. In a simulation model delays can be specified using the **after** clause in the signal assignment statements. During synthesis the delay values of the operations are derived from the synthesized implementation. This may differ from the values that the designer specified for simulation.

26. Comparisons may be modeled in the simulation differently from that actually synthesized into hardware. For example consider the selected signal assignment statement used to model a priority encoder as follows:

```
with datain select
result <= "00" when "---1",
          "01" when "--10",
          "10" when "-100",
          "11" when "1000",
          unaffected when others;
```

The character "-" represents don't care value in the IEEE 1164 logic system. However, remember that digital hardware can only distinguish between ones and zeros. Comparisons to don't care, high impedance, or other literals do not have meaningful hardware counterparts. Equality tests to other than 1/0 values always return false for synthesis. This does not necessarily agree with the semantics for simulation where signals can actually be assigned values such as Z or U.

27. Include all signals in a process in the sensitivity list of the process to avoid pre-synthesis and post-synthesis simulation mismatches. Otherwise the problem is that one can write processes where the sensitivity list includes only a few of the signals that are manipulated in the process. Thus during functional simulation processes are executed only when events occur on these signals. However if the synthesis process produces combinational logic for a process then this logic will respond to events on *any* of the input signals. This is the nature of combinational logic. Synthesis compilers will expect the process to be sensitive to all of the signals that are manipulated in a process. As a result the behavior of the synthesized hardware will not follow exactly the simulated behavior of the process. For example consider the following code:

```
process (sel) is
begin
if (sel = '1' and En = '0') then
A <= 1;
else
A <= '0';
end if;
end process;
```

During simulation events on signal En will not cause the process to execute. For example if sel = 1 and at some later point in time the value of En changes from 0 to 1 the process will not execute. However, after synthesis the resulting combinational logic will be sensitive to events on signal En. Synthesis compilers may in fact ignore the sensitivity list of the process or provide warnings if the sensitivity list is incomplete.

28. Imagine the following sequence of signal assignment statements in a process:

```
process(x, y, z)
begin
L1: s1 <= x xor y;
L2: s2 <= s1 or z;
L3: w <= s1 nor s1;
end process;
```

Let x, y, and z be input signals that are declared as input ports in the corresponding **entity** and let s1 and s2 be signals declared in the architecture. The simulation semantics state that the values of s1 and s2 used in statement L3 should be the values of the signals s1 and s2 when the process in invoked and not the new values that are assigned when the process is executed. However synthesis compilers will generally optimize this sequence to produce combinational logic and avoid latches.

29. The behavior captured in conditional and selected signal assignment statements have equivalent representations using the **process** construct (see Section 6.1). The former are always active and generally have more simulation overhead but are better for synthesis. Remember that in general optimizations for simulation may be at odds with synthesis.

30. Use of variables will lead to faster simulation. This follows form the need to maintain and manipulate the driver data structure for each signal. However the use of processes obscures concurrency within a process and may reduce the effectiveness of the inference mechanisms. The lesson is that writing code for optimal simulation speed is not the same as optimal synthesis

Part of the difficulty in developing synthesizeable models is in getting out of the habit of writing models for simulation where some behaviors can be modeled but not necessarily implemented. The process of synthesis is hardware design. The preceding observations essentially capture elements of hardware design as implemented by synthesis compilers.

A.2 Suggestions for Managing Models and Course Projects

When beginning your first class project it is often difficult to decide just where to start. There are several tools and levels of abstraction with which to build models. Even a simple design flow will help enormously in organizing our efforts and focusing our energies on the most profitable activities. One common sequence of design activities is shown in Figure A-1.

We start with the construction of a behavioral simulation model that we will simulate prior to synthesis. The simulation model is used to validate the functional correctness of the design. It is beneficial to keep in mind that this model will eventually be synthesized when writing this model. Once functional correctness has been established to our satisfaction we then concern ourselves with the synthesis. The synthesize design can be simulated prior to place and route. This will give us an opportunity to resolve any mismatches between the simulated and synthesized designs that may be due occurrences of model specific features like the use of incomplete sensitivity lists. Once these are resolved we can place and route the design and simulated the placed and routed design to obtain accurate timing information.

Although our tendency may be to dive in to the synthesis process the sequence of activities shown in Figure A-1 can actually save us time overall and will produce more robust models. In effect different aspects of a design are examined at each point and it provides natural checks to ensure the progress of a project through a course. Here are a few suggestions while you proceed from simulation through synthesis to validation:

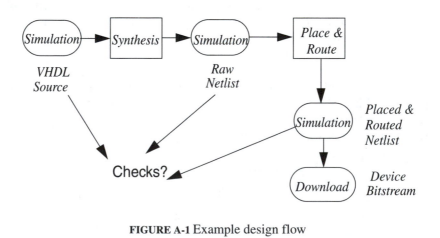

FIGURE A-1 Example design flow

- First start with a high-level block diagram of the design and proceed to refine the schematic to a functional block diagram such that we have combinational and sequential components.

- Place all entity descriptions and architecture descriptions in separate files. Write a configuration declaration for each design entity in a separate file. This promotes independent development and cooperation within design groups. Remember the structure of the design hierarchy is maintained through the names of the entities and architectures and not the file names.

- Use IEEE standard libraries for data types to improve portability.

- Tightly control the latest revision of the entities. Architecture development is easily partitioned among project group members. Configurations create a specific instance of a design that is to be simulated. Project members meet primarily to meet and discuss entity descriptions.

- After the behavioral simulation is complete we are ready to proceed to synthesis. Armed with what we know about common inference rules for VHDL we can write the combinational components in manner that will generate combinational logic using either processes or signal assignment statements. Reference Section A.1.

- The sequential components can be written in a form that will infer flip-flops or latches depending on whether edge-sensitive or level-sensitive expressions are used. Reference Section A.1.

- If it is necessary or convenient to write components that must contain both sequential or combinational blocks, use processes with **if-then-else** conditionals to isolate the sequential components that are inferred in a design without requiring that flip-flops or latches are inferred for all components design. This will give you control over the character of your design.

- Take global signals such as clocks and map them to low-skew resources on the chip. This is usually achieved by instantiating chip-specific components in a design such as special buffers and connecting your design's global signal to the input of this component.

- Explicitly instantiate components that will provide global reset to ensure all flip-flops are correctly initialized. Modern synthesis compilers will attempt to infer global reset signals that you may have in your design but you can ensure the presence of global reset explicitly.

- For commonly used components such as adders, multiplexors, and clock dividers you can use the vendor tools that generate usable cores and place them in your project directory. These are synthesized modules.

VHDL 1987 vs.
VHDL 1993

There are several classes of differences between the two versions of the language. Although VHDL 1993 is now the official version, at the time of this writing many synthesis tools in particular have not yet fully supported VHDL 1993.

Some of the major differences between VHDL'87 and VHDL'93 are the following. Note that because this text does not cover all of the features of the language not all differences are listed here.

1. Whereas file types were a variable object in VHDL'87 they are not a separate class of objects in VHDL'93.

2. The syntax is has been modified in many instances for example as shown Section 4.2. However, tools sets such as Foundation Express will accept both VHDL'87 and VHDL'93 differences in syntax as described in Section 4.2.

3. We can label all statements in a process in VHDL'93.

4. The input/output functionality has been changed significantly and are quite different between the two versions.

5. VHDL'93 has included the **xnor** and many several shift and rotate operators. These differences are identified in Chapter 12.

6. The delay models used in simulation models have been changed. VHDL'93 supports pulse rejection width specifications for inertial delay models.

7. The signal value **unaffected** was introduced. For example, these values can be used in selected signal assignment statements (see Section 4.3.5).

The preceding are the major differences in the aspects of the language covered in this text. As we delve deeper we can move to any one of a number of texts that discuss the language in greater detail.

Active-HDL Tutorial

The Active-HDL environment is one that is tightly integrated into the Xilinx Foundation toolset and represents at the current time the state-of-the-art in functional VHDL simulators. By functional we refer to the fact that the models may not necessarily be synthesizeable. In a typically design methodology functional VHDL simulation may be used early in the design process to verify the correctness of a model and to generate test vectors for subsequent testing of the synthesized design. We may then proceed to successively refine this model to a form that is amenable to hardware inference and synthesis.

C.1 Using Active VHDL

This tutorial assumes that we are starting with the creation of a new design. The sequence of steps proceeds through the creation and simulation of a VHDL model. This tutorial is for Active HDL 3.5 SE – the student edition of the full Active-HDL toolset (http://www.aldec.com).

Step: 1 Creating a Project

In most VHDL environments the first step is to create a project that will serve as the repository for the design files, intermediate files, and information concerning the options for the CAD tool environment. The Active-HDL environment maintains an analogous concept of a design. As terminology goes this may be a better match to the normal set of design activities associated with a simulation environment where we are generally interested in simulating a VHDL model of specific design, for example, a gate-level digital design, a datapath, or communication protocol implementation.

When you first start Active-HDL you will be prompted to open an existing design or to create a new one. Create a new design and name this design **example**. This will lead to the creation of a directory named **example** that contains several sub-directories and files. The Active-HDL window should appear as shown in Figure C-1 (a default message may appear in the upper part of the window rather than an empty canvas). Note that there is a distinction between files and directories. You could create a VHDL file in the directory corresponding to the design. However, the VHDL model is not part of the design until you explicitly add it to the design. This step is covered next.

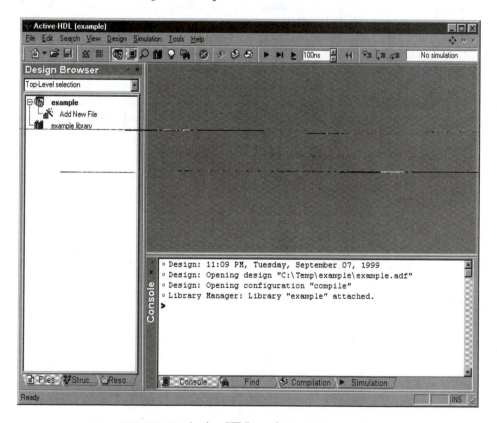

FIGURE C-1 Active-HDL environment on start-up

Step: 2 Creating a VHDL Model

The workspace for the design has been created in the form of directories and all other environment variables have been initialized. We can now add files to this design. From the menu select File->New ->Text Document. This will open the Active-HDL text editor. Type in the full adder model shown in Figure C-2. Save the model as the file *full.vhd*. The default directory in which the file is saved should be example/src, where example is the design directory. Once the file is saved it can be added to the design by selecting Design->Add Files to Design from the menu and adding the file *full.vhd*. This file should now appear in the Design Browser portion of the Active-HDL window with "?" next to the file name.

Alternatively we could have created a model by selecting File->New->VHDL Source from the file menu. This option would have started the source file wizard, which provides a convenient graphical interface to specify the names of the entity, architecture, and files, as well as the name and mode of all interface signals. The wizard can then create templates of the entity and architectures and we need only manually fill in the code bodies. If we use this approach the file can be automatically added to the design.

```
library IEEE;
use IEEE.std_logic_1164.all;
entity full_adder is
port (In1, In2, c_in : in std_logic;
      sum, c_out : out std_logic);
end entity full_adder;

architecture behavioral of full_adder is

begin
sum <= In1 xor In2 xor c_in;
c_out <= (In1 and In2) or (in1 and c_in) or (in2 and c_in);
end architecture behavioral;
```

FIGURE C-2 VHDL model of a full adder

Step: 3 Compiling a Design

After we have edited a text document to create the design the file name shows up the Design Browser with a "?" next to the filename to denote the fact that the file has been modified and the design should be re-compiled. We can compile the design by selecting Design->Compile from the menu. Any error messages will show up on the console window. After compilation the Active-HDL window should appear as shown in Figure C-3.

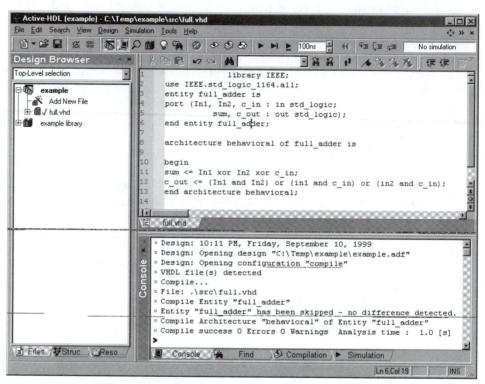

FIGURE C-3 The Active-HDL window after the design has been successfully compiled

The console window can be replaced with one that only shows messages relevant to the compilation or simulation by selecting the appropriate tab at the bottom. If there are compilation errors you can use the text editor to correct the model, save the design, and then recompile the design. Complete this loop until the design compiles without errors.

Step: 4 Simulating a Design

We are now ready to simulate a design. In general we may have many files in our design and may wish to simulate only one of then. We should first select the top-level design that we wish to simulate. We can do so in the **Design Browser** part of the Active-HDL window by selecting the module full_adder from the pull down menu. After we do so the **Design Browser** window should appear as shown in Figure C-4. Note that at the bottom of the **Design Browser** window there are three tabs that permit three different views of the design to be simulated, each view serving a different purpose. For example, if we wish to make some changes in the source file and re-compile the design we would clearly wish to have a **Files** view.

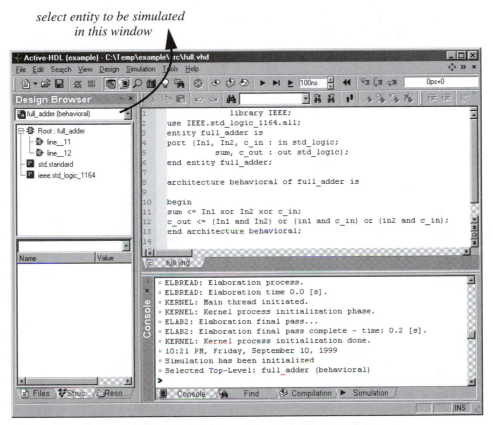

select entity to be simulated in this window

```
                                library IEEE;
                   use IEEE.std_logic_1164.all;
                   entity full_adder is
                   port (In1, In2, c_in : in std_logic;
                               sum, c_out : out std_logic);
                   end entity full_adder;

                   architecture behavioral of full_adder is

                   begin
                   sum <= In1 xor In2 xor c_in;
                   c_out <= (In1 and In2) or (in1 and c_in) or (in2 and c_in);
                   end architecture behavioral;
```

```
  ELBREAD: Elaboration process.
  ELBREAD: Elaboration time 0.0 [s].
  KERNEL: Main thread initiated.
  KERNEL: Kernel process initialization phase.
  ELAB2: Elaboration final pass...
  ELAB2: Elaboration final pass complete - time: 0.2 [s].
  KERNEL: Kernel process initialization done.
  10:21 PM, Friday, September 10, 1999
  Simulation has been initialized
  Selected Top-Level: full_adder (behavioral)
>
```

FIGURE C-4 Selecting a design entity for simulation

Simulation can verify the functional properties of a design. How can we verify that a circuit does what we think (or intend) it does? Design verification and validation is an increasingly large percentage of the design cycle for digital systems. A common technique is to provide input values and compare the output values with known correct output values. Generation of such input vectors and associated correct output vectors is a complex task for any but the simplest of systems. Like most simulators Active-HDL provides the ability to test simulation models in this fashion and in fact supports the automatic generation of testbench templates. Check the vendor documentation for this capability, which is omitted in this quickstart tutorial and is not available in the current student version.

Because the circuit is simulated by stimulating the input signals with a known sequence of values and examining the outputs, we would like to be able visualize the waveforms on the input and output signals. The basic activities in using most any simulator at this point, and the corresponding Active-HDL commands, are the following:

- *Select the signals to be traced*: From the menu select **File->New->Waveform**. This will open a trace window in the Active-HDL window. You will notice that the trace window is empty. We need to specify the signals we wish to trace. We can do so by selecting Waveform->Add Signals from the menu. This will produce the dialog box shown in Figure C-5. Select each signal and click Add. For this exercise add all of the signals to the trace.

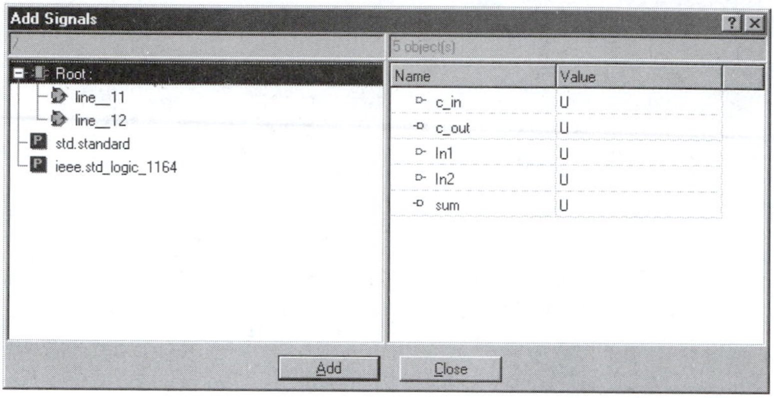

FIGURE C-5 Dialog box to add signals to the trace

- *Generate the stimulus for the input signals*: The next step is the generation of a stimulus on each of the input signals. Select a signal in the trace window and then select Waveform-> Stimulators from the menu. This will open the stimulator window shown in Figure C-6. There are several ways in which to stimulate the values of an input signal. The preceding formula can be interpreted as follows:

  - *Hot Key*: You can select a key on the keyboard that can toggle the value of an input signal. Whenever you press the hot key the value of the signal toggles between 0 and 1. Thus you can simulate for 100 ns, toggle the value of an input signal, and then simulate for another 100 ns.

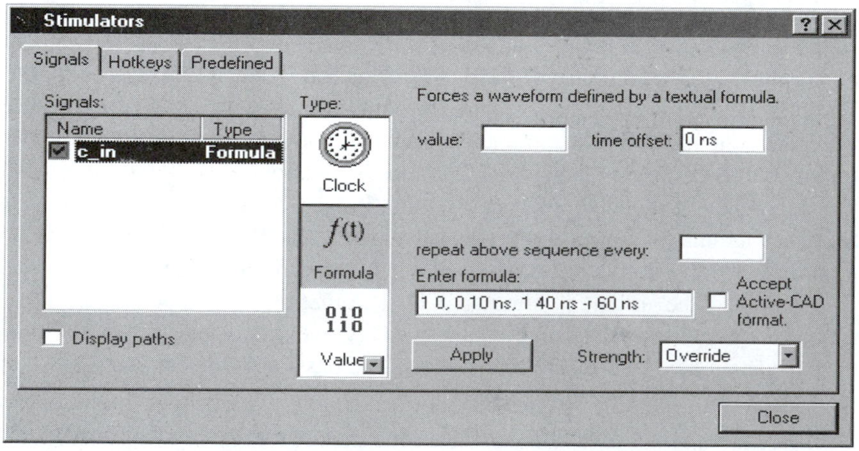

FIGURE C-6 The Stimulator dialog box

- *Clock Signals*: What if we chose to generate an arbitrary clock signal? How can be specify the pulse widths and the pulse separations? We can do so by clicking the clock button at the top of the list of options in the stimulator window. We can edit the clock information for any desired frequency. We can also select any duty cycle by clicking and dragging the rising edge of the clock signal shown in the window.

- *Formula*: In this example select the formula option and fill in the formula as shown below.

1 0, 0 10 ns, 1 40 ns -r 60 ns

The formula can be interpreted as follows. Each pair of numbers specifies a value and a time. The preceding formula states that the signal has the value 1 at time 0 ns, the value 0 at time 10 ns, and the value 1 at time 40 ns. The pattern repeats 60 ns later.

- There are also several other options for specifying the values of a signal including constant values as well as some predefined clock waveforms.

Now we are ready to start the simulation. Under the Simulation menu item we will find options to Initialize the simulation, End Simulation and Run Until a specified period of time. Run the simulation for 500 ns. Now examine the trace window. It should appear as shown in Figure C-7. By examining the values of the signals in the trace window we can determine whether the model is functioning correctly.

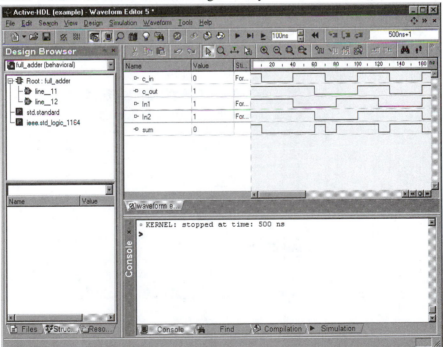

FIGURE C-7 Trace window after simulation

Once we have determined that the design is functioning correctly we are ready to proceed to the synthesis and device programming tools to generate a configuration that will program an FPGA device to implement this circuit.

C.2 Miscellaneous Features

There are many useful features of the Active-HDL environment that go beyond what we find useful in a quickstart tutorial and that can be found in the on-line help or vendor documentation. However, there are two particularly noteworthy features.

The first is the language assistant that is available by selecting **Tools->Language Assistant** from the menu. This will provide a dialog box with a menu of language constructs to select from. For example, Figure C-8 shows the contents of the dialog box after selecting a for-loop from the list of Language Templates. We can cut and paste from the window into our text editor. There are a wide variety of templates for simulation as well as for VHDL constructs that are synthesizeable.This **Language Assistant** is a handy reference and is enormously helpful when developing VHDL models.

A second particularly noteworthy feature is the automatic generation of a testbench for the design (see Section 10.3). The selection of **Tools->Generate Test Bench** from the menu will invoke the **Test Bench Generator Wizard**, which will guide you through the creation of a test bench template, including the use of a file that contains the test vectors. This feature is not available in the current student version.

FIGURE C-8 Language Assistant

C.3 Chapter Summary

This chapter has focused on a quickstart tutorial for Active-HDL version 3.5 SE. I have focused on the minimal set of activities/steps necessary to exercise the environment to simulate a single design. Early in digital logic and computer architecture courses students are more likely to be constructing single monolithic models of relatively simple components. This tutorial is intended to help them get to the simulation of these monolithic models quickly and as painlessly as possible so that they may concentrate on the digital logic and computer architecture concepts they are learning. I hope that the resulting familiarity will breed confidence in the readers to venture into the depths of these toolsets as necessary to avail themselves of the powerful capabilities these environments have to offer. It has been my aim to first reinforce the foundational material being taught in the classroom and subsequently to teach students to productively use industrial strength CAD tools. The steps covered here include the following:

- Creating a design
- Adding VHDL files to a design
- Compiling VHDL files
- Simulating the design
  - generating a stimulus input signals
  - creating a trace of the input and output signals
- Use of the Language Assistant

The environment provides for many more advanced design activities described in the vendor documentation.

Xilinx Foundation Express Tutorial

The Xilinx Foundation series of tools and associated devices have long held a dominant position in the configurable logic industry. This section describes a quickstart tutorial for Xilinx Foundation series student edition tools version 2.1i that is bundled with this text. The goal of the tutorial is to provide a quick start to the basic activities in creating, synthesizing, simulating, and creating an FPGA implementation of a VHDL design. Students can then proceed to more advanced activities by following the vendor provided tutorials and documentation.

D.1 Tutorial

The following sequence of steps will take the user through the essential steps in creating an FPGA implementation. We start from an empty design and end with a bit stream that can be used to configure an XC400XL device.

Step: 1 Create a Project

As with most VHDL environments the first step is to create a project that will serve as the repository for the design files, intermediate files, and information concerning the options for the Xilinx Foundation environment. When you first start Foundation you will be prompted to either open an existing project or to create a new project. Select the creation of a new project. You will then be presented with the dialog box shown in Figure D-1. Ensure that you have selected the Type as Foundation Series 2.1i and Flow as HDL (hardware description language). The alternative Flow is based on the use of schematic capture tools where you can draw a hardware design using graphical representations of hardware primitives. This tutorial assumes an HDL flow. You can browse to a directory where you wish to create the project and provide a project name. In this example we have chosen the name example. By clicking OK a new project is created and the Foundation tools Project Manager window opens and initializes the project. After initialization the Project Manager window appears as shown in Figure D-2. Note that the Constraint Manager is not available in the student edition of the tools. Before you proceed to the next step it is useful study the makeup of the Project Manager window.

The Project Manager window has three main areas: messages, project files, and design flow. The message window is for errors, warnings, and general messages concerning the status of simulations or synthesis activities in progress. We will see examples of such messages later in this tutorial. The upper left portion shows the files in the current project. By selecting the flow tab in upper right portion we will see a graphical representation of the core activities that take place within the Foundation Express toolset. We will refer to this as the *design flow*. The first rectangle in the design flow provides buttons for model creation. There are three ways to construct a model. The first is by using a schematic editor and constructing hardware models from library components. The second is a state machine editor that provides a graphical interface for the construction of state machines. The third approach to model construction is using a text editor and entering HDL code. In this tutorial we will be using the third approach with VHDL as the hardware description language.

FIGURE D-1 Dialog box for project setup

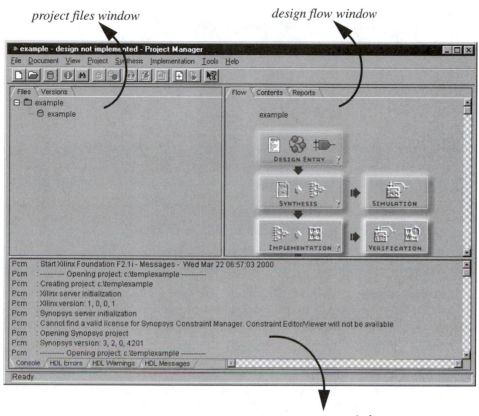

project files window   *design flow window*

FIGURE D-2 The Foundation Project Manager

Step: 2 Creating a VHDL Model

Now we are ready to create a VHDL model using the Design Entry tools button. Invoke the HDL editor by clicking the **HDL** icon in the Design Entry button. A dialog box shown in Figure D-3 will be appear. From the dialog box we can open an existing file or create a new one. A new VHDL model can be created in one of two ways. The first is by invoking the design wizard, which will generate a sequence of dialog boxes to select the mode, type, and names of the signals in the entity description. The VHDL text for the entity description and the text for an empty architecture description are created automatically.

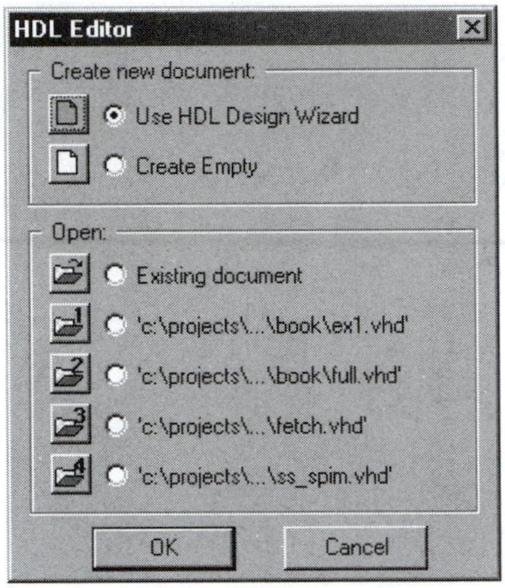

FIGURE D-3 HDL editor dialog box

The idea is that we only need to fill in the VHDL code for the architecture. It is useful wizard but really does not save us that much time if we know what we wish to model. The second approach to constructing a VHDL model is to simply type our model in an empty document using the text editor. Let us pick this latter option. Create an empty document and then type in a VHDL model of a full adder shown in Figure D-4. Note the absence of any timing or delay information as we are dealing with synthesis. Save the file as *full.vhd*. Ensure that the entity name is full_adder and the name of the architecture is behavioral as shown in the figure. Save this file in the directory example.

```
library IEEE;
use IEEE.std_logic_1164.all;
entity full_adder is
port (In1, In2, c_in : in std_logic;
      sum, c_out : out std_logic);
end entity full_adder;

architecture behavioral of full_adder is

begin
sum <= In1 xor In2 xor c_in;
c_out <= (In1 and In2) or (in1 and c_in) or (in2 and c_in);
end architecture behavioral;
```

FIGURE D-4 VHDL model of a full adder

Although the file *full.vhd* may exist in the directory **example**, it must be explicitly added to the project. Now in the **Project Manager** click on **Project** and select **Add Source Files**. Browse and select the correct source file in the project directory **example**, namely, *full.vhd*. When this VHDL file is included in the project it is automatically analyzed, that is, checked for syntactic correctness and then translated into internal form. If the model is analyzed successfully then a green check mark appears next to the filename as shown in Figure D-5. If the "+" next to the filename is selected the files will be expanded to display the name of the entity, full_adder, as shown in the figure. Any error messages will be displayed in the console window. To correct any errors the file can be opened in the Foundation text editor. When the file is opened errors can be identified in the source file. After fixing any errors save the file. Right mouse click on the filename and select **Analyze** from the resulting menu. Alternatively select **Synthesis->Analyze All HDL Files** from the menu. Continue the analyze-edit loop until the file is free from errors during analysis. We are now ready to synthesize the analyzed design.

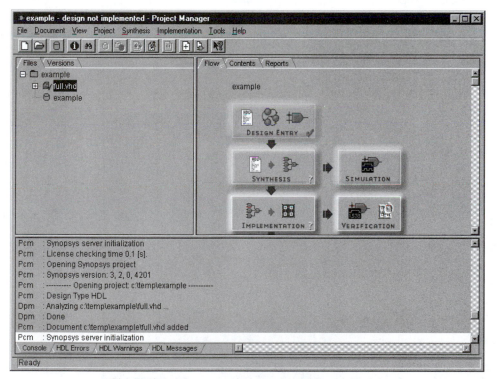

FIGURE D-5 The Project Manager window after adding *full.vhd* to the project

Step: 3 Synthesizing a VHDL Model

The Foundation environment incorporates Synopsys FPGA Express for VHDL synthesis. Once a VHDL model compiles with no errors we can select the filename name, in this case *full.vhd*, and click on the **Synthesis** button in the design flow shown in the upper right corner of the **Project Manager** Window. The synthesis dialog box shown in Figure D-6 appears. We are now ready to select the options for the synthesis process. Select the family of devices and speed grade as shown. For this simple example we have selected a modest- sized chip.

There are several classes of parameters to be selected for synthesis. First we must select the specific chip that will be hosting the design. To do so we must select the vendor of the specific chip (device), the family of devices, and the speed grade. These specifications collectively determine the hardware primitives available to us to implement the design specified in the VHDL model. Select the parameters as shown in the dialog box in Figure D-6.

Now select the SET button. In the resulting dialog box shown in Figure D-7 we will notice that we can optimize the design for speed or area. Generally high-speed designs will be realized by performing more computations concurrently, that is, using more hardware. On the other hand we can chose to implement a design with less hardware at the expense of greater delay. It is also possible to choose the level of effort in optimizing the design. The CAD tools are typically based on heuristics that search for the best solutions.

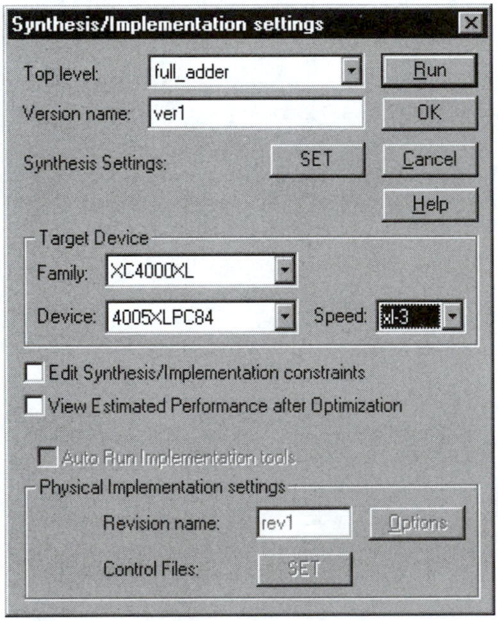

FIGURE D-6 Synthesis dialog box

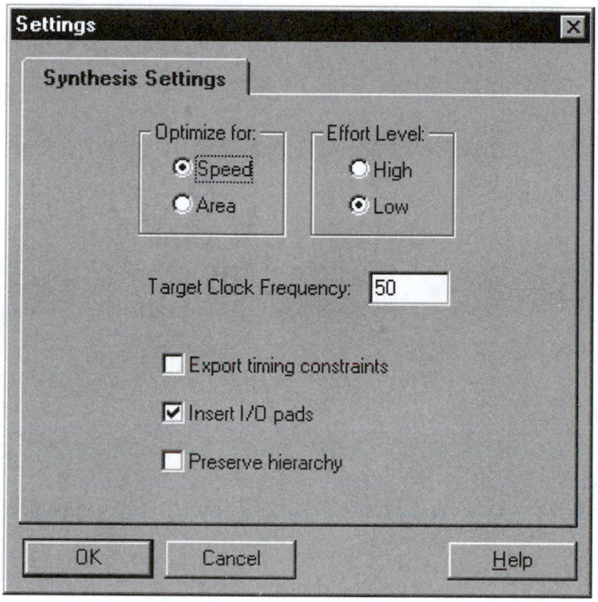

FIGURE D-7 Selecting synthesis options

Higher levels of effort usually imply searching among a larger set of options and therefore longer execution times but generally with better quality results. Finally, note the **Preserve Hierarchy** and **Insert I/O Pads** options. The former prevents optimizations across hierarchical components when a hierarchical design is flattened. The latter is not selected if the design is a component to be embedded within a larger design. In this case none of the entity signals will be connected to off-chip signals and therefore will not have to be routed through IOBs (see Section 3.3.3). Our simple design will be the only circuit mapped to the FPGA and therefore we wish to have the entity signals mapped to I/O pins on the chip. Therefore we should select the **Insert I/O Pads** option. We can also set a target clock rate for the physical design.

Finally note the use of version numbers in Figure D-6. Each time we synthesize a design the toolset will assign a new version number. The set of versions that we have available at any given time can be seen by selecting the **version** tab in the project files portion of the **Project Manager** Window. When the synthesis process is complete the **Project Manager** window will now appear, as shown in Figure D-8. Note the check marks on the first two buttons in the design flow.

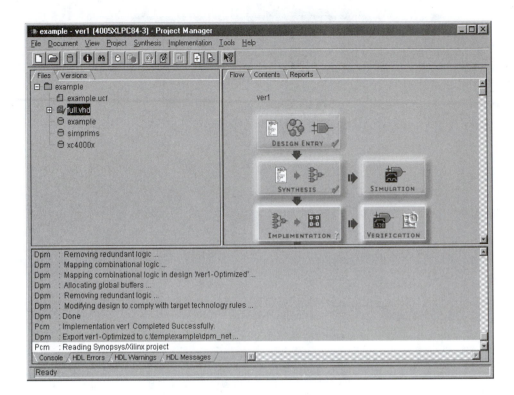

FIGURE D-8 Project Manager window after synthesis of *full.vhd*

Step: 4 Simulation of the Synthesized Design

The next logical step in the design flow is simulation. This activity can verify the functional properties of a synthesized design. How can we verify that a circuit does what we think (or intend) it does? The business of verifying designs is a complex task in its own right, something we will not go into detail here. Suffice to say that we will provide inputs and check the outputs. We know the outputs that a full adder should produce for any set of inputs. Thus in our case it is relatively simple to verify the operation of the full adder circuit. In more complex circuits errors are often very subtle and the generation of input–output pairs to check a design is often not so easy.

The circuit is simulated by stimulating the input signals with a known sequence of values and examining the outputs. Therefore we would like to be able visualize the waveforms on the input and output signals. Clicking on the simulation button in the design flow will start the logic simulator, which will open a empty simulator window. The basic activities in using most any simulator at this point in the design flow are the following:

- *Select the signals to be traced*: In the logic simulator window select Signal ->Add Signals. This will bring up a dialog box shown in Figure D-9 with all of the available signals including the input and output signals in the entity description. In general we would select the signals to trace by double-clicking on the signal name. In this model select the input/output signals of the entity full_adder, namely In1, In2, c_in, c_out and sum. Once we have selected the signals we wish to trace the simulator window will now appear as shown in Figure D-10. Note the "i" or "o" designation next to the selected signals denoting whether this signal is an input or outout signal.

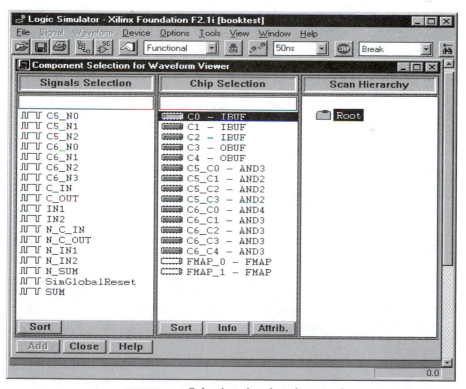

FIGURE D-9 Selecting signals to be traced

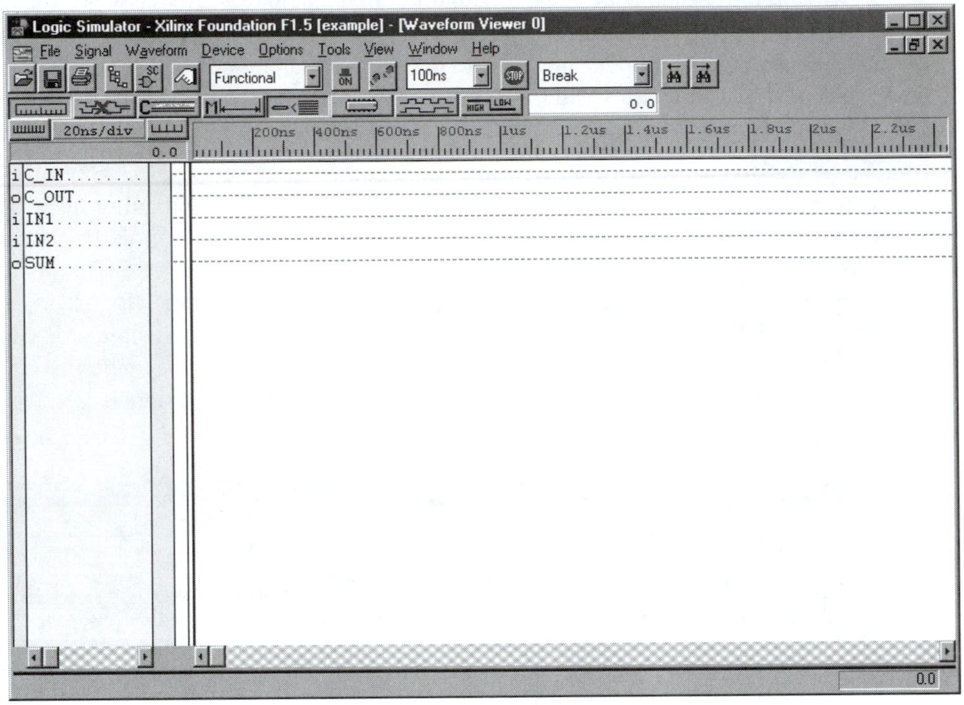

FIGURE D-10 Simulator with selected signals

- *Generate the stimulus for the input signals*: The next step is the generation of a stimulus on each of the input signals. From the menu click **Signals->Add Stimulators**. This will open the window shown in Figure D-11. There are several ways in which to stimulate the values of an input signal.

  - *Toggle*: You can select a key on the keyboard that can toggle the value of an input signal. Select an input signal on the trace and then a character on the keyboard shown in the stimulator window. Whenever you press the key the value of the signal toggles between 0 and 1. This you can simulate, for example, 100 ns, toggle the value of an input signal, and then simulate for another 100 ns.

  - *Synchronous counters*: A 16-bit synchronous counter is available. The frequency of the counter input, which is the rate at which the least significant bit toggles, is set from the **Options->Preferences** dialog box. The frequency of bit 1 is half the frequency of bit 0 whereas the frequency of bit 2 is one fourth the frequency of bit 0, and so on. Each of the 15 bits in the counter can be used as a stimulators with its frequency derived from that of bit 0. A signal can be connected to one of

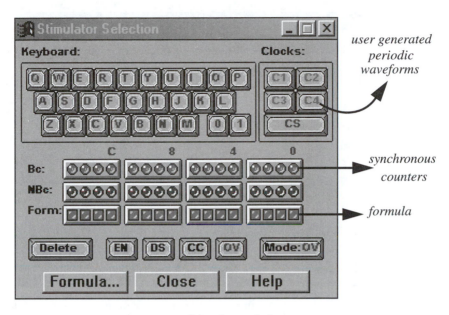

FIGURE D-11 Stimulator window

these signals by selecting the signal in the logic simulator window and then selecting one of the 16 yellow buttons that corresponds to the counter output signals. The red signals below the 16 counter bits are the complements of the counter signals.

- *Clock Signals*: What if we chose to generate an arbitrary clock signal? How can we specify the pulse widths and the pulse separations? We can do so by clicking the formula button in the stimulator window. This will produce the dialog box, shown in Figure D-12. The top half of the window shows four clock signals, C1, C2, C3, and C4. Select a signal and type in a formula in the text box at the bottom of the window. Specify how long the signal is high and how long the signal is low. For example, h15l20 states the signal is high for 15 ns and then low for 20 ns (the "l" is lower case L). We can specify any pattern here and this stimulus is applied repeatedly. The figure shows a pattern defined for C1. If we select accept, the C1 button in the upper right of the stimulus window will be highlighted. To apply this repeated pattern to an input signal, select the signal in the logic simulator window and then click the C1 button in the stimulator window. Finally, we can also a wizard to describe the formula, although once we understand the syntax it is quite easy and faster to simply write the formula.

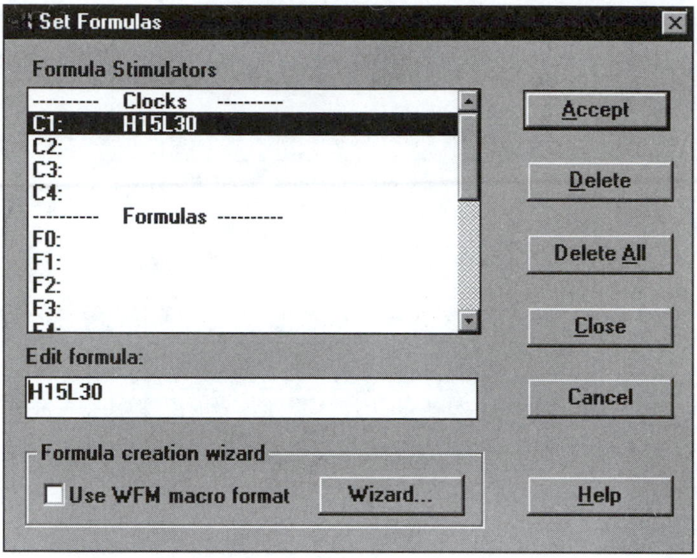

FIGURE D-12 Generating arbitrary waveforms as input stimulus

- *Formula*: Finally we can define up to 16 formulas. A formula is defined exactly as described in the preceding paragraph for clocks. However, formulas are only applied once and are not repeated. The signal retains the last value defined in the formula. For example in Figure D-12 a formula is defined for F0. If this formula is applied to an input signal this sequence of values is applied once and then the signal retains the value of 0. A formula is applied to an input signal by selecting the signal in the trace window and then selecting the formula button in the stimulator window. Formulas are numbered from right to left, that is, the right-most button is formula F0.

- *Simulation*: Now we are ready to start the simulation. By clicking on the simulation button (the "footprints" as shown in Figure D-13) we can run the simulation for a period set in the box shown in the simulator window. The default is usually set to 100 ns. We can also select Options->Start Long Simulation from the menu. Using the stimulus that we generated in this tutorial we obtain the waveforms shown in Figure D-13. Note the labels next to the input signals. They identify the source of the stimulus, that is from a key, clock formula, or regular formula. Now we can examine the trace and ensure that the circuit is indeed functioning correctly.

Once we have determined that the synthesized design is functioning correctly we are ready to generate a configuration that will program the FPGA device to implement this circuit.

starting and controlling the simulation time

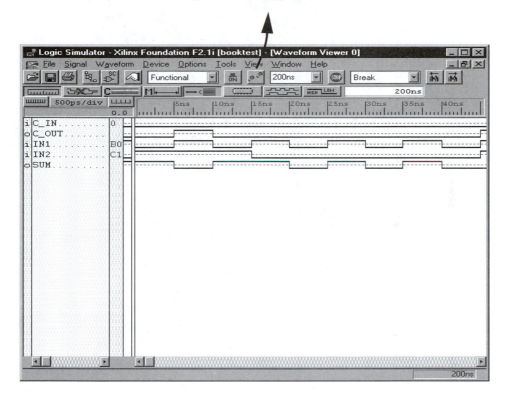

FIGURE D-13 A trace of the simulation of the full-adder circuit

Step: 5 Design Implementation

The last step is the generation of the bitstream used to configure an XC4005XL part to implement the full-adder circuit. In the Project Manager window select the Implementation button in the design flow. This will start up the flow engine as shown in Figure D-14. As is evident from the figure the process has several steps. The first step is to translate the design, which includes combining any netlists created with core generators such as the LogiBLOX. This step produces a complete hardware design. The map step translates the gate-level design into hardware primitives available in a XC4005XL device. These primi-

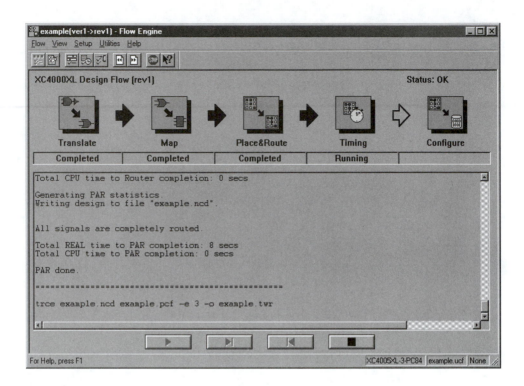

FIGURE D-14 The steps in the generation of a configuration bit stream for a FPGA device

tives include look-up tables to implement combinational logic as well as latches and edge-triggered flip-flops. There are also clock generators and global buffer resources for distributing signals such as clocks. Once the design has been mapped to these primitives we must now assign these primitives to physical locations on the chip and route the connections between them. This task is the function of the place and route step. Once the design has been placed and routed accurate timing information about the design can be generated and the configuration bits for each CLB and interconnect switch point can be determined. If you check the project directory you will now find a file named *example.bit*. This file contains the configuration bits for the XC4005XL device. We must now rely on other tools specific to the development board we are using to program a real device.

Step: 6 Examining a Design

When the process of generating a device-level implementation is complete we can examine the result in several ways. From the menu we can select Tools->Implementation->FPGA Editor. This shows the resulting device layout. Alternatively we might choose Tools->Implementation->Floorplanner. The result of this latter choice is shown in Figure D-15, where the CLBs and IOBs that are used by the design are marked and on the left are shown the signals as well as operators. If the resource graphics icon shown in Figure D-15 is toggled we can also see the resources that are used within each CLB, as shown in Figure D-16. This figure shows that two LUTs within one CLB are utilized. One is used to compute the sum and the other is used to compute the carry. Other icons on the top of the window can be used to displ*y the interconnections between the mapped CLBs and IOBs.

toggle resource graphics

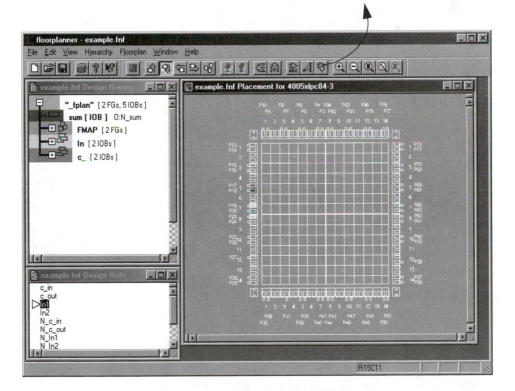

FIGURE D-15 Chip floorplan

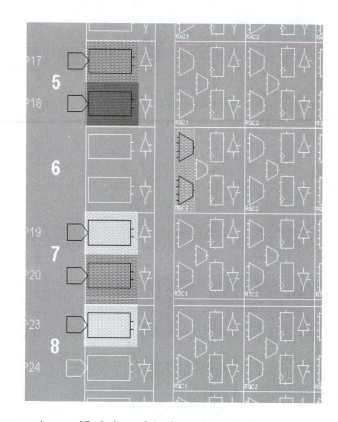

FIGURE D-16 A magnified view of the floorplan with the resouce graphics turned on

By selecting various options in this window you can control the level of detail that is visible. Play with various options. The full-adder circuit used in this example is very small and hardly occupies a few CLBs/IOBs shown on the left side of the chip. Larger designs will be more visible.

D.2 Chapter Summary

This chapter has focused on a quickstart tutorial for Xilinx Foundation Express 2.1i student edition that is available with this text. I have focused on the minimal set of activities/steps necessary to exercise the environment to synthesize a single design. Early in digital logic and computer architecture courses students are more likely to be constructing single monolithic models of relatively simple components. This tutorial is intended to help them get to the synthesis and simulation of these monolithic models quickly and as painlessly as possible so that they may concentrate on the digital logic and computer architecture concepts they are learning. It is hoped that the resulting familiarity will breed confidence to venture into the depths of these toolsets as necessary to avail themselves of the powerful capabilities these environments have to offer. The steps covered here include the following:

- Creating a project
- Adding VHDL files to a project
- Analyzing VHDL files
- Simulating synthesized circuits
- Translating synthesized circuits into FPGA implementations
- Viewing the chip floorplan after a design has been implemented

The environments provide for many more advanced design activities including manual optimization of a design. Access to such capabilities are available through the vendor documentation.

APPENDIX E

Synopsys FPGA Express Tutorial

Synopsys FPGA Express is a synthesis tool that is widely regarded as one of the leading CAD tools in this arena. This appendix provides a tutorial for using Synopsys FPGA Express 3.2 to synthesize VHDL models to Xilinx XC4000 series FPGA chips. When used in stand-alone mode the output can be a netlist in Xilinx Netlist Format (*.xnf*). When used in CAD environments such as Xilinx's Foundation series, FPGA Express is simply a transparent bridge to the implementation tools and we do not explicitly interact with FPGA Express. This tutorial is based on the use of Synopsys FPGA Express in stand-alone mode. It is useful to directly interact with the synthesis compiler so that we can view the hardware we have generated, be they gate-level designs or designs mapped to Xilinx primitives. By iterating through the model-synthesize-view sequence of steps we begin to generate first the intuition and then the expertise in creating efficient FPGA designs.

This tutorial assumes that we are starting with the creation of a new design. The sequence of steps proceeds through the creation, synthesis, and mapping of a design to a Xilinx XC4000 FPGA. The resulting design can be saved as a netlist for use by tools that will generate the configuration bits for programming the chips. Note that the viewing of the schematics of the synthesized designs is possible only with the appropriate license files.

E.1 Using FPGA Express

This section sequences through the most common steps in the synthesis of VHDL models for FPGA devices using Synopsys FPGA Express 3.2. My intention is to get the students productive in the use of this tool as soon as possible. Thereafter students can grow into more complex tasks using larger VHDL models by accessing the vendor documentation as they encounter new tasks. For classes in digital logic and introductory computer architecture the following tutorial is sufficient to get started for most class projects.

The basic steps involve creating a project, synthesizing the designs, and mapping these designs to FPGA primitives.

Step: 1 Creating a Project

The first step is the creation of a project. The project is structured as a directory that contains the directory **WORK** (see Chapter 11) and a project file that contains vendor-specific information. As we include source files in the project directory and synthesize the designs other sub-directories and files will be created in this project directory. We can think of a project as a set of directories containing all of the data files and source files related to our design project.

To begin start FPGA Express from the **File** menu and select **New Project**. Now browse to a directory where you wish to create your project and enter the project name **example** in the dialog box. When you have completed this step another dialog box will open up asking for source files to include in this project. We will include some files later, so for the moment we can click **cancel**. The FPGA Express main dialog box will now appear as shown in Figure E-1. If we were to check the directory within which we created the project we will find a sub-directory named **example** and in this directory one folder name **workdirs** and a FPGA Express file named **example**. An empty directory named **WORK** will appear in the folder **workdirs**. Having created the project directory we can now create VHDL source files in this project.

Step: 2 Adding Source Files

The project we have created is currently empty and we need to add the VHDL source files to the project. Using a text editor create a VHDL model of a full adder in a file named *full.vhd*. Ensure that the entity name is **full_adder** and the name of the architecture is **behavioral**. Save this file in the directory **example**.

Now in FPGA Express click on **Synthesis** and select **Add Source Files**. Browse and select the correct source file in the project directory **example**, namely, *full.vhd*. When this VHDL file is included in the project it is automatically analyzed, that is checked for syntactic correctness and then translated into internal form. If the model is analyzed successfully then a green check mark appears next to the filename as shown in Figure E-2.

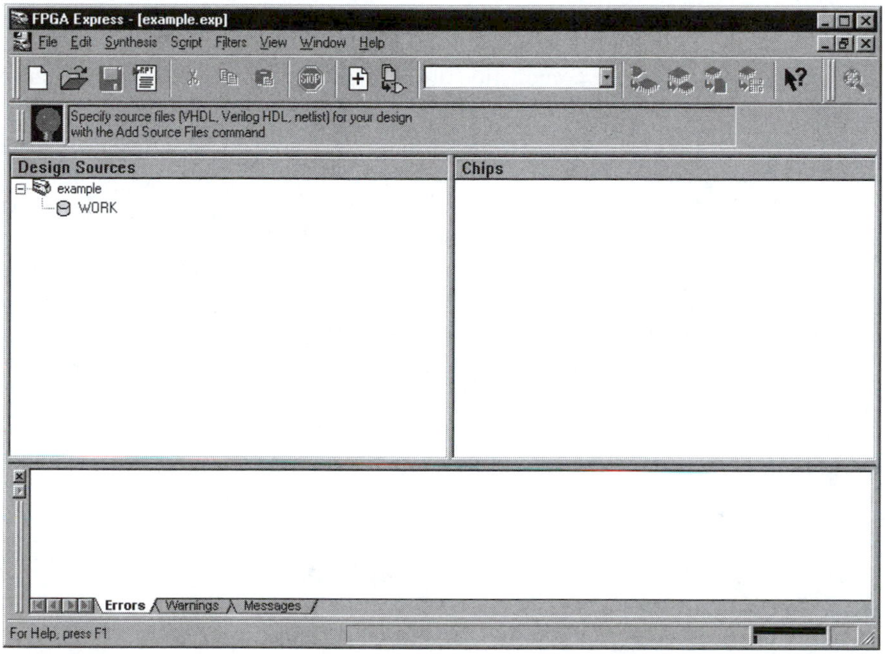

FIGURE E-1 The FPGA Express main window after creating a new project called example

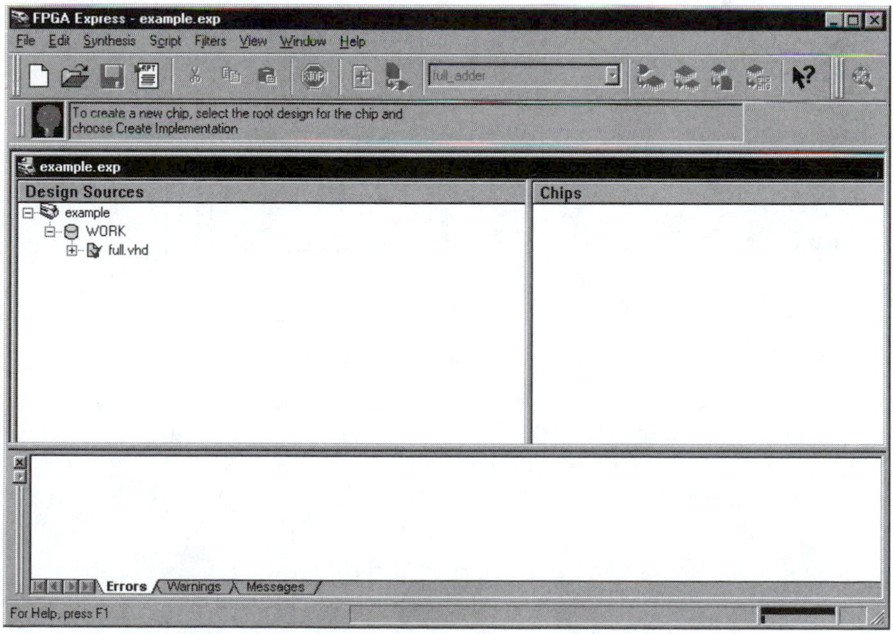

FIGURE E-2 State after the VHDL model has been successfully analyzed

Note how the filename appears under the directory WORK. This is the default directory into which all of the files created by the VHDL analyzer (compiler) are placed. If there were error messages in the compilation of the VHDL model these would appear in the dialog box at the bottom of the FPGA Express window. Note that you can select a tab to view errors, warnings, or messages. If we click on the "+" next to the filename the display shows the entity name.

If there are errors these errors will appear in the dialog box in the lower part of the window. By double-clicking on the error message a text editor will open with the VHDL design and the source at which the error was detected will be highlighted in red. Alternatively we can place the cursor over the filename and click the right button on the mouse. From the resulting drop down menu select Edit File. This will also open the text editor with the VHDL source and the appropriate source line highlighted. Correct the error. Now File->Save will save the file. Finally by selecting Synthesis->Update we can re-analyze the file. We can also re-analyze the file by placing the cursor over the filename and with a right click of the mouse, select Update from the resulting menu.

Step: 3 Creating a Design Implementation

Now we are ready create an implementation of the design. Click on the "+" sign next to the filename and make sure that the entity name, full_adder, appears below the filename. Now select Synthesis->Create Implementation. A new dialog appears as shown in Figure E-3.

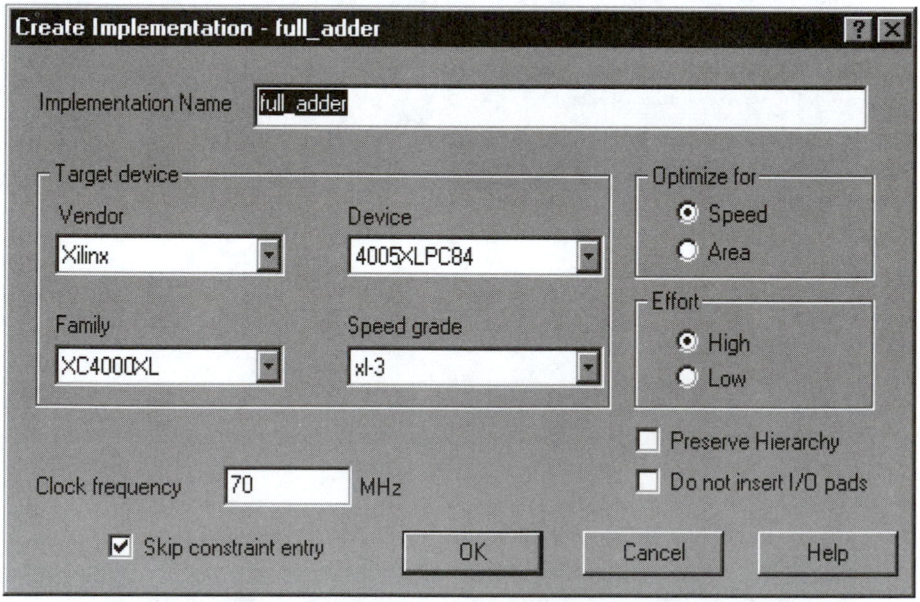

FIGURE E-3 Selecting parameters for synthesis

There are several classes of parameters to be selected for synthesis. First we must select the specific chip that will be hosting the design. To do so we must select the vendor, the specific chip (device), the family of devices, and the speed grade. These specifications collectively determine the hardware primitives available to us to implement the design specified in the VHDL model. Select the parameters as shown in the dialog box in Figure E-3. On the right side of the dialog box we will notice that we can optimize the design for speed or area. Generally high-speed designs can be realized by performing more computations concurrently, that is, using more hardware. On the other hand we can chose to implement a design with less hardware at the expense of greater delay. It is also possible to choose the level of effort in optimizing the design. The CAD tools are based on heuristics that search for better solutions. Higher levels of effort usually imply searching among a larger set of options and therefore longer execution times but with better quality results. Finally, note the **Preserve Hierarchy** and **Do Not Insert I/O Pads** options. The former prevents optimizations across hierarchical components when a hierarchical design is flattened. The latter is selected if the design is a component embedded within a design. In this case none of the entity signals will be mapped to pins on the FPGA and therefore I/O pads will not be necessary.

When all of the options have been selected click **OK**. Note the implementation name. If we make some changes to the design and re-synthesize the design a new implementation will be created with a unique name. The old implementation will not be overwritten. This is especially useful when we create multiple variants of a design that we wish to compare. When the synthesis process is complete in the right hand window we will see two designs, one of which is labeled optimized as shown in Figure E-4.

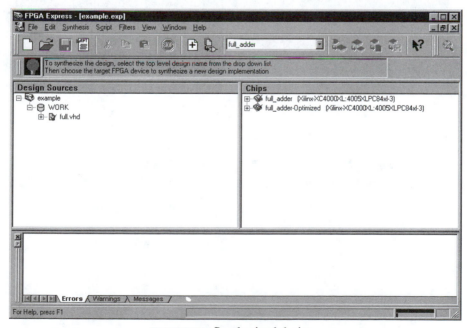

FIGURE E-4 Synthesized design

Step: 4 View Schematic

We would like to view the results of the synthesis. The first implementation of the design simply read full_adder and the second element reads full_adder-Optimized. If your dialog box only shows full_adder then select the first design implementation and then Synthesis->Optimize Chip. Now the right side of the main FPGA Express window should appear as in Figure E-4.

Select the implementation full_adder and then Synthesis->View Schematic. The hardware schematic will appear as shown in Figure E-5. By selecting the implementation full_adder-1-Optimized will see the mapped design, that is, the gate-level design of Figure E-5 implemented using the hardware primitives available within the XC4000XL FPGA devices. The corresponding mapped design is shown in Figure E-6.

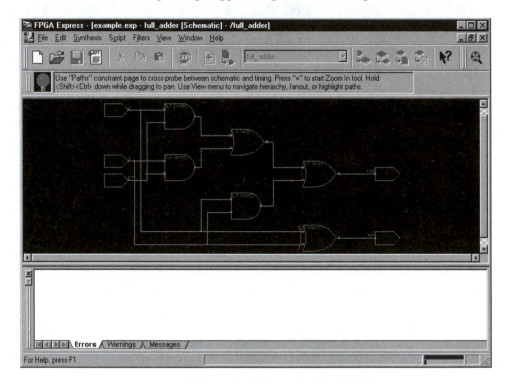

FIGURE E-5 Schematic of the synthesized design

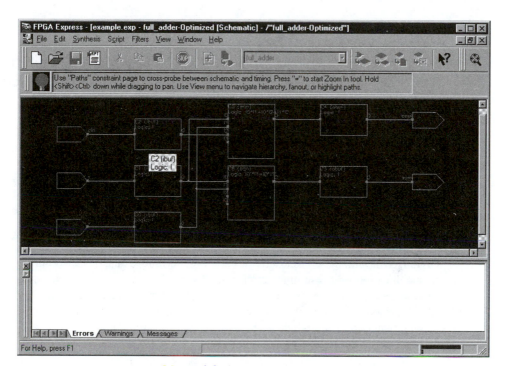

FIGURE E-6 Mapped design corresponding to the gate-level netlist shown in Figure E-5

Step: 5 Miscellaneous

The preceding steps form the minimal steps to synthesize and map a design. The toolset is quite powerful and provides for control over many other aspects of the design. For example, place the cursor over full_adder-Optimized and click the right mouse button. We will see two options: Export Netlist and Chip Report. The former can be used to create a description of the synthesized design than can be used by other CAD tools to create the configuration bits for a chip. The second is used for obvious purposes, that is, to see how well the synthesis process performed and to provide an analysis of the performance of the implementation.

E.2 Chapter Summary

This chapter has attempted to provide a quick start capability for the use of the Synopsys FPGA Express toolset. I have focused on a minimal sequence of steps required to synthesize and map a design. The steps required include the following:

- Create a project
- Analyze the design
- Synthesize the design
- Create a gate-level implementation
- Map the gate-level implementation to FPGA primitives
- View the gate-level schematic
- View the FPGA-level schematic

Organized around these basic activities are more advanced analysis and control tasks such as specification of constraints creation of netlists for manipulation by other CAD tools and the generation of reports that provide detailed chip-level statistics on the utilization of FPGA resources. I hope that this chapter will enable students in introductory digital logic and computer architecture classes to get a quick start in the productive use of FPGA Express.

Standard VHDL Packages

This appendix contains listings of interfaces to standard packages available with the VHDL distributions. The STANDARD and TEXTIO packages are provided as part of the implementation of the VHDL environment. The package std_logic_1164 is an implementation of the IEEE 1164 value system and is generally provided by all vendors to support the generation of portable VHDL models. There are several other packages that are also typically made available by vendors. The reader is encouraged to browse through the package headers at your installation and study the contents.

F.1 Package STANDARD

The package STANDARD is distributed by all vendors. This package provides the definitions of the predefined types and functions for the language. The package header contents shown here is from the 1993 IEEE Standard VHDL Language Reference Manual. The implementation of this package will be consistent across all vendors. The listing of the package header shown below omits the definition of all of the operators for each type.

```
-------------------------------------------------------------------------------
-- ANSI/IEEE Std 1076–1993
-- IEEE Standard VHDL Language Reference Manual
-- Copyright ©1993 by the Institute of Electrical and Electronics Engineers, Inc.
-- The IEEE disclaims any responsibility or liability resulting from the placement
-- and use in the described manner. Information is reprinted with the permission
-- of the IEEE
--
-------------------------------------------------------------------------------
--
--Predefined enumeration types
--
package STANDARD is
   type BOOLEAN is (FALSE, TRUE);
   type BIT is ('0', '1');
   type CHARACTER is (
      NUL, SOH, STX, ETX, EOT, ENQ, ACK, BEL,
      BS, HT, LF, VT, FF, CR, SO, SI,
      DLE, DC1, DC2, DC3, DC4, NAK, SYN, ETB,
      CAN, EM, SUB, ESC, FSP, GSP, RSP, USP,
      ' ', '!', '"', '#', '$', '%', '&', ''',
      '(', ')', '*', '+', ',', '-', '.', '/',
      '0', '1', '2', '3', '4', '5', '6', '7',
      '8', '9', ':', ';', '<', '=', '>', '?',
      '@', 'A', 'B', 'C', 'D', 'E', 'F', 'G',
      'H', 'I', 'J', 'K', 'L', 'M', 'N', 'O',
      'P', 'Q', 'R', 'S', 'T', 'U', 'V', 'W',
      'X', 'Y', 'Z', '[', '\', ']', '^', '_',
      '`', 'a', 'b', 'c', 'd', 'e', 'f', 'g',
      'h', 'i', 'j', 'k', 'l', 'm', 'n', 'o',
      'p', 'q', 'r', 's', 't', 'u', 'v', 'w',
      'x', 'y', 'z', '{', '|', '}', '~', DEL);
--
-- there are a host of other characters here including some special characters which
-- are omitted from this presentation
--
   type SEVERITY_LEVEL is (NOTE, WARNING, ERROR, FAILURE);
   type universal_integer is range implementation_defined;
   type universal_real is range implementation_defined;
--
-- in implementations of this package the statement below would define
-- numeric values in the range field
--
   type INTEGER is range implementation_defined;
```

type REAL **is range** *implementation_defined*;
type TIME **is range** *implementation_defined*
  units
    fs;   -- femtosecond
    ps = 1000 fs;   -- picosecond
    ns = 1000 ps;   -- nanosecond
    us = 1000 ns;   -- microsecond
    ms = 1000 us;   -- millisecond
    sec = 1000 ms;   -- second
    min =   60 sec;   -- minute
    hr =   60 min;   -- hour
  end units;
subtype DELAY_LENGTH **is** TIME **range** 0 fs **to** TIME'HIGH;
-- function that returns the current simulation time:
impure function NOW **return** DELAY_LENGTH;
  -- predefined numeric subtypes:
  subtype NATURAL **is** INTEGER **range** 0 **to** INTEGER'HIGH;
  subtype POSITIVE **is** INTEGER **range** 1 **to** INTEGER'HIGH;
  -- predefined array types:
  type STRING **is array** (POSITIVE **range** <>) **of** CHARACTER;
  type BIT_VECTOR **is array** (NATURAL **range** <>) **of** BIT;
--
--predefined types for opening files
--
type FILE_OPEN_KIND **is** (READ_MODE, WRITE_MODE, APPEND_MODE);
type FILE_OPEN_STATUS **is** (OPEN_OK, STATUS_ERROR, NAME_ERROR,
MODE_ERROR);

attribute FOREIGN: STRING;

end STANDARD;

F.2 Package TEXTIO

The TEXTIO package is distributed by all vendors. This package provides the definitions of the predefined types and functions of the language for performing input/output operations on text files. The package header contents shown here is from the 1993 IEEE Standard VHDL Language Reference Manual. The implementation of this package will be consistent across all vendors. The listing of the package header shown below omits the definition of the operators for each type.

```
---------------------------------------------------------------------------------
-- ANSI/IEEE Std 1076–1993
-- IEEE Standard VHDL Language Reference Manual
-- Copyright ©1993 by the Institute of Electrical and Electronics Engineers, Inc.
-- The IEEE disclaims any responsibility or liability resulting from the placement
-- and use in the described manner. Information is reprinted with the permission
-- of the IEEE
--
---------------------------------------------------------------------------------
package TEXTIO is
-- Type Definitions for Text I/O
--
    type LINE is access STRING;      -- A LINE is a pointer to a STRING value.
    type TEXT is file of STRING;      -- A file of variable-length ASCII records.
    type SIDE is (RIGHT, LEFT);      -- For justifying output data within fields.
    subtype WIDTH is NATURAL;      -- For specifying widths of output fields.
--
-- Standard text files:
-- Note these are different from VHDL'87
--
    file INPUT: TEXT open READ_MODE is "STD_INPUT";
    file OUTPUT: TEXT open WRITE_MODE is "STD_OUTPUT";
--
-- Input routines for standard types:

    procedure READLINE (file F: TEXT; L: out LINE);
    procedure READ (L: inout LINE; VALUE: out BIT;      GOOD: out BOOLEAN);
    procedure READ (L: inout LINE; VALUE: out BIT);
    procedure READ (L: inout LINE; VALUE: out BIT_VECTOR; GOOD: out BOOL-
EAN);
    procedure READ (L: inout LINE; VALUE: out BIT_VECTOR);
    procedure READ (L: inout LINE; VALUE: out CHARACTER; GOOD: out BOOL-
EAN);
    procedure READ (L: inout LINE; VALUE: out CHARACTER);
    procedure READ (L: inout LINE; VALUE: out INTEGER; GOOD: out BOOLEAN);
    procedure READ (L: inout LINE; VALUE: out INTEGER);
    procedure READ (L: inout LINE; VALUE: out REAL; GOOD: out BOOLEAN);
    procedure READ (L: inout LINE; VALUE: out REAL);
    procedure READ (L: inout LINE; VALUE: out STRING; GOOD: out BOOLEAN);
    procedure READ (L: inout LINE; VALUE: out STRING);
    procedure READ (L: inout LINE; VALUE: out TIME; GOOD: out BOOLEAN);
    procedure READ (L: inout LINE; VALUE: out TIME);

-- Output routines for standard types
```

```
        procedure WRITELINE (file F: TEXT; L: inout LINE);
        procedure WRITE (L: inout LINE; VALUE: in BIT;
                JUSTIFIED: in SIDE := RIGHT; FIELD: in WIDTH := 0);
        procedure WRITE (L: inout LINE; VALUE: in BIT_VECTOR;
                JUSTIFIED: in SIDE := RIGHT; FIELD: in WIDTH := 0);
        procedure WRITE (L: inout LINE; VALUE: in BOOLEAN;
                JUSTIFIED: in SIDE := RIGHT; FIELD: in WIDTH := 0);
        procedure WRITE (L: inout LINE; VALUE: in CHARACTER;
                JUSTIFIED: in SIDE := RIGHT; FIELD: in WIDTH := 0);
        procedure WRITE (L: inout LINE; VALUE: in INTEGER;
                JUSTIFIED: in SIDE := RIGHT; FIELD: in WIDTH := 0);
        procedure WRITE (L: inout LINE; VALUE: in REAL;
    JUSTIFIED: in SIDE := RIGHT; FIELD: in WIDTH := 0; DIGITS: in NATURAL:=0);
        procedure WRITE (L: inout LINE; VALUE: in STRING;
                JUSTIFIED: in SIDE := RIGHT; FIELD: in WIDTH := 0);
        procedure WRITE (L: inout LINE; VALUE: in TIME;
            JUSTIFIED: in SIDE := RIGHT; FIELD: in WIDTH := 0; UNIT : in TIME;= ns);
end TEXTIO;
```

F.3 The Standard Logic Package

This package defines the types and supporting functions for the implementation of the
IEEE 1164 value system. It is made available by most if not all vendors and is placed in
the library IEEE.

```
-- ----------------------------------------------------------------------------------
-- IEEE Std 1164–1993
-- IEEE Standard Multivalue Logic System for VHDL Model Interoperability
-- Copyright © 1993 by the Institute of Electrical and Electronics Engineers, Inc.
-- The IEEE disclaims any responsibility or liability resulting from the placement
-- and use in the described manner. Information is reprinted with the permission
-- of the IEEE
--
-- ----------------------------------------------------------------------------------
-- Title        : std_logic_1164 multi-value logic system
-- Library      : This package shall be compiled into a library
--               : symbolically named IEEE.
--               :
-- Developers   : IEEE model standards group (par 1164)
-- Purpose      : This packages defines a standard for designers
--               : to use in describing the interconnection data types
--               : used in vhdl modeling.
```

```
--                   :
-- Limitation        : The logic system defined in this package may
--                   : be insufficient for modeling switched transistors,
--                   : since such a requirement is out of the scope of this
--                   : effort. Furthermore, mathematics, primitives,
--                   : timing standards, etc. are considered orthogonal
--                   : issues as it relates to this package and are therefore
--                   : beyond the scope of this effort.
--                   :
-- Note              : No declarations or definitions shall be included in,
--                   : or excluded from this package. The "package declaration"
--                   : defines the types, subtypes and declarations of
--                   : std_logic_1164. The std_logic_1164 package body shall be
--                   : considered the formal definition of the semantics of
--                   : this package. Tool developers may choose to implement
--                   : the package body in the most efficient manner available
--                   : to them.
--                   :
-- -------------------------------------------------------------------
-- modification history :
-- -------------------------------------------------------------------
-- version | mod. date:|
--  v4.200 | 01/02/91 |
-- -------------------------------------------------------------------


PACKAGE std_logic_1164 IS
    -------------------------------------------------------------------
    -- logic state system (unresolved)
    -------------------------------------------------------------------
    TYPE std_ulogic IS ( 'U', -- Uninitialized
                         'X', -- Forcing Unknown
                         '0', -- Forcing 0
                         '1', -- Forcing 1
                         'Z', -- High Impedance
                         'W', -- Weak    Unknown
                         'L', -- Weak    0
                         'H', -- Weak    1
                         '-'  -- Don't care
                       );
    -------------------------------------------------------------------
    -- unconstrained array of std_ulogic for use with the resolution function
    -------------------------------------------------------------------
    TYPE std_ulogic_vector IS ARRAY ( NATURAL RANGE <> ) OF std_ulogic;
    -------------------------------------------------------------------
```

-- resolution function

FUNCTION resolved (s : std_ulogic_vector) **RETURN** std_ulogic;

-- *** industry standard logic type ***

SUBTYPE std_logic **IS** resolved std_ulogic;

-- unconstrained array of std_logic for use in declaring signal arrays
----
TYPE std_logic_vector **IS ARRAY** (NATURAL **RANGE** <>) **OF** std_logic;

-- common subtypes

SUBTYPE X01   **IS** resolved std_ulogic **RANGE** 'X' **TO** '1'; -- ('X','0','1')
SUBTYPE X01Z   **IS** resolved std_ulogic **RANGE** 'X' **TO** 'Z'; -- ('X','0','1','Z')
SUBTYPE UX01   **IS** resolved std_ulogic **RANGE** 'U' **TO** '1'; -- ('U','X','0','1')
SUBTYPE UX01Z   **IS** resolved std_ulogic **RANGE** 'U' **TO** 'Z'; --
('U','X','0','1','Z')

-- overloaded logical operators

FUNCTION "and" (l : std_ulogic; r : std_ulogic) **RETURN** UX01;
FUNCTION "nand" (l : std_ulogic; r : std_ulogic) **RETURN** UX01;
FUNCTION "or"   (l : std_ulogic; r : std_ulogic) **RETURN** UX01;
FUNCTION "nor" (l : std_ulogic; r : std_ulogic) **RETURN** UX01;
FUNCTION "xor" (l : std_ulogic; r : std_ulogic) **RETURN** UX01;
-- function "xnor" (l : std_ulogic; r : std_ulogic) return ux01;
FUNCTION "not" (l : std_ulogic   ) **RETURN** UX01;

-- vectorized overloaded logical operators

FUNCTION "and" (l, r : std_logic_vector) **RETURN** std_logic_vector;
FUNCTION "and" (l, r : std_ulogic_vector) **RETURN** std_ulogic_vector;
FUNCTION "nand" (l, r : std_logic_vector) **RETURN** std_logic_vector;
FUNCTION "nand" (l, r : std_ulogic_vector) **RETURN** std_ulogic_vector;
FUNCTION "or"   (l, r : std_logic_vector) **RETURN** std_logic_vector;
FUNCTION "or"   (l, r : std_ulogic_vector) **RETURN** std_ulogic_vector;
FUNCTION "nor" (l, r : std_logic_vector) **RETURN** std_logic_vector;
FUNCTION "nor" (l, r : std_ulogic_vector) **RETURN** std_ulogic_vector;
FUNCTION "xor" (l, r : std_logic_vector) **RETURN** std_logic_vector;
FUNCTION "xor" (l, r : std_ulogic_vector) **RETURN** std_ulogic_vector;
-- --
-- Note : The declaration and implementation of the "xnor" function is

-- specifically commented until at which time the VHDL language has been
-- officially adopted as containing such a function. At such a point,
-- the following comments may be removed along with this notice without
-- further "official" ballotting of this std_logic_1164 package. It is
-- the intent of this effort to provide such a function once it becomes
-- available in the VHDL standard.
-- ---
-- function "xnor" (l, r : std_logic_vector) return std_logic_vector;
-- function "xnor" (l, r : std_ulogic_vector) return std_ulogic_vector;
   FUNCTION "not" (l : std_logic_vector) RETURN std_logic_vector;
   FUNCTION "not" (l : std_ulogic_vector) RETURN std_ulogic_vector;

   -- conversion functions

   FUNCTION To_bit   (s : std_ulogic;   xmap : BIT := '0') RETURN BIT;
   FUNCTION To_bitvector (s : std_logic_vector ; xmap : BIT := '0') RETURN
BIT_VECTOR;
   FUNCTION To_bitvector (s : std_ulogic_vector; xmap : BIT := '0') RETURN
BIT_VECTOR;
   FUNCTION To_StdULogic   (b : BIT   ) RETURN std_ulogic;
   FUNCTION To_StdLogicVector (b : BIT_VECTOR) RETURN std_logic_vector;
   FUNCTION To_StdLogicVector (s : std_ulogic_vector) RETURN std_logic_vector;
   FUNCTION To_StdULogicVector (b : BIT_VECTOR   ) RETURN
std_ulogic_vector;
   FUNCTION To_StdULogicVector (s : std_logic_vector) RETURN
std_ulogic_vector;

   -- strength strippers and type convertors

   FUNCTION To_X01 (s : std_logic_vector) RETURN std_logic_vector;
   FUNCTION To_X01 (s : std_ulogic_vector) RETURN std_ulogic_vector;
   FUNCTION To_X01 (s : std_ulogic   ) RETURN X01;
   FUNCTION To_X01 (b : BIT_VECTOR   ) RETURN std_logic_vector;
   FUNCTION To_X01 (b : BIT_VECTOR   ) RETURN std_ulogic_vector;
   FUNCTION To_X01 (b : BIT   ) RETURN X01;
   FUNCTION To_X01Z (s : std_logic_vector) RETURN std_logic_vector;
   FUNCTION To_X01Z (s : std_ulogic_vector) RETURN std_ulogic_vector;
   FUNCTION To_X01Z (s : std_ulogic   ) RETURN X01Z;
   FUNCTION To_X01Z (b : BIT_VECTOR   ) RETURN std_logic_vector;
   FUNCTION To_X01Z (b : BIT_VECTOR   ) RETURN std_ulogic_vector;
   FUNCTION To_X01Z (b : BIT   ) RETURN X01Z;
   FUNCTION To_UX01 (s : std_logic_vector) RETURN std_logic_vector;
   FUNCTION To_UX01 (s : std_ulogic_vector) RETURN std_ulogic_vector;
   FUNCTION To_UX01 (s : std_ulogic   ) RETURN UX01;

```
FUNCTION To_UX01 ( b : BIT_VECTOR    ) RETURN std_logic_vector;
FUNCTION To_UX01 ( b : BIT_VECTOR    ) RETURN std_ulogic_vector;
FUNCTION To_UX01 ( b : BIT          ) RETURN UX01;
----------------------------------------------------------------
-- edge detection
----------------------------------------------------------------
FUNCTION rising_edge (SIGNAL s : std_ulogic) RETURN BOOLEAN;
FUNCTION falling_edge (SIGNAL s : std_ulogic) RETURN BOOLEAN;
----------------------------------------------------------------
-- object contains an unknown
----------------------------------------------------------------
FUNCTION Is_X ( s : std_ulogic_vector ) RETURN BOOLEAN;
FUNCTION Is_X ( s : std_logic_vector ) RETURN BOOLEAN;
FUNCTION Is_X ( s : std_ulogic        ) RETURN BOOLEAN;
END std_logic_1164;
```

F.4 Other Useful Packages

In addition, users should be aware that vendors will provide other packages that encapsulate many useful functions such as those for arithmetic, and for handling real numbers, as well as miscellaneous utility functions such as type conversion. Some of these packages are vendor specific, whereas others are currently subject to efforts to arrive at some standards of use.

Check the vendor documentation for other packages that may be available on your system. It is useful to browse through the package headers to obtain an idea of the sets of functions, procedures, or data types that are supported within these packages and thereby understand the motivation for their development. Packages for mathematical functions and type conversion are perhaps the first themes that come to mind. When we think in terms of hardware design, several other needs also become evident. For example, given a specific gate-level design, we may have packages containing various implementation alternatives for the same set of components. One package may contain models for the high-speed implementation of the components, whereas another may contain models corresponding to the low-power implementation of the same components. The structuring mechanism provided by packages is put to good use in creating libraries of component models used within an organization. Often these packages are proprietary products of the parent organization.

A Starting Program Template

This appendix serves as a quick reference guide to the structure of a first VHDL model. A template for a general VHDL model is presented. This template can help with the syntactical arrangement of programming constructs. It is useful when trying to remember where to place statements within a program relative to other program constructs. This template can serve as a handy reference for quickly constructing our first VHDL models. The goal here is to provide a template that contains the most basic and common (and therefore, for our purposes, important) language features and will enable the reader to rapidly proceed to the construction of useful VHDL models.

G.1 A Simulation Template

We can combine the procedures for constructing behavioral and structural simulation models that are described in the early chapters and identify a sequence of common operations. The first step is the construction of a schematic of the system being modeled.

G.1.1 Construct_Schematic

1. Represent each component (e.g., gate) of the system to be modeled as a *delay element*. The delay element simply captures all of the delays associated with the computation represented by the component and propagation of signals through the component. For

each output signal of a component associate a specific value of delay through the component for that output signal.

2. Draw a schematic interconnecting all of the components. Uniquely label each component.

3. Identify the input signals of the system as input ports.

4. Identify the output signals of the system as output ports.

5. All remaining signals are internal signals and should be uniquely labeled.

6. Associate a type, such as **bit**, **bit_vector**, or std_logic_vector, with each input port, output port, and internal signal.

7. Ensure that each input port, output port, and internal signal is labeled with a unique name.

This schematic can now be translated into a VHDL model containing behavioral and structural models of the components that compose the system. In fact, the architecture body shown in Figure G-1 can be structured as a series of program statements. Each statement can be one of the following:

1. A concurrent signal assignment statement

   • simple signal assignment

   • conditional signal assignment

   • selected signal assignment

2. A process

   The process may have a sensitivity list, and may be composed of a large block of sequential code. Recall that a process execution takes no simulation time and may produce events on signals that are scheduled at some time in the future.

3. A component instantiation statement

   If components have been declared in addition to signals, these components may be instantiated and their input and output ports mapped to signals declared in the architecture. In this manner, these components can be "connected" to, or communicate with, other components, CSAs, or processes.

This leads to the following procedure for constructing general models reflecting the behavior of the digital system.

G.1.2   Construct_Behavioral_Model

1. At this point I recommend using the IEEE 1164 value system. To do so, include the following two lines at the top of your model declaration:

   ```
   library IEEE;
   use IEEE.std_logic_1164.all;
   ```

Single-bit signals can be declared to be of type std_logic whereas multi-bit quantities can be declared to be of type std_logic_vector.

2. Select a name for the entity (entity_name) for the system and write the entity description specifying each input or output signal port, its mode, and associated type.

3. Select a name for the architecture (arch_name) and write the architecture description. Within the architecture description, name and declare all of the internal signals used to connect the components. These signal names are shown on your schematic. The architecture declaration states the type of each signal and possibly an initial value.

4. For each delay element decide if the behavior of the block will be described by concurrent signal assignment statements, processes, or a component instantiation statement. Depending upon the type, perform the following:

    4.1 *CSA*: For each output signal of the component select a concurrent signal assignment statement that expresses the value of this signal as a function of the signals that are inputs to that component. Use the value of the propagation delay through the component provided for that output signal. The output signal and/or one or more input signals may be a port of the entity.

    4.2 *Process*: Alternatively, if the computation of the signal values at the outputs of the component are too complex to represent with concurrent signal assignment statements, describe the behavior of the component with a process. One or more processes can be used to compute the values of the output signals from that component. For each process perform the following:

        4.2.1 Label the process. If you are using a sensitivity list, identify the signals that will activate the process.

        4.2.2 Declare variables used within the process.

        4.2.3 Write the body of the process computing the values of output signals and the relative time at which these output signals assume these values. If a sensitivity list is not used, specify wait statements at appropriate points in the process to specify when the process should suspend and when it should resume execution. It is an error to have both a sensitivity list and a wait statement within the process.

        4.2.4 Complete the process with a set of signal assignment statements, assigning the computed values to the output signals. These output signals may be signals internal to the architecture or may be port signals found in the entity description.

    4.3 *Component Instantiation*: For those components for which entity–architecture pairs exist.

        4.3.1 Construct component declarations for each unique component that will be used in the model. A component declaration can be easily constructed from the component's entity description. For example, the port list is identical.

        4.3.2 Within the declarative region of the architecture description (i.e., before the **begin** statement), list the component declarations.

4.3.3 Within the declarative region of the architecture description (i.e., before the **begin** statement), list the configuration specification if not using the default binding for the component entities.

4.3.4 Write the component instantiation statement. The label is derived from the schematic followed by the **port map** construct. The port map statement will have as many entries as there are ports on the component. If necessary, include a **generic map** statement.

5. If there are signals that are driven by more than one source, the type of this signal must be a resolved type. This type must have a resolution function declared for use with signals of this type. For our purposes use the IEEE 1164 types std_logic for single-bit signals and std_logic_vector for bytes, words, or multi-bit quantities. These are resolved types. Make sure you include the **library** clause and the **use** clause to include all of the definitions provided in the std_logic_1164 package.

6. If you are using any functions or type definitions provided by a third party make sure that you have declared the appropriate library using the **library** clause and declared the use of this package via the presence of a **use** clause in your model.

These steps will produce a fairly generic model. In particular, this approach implies that all design units (entity, architecture, and configuration information) is placed in one physical file. This is clearly not necessary. For example, we know from Chapter 8 that configurations are distinct design units that may be described separately. However, it is often easier to start in the fashion shown here. As our expertise grows, we will be able to avail ourselves of the advantages of dealing with design units separately and managing them effectively. Finally, note that in Figure G-1 the location of the packages is shown as library IEEE. Depending on the packages, this may not be the case, and when writing models we must have knowledge of the location of any vendor-supplied packages that are being used. We may also be creating our own libraries for retaining user packages.

G.2 A Synthesis Template

The construction of a synthesis template largely mirrors that of the simulation template with a few important exceptions.

1. Do not specify any delays within the design. They will be generally be ignored.

2. Follow restrictions required of synthesis compilers. For example, only one wait statement is permitted in a process. Check with hints listed in Appendix A.

3. Synthesis compilers may not support configurations

4. Support for resolved types may differ across synthesis compilers. Use the IEEE 1164 value system and associated packages if at all possible.

With these exceptions the template shown in Figure G-1 can also be used as a starting point for synthesis templates.

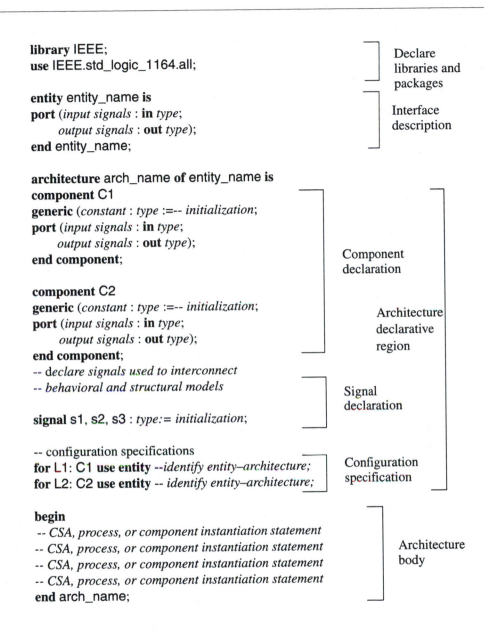

```
library IEEE;                                             Declare
use IEEE.std_logic_1164.all;                              libraries and
                                                          packages

entity entity_name is                                     Interface
port (input signals : in type;                            description
      output signals : out type);
end entity_name;

architecture arch_name of entity_name is
component C1
generic (constant : type :=-- initialization;
port (input signals : in type;
      output signals : out type);
end component;                                    Component
                                                  declaration

component C2
generic (constant : type :=-- initialization;            Architecture
port (input signals : in type;                           declarative
      output signals : out type);                        region
end component;
-- declare signals used to interconnect
-- behavioral and structural models               Signal
                                                  declaration
signal s1, s2, s3 : type:= initialization;

-- configuration specifications
for L1: C1 use entity --identify entity–architecture;    Configuration
for L2: C2 use entity -- identify entity–architecture;   specification

begin
 -- CSA, process, or component instantiation statement
 -- CSA, process, or component instantiation statement   Architecture
 -- CSA, process, or component instantiation statement   body
 -- CSA, process, or component instantiation statement
end arch_name;
```

FIGURE G-1 Anatomy of a VHDL model

References

1. J. Bhaskar, *A VHDL Primer*. Englewood Cliffs, NJ: Prentice Hall, 1995.

2. B. Cohen, *VHDL Coding Styles and Methodologies*. Boston, MA: Kluwer Academic, 1995.

3. D. Gajski and R. H. Kuhn, "Guest Editors Introduction—New VLSI Tools," *IEEE Computer*, vol. 16, no. 2, 1983, pp. 14–17.

4. J. Hayes, *Introduction to Digital Logic*. Reading, MA: Addison-Wesley, 1993

5. *IEEE Standard VHDL Language Reference Manual: ANSI/IEEE Std 1076–1993*. New York: IEEE, June 1994.

6. R. Lipsett, C. Schaefer, and C. Ussery, *VHDL: Hardware Description and Design*. Boston: Kluwer Academic, 1989.

7. V. K. Madisetti, "Rapid Digital System Prototyping: Current Practice and Future Challenges," *IEEE Design and Test*, Fall 1996, pp. 12–22.

8. V. K. Madisetti and T. W. Egolf, "Virtual Prototyping of Embedded Microcontroller–Based DSP Systems," *IEEE Micro*, pp. 9–21, 1995.

9. D. Patterson and J. Hennessey, *Computer Organization & Design: The Hardware/Software Interface*. San Francisco: Morgan Kaufmann, 1994.

10. D. Perry, *VHDL*. New York, NY: McGraw Hill, Second Edition, 1994.

11. M. Richards, "The Rapid Prototyping of Application-Specific Signal Processors Program," *Proceedings of the First Annual RASSP Conference*, Defense Advanced Research Projects Agency, 1994.

12. K. Skahill, *VHDL for Programmable Logic*. Reading, MA: Addison-Wesley, 1996.

13. D. E. Thomas, C. Y. Hitchcock III, T. J. Kowalski, J. V. Rajan, and R. A. Walker, "Automatic Data Path Synthesis," *IEEE Computer*, vol. 16, no. 12, December 1983, pp. 59–70.

14. R. Walker and D. E. Thomas, "A Model of Design Representation and Synthesis," *Proceedings of the 22nd ACM/IEEE Design Automation Conference*, 1985, pp. 453–459.

Index